SPREADING MISANDRY

Spreading Misandry

The Teaching of Contempt for Men in Popular Culture

PAUL NATHANSON

AND KATHERINE K. YOUNG

McGill-Queen's University Press

Montreal & Kingston · London · Ithaca

Legal deposit fourth quarter 2001
Bibliothèque nationale du Québec

Printed in Canada on acid-free paper
Reprinted 2002

McGill-Queen's University Press acknowledges
the financial support of the Government of
Canada through the Book Publishing Industry
Development Program (BPIDP) for its
publishing activities. It also acknowledges
the support of the Canada Council for
the Arts for its publishing program.

**National Library of Canada Cataloguing
in Publication Data**

Nathanson, Paul, 1947–
Spreading misandry : The teaching
of contempt for men in popular culture
Includes bibliographical references and index.
ISBN 0-7735-2272-7
1. Misandry. 2. Men in popular culture.
3. Sex discrimination against men.
4. Men – Identity. I. Young, Katherine K.,
1944– II. Title.
HQ1090.N37 2001   305.31   C2001-900819-8

Typeset in Sabon 10/12
by Caractéra inc., Quebec City

Contents

vi   Contents

Acknowledgments

We thank the Donner Canadian Foundation for its extremely generous financial support beginning in 1988 (which was part of its Program on Medicine, Ethics and Law and the Contemporary Canadian Family, established at the McGill Centre for Medicine, Ethics, and Law). In addition, we acknowledge with deep appreciation the Social Sciences and Humanities Research Council of Canada (which awarded Paul Nathanson a Canada Research Fellowship, held between 1989 and 1994), and the McGill Centre for Medicine, Ethics, and Law (which provided matching funds). We are grateful to the McGill Faculty of Religious Studies, which supported Nathanson's Canada Research Fellowship and provided Katherine Young with teaching-release time at several critical stages of this project. Finally, we thank our research assistant, Harold Wilson, and our editor, Maureen Garvie, for her many perceptive comments.

Preface

We began this book, the first volume in a trilogy called *Beyond the Fall of Man*, by noting that many pop cultural artifacts and productions from the 1990s said very negative things about men. This led to our initial hypothesis: that misandry, the sexist counterpart of misogyny, had become pervasive in the popular culture of our society – that is, of Canada and the United States – during that decade. But how pervasive? And why? These questions presented us with several problems: (1) defining popular culture; (2) overcoming conventional wisdom; (3) describing the artifacts and productions of popular culture in a disciplined way; (4) interpreting them as potential carriers of misandry; (5) demonstrating that misandry in popular culture has become a significant phenomenon and is thus worth being taken seriously by scholars; and (6) examining our evidence in relation to the many studies on misogyny in popular culture.

In some ways, our work presupposes the existence of a more or less unified popular culture. This is unlike traditional folk cultures in at least one important way: it is not created by and for a non-literate segment of the population. It is carried to everyone, moreover, through the mass media made possible by an industrial society. Contemporary popular culture is the property of all people, regardless of traditional barriers such as class or religion (except for the Amish, the Hasidim, and other groups that deliberately isolate themselves from the larger society). The poorest residents of rural communities are thus united in at least one respect with the richest residents of gated communities: they all listen to popular singers, watch popular movies and television shows, read popular books or magazines, and so on. There are "taste communities," it is true. Consider the case of music. Some people prefer country and western, others heavy metal, and still others the sentimental ballads of divas. But all are exposed every day to the full range of popular styles, and most find some gratification in at least one of them. Preference is by no means dictated by race and other traditional boundary markers. Whites are as likely as blacks, for instance, to enjoy hip hop. Even so, many enjoy classical (elite) music as well. Applicants to the Juilliard School are hardly restricted to members of an upper class. Although many people do prefer either elite or popular music, in short, these categories cannot be considered mutually exclusive. The same can be said of other media. Just because some people enjoy the "art films" of Ingmar Bergman, for instance, does not necessarily mean that they dislike romance or adventure movies. But the point here is merely that popular movies are accessible to everyone. All people are addressed. All potential ticket-buyers are expected to understand the cinematic conventions, be familiar with the imagery, and so forth. To put this another way, popular culture is not merely the opposite of elite culture: the two are related in ways that are much too ambiguous and too fluid for so stark an opposition.

Both conventional wisdom (as revealed in the anecdotal evidence of everyday life and, not coincidentally, in the stereotypes purveyed by countless talk shows, sitcoms, movies, or whatever) and academic fashions (as revealed in the burgeoning literature of women's studies) have been preoccupied with the problem of misogyny. Until very recently, no scholar recognized even the *possibility* of misandry, let alone of widespread misandry. Consequently, no systematic study of misandry in popular culture has been produced. This first volume in our trilogy was written for precisely that reason. Our aim here is primarily to collect evidence and thus demonstrate the existence of widespread misandry in contemporary popular culture, a phenomenon that appears not merely now and then or here and there but on a massive scale and in consistent patterns.

Our method of description is not scientific, to be sure, but it is far from haphazard. We did not seize the odd motif or metaphorical allusion. We looked for *patterns*, ones that recur over and over both within and across genres. To see any patterns at all, of course, requires a systematic effort. That meant relying on the systematic use of what art historians call "formal analysis," observing what is actually presented in visual or verbal terms, to provide a close and disciplined "reading" of every "text." Formal analysis was used very effectively by one of the present authors, Paul Nathanson, in *Over the Rainbow: The Wizard of Oz As a Secular Myth of America*. That analysis began with the careful observation of consistent patterns in the use of formal properties. In the case of a movie, of course, those were cinematic properties such as colour, music, mise-en-scene, time, space, and so on.

At this stage, description, there is no need to speculate about accuracy; the patterns are either there or not there, and anyone can check merely by looking and allowing the evidence to speak for itself. What all this *means*, however, is another matter.

We argue that the "documents" discussed here can be interpreted as evidence of pervasive misandry (although we do not claim to have exhausted the interpretive possibilities of any item). This is our interpretation, but is it what the people who produce this stuff have in mind? It could be argued – it was once assumed – that "correct" interpretations are whatever the creators have in mind. In this respect, we follow the current tendency to argue that "the author is dead." With a few exceptions, we are not interested in what the creators wanted to say; we are interested primarily in what their creations do say. But wait. Can we know what they say? Can we know, in other words, how viewers or readers *interpret* them?

One way of finding out how they do so – or to put it another way, how they are affected – would be simply to ask them. But that would require elaborate surveys. And the results, based not only on how questions are selected and phrased but also on the particular people whose opinions are solicited and how they feel that day, would not necessarily establish anything remotely like a "true interpretation."

For decades, experts have debated the effects on children of violence on television. There have been many studies but no conclusive proof to support any one position; otherwise, governments would have intervened long ago with legislation. Everyone agrees that violence on television has some effect on some children in some circumstances. But precisely which effect? And on precisely which children? And in precisely which circumstances? The answers are not obvious, to say the least, because too many variables are involved. These include class, region, age, religious environment, educational resources, and family situation. Among the most important variables, however, is the personal psychology of every child. Some children are indeed motivated by television to behave in antisocial ways. But most children who watch the same shows are not.

The same thing applies to pornography. Many feminists believe that (heterosexual) pornography is dirty and vulgar. But probably far fewer agree with anti-pornography activists, some of whom consider even (heterosexual) erotica an indirect cause of violence against women. And with good reason. That belief has not been substantiated with empirical evidence. It probably cannot be, moreover, because once again there are too many variables for any simple cause-and-effect relation.

Not being sociologists or psychologists, in any case, we do not rely on polls or questionnaires. But there are precedents for drawing conclusions in other ways about how people are affected by popular (or elite) culture. In the 1970s, anthropologists such as Dick Hebdige observed that cultural artifacts or productions created by and for one group are often reinterpreted, adapted, appropriated, and absorbed by others. Subcultural artifacts and productions can go mainstream, which is what happened, at least among teenagers, to the styles of music and clothing favoured in the worlds of punk, say, and hip hop. Or the process can work in reverse, moving from mainstream to subculture.

An obvious example from the United States would be *The Wizard of Oz*. This movie was intended as pure entertainment for Americans in general and American children in particular, and it has indeed become an American "classic." In addition, it has become a "cult" movie – which is to say, one that has been appropriated by specific segments of the population and interpreted in view of their own needs or interests. Hippies liked it, for example, because Dorothy's "trip" in Oz reminded them of their own experiences with hallucinatory drugs. Gay people like it, on the other hand, because (among other reasons) Dorothy's isolation from society and yearning for community reminds them of their own isolation and yearning.

The artifacts and productions under discussion here could all be described as mainstream. They are commercially successful to the extent that they "speak" to people. And some have been notably successful. Many of the movies, for instance, were box-office hits. It is easy to know which are financially successful and which are not, but precisely why is more difficult to establish with any accuracy – even when people are asked for explanations of their likes or dislikes (partly because the questions are notoriously subject to biases or expectations of one kind or another). Why do so many artifacts and productions show signs of misandry? To put it another way, why do so many people respond favourably to misandry – or at least not complain of sexism? Our hypothesis is that, like misogyny once upon a time, misandry has become so deeply embedded in our culture that few people – including men – even recognize it. Those who do, moreover, seldom recognize it as a pervasive problem. And those who do that, it must be added, seldom know what to make of misandry in the face of so much debate over misogyny. In formulating our hypothesis, however, we are doing nothing that social scientists do not do. Faced with statistical anomalies or surprises, they rely on logic or even common sense to suggest explanations.

Pervasive misandry is surely a "statistical" surprise (though not a statistical anomaly in the technical sense). Nevertheless, we have examined not one or two but many genres and not one or two examples within each but many. The patterns we identify can be found everywhere in the popular culture of our time – that is, the 1990s. This phenomenon cannot be explained adequately, or explained away, as accidental. It surely indicates *something*. It is true that interpretations will almost inevitably differ to some extent from one period to another, from one community to another, and even from one individual to another. This is obvious to anyone who has examined the history of literary criticism, say, or biblical exegesis. And it is true that no one can "prove" the legitimacy of an interpretation. This is not chemistry or even experimental psychology. Even so, we need not succumb to relativism. Some interpretations offer more fruitful possibilities than other interpretations.

These problems should sound very familiar. Precisely the same ones arose thirty years ago in connection with discussions of *women* as portrayed in popular culture. Feminists discerned patterns that they believed were significant, ones that anyone could see once they had been pointed out. But most people – including women – had either not noticed or not taken seriously portrayals of women as submissive at best and threatening at worst. After enough evidence had accumulated, it was hard not to see these patterns and equally hard to see *other* patterns.

As for the extent to which feminist interpretations of popular culture have been helpful, well, that is another matter. In some ways, they have been helpful. We are all much more aware now of how problematic representations of gender can be and of the specific ways in which women have been represented unfairly. In other ways, feminist interpretations have not been so helpful. For one thing, their exclusive preoccupation with portrayals of women has meant either ignoring or trivializing portrayals of men. Moreover, many of the most influential feminists have insisted that portrayals of women are due ultimately and primarily to a deeply rooted misogynistic conspiracy – even though it was once far from obvious that white, middle-class women were an "oppressed class."

At any rate, we have discerned another pattern. This misandric one can coexist uneasily and ironically (sometimes in the same medium or genre and sometimes in the same artifact or production) with the misogynistic one described by feminists and now considered virtually self-evident. But there are some important differences between misandry and misogyny in popular culture. Misogyny has been studied and taken seriously for decades. Misandry, on the other hand, has been either ignored or trivialized for decades. Also, political pressure has eliminated (or at least hidden) a great deal of misogyny. Not only has no political pressure been used to eliminate (or hide) misandry but some of the political pressure used against misogyny has directly or indirectly exacerbated misandry. As a result, we suggest, the worldview of our society has become increasingly both gynocentric (focused on the needs and problems of women) and misandric (focused on the evils and inadequacies of men).

How did we reach this point? We have concluded that one form of feminism – one that has had a great deal of influence, whether directly or indirectly, on both popular culture and elite culture – is profoundly misandric. It would be hard to argue that the artifacts and productions discussed in this book have nothing at all to do with its relentless hostility towards men as a class of enemy aliens. How could it be otherwise in a worldview based precisely on "gender"? It is impossible to discuss women per se without also discussing men, after all, or men per se without also discussing women. The precise relation between ideological feminism and misandry, however, will be discussed more fully in the second and third volumes of this trilogy.

We argue that ideological feminists have played an important role in creating the gynocentric worldview and disseminating it. But the process of embedding that worldview in popular culture is very complex. For one thing, many negative stereotypes of men (as of women) had long been part of our culture. But feminists have made it acceptable, in one way or another and for one reason or another, to exploit them. This, and the fact that feminists of all kinds have made it unacceptable (though still not quite impossible) to exploit negative stereotypes of women, has led to not only a cultural preoccupation with misogynistic stereotypes but also a cultural indifference to misandric ones.

Not all feminists will appreciate this "intrusion" onto what has for decades been their turf. Having examined deconstructionist theory (see appendix 5), we are well aware that the first response of some will probably be to explain away our unflattering portrait of what we call "ideological feminism." We know that feminism is "diverse," that there are different and even conflicting schools of feminism. Not all of them promote the kind of gynocentrism (and accompanying misandry) we describe. But at the end of the day, gynocentric ideas (and their misandric results) have become so pervasive – trickling down to popular culture – that they cannot be explained away as the results of a few academic loonies. The variety of "feminisms" is a second-order phenomenon. The first-order phenomenon is gynocentrism, because that is surely the one thing that all schools of feminism have in common: primary concern for the needs and problems of women.

We hope that this volume suggests new topics of research and encourages other scholars to take a second look at the ways in which gender is portrayed in popular culture – the gender not only of women but of men as well.

SPREADING MISANDRY

CHAPTER ONE

Introduction:
Misandry in Popular Culture

I am told that I would do better to devote myself to some constructive task rather than denounce the teaching of contempt. Why not initiate the teaching of respect? But the two ends are inseparable. It is impossible to combat the teaching of contempt ... without thereby laying the foundations for the teaching of respect and conversely, it is impossible to establish the teaching of respect without first destroying the remnants of the teaching of contempt. Truth cannot be built upon error.[1]

Hath not a Jew eyes? Hath not a Jew hands, organs, dimensions, senses, affections, passions? Fed with the same food, hurt with the same weapons, subject to the same diseases, healed by the same means, warmed and cooled by the same winter and summer, as a Christian is? If you prick us, do we not bleed? If you tickle us, do we not laugh? If you poison us, do we not die?[2]

Western society is obsessed with women to the point of mass neurosis ... Trouble is, people are so busy looking at the men on top of the heap that no one notices them when they fall.[3]

Given all the stereotypical nonsense and political rhetoric that now govern our culture's perceptions of men, it will take great effort of the imagination, at least for many people, even to think about men as real people. In a different but analogous context, Shakespeare made a similar point in the famous lines from his perhaps most infamous play, *The Merchant of Venice*, quoted in the second epigraph.

Why infamous? Because its title role, that of the merchant Shylock, corresponds closely to a classic stereotype of the Jew: a sinister, opportunistic, and legalistic miser for whom the accumulation of wealth is the sole purpose of life. Even though Portia collects more than enough money to pay Antonio's debt, Shylock exploits the situation for his own nefarious purpose, insisting that the letter of the law be fulfilled by his collecting one pound of flesh from Antonio's body. Those who consider this play anti-Semitic seldom call for a ban on its publication. Even they grudgingly acknowledge it as a literary classic. Nevertheless, they often try to mitigate its impact. Attempts have been made to prevent its use as a text in high-school English classes, and to delete it from the repertoires of theatrical companies. Reduced to the simplistic categories of a syllogism, their point is this: Shylock represents the Jews; Shylock is a villain; ergo, the Jews are villains. But is this what Shakespeare intended? More importantly, is this what the play actually says to people? If Shylock's speech is taken seriously, the answer in both cases would have to be no.

Because the Jews had been expelled from England in 1290, Shakespeare himself probably never met one.[4] All he knew of Jews was gleaned either from biblical references interpreted in sermons or from popular animosity passed from one generation to the next in folklore. The wonder is not that someone as insightful as Shakespeare could accept the prevalent stereotype of Jews but that he could capture something of their underlying humanity in spite of it. Shylock is an anti-Semitic[5] stereotype, but he is also a real person. To recognize the underlying humanity common to both Jews and Christians and the vulnerability of those presumed to be enemies, something not always recognized even among Christians of opposing persuasions during the Reformation, was an astonishing achievement and one that should still command our respect four hundred years later.[6]

Why begin this book about men with these words about Jews? Because in our time, surprising though it might sound, belief in the full humanity of *men* has been dangerously undermined by stereotypes based on ignorance and prejudice, just as that of Jews was. This is even more surprising in view of the fact that, after centuries, the problem of misogyny has been finally exposed and effectively challenged. The cultural face of woman, as it were, has been transformed in a positive way. And that has had a profound effect on society. Women are no longer confined to the private realm. They are now expected to participate with men in all aspects of public life, which is as it should be. (The distinctive needs and problems of women are by now so well documented that we will not repeat what has been written elsewhere.) Unfortunately, mutual respect between men and women remains as elusive as ever.

Here is the central problem to be explored in this book. Feminists have claimed that gender is the most important feature – for some feminists, it is the only important feature – of any society's worldview.[7] They argue that the worldviews of most societies focus on men, moreover, not women. In other words, these worldviews are androcentric. The world revolves around men: the needs of men, the problems of men, the political interests of men, the private desires of men, and so on. We agree that the worldview of our society was androcentric until recently, at least to the extent that it focused on gender (although we do not agree with many feminists on how or why androcentrism came to prevail). But conditions have changed, partly as a result of feminism. By the 1990s, androcentrism was increasingly being replaced by gynocentrism in popular culture and much of elite culture. In our time, public discourse assumes that the world revolves around *women*. There has been a corresponding change, not surprisingly, in public expressions of sexism. In the past, it took the form of misogyny. Now, in our gynocentric world, misogyny is closely monitored. It is considered morally and often legally unacceptable. Not everyone has internalized that point of view, no doubt, but everyone knows that the cost of giving public expression to misogyny is high. This is not the case with misandry, the sexist counterpart of misogyny. Like misogyny, misandry is culturally propagated hatred.[9] And like misogyny, it is often expressed as negative stereotypes of the opposite sex. But unlike misogyny, misandry is not closely monitored, because, from a gynocentric perspective, it is considered morally and legally acceptable. Even though misandry is clearly visible to anyone with eyes to see and ears to hear, it is not visible to many people *as a problem*. On the contrary, most people ignore it. In fact, they have found at least three ways of doing so: they try to excuse it, trivialize it, or even justify it. The face of man, as it were, has been so distorted by public expressions of misandry that it has become virtually unrecognizable *even to men themselves*. This book is about misandry in popular culture, but the mentality is equally pervasive in many venues of elite culture,[10] including universities (but two more volumes will be required to deal with that aspect).

Now, consider the first epigraph. It was because of Jules Isaac's provocative book, *The Teaching of Contempt*, that Pope John XXIII asked Isaac to attend the Second Vatican Council in an advisory capacity. In his submission to the committee working on relations between the church and the Jews, Isaac referred to the image of Jews presented to generations of Christian children. Even though Christian preachers sometimes incited anti-Jewish violence, Christian leaders never actually advocated the murder of Jews. Still, as Isaac pointed out, they did encourage Christians to look with contempt at a people believed to live in darkness and error. This negative presentation of the Jews and Judaism had so corrupted the mentality of some Christians that even murder occasionally seemed justifiable retaliation against those who had allegedly murdered Christ. Of importance here is not the ultimate result of prejudice but its *inherent nature*. What

Isaac did was to reveal the ways in which Christian education, supposedly representing the highest moral and spiritual standards, directly
or indirectly and consciously or subconsciously supported not only
contempt but also hatred (a problem that many Christian communities,
most notably the Roman Catholic Church, have recognized and taken
steps to avoid in future).[11] The same problem that long prevented
mutual respect between Jews and Christians, the teaching of contempt,
now prevents mutual respect between men and women.

Isaac referred specifically to the Christian tradition of theological
anti-Judaism, which was later translated into the secular terms of racial
anti-Semitism. Applying this larger thesis more generally must be
considered with extreme caution. Isaac himself would have been the
first person to deplore facile analogies between the ultimate results of
anti-Semitism – death camps – and those of other ideologies. Nevertheless, we believe that some analogies are legitimate.[12] As feminists
have pointed out, the teaching of contempt for women has been
endemic in our society and had disastrous consequences. And disastrous consequences are likely to occur also as a result of pervasive
contempt for men. So far, however, this possibility is seldom taken
seriously or even acknowledged.

Misogyny in popular culture is no longer a dark secret. For decades,
feminists have been exposing it.[13] Misandry in popular culture, on the
other hand, remains a dark secret. Or, to put it another way, gender
watchdogs use a double standard. In a review of *The Hand That Rocks
the Cradle* (a movie discussed more fully in appendix 1), Owen Gleiberman writes that this thriller about a crazed nanny "trades on the most
retrograde images of women imaginable – they're either '90s Doris Days
or murderous destroyers."[14] But when it comes to the way *men* are
portrayed on screen, Gleiberman has been notably silent. Other critics
have reacted precisely the same way to *Fatal Attraction* (Michael Grant,
1985), which is about a psychologically unstable woman who has a
brief affair with a married man, is spurned by him, and sets about to
get her revenge. Even though movies with female villains are extremely
rare – and the leading male characters in both these movies are themselves far from exemplary – critics have attacked them as unfair only
to women. These movies do not "represent" women, they argue, but
instead pander to stereotypical notions of women.

In her famous response[15] to a movie "glorifying" the publisher of
Hustler, The People vs Larry Flynt (Milos Forman, 1996), Gloria
Steinem declared that "womanhating" is the only form of prejudice
America still finds acceptable. In other words, if Flynt had championed
the right of any other cause to freedom of expression – racism, anti-

Semitism, even cruelty to animals – no one would have thought of glorifying him. But where was Steinem when another movie, *I Shot Andy Warhol* (Mary Harron, 1996), glorified Valerie Solanas, the woman whose stated aim was not only to kill one man but to exterminate all men? Steinem, no doubt, would deny that Solanas was glorified; on the contrary, she would argue, Solanas is portrayed as crazy. Steinem might have more difficulty with the fact that so many women, including the director herself, find Solanas "sympathetic" nonetheless. Clearly, the definition of "glorification" is never entirely objective. If it can be argued that Solanas is not glorified in *Warhol*, then it can surely be argued that Flynt is not glorified in *Flynt*.

The fact is that many people do not, cannot, or will not *see* the evidence of misandry around them. Well, they see some of it, but not the fact that it is pervasive or that it represents a cultural pattern. One segment of a *Today* series on gender was devoted to Hollywood,[16] for example, but almost the entire segment focused on the representation of *women* in the movies – as if that of men were *not* just as problematic. Only in the last fifteen seconds was there a tongue-in-cheek reference to men. It was noted that in a scene from *Mrs Doubtfire* (Chris Columbus, 1993), Robin Williams asks Harvey Fierstein, his gay brother, to make him over into a woman!

Like misogyny, misandry can be found in almost every genre of popular culture[17] – books, television shows, movies, greeting cards, comic strips, ads or commercials, and so on – and in every sub-genre within some of those. This book is about misandry in popular culture, primarily that of Canada and the United States in the 1990s. In addition, it is about the way people, primarily journalists and academics, do or do not *respond* to misandry in popular culture.

The misandric artifacts and productions of popular culture promote a particular worldview. It is not a complex one. On the contrary, it is very simplistic. Symbolically encoded in each movie is what we call the "conspiracy theory of history." One specific group of people is identified as the threatening source of all suffering and another as the promising source of all healing. There is nothing new about this theory; only the names have changed. At various times over the past century, nations, classes, and ethnicities have replaced religions as the representatives, or incarnations, of good and evil.[18] Today, that is true of the two sexes as well.

Of interest to most people is not so much biological sex per se but culturally transmitted notions of what that means: in a word, gender. For many people, gender is not merely one important feature of human existence; it is the *only* important one. By the 1980s, the word "gender" was used routinely as a synonym for "women." To study gender is still, by implication, to study women. More specifically, it is to study the victimization of women by men. College courses on "gender" are usually courses on women trying to survive patriarchal tyranny. Men are always mentioned in courses on "gender," even featured, but almost invariably as those who created the problem of "gender" in the first place. This has meant that (1) men are society's official scapegoats and held responsible for all evil, including that done by the women they have deluded or intimidated; (2) women are society's official victims and held responsible for all good, including that done by men they have influenced or converted; (3) men must be penalized, even as innocent individuals, for the collective guilt of men throughout history; and (4) women must be compensated, even as undeserving individuals, for their collective victimization throughout history. Two underlying assumptions are that *the end justifies the means* and that *collective rights trump individual rights*.

Misandric popular culture has defining features that are derived from these assumptions. Artifacts and productions that take narrative form, at any rate, feature several characteristics: (1) Every major female character is heroic (both willing and able to defend the good, including herself), virtuous, or both. (2) Every major male character is psychotic (unable to choose the good), evil (unwilling to do so), less than adequate, or all of these things. (3) Until they develop the inner resources to fight back, either individually or as a group, female characters are the victims of male ones. (4) Until their true nature is revealed, male characters often appear to be charming, benevolent, and trustworthy. (5) Female characters are either already feminists or ready for conversion by remembering traumatic events in their own lives. And (6) evil or psychotic male characters are often eliminated through death or "surgery," and inadequate ones converted through contact with female friends into honorary women. Token minority men, in particular, are often given that status as a way of showing that feminism opposes both sexism and racism.

The primary message is very clear: there is nothing about men as such that is good or even acceptable. Therefore, men should be tolerated only to the extent that they can either become women (through physical castration) or be like women (through intellectual or spiritual castration). In short, the only good man is either a corpse or a woman. After annihilating, or "deconstructing," everything distinctive to men, whether physical or otherwise, what is left? Only whatever affirms women and honorary women. There is no room in this universe for *men per se*.

The misandric artifacts and productions of popular culture are not necessarily intended as political statements. Most merely reflect assumptions already prevalent in our society. But others *are* consciously intended as weapons in a revolutionary crusade. In cinema, these are the functional equivalents of what used to be called "message pictures." All that has changed is the particular message they convey. Because they are obviously *intended* to manipulate readers or viewers into accepting new political positions rather than thinking through complex problems for themselves, they could be classified as propaganda. But defining that word is notoriously tricky, so tricky that using it at all makes no sense.[19]

One current tendency in literature is,[20] as we say, the promotion of an implicitly or even explicitly misandric worldview. This has been described succinctly by Robert Plunket in a review of *Welcome to the World, Baby Girl!* by Fannie Flagg (author of *Fried Green Tomatoes at the Whistle Stop Cafe*). Plunket is resigned to the fact that he will never be a "beloved author." He is referring to those authors who become known not merely as great artists but as moral or "spiritual" authorities. These authors, "who make a difference in people's lives," are strongly favoured by Oprah Winfrey and her counterparts all over the world. They "both comfort and inspire," writes Plunket. "When they pontificate, people listen. Most beloved authors are women, and many are from minority groups (think of Toni Morrison, who literally wrote the book when it comes to being 'Beloved'). Some appeal to more than one minority group (like Alice Walker, who with her increasing emphasis on lesbian erotic self-empowerment may be losing some readers who don't wish to be inspired quite that much). But male or female, beloved authors are always 'womanist' in tone and concern. Bullies (i.e., men) do terrible things and the wounds they inflict must be healed, and beloved authors know just how to do it."[21] (Plunket does, however, find that *Baby Girl* is less effective than many similar books, because "not enough women are battered into submission" by wicked men.)

Consider Laura Zigman's *Animal Husbandry*.[22] The title is self-explanatory. Men are beasts. One reviewer, Laura Miller, put it this way: "It's a bit of a stretch to call any of the callow fellows in [the protagonist's] orbit 'men' – that is, in anything but the most literal sense of the word. But when applied to boys in men's bodies ... [her] theory is right on the money. She trades in her starry-eyed romanticism for a brutal evolutionary view of sexual relations."[23] And what about *The Inland Ice and Other Stories* by Eilis Ni Dhuibhne? Suzanne Ruta admits, reluctantly, the presence of a "weakness, perhaps: the male characters are all either boring and dependable or alluring and treacherous. Only one heterosexual male – smug, defensive Michael in 'The Woman with the Fish' – is allowed the dignity of self-awareness, and he's lifted wholesale from Chekhov's story 'The Lady with the Lapdog.'"[24] Or *The Itch*, by Benilde Little?[25] One reviewer predicted that

"you might want to listen to Gloria Gaynor's 'I Will Survive' a few
thousand times – and then lower your expectations of the male species
to zero ... The villains are the men, every last one of them."[26]

The list could be extended almost infinitely. The trend is so pro-
nounced that Valerie Frankel was happily surprised to find a novel
about single women that is *not* based on the belief that men are all
demons and women all angels. "The recent slew of books by and about
single women in their 30's," Frankel writes, could be described as
stories "of striving, seduction and betrayal ... Man may be Fallen,
these authors want us to know, but Woman is Blameless. It's old whine
in new bottles."[27] Of *Cupid and Diana*, by Christina Bartolomeo, she
notes with amazement that "[a]ll the cheaters in this book are women
– and none of the men are evil."[28]

In Joanne Harris's novel *Chocolat*,[29] too, good and evil are gendered.
The protagonist, Vianne, arrives in a small French town and opens a
chocolate shop. It becomes clear soon enough that Vianne is more than
a character – she is an archetype. She represents some primordial female
essence, one that Harris identifies with pagan, worldly, and life-affirming
sensuality. Her male counterpart is also an archetype. Reynaud, whose
name means "fox," is the local priest. He represents some male essence,
one that Harris identifies with the patriarchal, otherworldly, and life-
denying mentality of Christianity. Harris by no means invented this
dichotomy. It could have been lifted whole from the pages of *Beyond
Power* by Marilyn French[30] or dozens of other feminist polemics on
this topic. Reynaud and Vianne are natural enemies in this fictional
world. By implication, so are men and women. And women, judging
from what Harris implies, are on the side of the angels.

The same mentality is often characteristic even of more "serious"
writers. We have already mentioned Toni Morrison and Alice Walker.
The latter is famous for "literary fiction" about the complexities of
black American life. Nevertheless, she maintains the facile belief that
the "human spirit needs to believe that someone has escaped the
general pressing down of life that passes for the male notion of
civilization."[31] No wonder Tobin Harshaw wrote in the *New York
Times Book Review* about a book of memoirs, "[The author] may be
a braggart and a blowhard ("God the Father on the throne, a bottle
of stout for his crozier"), but he is also that rarest of birds in this age
of victimography, a decent man."[32] The point here is not that contam-
ination by misandry was ubiquitous in the 1990s. Our point is merely
that it was very common – common enough, even among "serious"
writers, to be considered a phenomenon worthy of study.

The story of misandry on television has been very similar and for
obvious reasons. By the 1990s, it had become pervasive. Like film,

television is far from being consistently "noncensorious." It presents an open-minded approach to many topics, but not all of them. On no television show, for example, is racism or sexism – in the form of misogyny – considered an "alternative lifestyle." Women are seldom if ever criticized as a group except by men who are presented as buffoons and thus need not be taken seriously. Men, on the other hand, are routinely ridiculed or trivialized as a group. Obviously, sexism in the form of misandry is considered "politically correct" (more about that egregious phenomenon in chapter 7).

In a somewhat glib article for *Entertainment Weekly*, Bruce Fretts comments on the high quality of television in the 1990s. He provides ten reasons for claiming that the quality is higher, in fact, than that of film. His first reason is worth noting. Television is better than film, he avers, because the former appeals primarily to women and the latter to men, or at least to adolescent boys: "Are TV execs feminist and movie execs sexist? Nope. It all comes down to money. The key to huge opening weekends for movies is young men; they're also the most likely to give a film repeat business. As a result, says [Elizabeth] McGovern, 'parts in movies for women tend to be less interesting, more the young girlfriend.' On the other hand, she adds, 'TV advertisers are going after women, and women have the need to see themselves reflected in interesting, dimensional characters.'"[33]

The trouble with this explanation is that it makes the wrong comparison. It is based on the longstanding belief in America, noted by McGovern,[34] that women are more "cultured" than men, that women have higher "artistic" standards than men. But if that were the case, how could we explain what is presented on *daytime* television? No one would argue seriously that daytime TV has not always been the domain primarily of female viewers. Prime-time shows, on the other hand, are enjoyed by both female *and* male viewers. If women have such high standards, artistic or intellectual, how can we explain the sleazy, sordid, trivial world inhabited by aficionados of talk shows, game shows, and soap operas?

It is usually assumed that talk shows, for example, are educational at best and trivial at worst. But some of them are not merely trivial. The *Jerry Springer Show* is famous not for its sentimentality but for its violence. "So what's put the spring in *Springer*?" asks Kristen Baldwin for *Entertainment Weekly*. "Can you say *bitch slapping*, boys and girls? When Universal Television bought the show from Gannett in January of '97, execs told *Springer*'s producers to stop editing out wild fracases that had been happening all along but had rarely made it to the screen."[35] By 1998, this show was doing as well as the more high-minded one hosted by Oprah Winfrey and the more "refined" one hosted by Rosie O'Donnell. Says programming consultant Dick

Kurlander, "There are some markets where literally half the available female audience is viewing *Springer*."[36]

But our point here could be made without referring to the notorious Springer. Winfrey's and O'Donnell's talk shows are more civil, but they do not exactly compete for the attention of those who watch PBS. Fretts and other critics are being honest when they deplore the filmed scenes of car-chasing cops or drug-dealing thugs that intrigue male viewers, true, but they are being dishonest when they ignore the televised scenes of boyfriend-stealing mothers or bed-hopping spouses that intrigue female viewers. To say that the latter are really about "relationships" would be like saying that the former are really about "sociology." In both cases, viewers are presented with entertainment based on vicarious thrills. There is nothing very inspiring or edifying about either.

Now consider another journalistic foray into the realm of popular culture, this one from the *Orlando Sentinel*: "Men Drag Down TV: Bad Taste Reduces Quality of Shows." Men are called "low-brow" and women "high-brow." (When this hot item was reprinted in the *Montreal Gazette*, it was prefaced by a revealing byline: "A Look on the Bright Side.") Fortunately for the future of Western civilization, the author implies, women control the television industry because they buy most of the products sold on television. And women "tend to throw their heaviest support to series that get remembered at Emmy time – *Roseanne, Murphy Brown, Home Improvement, Northern Exposure*."[37] The author might have added *Men Behaving Badly*: the title says it all.

If any further proof were needed, here is the scoop from *Entertainment Weekly*: "Talk to the folks involved in this reworking of a big British TV hit, and you get a lot of canine comparisons. Executive producer Matthew Carlson says the show is about 'what men are capable of doing ... it's not necessarily that men are pigs, it's just men are capable of being idiots. And, I think, more dogs than pigs.'"[38] But if these shows are popular with women, it is surely not because of their sophistication or subtlety. (Of the shows named, only *Northern Exposure* could be considered highbrow, in both the best and the worst senses of that word.) It is more likely because each tells women what they want to hear. It would be rash indeed to suggest that *only men* "drag down" the quality of commercial television.

In this book, therefore, we examine several television genres. Misandry was pervasive on television in the 1990s. During any one week, viewers could see many shows that ridiculed or dehumanized men. (See appendix 2 for weekly listings of misandric programs in 1992, 1994, and 1999.)

Misandry could be found also in every conventional cinematic genre, to the extent that a case could be made for the existence of a new genre, the misandric one, that cut across the lines of all other genres. For our present purpose, however, that is unnecessary. (See appendix 3 for a discussion of misandry in traditional cinematic genres.)

Here is a brief analysis of what could be considered a prototype: *The Color Purple* (Steven Spielberg, 1985). Though not necessarily the first of its kind, this movie can now be seen as a kind of cinematic watershed. It was a sign of the times but also of things to come: what was still unusual in 1985 would become commonplace by 1990. Since then, movies based on this mentality have become pervasive.

Purple was based on Alice Walker's critically acclaimed and best-selling novel of the same title. When it failed to win an Academy Award, critics were outraged. Here was a powerful movie about the experience of black people, especially black women, and it was virtually ignored by the Hollywood establishment. Charges of racism were heard throughout the land. But those were not the only charges. Black men charged that the movie was sexist (for perpetuating negative stereotypes of black men) as well as racist (for pitting black men and women against each other instead of white society). And they did so right in the public square on talk shows such as *Donahue*.[37] What caused their fury? In a nutshell, it was that every male character, without exception, is either a hopelessly stupid buffoon, a fiendishly evil tyrant, or both. And every female character, without exception, is a purely innocent victim, a quietly enduring hero, or both. In short the world presented to viewers is one of an eternal struggle between "us" and "them." (We present a more detailed discussion of that mentality, a worldview known to philosophers and theologians as "dualism," in chapter 7.)

In *Purple*, this cinematic world – viewers know it only from what they actually see and hear in movie theatres or on television – consists ultimately of a battle between the forces of light represented by women and those of darkness represented by men. Unless viewers supply other information from their own world (and thus contradict what is "said" by the movie itself) or from Walker's novel (and thus add at least some depth of humanity to the male characters), they must reach the conclusion that men are inherently worthless. In fact, they might as well be aliens from some other world. Whether viewers are consciously aware of it or not, that is the inherent inner logic of this movie. "Men are the gremlins of Celie's world," writes April Selley about the filmed version; "they are released to wreak havoc, but since they do not belong, they return to their own sphere, wherever that is. Spielberg's skill in earlier films to bring alien creatures, whether evil or benign, into the ordinary world and then to return them to their own universes backfires in *The Color Purple*. For men are not E.T. or the visitors in *Close Encounters*. Their disappearance cannot preserve or restore order or the status quo."[40]

What has made the male characters so worthless or evil is never shown; they just *are* that way. Was it because of the appalling conditions black people endured in the rural South of sixty years ago? Possibly. But if the situation was so destructive, why did only the female characters emerge with their dignity and humanity intact? From what viewers are shown, only one conclusion is possible: something innate in women allows them to rise above degradation, while something innate in men prevents them from doing so. Four women are triumphant and four men defeated. Harpo, the oaf who keeps falling through the ceiling as if in a rerun of *Amos 'n Andy*, is taken back at the very end by his long-suffering wife. No discernible change has taken place in him, while she has grown in wisdom and tolerance. Mister, a kind of black Simon Legree, eventually repents of his evil ways. But the last scene finds him so crushed by guilt that he cannot bring himself even to ask for Celie's forgiveness. She, meanwhile, has successfully transcended the past and can thus move on into the future. Even in contrition, then, the men are worthless. At their *best*, in other words, they are irrelevant anachronisms.

Given the *dramatis personae*, the only people who can actually identify themselves with the characters on-screen are women, whether black or white. No healthy man, black or white, could possibly do so, not only because all male characters are so unspeakably vile and so incredibly stupid but also because they are so uncinematically lifeless. Unlike the women, the men are not really people at all. They are wooden caricatures who represent crimes or pathologies, cardboard cutouts that exist in only one dimension, straw men set up to be knocked down – in short, not complex human beings in whom male and female viewers can see some of the good and evil in themselves. Never mind: this movie is not addressed to male viewers, not even to racist, white, male viewers. Apparently, the possible reaction of male viewers was considered irrelevant. The movie indicates that men are irrelevant once they stop persecuting women. In the final shot, the camera looks upward at the women, thus conferring visual monumentality and dignity on those who have escaped from their men and gone off to live together. Their pride and independence is thus emphasized in precisely the same way as the brutality and evil of the men, Celie's father and husband, were at the beginning.

Like the "docudramas" on television, *Purple* purports to be two very different, even opposing, things at the same time. On the one hand, there is an apparent link between the story and history. After the opening credits, viewers are informed that the story takes place in the 1920s. This information is verified by the historically accurate use of sets, costumes, and other props. But even docudramas are never scientific descriptions of the world, sociological treatises in narrative form. The events and characters depicted are clearly *selected* for some purpose, not thrown together at random as they allegedly are in cinéma vérité. They are not merely observed in the process of documentation, because raw data are always mediated by the senses and filtered through the mind as formed by culture. They have obviously been *interpreted* in the context of a particular worldview, whether that of the director, the author, or both. As feminists are so fond of asking when confronted with what they consider patriarchal cultural productions, What is wrong with this picture? What is left out, and why?

Purple was made in 1985. Whatever it says about life among rural blacks in the 1920s, it says at least as much about life among urban blacks and whites in the 1980s. Otherwise, only historians or anthropologists would buy tickets. Thus the evaluation of this movie should have less to do with its historical veracity than with what Walker calls its "womanist" perspective. By that, she means its ability to satisfy the psychological needs and serve the political interests not only of contemporary black women and feminists but also, by extension, those of potential "converts" among other women who identify themselves with female victims. Feminists often argue that there is no such thing as an "innocent" movie, that every movie promotes a subjective or "biased" point of view designed to legitimate class or gender power. It is very ironic, therefore, that they have legitimated this one on the grounds that it does present an objective point of view, accurately describing "the way it was." A double standard is clearly operating here. Many believe that the whole notion of unbiased truth, whether in terms of historical accuracy or scientific objectivity, is preposterous and must be "deconstructed." They might ridicule this notion as a naive illusion resulting from "the male model" of linear thinking. Or they might condemn it as a sinister attempt by men to define truth and scholarship in a way that denies equality to the "alternative logic" or "lateral thinking" of women. But when it comes to "feminist knowledge" about the "oppression" of women by men, they seldom hesitate to claim historical accuracy and scientific objectivity.

On the other hand, there is an apparent link between the story and art. The narrative structure, for example, corresponds perfectly to established conventions for fiction. It has a plot, heroic characters, villainous ones, and so forth. But does it correspond at a deeper level to the avant-garde notion of art? Consider the criteria usually used to evaluate art according to that definition, which now prevails in Western societies. Art explores complex problems without presenting simple explanations or proposing easy solutions. In other words, art reveals the paradoxical and ambiguous nature of human existence. To achieve this, artists must try to stand apart from society and challenge conventional wisdom, attack the status quo, undermine normal perceptions of reality, and so on. Is *Purple* art in that sense? Hardly. It challenges, attacks, and undermines, to be sure, but only in order to replace older forms of smugness, self-righteousness, and complacency with new ones.[41] It proposes a very simple solution to the problem of hostility between the sexes. Women need to escape from suffering. Their suffering is due primarily or even solely to the evil of men. Ergo, women need to escape from men. Sure enough, four innocent and heroic women escape from four evil and stupid men.

But *Purple* cannot be considered good art even in purely aesthetic terms. According to film critics and theorists, cinematic artistry is indicated by innovation rather than cliché and subtlety rather than blatancy. This movie is anything but innovative or subtle. It is more like a black version of Cinderella. Think of these scenes from the first half-hour: Celie having her baby torn out of her arms and sold by her own incestuous father; Celie being sold to Mister; Celie being slugged by Mister; Celie's stepson throwing a rock at her; Celie on her hands and knees scrubbing the floor while the others continue wallowing in their own slop and filth ... Narrative subtlety never rears its head. This is art?

Then too, art is usually defined in connection with communication. At its best, art bridges the social[42] and cultural chasms that separate people by revealing their common humanity. This gives art a universal quality. In fact, it is through particularity, and not in spite of it, that universality is attained. No matter how different we are from the ancient Chinese or the medieval Europeans, we can still see something of ourselves in the art they produced. Whether consciously and intentionally or not, the greatest artists speak to everyone. Directly or indirectly, they reveal whatever lies at the core of human identity and whatever defines the human condition. *Purple* addresses only women, albeit white as well as black women. It explores only the condition of women. It reveals the humanity only of women. It actually prevents viewers from seriously considering the hopes and fears of men, black or white, as real members of the same species. Its claim to kinship with works of art, therefore, is tenuous indeed.

This movie implicitly claims both the objectivity of being "true to life" or even "fact-based" *and* the subjectivity protected by "artistic licence." It is a story of people who never lived but could have or "should" have. (This matter is further complicated by the fact that many of the characters are said to have been based on people actually known to Walker.) These contradictory claims should provoke suspicions of duplicity. Among the viewers for whom it did not were both women and racists. For quite different but analogous reasons, both said that "it's only a movie." At the same time, many made contradictory claims. "That's the way men were (or are)," claimed women. "That's the way blacks were (or are)," claimed racists.

But if *Purple* does not fit well into the standard categories used to interpret movies – art, history, education – where does it fit? The word "myth" could describe the movie either negatively or positively. But that word is subject to the same problem as "propaganda." In popular usage, it is virtually a synonym for something childish, ignorant, false, deceptive, illusory, or primitive. People commonly use it to ridicule or attack the stories of "those others." Unlike "propaganda," however, "myth" can be defined on some basis other than pure subjectivity. It is used in this way, for example, by scholars in fields such as anthropology and religious studies. We suggest that *Purple* and movies like it are "secular myths,"[43] stories that function in secular communities much the way traditional myths function in religious communities. In symbolic terms, they explain the confusing or lamentable way things are now in relation to the way things could be, should be, will be, and, in some cases, once were. Myths are about communal identity. They confer meaning and purpose on those who tell them. Clearly, *Purple* functions very effectively in precisely these ways for feminists, "womanists," and women in general. In this sense, "myth" is a descriptive term, not an evaluative one.

Having accepted the idea that myth is a legitimate and even universal human phenomenon, and that secular myth is a variant of traditional myth, we can nevertheless consider the relative value of particular myths from a wide range of perspectives: aesthetic, intellectual, moral, functional, or whatever. Considering the use made of myth in Nazi Germany, to take only one extreme example, it is clear that not all myths are of equal moral value; the Nazi myth promoted hatred and murder, not love and compassion. Is *Purple* a good myth, then, or a bad one? Is it a true myth or a false one? At issue is not whether the characters depicted in *Purple* ever existed. Clearly, they did not. At issue, moreover, is not whether people *like* them ever actually existed. Just as clearly, they did and still do. At issue is whether they are presented in such a way that oversimplifies or in some other way distorts the reality of past, present, or both. *Purple* was a prototype. It was the first and, in some ways, the ultimate example of a cinematic myth that continues to flourish in movie houses across the land.

In early 2000, the director, Steven Spielberg, was awarded the Image Award of the National Association for the Advancement of Colored People.

Our point in this book once again is not that misandry is universal. Trying to prove that something occurs everywhere is as futile as trying to prove that it occurs nowhere. Our point is not, moreover, that

misogyny is no longer a problem. This controversy is not about
political one-upmanship, or whatever the politically correct form of
that word might be. It is about a complex, sometimes ambiguous
phenomenon. We make two basic points in this book about misandry
in popular culture.

First, it is pervasive, far more so than most people imagine and far
more so (at least on the explicit level) than misogyny. Unlike misogyny,
misandry is still generally unrecognized *as a problem*. Many people
can point to this or that example of blatant or even grotesque misandry, to be sure, but these are easy to dismiss as trivial exceptions. Some
people even try to justify them. (For a discussion of those phenomena,
see chapter 7.) But few people recognize subtler, more sophisticated
expressions of misandry. As a result, few attempts are made to expose
or challenge it, and therefore it continues to be extremely pervasive.
That brings us to our second point.

The mere fact that misandry, unlike misogyny, is seldom seen as a
problem – it is ignored, tolerated, or even justified – suggests the
prevalence of gynocentrism. Not everyone has adopted that way of
thinking. Not even all women see the world revolving around themselves. But what people think or feel in private is not necessarily what
they say and do in public. And the result, an "official" view of men,
is not something to be trivialized as a superficial veneer that hides
reality. Feminists have long pointed out that the way women are
represented in movies or on television can have profound effects on
the way men see women in real life and – even more important – on
the way women see themselves in real life. And the process works both
ways. Popular culture, in turn, is heavily influenced by the way men
see women and the way women see themselves. The same thing
happens in connection with men: the way women see men and the
way men see themselves. To the extent that our society recognizes the
needs of women (including the need to eliminate misogyny) but fails
to recognize those of men (including the need to eliminate misandry),
its worldview can be considered not only gynocentric but misandric
as well.

Although we focus attention in this book on misandry in popular
culture, bear in mind that the scope of this phenomenon and its
implications are far reaching. The penultimate goal of our research,
though not fully realized here, is to show that our society has not only
silenced men per se but also dehumanized them. And this is so to such
an extent that even men can now find it difficult to recognize their
own humanity, let alone their equality with women. Many find it
impossible to establish a collective identity based on something publicly acknowledged as both distinctive and valuable. And no healthy

identity – healthy for both men, in this case, and society in general – can be based on anything less.

Our ultimate goal is a *moral*[44] one, however, not merely a sociological or psychological one. The problem of sexual polarization, which is the end result of sexism in the forms of both misandry and misogyny, should be faced not only because tolerating it is inherently dangerous (a practical position) but also because reversing it is inherently good (a moral position).

CHAPTER TWO

Laughing at Men:
The Last of Vaudeville

TED: I can't believe you actually entered a contest to have lunch with the hunk from the Diet Coke commercial.
SALLY: Marcie made me.
TED: Yeah, right. That's a sexist ad, you know.
SALLY: No, it's not.
TED: Are you kidding? Women furtively ogling a shirtless guy isn't sexist?
SALLY: Sexism is a one-way street, Ted. Haven't I explained that to you before?[1]

Vaudeville was not what many people would now consider a politically correct form of entertainment. Ethnic humour was characteristic of many comedy acts. This tradition was partly an outgrowth of nineteenth-century minstrel shows, in which white actors impersonated black character "types." In the early twentieth century, for instance, Al Jolson became famous as a "blackface" performer, his most memorable song "Mammy." But black people were by no means the only ones to be stereotyped or ridiculed, sometimes affectionately, on stage. The same thing was true of most (though not quite all) identifiable groups: people who stuttered and men who were effeminate, stingy people and clumsy people, the Jews and the Irish, and so forth. Today, people often say that they are embarrassed by recorded vaudeville shows or vaudeville as it was portrayed in early movies. In any case, very few performers would dare to mock blacks, Jews, or women. (Those who do find themselves isolated and attacked, as Andrew "Dice" Clay was for a stand-up routine that mocked women.) But the vaudeville tradition survives. One group of people is considered the legitimate object of ridicule: that of men.

The direct successor to vaudeville is stand-up comedy. Listen to Brett Butler, of *Grace under Fire* fame. "My mom always said men are like linoleum floors," she says. "Lay 'em right and you can walk all over them for thirty years."[2] Of interest here is not that someone might have said this a generation ago but that someone was repeating it in our time. Maybe you had to be there on both occasions. Maybe everything can be explained by context. Maybe. It would be hard to imagine any acceptable excuse for a similar statement about wives. It would be equally hard to deny that misandry of this kind is a prevalent and accepted form of comedy.

Stand-up comedy often encourages a misandric take on relations between the sexes. Whoopi Goldberg's comedy routine at the sixty-sixth Academy Award ceremony included jokes such as the following: "One of our next presenters starred in a movie in which she played a man who had the heart of a baboon, which, in my experience, is not all that unusual," and "Lorena Bobbitt, please meet Bob Dole."[3] The problem is not that she said these things or even that people found them amusing. In a healthy society, people can laugh about almost any aspect of everyday life. The problem is a double standard. Similar remarks about women clearly would be considered politically incorrect. In its review of the Oscar ceremony, *Entertainment Weekly* had two comments on Goldberg's performance. In one way, she was praised: "Her elegant appearance (at least during the first half), her uncharacteristic restraint (she didn't cuss), and her ability to make it funny (despite the very sombre speeches) made the ho-hum telecast worth watching." In another way, it is true, she was not praised. "Sure, she didn't curse, but her insults packed plenty of venom. Whoopi took pot-shots at Nancy Reagan, the *Los Angeles Times*, and as much of Hollywood as she had time for – proving she was, as promised, 'an equal-opportunity offender.'"[4] Well, not quite: her jokes about men, apparently unnoticed, had no counterparts in jokes about women.

Not only do some female stand-up comedians – Jenny Jones, say, or Judy Tenuta – consider men the one segment of society that can be ridiculed without fear of personal snubs or professional reprisals; so do some of their male counterparts. There is a difference between all of these entertainers and those who are ready, at least in theory, to ridicule everyone.

The first category is illustrated by Jay Leno. During one monologue on the *Tonight Show*, he mentioned the strange case of 2,500 pigs that got drunk because their feed had fermented. "You know how you can tell when pigs are drunk?" asked Leno. "They start acting like men."[5] Had he said that or anything remotely like that about women, Leno would have been fired within twenty-four hours. As it was, he received sustained applause. But Leno occasionally makes fun of women as well.

Jim Carrey's humour is more ambiguous in this respect. Of his own comedy routine from "In Living Color," he says that "nobody gets off the hook." One of his most famous characterizations on that show was Fire Marshall Bill, a badly burned man who "dispenses handy home-safety tips." Another was Vera de Milo, a woman "who's ingested a few steroids too many"[6] and thus transformed her body into a parody of male vigour. Is he making fun of women, men, or both? But Carrey himself has indicated a preference for the ridicule of men. "I don't mind making fun of stereotypical WASP guys or bigots. That's something that has to be done"[7] (words that are featured under Carrey's portrait in this article). Even though he makes fun of other groups too, the implication here is that men who happen to be white, Anglo-Saxon, and Protestant are *legitimately* stereotyped as bigots and, therefore, *legitimately* mocked. If so, then we could conclude that Carrey mocks men in earnest, possibly as a moral or political state- ment, but mocks other people merely in the spirit of good fun.

Some comedians belong unambiguously in the second category, because they caricature primarily or even *only* men. They consider themselves exempt from criticism on two counts. With "all the power," men are supposedly immune to the psychic damage inherent in sus- tained attacks on their identity. In that case, presumably, the "golden rule" may be set aside. Then too, these comedians, as men, are sup- posedly satirizing themselves. In that case, the "golden rule" would not apply in the first place. Neither form of rationalization rests on a solid foundation. For one thing, the evidence indicates that men are *not* immune to the relentless attack on their identity, which is now a normal feature of everyday life. In fact, they are probably more vulnerable to that sort of thing than any other group, because every other group is expected either to defend itself or to seek protection. It could be argued, and we do argue elsewhere, that radical loss of identity has become an urgent problem for men in our society. Also, self-mockery might or might not be sincere. Jackie Mason's exaggerated Jewish accent and mannerisms make it clear that when he laughs at Jews he is laughing at himself as well. But Mason laughs at almost every other religious and ethnic group too, occasionally getting into trouble with "sensitive" ones for being politically incorrect. Jews love him, but they would angrily reject him if he laughed *only* at Jews, either as a cynical oppor- tunist cashing in on anti-Semitic stereotypes or as a neurotic "self- hater" begging for acceptance from the anti-Semites.

Comedians who lampoon only men, therefore, could be playing a dangerous game. If people expect "women and minorities" to project negativity on to other groups, why should they be shocked when men do precisely the same thing? It is surely not entirely coincidental that just as some comedians have risen to prominence recently by isolating men as the only group that may be treated with derision and contempt, others have risen by isolating men as the only group that may *not* be treated with derision or contempt. As the popularity of Andrew "Dice" Clay indicated in the 1990s, there is no reason to assume either that "men can take it" or, indeed, that they will take it.

Yet even men often fail to appreciate the double standard. Charlie Gibson, the affable and popular host of *Good Morning, America*, complained about the prevalence on cable television of stand-up comedians who tell jokes that are "demeaning to women."[8] Was he unaware that the stand-up comedians not only tell jokes that are demeaning to men but do so without the slightest fear of reprisal?

Misandry is considered lucrative, not merely funny. One commercial for Polaroid[9] makes this clear. A female ethologist says, obviously recording a field trip: "After miles of searching through remote territories, my efforts were rewarded ... a group of nomadic males. Strong, powerful, magnificent! They truly are impressive beasts." And she means *beasts*. The camera shows a group of very paunchy, middle-aged men getting out of their car. They yawn, scratch themselves, discover that they're locked out of the car, and proceed to get drunk. It would be unthinkable for any company to advertise its products by exploiting stereotypes of women, even though women are not a minority. Or Jews, even though Jews are not an oppressed minority.

Another commercial, for the Pontiac Sunfire,[10] is equally grotesque. A young man and his date sit down for dinner at a fancy restaurant. He is a stereotypical boor. He grabs some rolls from the basket being held in front of her. He tosses his napkin on the floor. He chokes on the wine, blowing the contents of his mouth into her face. Not surprisingly, when they leave the restaurant, she locks him out of the car and drives off alone.

Some trade books aimed at the mass market, especially those of the "self-help" genre, are supposed to be taken seriously. Others, especially those classified as humour, are not. Both types often become best-sellers, featured on display racks near the cash register. And both often rely heavily on negative stereotypes of men. Many are based on the traditional and widespread premise that men and women are profoundly different from each other and, as a result, find it very hard to communicate effectively with each other. But the underlying assumption, one that was not always made in the past, is that only men have any learning to do. By the late 1980s, this mentality had produced an avalanche of popular books that included *Men Who Hate Women and the Women Who Hate Them: The Masochistic Art of Dating*, by Nancy Linn-Desmond;[11] *Men Who Hate Themselves: And the Women Who Agree with Them*, by David A. Rudnitsky;[12] *Men Who Hate*

Women, by Susan Forward and Joan Torres;[13] and *Men Who Love Too Little,* by Thomas Whiteman and Randy Petersen.[14] The dedication of *Why Dogs Are Better Than Men,* by Jennifer Berman,[15] reads as follows: "This book is for any woman who has steadfastly resisted the frequent urge to feloniously resolve her relationship with our hormonally challenged counterparts." Even as satire, the reverse would be unthinkable. Not all popular books on this topic are so grotesque. Included in this category are John Gray's best-selling *Men Are from Mars, Women Are from Venus*[16] and its sequel *Mars and Venus in the Bedroom.*[17] Though more benign, they are equally superficial. But they are meant to be taken more seriously.

Some comic strips would be utterly inconceivable if their "humour" were associated with stereotypes of women rather than those of men. Actually, comic strips have poked fun at men for many decades. The classic of this genre, possibly the prototype, was *Bringing up Father.* Jiggs was the hapless, henpecked husband. That was demeaning to men. On the other hand, Maggie was the snobbish and even violent wife. She repeatedly belted him with a rolling pin for failing to support her social pretensions. Both husband *and* wife, in short, were parodied. Things had changed by the time *Blondie* arrived on the scene. Dagwood is treated well by his patient wife, Blondie, but he is even more pathetic than Jiggs. Like Jiggs, nevertheless, Dagwood evokes sympathetic responses from readers. In this comic strip, the classic pattern remains. Modern variants of that pattern make gender politics more explicit. Consider *Sally Forth.* Ted complains to his wife: "I don't mind a good ribbing, Sal, but it seems as if the whole trend in comedy is to make men the butt of the jokes." She replies: "Everyone else is on the protected-group list ... ethnic groups, racial minorities, religious groups ... it's even getting hard to joke about women. You male WASPs are the last group we can ridicule." The whole point being made, presumably, is that Ted's observation is ridiculous. When Sally tells him that he is exaggerating the problem, he replies, "Oh, sure, lump us in with lawyers and politicians. You really know how to hurt a guy." Says she: "You forgot TV evangelists."[18] Elsewhere, Sally tells Ted, "I'm trying to get a handle on this angry white male phenomenon. How can the most advantaged group of humans be angry? It doesn't make sense. What makes you angry?" And Ted, busy reading, replies impatiently, "Not being allowed to finish the last chapter of an exciting book."[19] Ted is not treated with contempt, but men are.

At the moment, pathetic men are de rigueur in comic strips. Evoking sympathy for them, however, is definitely not. Sometimes, they are merely stupid. In *Herman,* a woman looks at her infant son and says,

"Smarten up! Sometimes, I think your father's got more brains than you have."[20] Or in *Real Life Adventures*, a caption reads: "We use only 10 percent of our brain. Some even less." The picture above shows a man talking to his wife. He: "Have you seen my keys?" She: "They're in your hand." He: "Oh, so they are. I wonder how they got there." She: "You picked them up." He: "Yep. I'll bet that's what happened."[21] In another case, the misandry is explicit: "As the number of males in the group increases, the collective IQ decreases exponentially." The picture shows one man guzzling beer and another saying, "Hey, I got an idea! Let's all take off our shirts and paint a different letter of our team's name on our stomachs … like this."[22] In a second case within the same month, the caption is slightly less explicit: "Catching your husband performing an unnatural act." It shows a man preparing his laundry, with his wife asking, "Are you *actually* picking up socks and putting them in the hamper?"[23] Yet another example of the same comic strip features this caption: "Why you don't hear more about Father Nature." The latter tells his wife, "Gee, normally I'd love to help you, hon, but there's a game on. Do you mind doing it yourself this time? I promise next time we'll change seasons together."[24] The joke in *Hagar the Horrible*, is a klutzy male Viking. In one strip, his long-suffering wife, Helga, tells their daughter: "There are just two things I'm sure of: number one: 'women are smarter than men!'" When the daughter asks what number two is, the answer is, "Never tell a man about number one."[25] Not all comic strips include cartoons. Jim Mullen's *Hotsheet*, for *Entertainment Weekly*, is entirely verbal. Under the heading of "Monday Night Football," he writes, "Viewership is down for the fourth year in a row. Because the Internet is an even better way for men to ignore their families."[26]

Comic-strip men are often overtly sexist. That makes them worthy of nothing but contempt. One disturbing sign in recent comic strips, although it appears in many other media and especially on television sitcoms, is the assumption that readers will define "sexism" in a way that makes sense only in misandric terms – which is to say, as a synonym for *misogyny*. Not only is the word "sexism" used exclusively in connection with men, as if women were somehow immune to it, but it is used routinely in connection with attitudes that do not in themselves involve hatred. Here is one example from *Beetle Bailey*, which is often about intersexual hostility. One standard situation ridiculed in this comic strip is the lecherous attitude of General Halftrack towards the two women who work in his office, Miss Buxom and Private Blips. In one strip, they approach him and offer their congratulations: "We've been keeping score, sir," says one. "For a whole month," says the other, "you haven't made a sexist remark." And the general's reply is characteristic of him: "Well, that deserves a big hug and kiss."[27] His remark, presumably a self-evident example of sexism, leads the women to tear up their score sheet and walk out. The problem here is sexual harassment, not sexism. It is surely not sexist to have heterosexual desire (although expressing it in inappropriate places or ways can constitute sexual harassment). Miss Buxom and Private Blips have identified General Halftrack's heterosexuality, per se, with sexism. Consider a slight alteration. Suppose the general had merely *thought* those words. Without saying them, he could not be accused of sexual harassment. But readers would still be expected to recognize this guy as a sexist pig merely for being attracted to the women. In the ideal world of misandry, the only acceptable men would be gay men or, possibly, straight men who were willing to repress their heterosexual urges. Except when women explicitly ask for heterosexual responses (and not then, either, according to Andrea Dworkin).[28] As it happens, even *ridiculing* the general's sexism is now considered too soft. After a scandal involving sexual integration in the military, cartoonist Mort Walker decided to send General Halftrack to "sensitivity training" classes and have him apologize to his secretaries. But Canada's biggest newspaper, the *Toronto Star*, was too prissy for that solution. Its own solution was simply to cancel the comic strip.[29] One encouraging development is the rise in "underground comics" by women. In these comics, women are portrayed as just as interested in sex as men.[30]

Often overlooked in studies of popular culture is the greeting card. It is unnecessary to be a rocket scientist, or even a sociologist, to realize that greeting cards say a great deal about the people who buy them – more, possibly, than about the people who create them. According to an article in the *New York Times Magazine*, a female writer for Hallmark Cards makes no secret of the double standard: "Men are always fair game ... But only women can make fun of women. House rule, you know."[31] It is worth noting here that "[m]ore than 85% of greeting cards are bought by women. And woman-to-woman 'friendship' cards have gone through the roof ..."[32] (Apparently, even women need help in expressing their feelings.) Here is one sample: A poutingly posed Adonis is stamped with a simulated F.D.A. contents label: "Man. Ingredients: vanity, self-centredness, arrogance, insensitivity, thoughtlessness, insincerity. Plus they may contain one or more of the following: communications skills of a chimp, obsessive love for his mother, and/or an ego the size of a landfill."[33] That kind of humour sells, big.

The title of an article by Kathy Jackson says it all: "'Man Jokes' Make Bucks."[34] (The *Montreal Gazette* placed this title directly below that of a column called "A Look at the Bright Side.") Jackson writes that *Men! The Cartoon Book* has made its author, Cindy Garner, "the darling of morning radio shows in the u.s." According to Jackson, "[S]ome people, even a few males, say that men finally are getting what they deserve and it's perfectly OK for entrepreneurs like Garner to profit by making fun of them with books, cartoons, even greeting cards. Others say such slams are blatantly sexist, the equivalent of dumb blonde jokes."[35] Those in the former group believe that promoting stereotypes and even bigotry is morally acceptable when the targeted victims "deserve it." They forget that the same way of thinking has always been used to legitimate prejudice and even crime. After all, people used to argue that some women "deserved" to be raped. Yet even Hallmark, known for the mass production of cards expressing inoffensive sentiment, has decided to cash in on the overtly offensive sentiments of many women:

As for the cards that bite, after complaints Hallmark pulled one from the shelves. On the outside it says, "Men are scum." On the inside it says, "Excuse me. For a second there, I was feeling generous." But Hallmark is still selling cards that say, "There are easier things than meeting a good man; nailing Jell-O to a tree, for instance." There are others with similar messages. Renee Hershey, a Hallmark representative, said the cards are intended to help build friendships between women by using a topic virtually all of them can identify with. "We also have cards in the Shoebox line that talk about positive relationships with men. And women can relate to those cards as well," she said.

So Hallmark is not just making money by pandering to popular prejudice. No, readers are told, this company is actually performing a valuable service to the community by promoting friendships among women. Never mind that it does so at the cost of undermining the prospect of respect between women and men. Of course, women can choose cards expressing other feelings, too. Contempt, respect ... these have nothing to do, according to Hershey, with moral choices. They merely reflect personal taste. Unlike misogyny, they claim, misandry is not inherently wrong; it merely expresses an "alternative lifestyle."

A popular singer, Helen Reddy, once said about her belief in reincarnation, "I've been a man many times. That's what I'm trying to atone for now."[36] This sums up the premise of *Switch* (Blake Edwards, 1991), a situation comedy about gender. Some lines are supposed to be funny, but the main reason for calling this a comedy (and discussing it in this chapter) is the "situation," or basic premise, that sets up the plot. Viewers are asked to see *that* as funny. Though hardly a classic, it did receive some favourable reviews.[37]

In the prologue, viewers are introduced to Steve Brooks, a confirmed bachelor who likes to sleep around. Almost immediately, he is established as a sleazy jerk, hated by the women he uses for his own pleasure. Even he is surprised when three ex-girlfriends invite him over for the evening. Relaxing together in the Jacuzzi, they suddenly force him under the water, drown him, and tie up his body with their underwear. Macho beast that he is, Steve recovers and staggers into the bedroom where Felicia, Margo, and Slick are making plans to dispose of the body. Margo pulls out a revolver and shoots him three times. After that, Steve is truly dead. In purgatory, he is informed of his impending resurrection, but God makes it clear that this second chance will be his last. To enter heaven instead of hell, Steve will have to find one "female" who likes him. He wakes up in his bedroom, the previous sequence seemingly a bad dream. But while he is in the bathroom, Satan convinces God to reincarnate Steve in the body of a woman. Attempting to urinate, Steve discovers that he is now missing the necessary equipment. He screams hysterically. His neighbour complains to the doorman. The two of them find a woman unconscious on the bathroom floor.

It takes Steve only a few moments to begin making plans. First, "she" phones "her" friend, Walter, but cannot convince him that "she" has been killed and reincarnated. Then "she" pays a visit to Margo. After the apparent stranger reveals details of their private relationship, including the murder, Margo begins to realize that this "woman" is really Steve. Afraid of what might happen if the police are notified, she agrees to help Steve and provides him with some clothes. Next, Steve introduces "herself" at the office as "Amanda," Steve's sister, and takes over his old job. That evening, she and Walter meet at their old hangout, Duke's Bar and Grill.

Life suitably reorganized, Amanda now begins her search for a female who likes her. At first, this seems impossible. Every time she calls a woman listed in Steve's little black book, the response is a screaming tantrum. With men, however, the situation is very different. Looking like a *Playboy* centrefold, Amanda is sexually attractive to friends (such as Walter), colleagues (Dan, the new executive at work), and strangers on the street (a sewer worker). After a while, though, she meets one woman who really does like her. Sheila, a lesbian, meets Amanda on business and invites her to a party. She reveals her sexual interest in Amanda, taking her out to an expensive restaurant. When the macho Amanda is uncomfortable in this refined atmosphere, Sheila takes her to Duke's. A man makes a pass at her there, and she reacts with hostility. But when they end up at a club that does suit Amanda, a lesbian one, it presents Sheila with a problem. She discovers that her own lover has been using her for business purposes. The bickering that follows attracts the attention of a female bodyguard. Amanda attacks her but to her surprise is promptly decked. Next day in the boardroom, Sheila gives her account to Dan instead of Amanda. That puts an end to the relationship. Once again, Amanda is left wondering how she will ever find a female to like her.

One night at Duke's, she and Walter have too much to drink. A brawl ensues. When they get home, Amanda manages to undress the semi-conscious Walter and tosses him into the bed. The two fall asleep side by side. Next morning, Amanda sees that Walter is half-naked and accuses him of rape. At that moment, Margo arrives for a visit. Walter and Amanda continue quarrelling, but Margo watches the news and learns that Steve's body has been found. With that in mind, she plants a gun behind some cushions on the sofa. The police find it and charge Amanda with Steve's murder. A trial follows. Once again, Margo and her friends are left unscathed. Amanda's bizarre story of death and reincarnation leads to a verdict of not guilty by reason of insanity. Instead of prison, she is sentenced to a mental institution. Several months pass. Through all this, Walter remains faithful to Amanda. When he finds out that a baby is on the way, he decides to marry her. Knowing that the pregnancy and birth will endanger her life, Amanda nevertheless decides against an abortion. The baby, a girl, is delivered safely and immediately responds to her mother. In other words, Amanda (Steve) has finally found a female who likes her (him). Now Steve is ready to die and enter heaven.

The epilogue shows Walter and his daughter visiting a cemetery. The tombstone clearly identifies Steve and Amanda as the same person. In a concluding and decisive voice-over, the "spiritualized" protagonist has trouble deciding whether to become a male angel or a female one. But even though Steve is no longer incarnated as a woman, his voice is still that of a woman. Amanda's voice, not Steve's, reminds the protagonist that there is no need to decide in a hurry. A woman has the last word in *Switch*, therefore, both literally and figuratively.

Steve has been threatened with eternal torment in hell for his sins. But what precisely are his sins? What is it that makes him so bad? On numerous occasions, characters refer to him as a "male chauvinist pig." What does he actually do to deserve this label? From the information provided, his primary sin seems to be what used to be called fornication. Because he has affairs with many women, moreover, all of them feel betrayed by him. There is no indication that he rapes these women, brutalizes them, or even seduces them. The women we meet are sophisticated, worldly, and cynical. Dressed in a fur coat, Margo is accosted by an animal-rights activist: "Do you know," he asks, "how

many animals were killed to make that coat?" She replies: "Do you
know how many such animals I had to *fuck* to get this coat?" But if
casual sex is now considered normal rather than sinful by both men
and women, why condemn Steve? What is so horrible about him?
Evidently, it is his view of women as sexual objects. Affronted by the
sexual overtures of one man, Amanda says, "I'm sick and tired of
being treated like a piece of meat!" Okay, but why does she consistently dress in a preposterously provocative way? If the clothes are
Margo's, then viewers must assume that Margo herself is in the habit
of exploiting sex. If not, then they must assume that Amanda has
deliberately set out to do so on her own.

In any case, *Switch* does not tell us about the attitude of Steve's ex-
girlfriends to men. If he was enjoying casual sex with them, after all,
it is at least possible that they were doing so with him as well. There
is certainly no indication that these women subscribe to religious,
philosophical, or moral precepts of a more elevated kind. Not only do
they never discuss the moral implications of revenge, they carry out a
cold-blooded murder. Viewers see them clothed in pure white robes,
nonetheless, perversely suggesting their innocence. (On at least one
television show, *Equal Justice*, viewers are expected to approve when
a woman is found not guilty for attempting to murder her husband
under similar circumstances. After discovering that he has a girlfriend,
she deliberately plans to kill them both and succeeds in killing the
woman. Even though this is not presented as a case of self-defence, in
which a wife plans to kill her abusive husband before he can assault
her again, the jury – composed, not coincidentally, mainly of women
– still finds her behaviour perfectly acceptable.)[38] Not only do Steve's
three ex-girlfriends murder him, moreover, they also arrange to have
him arrested for his own murder! Viewers are asked to believe that
promiscuity and boorishness are crimes worthy of personal attention
by the Devil; revenge and murder, on the other hand are legitimate
and even amusing. What kind of a moral universe is this?

The answer is simple: this is not a moral universe at all. It is a
misandric universe. The premise of *Switch*, that heterosexual men are
innately evil, is made clear immediately following the opening credits.
(The term "innately evil" makes no sense, being an oxymoron, but it
is useful to indicate a paradox in the way men are sometimes portrayed. Unless people are free to choose between good and evil, they
cannot be moral agents – which is to say, they can be neither moral
nor immoral. To suggest that men are "innately evil," therefore, is to
suggest that they are both moral agents, who consciously choose evil,
and amoral beings, who have no choice but to do evil.) Onscreen are
two objects: a golf ball and a golf club. Considering the cinematic

context that is presented over the next two hours, it is surely reasonable to assume that the ball represents "balls" and the club what women should do to them. Indeed, those responsible for this movie have left nothing to the imagination. Giving birth in the hospital, Amanda repeatedly clutches Walter's groin as if trying to tear it off his body. Time after time, she strikes the genitals of men. In one interesting scene, a sewer worker says, without making the slightest physical advance: "If you don't kiss me, I'm going to be sick." Amanda replies: "Oh yeah, then we've both got a problem," and aims her purse directly at his crotch. These scenes are considered extremely amusing by audiences. Viewers have clearly come a long way from the days when a mere slap across the face was considered the appropriate way for ladies to defend their dignity when confronted with the unwanted attention of cads. (That cinematic convention, "the slap," is as common now as it ever was. It is worth a study in itself.)

The real problem with Steve and every other man in this cinematic world is simply that they *are* men, heterosexual men. Their crime is expressing erotic interest in women. Although the sewer worker does so in a vulgar way, others do not. Arnold, Amanda's boss, asks her out for dinner. The implication is that he wants more than to have dinner with her. He receives an indignant refusal. But what, precisely, is wrong with what he really wants? Is it that he offers her a *quid pro quo*? *Switch* does not say so, but that is the clear implication. Is it that casual sex is wrong? If so, that has not prevented Margo and her friends from indulging in it. Or is it that *heterosexual* sex is wrong? Later on, Amanda tells her rather timid friend Walter that he is a good man, not like the others. "Maybe I'm not so good," Walter replies. When asked for an explanation, he continues, "Because I really want to go to bed with you." Clearly, the *desire* of a heterosexual man to enjoy sex with a woman, whether expressed rudely or politely, is considered reprehensible ("not so good"). The other women have sex with men and even enjoy doing so, it is true, but not because they *like* the men they have sex with. Margo uses men sexually in order to buy fur coats or other luxury items. Her female pals in the corporate world, presumably, use men sexually for similar purposes. Viewers might point to a cinematic link between the way these women exploit men and the way men exploit women, which would require them to indict the cynical opportunism of both sexes. But *Switch* encourages them to replace the parallel with a double standard: the men are not justified for exploiting women, of course, but the women are indeed justified for exploiting men.

Because every movie presents itself as a world, generalized conclusions are drawn from whatever is or is not shown. In this one, every

male character is bad; by implication, most or all men are bad in real
life, too. Sheila makes the point very directly when Amanda reveals
her true aims. With more accuracy about Amanda than she herself
realizes, Sheila says, "You're cruel like a man." But *Switch* would not
amount to much if it allowed only female characters to make misandric remarks. Misandry can now be expected from women, but not,
perhaps, from men. The "genius" of *Switch* is its imaginative use of
irony to achieve precisely this. Female viewers are obviously delighted,
judging from their laughter and applause, when Amanda confirms
their own stereotypes. Coming from the mouth of a man, albeit one
who appears to be a woman, rebukes directed at other men sound all
the more convincing. Amanda accuses Walter of rape and observes
that "every six minutes, a woman is raped in this country." (A
hallmark of misandric movies is the direct, though cinematically unre-
alistic, insertion of statistical or sociological information into the
dialogue.) Female viewers are invited to think, "See, even *men* know
how rotten they are." Women are invited to draw the obvious conclusion that men are not merely ignorant or stupid but consciously
and deliberately evil. The fact that Amanda's behaviour is both vulgar
and violent is significant because it reveals a double standard. Viewers
are unlikely to be offended by the fact that Margo and her female
friends are not only cold, calculating, and cynical but also murderous.
The very things female viewers despise in *men*, judging from what can
be heard in the theatre, they admire in *women*. This reaction exem-
plifies revenge, not justice.

Like many other movies of the 1990s, this one has metaphysical
overtones. In the cinematic world of *Switch*, the cosmos is governed
by a bisexual deity; the Creator, God, is both male and female. But
the Devil, Satan, is still, as always, male. Holiness (or, in secular terms,
virtue) can be associated, at least theoretically, with both maleness and
femaleness and thus can be accessible to both men and women. But
sin (in secular terms, vice) can be associated only with maleness and
can thus be attributable only to men. Sexual polarization has been
cleverly disguised and even reversed, in other words, not eliminated.
It is impossible to understand the prologue and epilogue of *Switch*
without this metaphysical background, no matter how secularized and
trivialized, because what is true "above" (of the satanic and the devine)
is true "below" (of soul and body, male and female, men and women).
The main premise of this movie is that Steve's soul, or spirit, can be
separated from his body. Even in the body of a woman, it is still that
of a man. In itself, this premise is not necessarily dualistic because the
soul is not necessarily in *conflict* with the body. In many Western
religious systems, the soul is differentiated from but intimately related

to the body.[39] The premise is used here, however, to establish another one that is necessarily dualistic.

Because Steve's soul inhabits the body of a woman but continues to function as that of a man, because the reincarnation does not immediately convert him from evil to good, we must conclude that it has been tainted or corrupted by years of contact with a male body. Nevertheless, Steve is eventually transformed, primarily because of his experience in a female body, culminating in his experience of pregnancy and childbirth. Thinking about the possibility of dying in childbirth, Amanda tells Walter, "You can't imagine what it is to have a life inside you." From this, two things are made clear. Vice is inherent in the male body, but virtue is inherent in the female body. And the body is primary, the soul secondary. That cinematic hierarchy corresponds symbolically to the biological reductionism of Marilyn French[40] and other misandric feminists. They associate men with transcendence, referring by that to their alleged invention of the soul, otherworldly monotheism, asceticism, science, technology, and so forth. Women are different. They associate woman with immanence, referring by that to their alleged affinity for nature, worldly polytheism, caregiving, healing, and so on.

Because Amanda has a female body in addition to a male soul, she is liberated. Her female body eventually purifies or decontaminates her male soul, thus bringing about salvation. Most men are not in Steve's "fortunate" position. Not being transsexuals – those willing to acquire female bodies by castrating themselves – men like Walter must find some other way of washing away the pollution of maleness. That amounts to emotional and intellectual surgery. Although he has the benefit of neither innate virtue (available only to women) nor radical surgery, Walter can still be "converted." Stained as he is by the "original sin" of maleness, he is not much better than Steve. He likes and admires Steve, a man universally hated by women. Walter is more acceptable to viewers than Steve, to be sure, but only because he is afraid to be himself. Even so, Walter is still redeemable.

In many forms of Christian theology, especially Protestant forms, redemption (or salvation) is a result of divine grace alone, not of the merit earned by doing good works. Christians can participate in their own salvation only by responding to the divine initiative with faith. Walter is "saved" because of his admiration for Amanda, not because of anything he himself has said or done. (We refer here to Amanda rather than Steve in this context, because it is her female body, not her male soul, that has cinematic priority.) Because virtue is allegedly inherent in the female body – the mere ability to give birth is a defining feature of female bodies – it is fair to say that salvation is due to

Amanda rather than Steve. Amanda sacrifices herself by refusing to
have an abortion, which conveniently affirms "a woman's right to
choose," even though the cost of doing so will probably be death.
Because of that, Walter finally grows up and takes on the adult
responsibility of fatherhood. In terms of our theological metaphor,
salvation is possible only through the mediation of a female Christ.
Steve himself is "saved" in a similar way: his child is a daughter, not
a son. Through the love of this female, the way to heaven is opened
and an eternity in hell prevented. Furthermore, it is Amanda's discovery of her own maternal love that causes her conversion to feminism.
Amanda, finally, represents Mary as well as Christ. Although the night
in bed with Walter technically included sex, Amanda was drunk at the
time and thus unaware of it experientially. This leads, therefore, to a
kind of "virgin birth." To sum up, the sexual hierarchy has not been
abolished in Switch, merely *reversed*. Salvation is through the daughters of Eve and damnation through the sons of Adam.

Because it features gender reversals, *Switch* invites comparison with
other movies based on the premise of men being mistaken for women.
One of the most successful has been *Some Like It Hot* (Billy Wilder,
1959).[41] Trying to escape from gangsters after witnessing the Valentine's
Day Massacre in Chicago, Gerry ("Daphne") and Joe ("Josephine")
join a female band on its way to Florida. When their real identities
are revealed in the end, both find happiness: Joe marries Sugar, a
beautiful singer with the band, and Gerry "marries" a (presumably
gay) millionaire yachtsman. The underlying and unifying theme in this
comedy of manners is gender. It focuses attention on the common
humanity that draws men and women together, not on the prejudice
that divides them. The foibles of *both* sexes, as understood at the time,
are revealed. Women look at men as "success objects," and men look
at women as "sex objects." In the end, through love, both Sugar and
Joe transcend the limitations imposed on them by stereotypes. In the
case of homosexuality, this movie rejects the notion of a clear distinction that separates heterosexuality from homosexuality. It affirms the
ambivalence that allows one, at least occasionally, to merge with the
other. Although Gerry is delighted by the physical closeness of Sugar
and the other women, he is intrigued by the forbidden delights of gay
romance. Entirely forgetting that he is a man until Joe reminds him to
keep saying, "I'm a boy, I'm a boy," he falls head over heels in love
with and announces his engagement to another man. In the end, even
the need for secrecy is abandoned when his "fiancé," on being told of
Gerry's true identity, says, "Well, no one's perfect." There is not a trace
of the self-righteousness that mars *Switch*. The humour is gentle and
affectionate, not savage and mocking. If we ever again reach the stage

of civility represented by *Some Like It Hot*, it will not be due to movies such as *Switch*.

Switch invites comparisons also with movies in which men learn what women are thinking. One example would be another "romantic comedy" called *What Women Want* (Nancy Meyers, 2000). Nick is a "chauvinistic advertising executive who never underestimates the selling power of a babe in a bikini."[42] Trouble is, his boss is a woman. After a freak accident, he is able to hear what the women around him are thinking. Nick realizes now that "his crude jokes are rarely appreciated, his charm is more like smarm, and frankly, his sexual technique could benefit from some pointers."[43] The obvious lesson here is that men are too stupid or too lazy to understand women, which explains the "cuckoo things" that men say or do. Men should therefore "listen" more carefully to women. Otherwise, they run the risk of retribution – a punch in the face, according to this "old-fashioned battle of the sexes."[44] The less obvious (but implicit) message is that men, not women, are to blame for any problems in relations between the sexes. Maybe the new decade, or at least the new century, will produce a cinematic counterpart in which women learn something from men.

No one expects television sitcoms to be taken very seriously by the viewing public. But they are taken seriously indeed by academics in fields such as women's studies and "cultural studies."[45] They argue that most sitcoms foster a bourgeois or patriarchal worldview. But is the argument well founded? As far as we can tell, it is not. Two approaches towards men are common on sitcoms (and other genres).[46] *Designing Women* takes a direct approach, referring explicitly to sexual politics. Very often, characters refer to events in the news. *Home Improvement* and *The Simpsons* take an indirect approach, referring implicitly to sexual politics: characters merely parade common stereotypes. *Ally McBeal* combines the two.

Sitcoms, which draw heavily on ridicule for their humour, have probably done more than any other genre to turn men into objects of derision. On *The Simpsons*, fathers, and men in general, are routinely mocked. Bart is, to be charitable, a fool. And then there is MTV's *Beavis and Butt-head*, its two characters described in overtly sexist language by Ginia Bellafante as "unwavering in their testosterone-fueled stupidity."[47] This series was turned into not only a movie, *Beavis and Butt-head Do America* (Mike Judge, 1996), but also a spin-off series: Fox's *King of the Hill*. The central characters, all of them male, are described sarcastically by Bellafante as "real men."

A most egregiously misandric sitcom was NBC's mercifully short-lived *Men Behaving Badly*, which aired from 1996 to 1997. The basic "situation" generating "comedy," as in *Home Improvement*, is the innate stupidity of men. "Sexist sentiments exploded by the stupidity of the guy expressing them," writes Ken Tucker of *Entertainment Weekly*, "is what this show's about."[48] Jamie and Kevin are not merely two characters who happen to be men: by default, they represent *all* men. Moreover, according to Tom Werner, one of the producers, the series justifiably "shows men as they really are."[49] This is made clear by the title. Also by default, Sarah, Kevin's long-suffering girlfriend, represents all women. This is made clear by her short monologues accompanied by clips from vintage films. Addressing female viewers, Sarah invariably makes some stereotypical allusion to the stupidity of men in general: "Men's fascination with technology is hard-wired into their brains." What follows is supposed to illustrate the timeless wisdom of this woman and, by implication, of women in general. It is true that one of the men, Kevin, is likeable despite his stereotypical masculinity. Though sloppy, animalistic, coarse, ignorant, and over-sexed, he is also cute and sweet. But that is the whole point – at least some men can be liked or even loved *despite* the fact that they are men, and supposedly so different from women, not because of it. In one episode, Sarah tells poor Kevin that she is attracted to him precisely because he makes her feel superior.[50] (She refrains from explaining that she finds him attractive because, in addition to anything else, he is a very handsome young man. To do that would be to admit that women are just as likely to "objectify" men as men are to "objectify" women, a complaint made repeatedly on the show.)

Given the politicized atmosphere of the 1990s, no one should be too surprised to find that every episode of this popular sitcom begins, during the opening credits, with a montage of old films in which women slap and punch men. (In some cases, the men are hurled through walls, over furniture, and onto the floor.) So much for the claim that female viewers have elevated the artistic level of television. But *Men Behaving Badly* is only one of the more blatant examples of misandric television. Other shows, some earlier and others more recent, require further comment.

Designing Women, both in its original run and in reruns, has been extremely successful in translating the hopes and fears, needs and problems, of women into familiar features of public discourse. Many episodes are intended very obviously to indoctrinate viewers with feminist convictions or to reinforce those already held. No attempt is made to help viewers see the complexity or ambiguity of reality by presenting other points of view that could, at least in theory, be taken seriously. No attempt is made even to disguise the use of polemical rhetoric. Episodes of this kind are blatantly misandric. It is not true that feminists have no sense of humour: they may sometimes find it hard to laugh at themselves as feminists, though not as women, but seldom find it hard to laugh at men.

In view of the fact that many episodes were about current political controversies – feminism, sexual harassment, domestic violence, and so on – most would agree that *Designing Women* was created largely by and for people who supported feminist causes. Linda Bloodworth-Thomasen, the show's creator, writer, and co-executive producer, made no secret of her close ties with the supportive Clinton White House. The political atmosphere on prime-time television, though, is supported indirectly as well directly. Consider the contrast between two other sitcoms: *The Golden Girls* and *The Fanelli Boys*. The former is about women. Although the women themselves are sometimes irritating, they are portrayed sympathetically. Sophia is a crotchety oldster, but she is also honest, unpretentious, and good-hearted. Blanche is a vain and promiscuous nymphomaniac, but she is also generous and good-hearted. Rose is a naive idiot, but she is also innocent and good-hearted. Dorothy is a self-righteous moralizer, but she is also forgiving and good-hearted. Despite the ups and downs of everyday life as it is portrayed on each episode, these women clearly support publicly endorsed moral values such as loving, caring, "sharing," friendship, and loyalty. *The Fanelli Boys*, created by the same talented production team, was notably unsuccessful. Aired directly following *The Golden Girls*, it was intended to be seen as an equivalent but contrasting show about men (even though one of its major characters is a woman).

Unlike the "golden girls," however, what could have been called the "brassy boys" are unsympathetic characters. Their image is at least partly determined by class. They supposedly represent the lower, not upper-middle class. At any rate, they are less educated, less articulate, and generally less refined than their female counterparts on *The Golden Girls*. This is in keeping with the stereotypical link between masculinity and coarseness or even brutality.

When the women make misandric remarks – and that happens often – the humour is supposed to lie in the situation attacked. In one episode, for example, Dorothy discusses the hardships of motherhood: "If it were easy," she says, "fathers would do it."[51] The audience is expected to laugh in recognition of the truth being imparted. When their male counterparts make misogynistic remarks – and that too happens often – the humour is supposed to lie in the characters themselves. Even when the same behaviour is featured on both shows, the expected audience response is different. Nearly every episode of *The Golden Girls* features bawdy remarks, generally from the lips of either Blanche or Sophia. The same is true of *The Fanelli Boys*. When vulgarity comes from women, it is presented as earthy honesty. When vulgarity comes from men, it is presented as sleazy. The audience is expected to laugh *at* them, not *with* them. In other words, sexism is acceptable when it comes from women but reprehensible when it comes from men.

The network executives flunked an opportunity to promote healthy male bonding, in short, whether among brothers or friends. Instead, they took an opportunity to ridicule men. Fortunately, we have not yet reached the stage at which merely ridiculing alone can maintain viewer interest. Because no discernible effort was made to probe the depth and richness of the characters' humanity, viewers found *The Fanelli Boys*, unlike *The Golden Girls*, boring. This show could not escape the fate – early cancellation – of a still earlier attempt to do the same thing. In 1989,[52] *Men* tried to "explore the bonding" among another bunch of neurotic, insensitive, and vulgar men. It failed to generate enough public sympathy or interest for a single full season. The same thing happened in 1997 to ABC's *The Secret Lives of Men*. That show too tried to cash in on the ugly stereotypes of men (albeit in a more sophisticated way).

It seems clear, therefore, that male human beings are unable to excite the imagination of good writers – even of male writers. For whatever reasons, whether emotional, intellectual, or political, our society is unable to use its creative resources to explore the condition of men or to take men seriously as real people in the context of humour. Television merely reflects what is prevalent in other genres of comedy.

One show, more than any other, has exemplified this state of affairs. Though no longer in production, it will be shown in syndicated reruns for decades to come. In the fall of 1991, ABC introduced a sitcom called *Home Improvement*. From the beginning, it was massively popular, the top-rated show week after week. Clearly, then, the phenomenon is of importance. "Some would argue," says Christopher Loudon in a *TV Guide* interview with the show's star, "that *Home Improvement* is all about men being jerks." Loudon is careful to add that he personally thinks "it's really a celebration of how smart – and tolerant – women are." Tim Allen responds by saying, "I think it's both," although he adds that he thinks Tim Taylor, the protagonist, has "grown" and that "what was politically incorrect when we started the show has since become the norm."[53] That last comment is extremely interesting. When the show began, it was still considered unwise to ridicule either women or men as groups. By this time, according to Allen, ridiculing men had become the norm. And lamentably, he was correct. One reviewer, Mike Boone, has outlined the formula:

Pigheaded husbands inflicting torment on long-suffering wives have been a staple of situation comedies since television began. Tim Taylor [in *Home Improvement*] is the 1990s heir to a tradition that extends back through Archie Bunker to Ralph Kramden. The Honeymooners didn't invent spousal spats. In adapting the battle of the sexes to TV, sitcoms slapped on a laugh track and simplified each skirmish to fit into a half hour of airtime. The opening block lays out details of a plan that the husband is trying to conceal from his wife. After the first commercial break, a security lapse – the kids blab, or the oaf leaves some incriminating evidence (sales slip, a fishing lodge reservation) lying around – results in [the wife] getting wise. Then, after more ads, action intensifies (he knows she knows; she knows he knows she knows) speeding toward a dénouement in which the man of the house sheepishly admits to being an unfeeling cretin and promises never to misbehave again. As the final credits roll, the man's act of contrition is rewarded by a kiss, a hug and a scratch behind the ears. As viewers are bathed in the warm glow of forgiveness, TV offers up the comforting illusion that all marital transgressions can be adjudicated in 30 minutes – and every transgressor gets off with a suspended sentence.[54]

Although Boone's description of the sitcom formula is accurate, his understanding of its moral and psychological implications is not. What is so comforting, after all, about the illusion that all husbands are "unfeeling cretins" to be treated condescendingly either as children who promise never to be naughty boys again or pet dogs who are rewarded for good behaviour with a scratch behind the ears? To put it differently, comforting to whom? And comforting in what way?

Home Improvement is about the host of a TV do-it-yourself show. Its star, Tim Allen, had made his reputation doing a stand-up comedy routine called "Men Are Pigs." In 1990, the routine was repackaged for Showtime as an hour-long television special. It won cable television's Ace award. According to Boone, the "beast has been domesticated. In every episode of *Home Improvement*, Jill Taylor [the wife] gets the last laugh – along with viewers who can't help succumbing to Tim's goofy charm. Sure, he's a jerk. But who isn't?" Well, not wives. Not if viewers are to believe what they see on television week after week. "The best sitcoms are therapeutic," continues Boone. "We watch our own foibles writ large and played for laughs."[55] Really? *Our own* foibles? The fact is that more of *Home Improvement*'s fans are women than men. "Network entertainment," according to Richard Zoglin, "is largely driven by the female audience … the great bulk of TV movies focus on women protagonists with either an empowering story to tell or a rapist on their trail; and most sitcoms have a female orientation even when they ostensibly revolve around men. (Watch Major Dad get tamed by the women in his life.)"[56]

Precisely what, then, is the attraction for female viewers? Their foibles are never played for laughs on *Home Improvement*. Jill is occasionally silly as an individual, true, *but not as a woman*. She delivers value-laden messages by virtue of being a woman. Men should learn to talk about their feelings, say, or washing clothes is just as important as repairing a machine.[57] She is clearly supposed to be taken seriously as a woman. Tim, on the other hand, delivers value-laden messages in spite of himself. He is really a sensitive guy underneath all his macho posturing. But he is surely not supposed to be taken seriously *as a man*. Or, to put it another way, he is supposed to be taken seriously as a man to the extent that men in general are slobs and fools but can be trained or "housebroken" by women. The show implies that Tim's sensitivity is learned, not innate. Without the civilizing influence of Jill's feminist lessons, Tim would be just another male barbarian. Female viewers can love him, yes, but only as someone remade in their own image. Their love for him, therefore, is a form of *self*-love.

This is not quite true of some other sitcoms featuring boorish men. Boone observes that "beer drinkers love Norm on Cheers. Dan Conner, Roseanne's big slob of a husband, appeals to the goober in all of us." *Cheers* and even *Roseanne* exist in a different, somewhat higher, moral universe. Sure, Dan is a slob, but so is Roseanne. Sure, Norm swills beer while Cliff pontificates and Sam brags about his sexual exploits, but Carla bitches about everything and Dianne looks down her nose at everyone. Those shows are about human foibles. *Home Improvement* is exclusively about *men's* foibles. Ken Tucker said it best: "Just as the men's movement's message seemed to boil down to 'guys can't help it if they're pigs,' so many of the jokes in *Home Improvement* revolve around the notion that Tim just can't help grunting like a baboon and talking like a jerk."[58]

Obviously, Allen "lampoons macho and other chauvinistic behaviour by men." Also lampooned are the men who read Robert Bly and prance around in the woods with tom-toms. In an interview, Allen once made a distinction between bad "machismo" and good "masculinism."[59] No distinction, though, is evident on the show. Compare Allen with Jenny Jones. She became famous for a misandric stand-up routine, openly barring men from admission, and was rewarded with a talk show of her own. Like Jones, Allen makes money by legitimating prejudice.[60] Like her, he cashes in on the morally dubious but "politically correct" fashion of ridiculing men. According to Mark Morrison, "what makes the act work and what allows it to translate so well to the role of Tim Taylor, a TV repair-show host à la Bob Vila, on *Home Improvement* is that Allen is able to celebrate and send up masculinity at the same time."[61] This presents us with a contradiction. To celebrate something is to point out its inherent value. To ridicule something is to point out its lack of value. Something – in this case, machismo – can either be celebrated or ridiculed but not both at the same – not unless it is either celebrated in some ways and ridiculed in others or celebrated by some people and ridiculed by others. In this case, the former proviso is inadequate to explain the phenomenon in question. *Everything* specifically identified as "masculine" on *Home Improvement* is overtly mocked, not celebrated.

The latter proviso, however, is much more likely to shed light on this phenomenon. It could be that not everyone interprets this ridicule in the same way. Male viewers, for example, might believe that Allen is indirectly celebrating stereotypical aspects of masculinity, and female viewers that he is simply ridiculing them. Allen himself agrees with this explanation. On the one hand, he says, "I love berating men, because we seem to like it. Men get a big kick out of laughing at themselves."[62] In other words, men are really "celebrating" themselves. Coming from one of their own, the ridicule need not be taken seriously. On the other hand, according to Morrison, Allen believes that women "can't take criticism like men [but] get a big kick out of laughing at their mates (or their fathers)."[63] In other words, women really *are* ridiculing men. Coming from a man, the ridicule merely confirms their own prejudice against those "others." How convenient for women: they have permission to scorn men, and it comes from the targets themselves! And how convenient for Allen: he is rewarded for doing so by both men and women! Authentically self-deprecating humour leads to transformation and reconciliation. Because we are all flawed, we all participate in a common humanity. But this premise is entirely absent on *Home Improvement*. Far from being authentically self-deprecating, Allen expects to be *admired* both by men for refurbishing the tarnished image of machismo and by women for subjecting machismo to the critique of feminism. The result is likely to be further polarization between men and women, not transformation or reconciliation.

Home Improvement propagates exceptionally crude stereotypes of men. Tim Taylor makes his living as the host of a show on home improvements. His passions are technology and power. Indeed, the two seem to be synonymous. Marilyn French, the author of *Beyond Power*, a compendium of every conceivable way in which women are superior to men, could have written the pilot episode.[64] At one point, Tim asks his son Mark if he knows what will happen when some new equipment is installed. Mark says, "More power!" His father replies, "You learn well, my little one." Later, Tim amplifies the message: "As soon as we install this bad boy, we're going to enter the Indianapolis 500." He refers to a souped-up lawn mower that can be driven like a motorcycle as a "bad boy." By implication, technology is associated not only with bad "boys" but also with "badness" itself. Tim sees himself as a member of what his wife mockingly calls "Hell's Mowers." Throughout the episode, her words and behaviour are condescending and self-righteous, as if women would never stoop to such an idiotic passion. Another stereotype is that of the allegedly male penchant for dirt. Tim tells Mark: "Grease is our friend ... As a matter of fact, I like grease all over ... kind of like war paint." Painting the boy's face with spots of grease, he says: "Chief Spark Plug." In this scene, dirt is symbolically associated not only with maleness (father and son) and the primitive (an Indian chief) but also with technology (spark plugs) and war (war paint).

Nevertheless, Allen acknowledges no moral accountability for the use of these stereotypes: "My act is not aggressive," he observes. "I'm not trying to teach a lesson. It's not about anything in the real world. There comes a point in life to have fun."[65] But if his material has *nothing* to do with real life, how can he explain the response he gets from viewers who live in the real world? Obviously, it has *something* to do with the real world. Where is the chorus of angry feminists who warned us long ago that the stereotypes we see on television week after week, no matter how entertaining, have a great deal to do with what we expect to find in real life? Did their logic apply only to the stereotypes that they found inconvenient from their own perspective as women?

According to John T.D. Keyes, "TV writers have been making fun of women for years, trivializing their concerns, painting them as two-dimensional creatures, often with big chests and no brains. Now the men are going to find out what it's like to be the butt of the joke. 'Home Improvement' may be overkill, but it's long overdue."[66] But television shows have been mocking and trivializing men for years, presenting them either as macho machines (cops and crooks, psychotics and gunslingers), or as bumbling idiots (incompetent husbands, fathers, and friends). Besides, Keyes explicitly endorses the principle of revenge. It is one thing to observe that polarizing society by appealing to the market for retaliation can be very lucrative. It is another thing to give this the veneer of moral legitimacy in reviews by those who supposedly place television shows in their larger cultural context. In 1992, Tim Allen won an Emmy Award for his creation of *Home Improvement*. In 1993, he received the People's Choice Award as favourite male television performer; his show won for favourite television comedy series. That was only the beginning. Allen became one of the most popular entertainers not only on television but also in the movies. Leo Benvenuti, Allen's friend, has observed that "Tim's comedy about men is *very* pro-woman."[67] That being "pro-woman" should involve being anti-man is a sad but telling comment on our society.

Given the consistently high ratings of *Home Improvement* – except during coverage of the summer Olympics one year, it seldom fell below fifth place and usually ranked second – it is hardly any wonder that other networks tried to imitate it. For its 1992 season, the Fox network introduced *Martin*, a black version. Martin Lawrence "plays a comic shock-radio host whose on-air macho-caveman routine does not sit well with his more enlightened girlfriend, Gina (Tisha Campbell), a marketing executive. At home, though, Martin is alternately a pit bull and a lapdog, and his funny, sexy sparring with Gina gives the show genuine heat. Lawrence is great at taking the edge off his macho posturing by showing the whimpering baby beneath; Campbell is great at staying cool while she watches him bluster and squirm. Their chemistry promises a lot."[68] Once again, the joke is on men. Men are supposed to laugh at themselves; women are supposed to laugh *at men*. As an isolated phenomenon, a show based on that premise might be appropriate. But as one of many? Both on its own and on a cumulative basis, the implication is that not merely this or that individual man is a stupid and sexist windbag but that *most or all* men are.

In the spring of 1991, Fox introduced a game show called *Studs*. In each episode, two stereotypical "studs" date three women who are then asked for a report on the men. Following this, the men try to match the comments to the women. What is the point of all this? Ostensibly, it is to see which man is the best date, the real "stud." He and his favourite date win $500 to use on a dream date they plan for themselves. The loser, of course, "receives only the once-in-a-lifetime chance to look like a schmuck on national television." According to Brian Garden, one of the show's creators, it "stems from the idea that if you're like I am, 5 foot 7 and average-looking – when you go to the bars, it's the studs that always get all the women. Well, this is a chance to get back at all the studs that ever took the babes from you." Garden continued, "Essentially what it does is turn the tables and give women the upper hand. The women roast the guys, but it's all in fun."[69] Sure it is. In 1991, the battle of the sexes was turning into a war. What looked like "fun" to Garden looked more like sexism to others. But what kind of sexism? Critics and feminists complained that *Studs* demeaned *women*. They claimed that allowing the public to eavesdrop even as women roasted men was *misogynistic*.

The female monopoly on virtue was made even more explicit in another situation comedy making its debut in the 1991 fall season. *Herman's Head* is set, quite literally, in the mind of its protagonist. In each episode, four personified aspects of his mentality – known as Animal, Genius, Wimp, and Angel – argue among themselves as to which course of action he should take. It should come as a surprise to no one that Angel, the sensitive voice of Herman's conscience, is the one aspect played by a woman. The other aspects are, well, not angelic.

A popular movie of the previous year, *Flatliners* (Joel Schumacher, 1990), followed the same pattern. In that movie, four medical students undertake an experiment to find out what death is like. After inducing a near-death experience, each discovers what lies ahead as an ultimate reward or punishment. Of the four, only one is a woman. And she is the only one found innocent. Due to the discovery that she was not so guilty or sinful, her return to the land of the living is joyous. The three men, on the other hand, discover that they are even more guilty or sinful than they had imagined. Their return, therefore, is less joyous. They – by symbolic extension, men in general – have been given a warning: shape up or expect to pay the consequences in eternity.

The trend continued in 1992. "Self-exiled from *Roseanne*, Tom Arnold's back, playing a loudmouth sitcom star in ABC's *Jackie Thomas Show*," burbled Ken Tucker. "Here's hoping it fulfills its great potential."[70] The public appetite for this sort of cliché apparently is insatiable. Like so many other male characters in a long tradition from Ralph Kramden in *The Honeymooners* to Tim Taylor in *Home Improvement*, Jackie Thomas is a "loud, lovable dope" who specializes in "barking orders and driving everyone crazy."[71] Like Tim Taylor, he is a negative stereotype. The lout is the functional equivalent for men of the bimbo for women – except, of course, that it is now considered highly offensive to portray women as bimbos but highly amusing to portray men as louts. Like all stereotypes, this one works by association. It depends on the willingness of viewers to associate specific qualities immediately with either men or women. Once again, an entire show is based on the interaction of two particular associations. In spite of being an insufferably dictatorial barbarian on the outside (that is, a man), Jackie is a sensitively vulnerable innocent on the inside (that is, a woman). This is the recurrent "situation," in fact, that makes *Jackie Thomas* a "situation comedy." Opines one critic, "Jackie is a funny guy who suspects he's really not *that* funny, who has somehow lucked into a show that millions of people watch every week. Jackie vents his insecurity … At the same time, Jackie's not an unlikable guy; he has the courage of his vulgar convictions."[72] That says it all. To be a man, according to those who pander to popular stereotypes, means to be vulgar, coarse, ignorant, and prejudiced. To be a woman, on the other hand, means to be genteel, refined, enlightened, and tolerant. For a man to be any of the latter, therefore, means that he cannot really be a man at all (except, possibly, a gay man). This way of "thinking" was at least challenged when Archie Bunker exemplified it on *All in the Family*. Twenty years later, the situation had deteriorated for men even as it had improved for women.

The most telling illustration of this problem can be found on a show that purports to be, and generally is, sympathetic to males if only because the protagonist happens to be a boy. Both a critical and a popular success, *The Wonder Years* is about the hopes and fears of Kevin Arnold, a slightly confused but thoroughly likeable teenager in the process of learning how to become a man. Kevin's older brother is a loutish bully. His father is a moody fellow but not unkind. And his mother is a slightly updated version of June Cleaver, Margaret Anderson, or Harriet Nelson. The series is set in the late 1960s and early 1970s. It was inevitable, therefore, that Mom would be "liberated." One day, she announces in a sprightly tone that she has decided to find a job. Although Dad refrains from screaming obscenities, he does trivialize her attempt to get a life. He offers to help her find a job at his factory, but he imagines that she would be satisfied to work as his secretary. Has he forgotten that she has just finished a college degree? In the end, he is able to accept the fact that she has been hired as a comptroller, but only because he assumes that she will continue her housework as before. To make the point, he sticks his foot in her face to let her know that his socks need darning. Kevin is no better. When Winnie, his girlfriend, scores much higher than he does on the SATs, Kevin becomes morose.

The problem is "settled" at a bowling alley. There, the men prove their male superiority over the women. The moral is clear as an older Kevin recalls this encounter with women: "In one important respect, we still had a lot to teach them: when it came to being jerks, they still had a lot to learn."[73] Like every show or movie set in the past, this one is intended to serve the "needs" of contemporary viewers. Unfortunately, it serves only those of women – and, in the long run, not even theirs. Otherwise, it would have acknowledged that men have good reasons for feeling threatened by female superiority.

It is true that boys often react the way Kevin does and that men often react the way his father does (although girls and women often either react the same way or find their own, distinctive, ways of acting badly). And it is true that doing so is unfair to women. It is not necessarily true, however, that this behaviour is generated by malice or even by stupidity. Identity is a real problem for males, and trivializing it will do nothing to help either men or the women who are part of their lives. Maybe no half-hour sitcom could deal with the problem adequately. In that case, even ignoring it might have been more appropriate than reducing it to absurdity through the kind of glib mockery that panders to a "politically correct" common denominator. And this from the creators of what was probably the *only* show on commercial television at that time to build its reputation on sensitivity to the experience of boys!

By 1997, misandric sitcoms had become much more sophisticated, which is to say, less obviously misandric. Fox's *Ally McBeal*, the continuing and soapy saga of some Boston lawyers, is a good example. Although each episode runs for a full hour and has no laugh track, this show is indeed a sitcom. In any case, it is about the private lives of these folks – that is, their emotional and sexual lives – both at the office and at home, not about their professional duties. What makes it sophisticated? Partly, its attempt to depict characters with at least some subtlety. Nevertheless, this is more effectively done for the female than the male characters, so it is not surprising that most viewers are women. It is they who have made the show a success, earning Calista Flockhart, who plays the title role, a Golden Globe award. Comments critic Richard Helm, "For a character who some viewers initially wrote off [as] a love-lorn whiner and total ditz in a miniskirt, Ally McBeal has quickly grown into something of an icon for young working and dating women."[74] Or, as James Collins puts it with greater precision, "Ally represents the modern female trying to remain true to herself in a harsh male world. Unfortunately, she represents that female so explicitly that the show seems hollow and calculated even by TV standards ... You feel as if [writer and producer David] Kelley gathered a list of themes from focus groups and then set about addressing them methodically and baldly."[75]

Women are by no means united on the cultural significance of this show. "In fact," writes Benjamin Svetkey, "not since *thirtysomething* has a series so divided the nation, with half the viewers enthralled, half aghast."[76] What troubles many female viewers is the way *women* are portrayed. Ally's personality is too neurotic. Her behaviour is too erratic. And her skirts are too short. "Even in New York," complains Joanne Watters (as a professional woman in precisely the demographic category the show is aimed at), "I never see women in court wearing skirts like that. Also, she isn't all that professional. She's not confident or aggressive. She seems like she's always waiting for her knight in shining armor. I wouldn't hire her for my attorney."[77] Ally has little but sex on her mind. "They're always turning her into a sexpot," says Susan Carroll, "like in that cappuccino scene [in which Ally shows the other women how to experience a coffee break as a sublimated sexual encounter]. It's all about her appearance and her social life. It's pretty sexist."[78] Even worse, the show is written by a man.

Kelley himself legitimates his scripts very simply. Being a romantic comedy, it is necessarily about Ally's search for love and sex. But

Svetkey argues there is much more to it than that. According to him, "what Kelley delivered was actually more subversive [than a replacement for the female-oriented *Melrose Place*]: a series that sneakily explores *male* preoccupations (one typical episode delved into the eternal question, Does Size Matter?) by filtering them through a female protagonist's perspective. In other words, a guy show dressed up in chick-show clothing."[79] In yet other words, female viewers have missed the point. The remaining question, then, is this: How sexist is this "guy show" from the perspective of *men*? This question is surprisingly difficult to answer. The male characters are sympathetic. Even Richard is likeable, for example, despite his wattle fetish and his careless remarks. Moreover, these men are complex. John is as neurotic and erratic as Ally. But as Svetkey himself points out, the male portrayals are filtered through female perspectives. And that does, in the last analysis, make this a "chick show."

Almost every episode pits the two sexes against each other. In one, the women are shocked to learn that John hires prostitutes. In another, they are shocked to learn that Richard and Billy look longingly at a beautiful woman who sells sandwiches. The result is usually a draw. But John is still obliged to make a speech defending his recourse to prostitution. And Richard is still obliged to offer an apology for admiring the sandwich seller. The result is that these men, presumably among the best of their kind, are let off the hook. But they do require women to let them off the hook. And the distinct implication is that other men – men in real life are presumably not quite as "intelligent," as articulate, or as politically correct – need not be let off the hook so easily. On this show, appropriately one with a legal context, men are always on trial. Fortunately, their female judges usually display more common sense than triumphalism.

Of the two classic patterns – smart man with dumb woman, dumb man with smart woman – it was the latter that prevailed at the end of the century. In 1997, Fox introduced *Dharma and Greg*. Dharma seems ditsy at first. Always "high," she and her family are refugees from the 1960s counterculture. But she is invariably more sensible, at least in the long run, than her straightlaced husband, Greg. In 1998, Fox introduced yet another misandric sitcom: on *Getting Personal*, the situation includes two goofy men, Milo and Sam, and their savvy female boss, Robyn. Though created by two men, Jeff Greenstein and Jeff Strauss, this show "confirms what we've suspected all along," writes Kinney Littlefield: "Women-smart. Men-dumber."[80] Illogically, given that assessment of inequality, Littlefield comes to the following conclusion: "Sure sometimes Robyn is a vulnerable klutz. But she

makes the ongoing war of the sexes look like an equal playing field."
Apparently, men and women are both equal and unequal.

Mocking specific groups of people is not necessarily dangerous – not
if the real or imagined foibles of all groups are considered grist for the
comedy mill. But that is hardly ever the case. Some groups, almost
invariably, are considered off limits. In the days of vaudeville, it was
okay for Jews and Italians to ridicule themselves and other "ethnics"
but not to ridicule their anglo "superiors." Today, it is okay for anyone
to ridicule men, at least straight white men, but not to ridicule women
or blacks. There is, and always has been, a double standard. Those
who fail to play by the rules, such as Jackie Mason, pay a heavy price.
But individual entertainers do not pay the heaviest price. That is paid
by the target groups in the coinage of self-respect and by society as a
whole in the coinage of enduring conflict.

CHAPTER THREE

Looking Down on Men: Separate but Unequal

It's not that I don't like men; women are just better ... A very wise friend of mine asked: "Have you ever noticed that what passes for a terrific man would only be an adequate woman?" A Roman candle went off in my head.[1]

There was a time – it is not easy now even to recall it – when people said of men and women: *vive la différence*. The idea was that life is better because both sexes have their own distinctive verbal and non-verbal ways of expressing themselves. But the lingering *différence* is no longer celebrated. Instead, it is either lamented on practical grounds or exploited for political purposes. What happened?

After the civil rights movement in the United States and the dismantling of apartheid in South Africa, few would declare, at least publicly, that racial segregation – under the heading, in the United States, of "separate but equal" – had been a good thing. Even if it could be argued that separation were morally acceptable, which is highly debatable, the fact remains that the *ancien régime* in both cases had failed to provide equality. In fact, though not in theory, the races had been separate but unequal. And many have argued that racial inequality is inherent in the whole notion of racial segregation because of its focus on the *differences* between whites and blacks.

Early feminists were drawn to the rhetoric of integration, which had been popularized by the civil-rights movement. They tried to focus on what made women like men (which would justify their integration into the public sphere), not on what made them different (which had been used to justify their segregation in the domestic sphere). By the 1980s, however, women were increasingly preoccupied with their identity, with what made them different from men and allegedly justified some degree of separation from men. A great deal has been said since then about the lack of "communication" between men and women, supposedly due to their innate differences.

Difference can make romantic encounters exciting, true, but it can also make communication difficult. And the consequences can be disastrous. Several major events – obvious examples would include the Clarence Thomas hearing, the William Kennedy Smith trial, and the Clinton-Lewinsky scandal – have made it clear that the failure of both men and women to "hear" the opposite sex could have the gravest legal and political consequences. Until these public spectacles made the problem impossible to ignore, many people thought of the differences between men and women mainly as a source of stereotypical humour. Now we know better.

But difference per se is not the problem. After all, men and women are and always have been different in some obvious ways. (In the past, people assumed that these differences were due entirely to nature.) The problem is how people *interpret* difference. The lamentable human tendency is to do so in connection with hierarchy, using difference as an excuse to assign superiority and inferiority. And, feminist theory notwithstanding, women are no more immune to that than men. After several decades of "identity politics" on behalf of women, feminists have convinced many people that women are somehow superior to men. For reasons of their own, even many men are convinced. That point of view is both reflected in and fostered by countless productions of popular culture.

We might as well begin with movies. By the late 1990s, people had come to think of "he said, she said," in connection specifically with Clarence Thomas and Anita Hill or President Clinton and Monica Lewinsky. But that expression had been familiar to everyone long before there was any lewd talk of pubic hairs and coarse jokes about subpoenas and grand juries and sperm-soaked dresses – familiar enough, at any rate, to be used as the title of a popular movie. Though not a cinematic milestone, *He Said, She Said* (Ken Kwapis; Marisa Silver, 1991) did well enough at the box office. Whatever its stylistic merits or flaws, its subject matter provides an excellent illustration of the difficulties faced by both men and women when communicating with the opposite sex. But there is more to this than meets the eye. It is one thing to say that the "language" of women is different from that of men but quite another to say, even implicitly, that it is *superior* to that of men. (More about that particular problem in due course.)

The story is about Dan Hanson, a journalist for the *Baltimore Sun*, and his love-hate relationship with another journalist, Lorie Bryer. The two are opposites in almost every way. He is a blue-eyed blond; she is a brown-eyed brunette. He is boyish and playful; she is serious and intense. He reads *Playboy*; she reads *Mother Jones*. He is a conservative

reactionary; she is a progressive liberal or socialist. His desk is decorated with a werewolf or vampire; hers is decorated with a flower. His
link to nature is represented by the bestiality of Wolfman; hers is
represented by the purity of Evian water and membership in the
Cousteau Society.

With these differences in mind, their employers decide that pitting
them against each other, first in print and then on television, is a good
way to make money. What happens in public corresponds almost
perfectly to what happens in private. It is precisely the thought that
they squabble on the air but make love in private that makes them
fascinating. Viewers are especially delighted when she throws a coffee
mug at him. And even more delighted when she does so again. As their
public battles over art and highway planning rage, so do private ones
over anxiety and jealousy. The cinematic structure is a series of doubled
episodes; the same events are shown from two points of view, first that
of one character and then that of the other. Eventually, Lorie and Dan
agree to separate both publicly and privately. Lorie watches Dan make
his final appearance on television and say that she had been right about
everything all along. Following this, her own statement is equally
gracious. On the air, they agree to marry. This development is as
predictable as it is implausible.

The public sphere of business is a metaphor, in this case, for the
private one of romance. The movie is thus really about gender, not
journalism. Unlike movies that undermine traditional notions about
gender, *He Said, She Said* reaffirms them. But it does so even as it
empties them of any real meaning. Several of these "traditional"
notions are worth discussing.

First, viewers are expected to affirm stereotypes of both men and
women. The script includes lines such as: "You men are all alike"
and "I thought all women love weddings." The dependence of this
movie on stereotypes is illustrated perfectly in its advertisement. Not
surprisingly, the words "he said" and "she said" are written in blue
and pink respectively. (In the movie, "he said" is typed on computer
paper, and thus associated with technological efficiency. "She said" is
handwritten, and thus associated with emotional spontaneity). Male
viewers are expected to confirm their assumptions through identification with the hero: "Women are illogical, fussy, manipulative, hormonally deranged creatures who play hard to get, then are hard to
take," reads the ad, "but then he met Lorie." And female viewers are
expected to do the same through identification with the heroine:
"Men are insensitive, messy, uncommitted, sexually obsessed clods
who just want hot sex followed by a cold beer," the same ad
continues, "but then she fell in love with Dan." The words "but then"

indicate an exception. At the same time, they indicate the rule that
will be proven by that exception.

Furthermore, viewers are expected to be familiar with the idea that
men and women are fundamentally more different than they are alike.
In the past, it was thought that complementary differences were for-
tuitously inherent in the natural order and not merely created by the
cultural order. Despite a brief interlude in which it was popular to
emphasize similarities, the idea that men and women are more different
than alike has once again become fashionable. At both ends of even
the moderate political continuum – conservative and liberal – the
primacy of difference is considered inherent in the natural order;
differences between men and women are explained at one end in terms
of complementarity and at the other in terms of conflict. (In *He Said,
She Said*, these two notions are fused uneasily in the marriage of Mr
and Mrs Spepik, an elderly and presumably traditional couple representing the possibility of closeness in spite of continual bickering.)

With this in mind, think about that ad in more detail. It is littered
with symbolic oppositions. "He said" is represented above by a picture
of Kevin Bacon looking towards the camera while Elizabeth Perkins,
eyes closed, waits for him to kiss her. "She said" is represented below
by a picture of Elizabeth Perkins looking towards the camera while
Kevin Bacon, eyes closed, waits for her to kiss him. Even so, these
oppositions are visually unified. Both upper and lower portions can be
described as follows: they include two faces joined at the lips or chin;
set against a mauve field, both are overlaid with white letters and
include diagonals that, when placed together, run from top left to
bottom right and from top right to bottom left as an "x" (two lines
coming together at the centre). The movie, not coincidentally, is struc-
tured in the same bipolar terms. The first part is introduced by a coffee
mug labelled "he said." The second part is introduced by a coffee mug
labelled "she said." Because the latter "corrects" the former, by the
way, it is what some academics would call the "privileged" version.
The epilogue is introduced by a split screen, showing "him" on one
side and "her" on the other. This dissolves into what purports by cinematic implication to be an objective or unified view of the relationship.
In fact, it is merely an affirmation of the story as told by "her."

Unlike Dan, Lorie ends up with what she wanted all along. From
the beginning, Dan sees marriage as a sexually confining trap, albeit
one that might provide the possibility of carrying on family traditions
and rearing children. That someone like Dan might actually consider
this sort of thing is indicated when he takes Lorie to his hometown
for Uncle Olof's wedding. After the Swedish folk dancing begins, Dan
encourages the reluctant Lorie to participate. Lorie, on the other hand,

sees marriage as a *professionally* confining trap, albeit one that might offer the promise of emotional stability and intimacy. By the conclusion, both realize that they must learn to overcome their neuroses. But Dan agrees to give up his sexual freedom *as well.* (After discussing marriage, he dreams of being guillotined by the window and of finding himself attached to a ball and chain.) Lorie, on the other hand, agrees to give up nothing at all – nothing, at any rate, that gives her pleasure. Unlike Dan, she does not want the sexual freedom that marriage forbids. There is certainly no question of her sacrificing her ambition as a journalist in order to become a traditional wife and mother. Dan needs Lorie, in short, more than Lorie needs him.

Because fictional characters always represent more than themselves, the implication is that men need women more than women need men. This represents a mere reversal of the old asymmetry. At one time, wives were expected to become both legally and economically dependent on their husbands and husbands to become emotionally dependent on their wives. Now, neither wives nor husbands are expected to become legally or economically dependent. But husbands are still expected to become emotionally dependent on their wives, even though not all wives like that idea. The message, familiar from Shere Hite[2] and her counterparts in print and on television, is clear. If men want the benefits of marriage, they had better emulate Dan by finding ways of adapting to the wishes of women. In other words, marital unhappiness is caused by husbands, not wives. To suggest that wives should adapt to the wishes of husbands would be unthinkable. For the sake of argument, consider the following scenario: giving husbands the freedom to indulge in occasional sexual relations with other women,[3] in which case marital unhappiness could be blamed on inflexible wives no less than on philandering husbands.

Even though this movie presents marriage from the perspectives of both men and women, even though it was directed by both a man and a woman, the fact remains that the virtues it promotes are those associated with women – especially women who identify themselves in one way or another as feminists. Men are invited to identify themselves with Dan, to be sure, but also to acknowledge the superiority of Lorie. Not all men will actually do so, because she often seems not admirably righteous but unbearably self-righteous. Still, it is Lorie, not Dan, whose newspaper columns – one of them is called "Art That Touches Our Lives" – reveal sensitivity to social justice or avant-garde movements. And it is Lorie whose plight is expected to evoke sympathy from viewers, including any "sensitive" male viewers.

Speaking of her need for better communication with Dan, she says, "We want different things. I don't think you're ever going to change.

I love you, but I need more from you." Again, speaking of her attitude towards fidelity after meeting Dan, she tells him, "For me, sleeping with another man became unthinkable. For you, sleeping with another woman remained thinkable." Given prevalent assumptions about fidelity in marriage, who could argue with her except an insensitive oaf? But speaking of his admiration for the Wolfman, a modern version of Don Juan, Dan opines: "He's strong, aloof, destined to live alone. He's his own man ... a night here, a night there." Also speaking for men, the florist discusses his preference for one-night-stands: "Love is a time bomb. There's always another one right around the corner that could be even better." Who could agree with any of this except an immature jerk? Obviously, the directors, both male and female, agree on one thing: men are justly regarded as inferior to women. From the beginning, Dan is ridiculed as a "reactionary."

There are two underlying assumptions in *He Said, She Said*. What men want, sexual freedom, is bad. What women want, economic or professional freedom, is good. (It might be worth noting here that the desire of men for sexual variety, though not necessarily permission to seek it, is commonly acknowledged cross-culturally. The same is not true of women, which does not necessarily mean that the desire for sexual variety is absent.[4]) But the logic here is severely flawed. Sexual freedom is generally called "promiscuity." More specifically, it is called "fornication" by theologians, "irresponsibility" by sociologists, or "escape from commitment" by psychologists and journalists. Until very recently, at least in our society, it has been universally condemned in public though sometimes tolerated in private. According to middle-class moral standards, sexual fidelity was expected from both men and women after marriage. It was expected also from women before marriage. Now that this particular double standard has fallen into disrepute, both men and women must ask themselves what equality means. And so they do in *He Said, She Said*. For Lorie, equality means that sexual fidelity is expected of both men and women, with or without marriage. Dan is condemned for merely wanting to have sex outside of marriage. Lorie is astonished that he could even think of it. The implication is that she, as a woman, is naturally faithful but that he, as a man, is naturally unfaithful. And because fidelity is considered a virtue and infidelity a vice, the further implication is that women are naturally good and men are naturally bad.

Even so, the rhetoric of equality is proclaimed. But equality of this kind, based on the sexual fidelity of both partners, is more apparent than real. Lorie is applauded for insisting on a career as well as marriage. But if she and Dan are equals, why does she not demand the same sexual freedom that he claims for himself? Possibly because she really wants emotional security, not sexual freedom. Ergo, this movie denies the assertion of some feminists, and not only the direct disciples of *Cosmopolitan* founder Helen Gurley Brown, that women want sexual freedom as much as men. A single moral standard is adopted, but if we take seriously what this movie says about men and women, it is one that punishes men without necessarily rewarding women. In fact, it punishes men *more* than women. Dan gives up his sexual freedom, because that is the price he must pay for marriage to Lorie. Lorie gives it up, on the other hand, because she does not really want it in the first place.

In real life, many women do make sacrifices for marriage. Until very recently, most women stayed home to raise families instead of establishing their own careers in the larger world. Some women did not want careers outside the home. For them, staying home did not represent a sacrifice. Other women wanted to stay home and raise families but also to establish their own careers in the outside world. For them, staying home was indeed a sacrifice. But Lorie is unlike the women in both of these situations. Unlike the former, she does not want to stay home and raise a family. But unlike the latter, she feels no ambivalence over establishing a career in the outside world. She represents one version of the "liberated woman." Women who identify themselves with her, the movie suggests, should expect to have both marriage and careers without having to sacrifice any fundamental need or desire. The implicit, though possibly unintended, message, then, is that the "liberated marriage" requires a sacrifice from men but no equivalent sacrifice from women.[5] In her review of *Divided Selves* by Elsa Walsh, Vanessa Friedman notes, "It's the never-ending dilemma for most modern women: family versus career. It's also an issue that is rarely discussed."[6] Rarely discussed? Please. Hardly a day goes by on which this topic is not discussed, either directly or indirectly, by Oprah Winfrey, Sally Jessy Raphael, Geraldo Rivera, Ricki Lake, Montel Williams, or any other talk-show host. In women's magazines ranging from *Ladies' Home Journal* to *Ms*, hardly an issue goes by in which this topic is not discussed. In the 1990s, only sheer dishonesty could explain Friedman's remark.

We are not arguing here for a return to any double moral standard. Nor are we arguing for a single moral standard based on equal rights to promiscuity. The fact is that promiscuity, no matter how attractive it might seem in view of either biological urges or cultural indoctrination, is not very satisfying as a way of life, because sexual "freedom," taken as an end in itself, is unhealthy. Statistics on men indicate that married men live longer than those who remain single. They remarry quickly after being widowed or divorced.[7] This is hardly surprising:

like women, men need the emotional stability and long-term intimacy of family life. Nonetheless, we want to point out two things. First, choosing monogamy involves a conscious decision to sacrifice something that most young men in our society continue to want very much, even though they usually discover that the sacrifice is worthwhile.[8] Second, the kind of marriage or heterosexual relationship idealized in this movie is geared to the presumed needs and desires of women,[9] not men.

Even for many women, though, the conclusion of *He Said, She Said* might prove less than satisfying. Maybe that is because the marriage between Lorie and Dan is to be a private affair based on nothing more substantial than personal gratification. Affirmed here is neither the traditional notion of marriage as a sacred union (in which both partners are ultimately responsible to God for all eternity) nor that of a public partnership (in which both members are responsible to the community both now and in future generations). Despite the traditional aspects of its rhetoric, therefore, marriage is effectively undermined.

Finally, viewers are expected to affirm the idea that men and women, no matter how polarized, will nevertheless find happiness in permanent heterosexual unions. Implicit here is a kind of Hegelian dialectic in which "analysis" turns into "synthesis." Unfortunately, the movie does not provide a satisfying answer to the question of how or why couples move from "he said" versus "she said" to "but then." After two hours of the former, the hero and heroine suddenly decide that they cannot live without each other. Here again, the movie departs significantly from tradition. In the past, men and women came together, despite the gender system fostered by culture, for the serious business of pooling their resources to start new families. In the recent past, it was assumed that stable marriages not only assured the community of biological continuity through children but also assured the parents of emotional fulfillment through family life. In this movie, the relationship hinges solely on the emotional gratification of each as an "autonomous" individual.

In theory, that should refer to both Lorie and Dan. Should anything interfere with the "autonomy" of either, the marriage would have no foundation. In fact, this principle refers primarily to Lorie. As defined in this movie, marriage offers her both professional freedom and emotional intimacy. She has to develop trust, but she does not have to choose between two mutually exclusive alternatives. If she should ever have to do so, moreover, it would be due to *Dan's* failure, not hers. Even though Dan could be called "autonomous" by virtue of freely deciding to enter a monogamous marriage, his free choice consists of eliminating other free choices in the future. (This interpretation, by the way, is supported by statistical surveys conducted in the mid-1990s.[10])

He retains freedom of choice, to be sure, but *not within marriage*. By choosing to sleep with other women, he would affirm his autonomy but, by definition, forfeit his marriage.

He Said, She Said does not encourage viewers to see beyond gender stereotypes by suggesting that "but then" is a reality that transcends them. On the contrary, it encourages viewers to say, "Yes, that's just what I've always said about men (or women), but I'll put up with one of them even so." Even so. In other words, we have come to the stage at which men can love women and women can love men only in spite of who they are, not because of who they are.

In this way, *He Said, She Said* is a characteristic product of our time. The same motifs have been taken up in countless popular movies,[11] books, sitcoms, and so on. Lorie and Dan are ostensibly equals. The world revolves around women from Lorie's perspective and around men from Dan's. In fact, the two are not equals. Lorie is not merely different from Dan but morally superior to him. To the extent that this movie conforms to popular stereotypes, it corresponds to the notion that women are good and men bad. Or, to put it another way, the standard of goodness is established by women rather than men.

Now, consider popular journalism. When a conference was held to honour Nancy Drew, the fictional teenager who brought criminals to justice in countless mystery novels addressed to adolescent girls, Richard Threlkeld announced on television that the heroine had taught several generations "that girls are every bit as good as boys, maybe better."[12] Why better? How did he know that this sexist remark would be considered acceptable on commercial television? Did that question even cross his mind? To find the answers, it is necessary to consider the role of journalists. They hold a special place among the power brokers of our time – special, because they are still associated at least by the naïve among us with the search for truth, not power. And yet they wield considerable power, too – not on their own behalf, it is true, but on behalf of those for whom they feel sympathy. Threlkeld's casual remark is unimportant in itself. It merely reflects common notions about what is acceptable in public discourse. Nevertheless, it draws attention to a related phenomenon that really is important: the deliberate use of journalism to promote personal convictions, especially those about gender.

A journalist at the *New York Times*, Anna Quindlen, was inter-viewed by Judd Rose on *PrimeTime Live*[13] in connection with the publication of her book, *Thinking Out Loud*.[14] Quindlen's claim to fame is a particular approach to journalism. "Unlike her stuffier neighbors on the op ed page," observes Rose, "Quindlen has a more

personal perspective. As she once put it, 'real life is the dishes.'"
Quindlen herself explains this expression: "It means that real life isn't
in fancy parties. And real life isn't in limos. Real life isn't talking to
Henry Kissinger. Real life is ordinariness, day in day out. Because for
every person riding around in a limo, there's a million of them loading
a dishwasher." Even though it is easy to agree with Quindlen's belief
that there is something wrong with journalists who do nothing more
than collect gossip at trendy venues or hobnob with government
officials at cocktail parties, it is not so easy to agree with her implication that there is something wrong with journalists who discuss politics
with public officials or diplomats. Kissinger does not stuff cups and
plates into a dishwasher every day, but what he says or does can have
a dramatic impact on the lives of those who do. Why, then, does
Quindlen imply that journalists who interview politicians or bankers
are wasting their time on what is "unreal" and thus trivial? Or, to put
it another way, why would it be "real" and thus important to interview
people who do wash their dishes every night?

At first, the answer to both questions seems simple enough: cynicism.
At a time when many citizens, maybe most, suspect all leaders of
corruption and decadence, it seems preferable to focus attention on
lesser but better folks. Nowhere is this more evident than in America,
with its long traditions of scepticism and populism, dismissing as
contemptible those who represent an elite, even an artistic or intellectual elite. Glorified as righteous, on the other hand, are those who
represent "the people." Anyone can feel heroic merely for putting up
with the humdrum routines of everyday life.

But there is more to the Quindlen story than that. As Rose says of
her, she "has a way of making even the political personal." He refers
to the famous slogan "the personal is political" that underlies all forms
of feminism. Quindlen, whose column is called "Public and Private,"
is astute enough to see both sides of it. If the personal is political, after
all, the political is personal. As a journalist, she uses this insight
effectively to advance the cause of feminism. Instead of writing theoretical essays on abortion, for example, she writes stories about particular women who want abortions. Ethical analysis is accessible and
relevant only to intellectuals, presumably, but emotional experience is
accessible and relevant to everyone. No wonder she dismisses the kind
of accountability demanded by moral and legal systems. "Let's remember the jurisdiction, gentlemen. This is it," she says, pointing to herself
as if any community could exist on the basis of subjectivity and
personal autonomy alone. "This is the jurisdiction. It's inside me."

Quindlen is not merely a journalist. She is not merely a feminist
journalist. She is a female journalist. She supposedly represents a

"female" way of thinking. Quindlen agrees with traditionalists in at least one way. She associates men with an abstract way of thinking and women with a concrete one. Some feminists and some traditionalists believe that the ways of both men and women are equally valuable. Other feminists believe that the way of women is superior to that of men, however, just as some traditionalists believe the reverse. Quindlen's appearance on *PrimeTime Live*, a show that features cutting-edge journalism and highlights new trends, indicates that feminists of the latter persuasion are gaining ground. This becomes very clear during the interview.

Elsewhere, in a column, Quindlen had opined: "It's not that I don't like men; women are just better." This from a winner of the Pulitzer Prize – how did she come up with this idea? "A very wise friend of mine asked: 'Have you ever noticed that what passes for a terrific man would only be an adequate woman?' A roman candle went off in my head." Does that sound sexist? "Look," she claims to Rose in the interview, "I love men. My father's a man. My brothers are all men." Sure they are. And some of her best friends too are men, no doubt. The fact remains that she has gone on record as identifying one class of people, defined in biological terms, as inherently inferior to her own. Only seconds later, she recalls playing with her daughter and thinking about the girl's future: "I had to work every day of my life to make sure that gender prejudice didn't endure." Evidently, she believes that her own gender prejudice is exempt. Even more revealing is Quindlen's attitude towards her own children. On *Live with Regis and Kathie Lee* a few days later, she discusses the differences between her sons and her daughter. Responding to a question about innate differences between the sexes, she notes that her daughter is complex, unlike her sons: "not a simple machine."[15] At issue here is not whether she loves her male children but whether she *respects* them.

Quindlen went on to write *Black and Blue*,[16] a novel about domestic violence. According to one reviewer, drawing on the author's own point of view, that term "surely trivializes the routine stalking, beating and murder of women that is epidemic in our culture." The female protagonist is a nurse, Fran, who represents the healing associated with women by both tradition and many forms of feminism. Fran is forced into hiding. Eventually, however, she decides to fight back for the sake of her son, and thus in addition represents the courage associated by feminists with women. It is worth noting that Fran's plight – by implication the plight of most or all women – is explicitly likened to that of Jews under Nazi rule. Any analogy with the Nazis should be thought out very carefully. This one might be disturbing for many Jews, but it should be disturbing to anyone who values common sense.

Not everyone who perpetuates the notion of a sexual hierarchy does so intentionally. Some at least try to move in the opposite direction. In her best-seller, *You Just Don't Understand: Women and Men in Conversation*,[17] sociolinguist Deborah Tannen says very little that could be called original. The fact that some words or phrases or gestures are characteristic of either men or women, for example, has always been obvious to everyone (although it was fashionable in some circles, for a while, to deny it). She spells out in great detail, and with copious illustrations, what is already known to viewers of sitcoms, readers of comic strips, and subscribers to *Psychology Today*. In addition, she provides a theoretical framework derived directly from that of Carol Gilligan, who coined the popular phrase "in a different voice" to describe the way women think in general and the way they perceive moral problems in particular.[18] But like so many followers of Gilligan, Tannen implies that the "voice" of women, including their way of perceiving moral problems, is not only different from that of men but superior. One interviewer noted this: "In reading parts of your book," said Bryant Gumbel on *Today*, "it's hard not to think that female modes of interaction are in some sense superior. Do men feel slighted by your work?" Tannen replied as follows:

Not at all. The reaction I've gotten from men has been very enthusiastic. I think men in particular are relieved to see a woman writing about this phenomenon in a way that doesn't blame them. A lot of self-help books ... imply that there's something wrong with men because they don't communicate like women ... I think it's crucial to realize that if the vast majority of men act like this starting from as early as two-and-a-half to three years old, there's a limit to how much you can say their behavior is pathological. We might say that men would be better off if they were different, but we don't want to say that they're sick.[19]

In short, she says, men would be better off if they were women. Men are not evil, not even sick, just inadequate. Men are less likely to respond with anger to Tannen than to Marilyn French and others who attack men for their shortcomings.[20] Being relieved about escaping the blame for inferiority, however, is like being grateful to someone for not hitting you.

Unlike some other writers on this subject, Tannen seems at least potentially sympathetic to men. In theory, she claims that both men and women should learn from each other. In fact, she makes it clear that men have a great deal to learn from women but women have hardly anything to learn from men – not even in mathematical, spatial, or other realms associated with men. Still, she offers men at least the possibility of overcoming innate inferiority and catching up to women; though patronising, she is not without generosity.

Tannen argues explicitly that women are egalitarian. Yet what kind of equality can there be if women are superior to men? According to Tannen, men can always learn to be different. By this, she means merely that they can learn to be like women. Christians used to argue similarly that Jews were not innately inferior: they could always convert to Christianity. In both cases, the price of equality is disappearance as a distinct group. Even if men come to believe that the only way they can improve their communication skills is to adopt those of women, it is unlikely that more than a few would choose to "convert." Tannen might be an expert on communication, but she is not necessarily an expert on human nature. Everyone, male or female, needs an identity. And *a healthy identity is always based on the ability to make some contribution to society that is both valued and distinctive.*

Unlike some feminists, Tannen allows men a way out. They can claim to be victims. And this is true. Most men have been taught to communicate in ways that would help them survive the fierce competition of business, politics, or war, but not taught to communicate in ways that would help them flourish in the intimacy of marriage, parenthood, and friendship. Yet being designated a class of victims will provide no consolation for men if, like being designated a class of victimizers, it means effacing the range of their culturally defined identities as well as their dignity. What men should be encouraged to develop is a way of communicating, or interacting, that is neither obsolete and inappropriate (because men, as individuals, need intimacy as much as women) nor trendy and inappropriate (because men, as a class, need an identity of their own as much as women do), but a way that is linked in some way with their distinctive qualities as men. Seeking a mediating solution of this kind would be much more difficult than simply asking men to use the model that works for women. But there are no short cuts or quick fixes when it comes to problems of this magnitude and complexity.

Tannen has oversimplified the situation of women, not only that of men. Gender roles are like scripts: some actors learn their lines and recite them on cue. Others, and "method actors" in particular, actually try to "become" the characters they portray. The importance of this point cannot easily be overestimated, because the discussion is not merely about communication. It is about morality as well. We live in a society that publicly, and often privately, values equality on specifically moral (as well as practical) grounds. When women are said to be more egalitarian than men, therefore, they are said to be more moral than men. That is the underlying problem here.

But if women were more egalitarian than men, how could we explain the fact that many women, like men, supported segregation in the United States or apartheid in South Africa? For that matter, how could we explain the fact that so many women, like men, were enthusiastic Nazis in Germany? Several female scholars have wondered about precisely that. Alison Owings, for example, began by hoping to demonstrate that German women had been morally superior to German men. After doing her research, however, she had to admit that this had not been the case.[21] Yet most of these women would no doubt correspond in some way to Tannen's model. It is at least possible, therefore, that Tannen confuses form or appearance and substance. Some people, both men and women, behave in specific ways because they have been taught that doing so is adaptive and failing to do so is maladaptive. Others, both men and women, behave in the same ways because they have internalized a value system that makes it mandatory.

Whatever her actual intentions, Tannen has reinforced what could be called feminist "triumphalism." By that term (used originally in connection with the ancient triumph of Christianity over paganism and Judaism) we mean the belief that men are dinosaurs who have been superseded by women. (That metaphor has found its way into cartoons, even those in publications addressed to academics.[22]) Although few men might be precisely aware why books like Tannen's make them angry, much less to give their anger careful verbal expression, most men are aware that they are being stereotyped by Tannen and others like her. It is most unlikely, in any case, that either approach – attacking men either directly or indirectly – will lead to greater harmony between the sexes.

But the venue par excellence for those who want confirmation of the notion that women are superior to men is surely television, especially daytime talk shows (which are addressed primarily to women) and prime-time news-magazine shows (addressed to the wider public).[23] Very few segments of these shows are devoted specifically to men, except to the extent that they cause problems for women. As women have learned, commercial television reflects only what viewers consider important. The paucity of programs dealing with problems faced by men does not necessarily mean that men have no cause for distress or anger. What it clearly means is that our society prefers not to watch programs acknowledging the causes for distress or anger among men. Both men and women have reasons, albeit different ones, for this kind of denial. Men are much more reluctant than women to acknowledge their own vulnerability, for example, let alone their victimization.

Even though talk shows often try to disseminate information by way of "experts," usually the authors of books on pop psychology or other forms of self-help for the masses, intellectual analysis of the information presented is seldom high on the list of priorities. *Immediate emotional reaction* by members of the studio audience, on other hand, is high on that list. In fact, it is the only thing that really matters. This state of affairs was not invented by talk-show hosts and psychologists, pop or otherwise. Its ultimate origin is in a romanticism[24] that can be traced back long before the period normally referred to by that name. Its immediate origin, however, is a popularized version of psychoanalysis. In an essay on President Clinton's call for a "national dialogue" on race, Charles Krauthammer observes:

Scientific ideas don't die, they just fade away into popular culture. Psychoanalysis is as dead a science as alchemy. But its central idea, that somehow catharsis leads to cure, lives on – rages on – in Oprah and Geraldo and Ricki Lake TV talk shows and the whole steaming psychic stew that is America's confessional culture. No serious scientist would credit the notion, both unverified and unverifiable, that recalling the repressed, articulating the instinctual, magically undoes the inhibitions and pathologies of life. But no matter. So thoroughly has this fable soaked into the culture that it is now mere conventional wisdom that if we Americans just let it all out from the deep recesses of our souls – the anger, the fear, the prejudice, whatever – we will all be better off.[25]

Krauthammer (who writes that he himself has practised psychiatry) points out how difficult psychoanalysis can be under even the most controlled of circumstances, "the privacy, confidentiality and highly ritualized setting of the doctor-patient relationship. But in large groups of strangers? On live national TV? Led by a well-meaning but astute and cunning pol?"[26] The whole concept of healing catharsis is highly improbable. On the contrary, the result of legitimating emotionalism – and this is true especially in connection with rage orchestrated by politically savvy talk-show hosts and their carefully chosen experts – is likely to do nothing more, and nothing less, than heighten mutual hostility.

The current fragmentation of our society – the growing polarization between increasingly segregated communities of rage – might have many causes, but this is surely one of them. Krauthammer refers specifically to relations between blacks and whites, but he might just as well have said the following about relations between men and women: "America's problem is not inhibition. It is exhibition. What the President and the polity and the pedagogues should be preaching is racial decency.

Respect. Restraint. Manners. The lesson ought to be: Whatever your innermost feelings – and we have no idea, despite the claims of pop psychology, how to change inner feelings – we demand certain behavior. That is what the civil rights laws are about. They do not mandate a pure society. They mandate right conduct amid impurity."[27] Just so. If dialogue[28] is to mean more than the allegedly cathartic experience of two sides screaming at each other, it will have to be based on something more than emotional manipulation.

Theoretically, the talk-show format should be ideal for dialogue. Dialogue, after all, is inherent in talking; by definition, it involves the coming together of at least two individuals or groups. Unfortunately, television is seldom used effectively when it comes to dialogue between men and women. In fact, it is often used to polarize men and women. Even when talk shows are ostensibly devoted to the needs or problems of men, moreover, they often focus indirectly on those of women. There is a startling discrepancy between the number of daytime talk shows devoted to women and the number devoted to men. The number of shows about men during any given week is statistically insignificant.

What follows is an example from one talk show, *Donahue*. Although that particular show is no longer on the air, all the precedents for the genre were set by its host, Phil Donahue. He invented the daytime talk show and for many years was its unique representative. Every talk show today has its own distinctive tone, based on the personality of its host. Some are rowdy. Others are trashy. Still others are relatively "refined." But Donahue established the basic mechanisms that govern interaction between the host and the studio audience. Moreover, he articulated the basic principles that are used to defend the talk show against detractors.

On one *Donahue* show about men,[29] it becomes obvious almost immediately that a public discussion of feminism from the perspective of men is going to be dominated by women, not men. As feminists have long argued, power relations must always be accounted for in analysing relations between men and women. The host makes it clear that he has no sympathy or even respect for his five male guests and actively encourages members of the largely female audience to attack them. His guests are basically on the show to argue for the mere right to be heard. One cannot help wondering how they were selected: of the five, only one is articulate, and his manner is so abrasive that any chance of his being heard is severely limited. Donahue could have chosen other men. Warren Farrell and Fred Hayward, more sophisticated and experienced as leaders of the "men's movement," were much better equipped both emotionally and intellectually for this sort of encounter. Why were they not chosen? Possibly because that would have tipped the balance of power in a direction unacceptable either to Donahue himself or to his female viewers in the studio and at home. That would have meant both the necessity of acknowledging ambiguity and the possibility of losing control.

When one guest points out that feminists blame men for everything wrong with the world, Donahue offers the standard feminist explanation: "We do cause all the trouble." Instead of taking seriously the problem raised by his guest, he merely notes the "general hostility on the part of far too many men against women." He has a point, but so does his guest – and that is supposed to be the topic of this particular show. Donahue's attitude is revealed very clearly when he opens the discussion by addressing the following sarcastic remark to the audience: "What's not to love about the five men on our program?"

The question of blame is a major feature of this show. According to one member of the audience, "women don't complain" about their work. Unlike men, she argues, they just do their duty. Really? Every political movement is based on complaint. And commercial television, including shows such as this one, gives the complaints of women a very adequate hearing every day of the week. Another female member of the audience admonishes the guests to examine their own behaviour for clues to the origin of problems: "Don't blame others." But the fact is that blaming men has become common in feminist circles.

Donahue takes the notion of blame a step further on the way to moral chaos when he comments on the observation by one of his guests that American men, not women, have traditionally been exposed to mutilation and death in combat. That is fitting, according to Donahue, because "men call wars." The implication is that when soldiers are killed in wars, most of them as conscripts, it is their own fault. That is precisely what feminists call "blaming the victim," when the victims are women.

One guest wears a skirt and long hair. A woman says that he looks "totally ridiculous." Even though he points out that women routinely wear pants and short hair, several other women repeat this at various times throughout the show. It is considered legitimate for women to challenge stereotypes, but not for men to do so. Yet one woman is applauded for stating that feminism could liberate men as well as women. That is by no means the only example of a "mixed message"[30] given to men by women.

Still another woman calls the men "pompous primadonnas" for daring to talk about their anger. She forgets that early feminists were called "aggressive bitches" when they first dared to talk about their own problems. The same attitude is taken by another woman who dismisses the men for "carrying grudges." By this, she implies that they cannot possibly have legitimate reasons for feeling angry: their attitudes can be explained only with reference to personal problems. Several women believe that the guests are "men who don't have any self-confidence." Men who criticize feminism must be "weak," in other words, or "paranoid." Never mind that those who dare to criticize conventional wisdom, as understood in this context by feminists, are precisely those with courage. Then too, feminists themselves have often been dismissed either as lesbians or as bitter and neurotic women who cannot find men to love them. And those who believe that men are collectively involved in a sinister conspiracy to oppress women place themselves within the clinical definition of paranoia. One might well ask, moreover, why men should be morally condemned – moral disapproval is always implied – for feeling insecure. Insecurity is a psychological condition, not a moral problem. The appropriate response is surely to find out precisely why people are feeling insecure and do something about it, not to attack them. Finally, and most importantly, women have historically used shame to manipulate men. They have sometimes used the taunt of cowardice, for example, to shame men into defending the family or community. In this case, they are using shame to prevent men from responding to a threat. In the face of a real threat, it is both healthy and necessary to acknowledge the source of danger and confront it. When feminists look down on men, they are indeed a threat to the self-esteem required by every individual or group.

It is noted on the show that earlier generations of women might have been responsible for not teaching their sons to be more fully human by allowing them to cry and express emotions other than anger. The response is that women should not be held responsible for what other generations of women have done or not done. But the women in this audience show no sign of applying the same moral standard to men. One woman clearly subscribes to both the theory of collective guilt and to the conspiracy theory of history by declaring that men have been oppressing women "since the beginning of time."

No one mentions feminists such as Andrea Dworkin,[31] Laurel Holliday,[32] and Mary Daly,[33] who argue that men are collectively and vicariously guilty for all human suffering, past and present. Some of these feminists hold influential positions in the academic world. Generally speaking, the women in this audience claim to be unaware of any feminists who hate men. According to them, feminism is only about equality and opportunity. They are sincere, no doubt, but also naive. Fortunately, most women do not read feminist literature based on the conspiracy theory of history. But they do absorb hostility toward men when it is filtered down to their level on shows such as Donahue and in other artifacts or productions of popular culture.[34]

The intellectual level of this show is low. Most of the men are not only inarticulate but also blinded by their own anger. In this way, they are no better than the women. But when one of the men says that a solution to sexual polarization is "for women to listen to what men are saying," a very sensible statement, he is booed by the audience. In effect, this proves his point. Men are silenced now, literally, just as women were silenced in the past. Listening to the other is the very essence of dialogue, the sine qua non. This show, in short, is the *reverse* of a dialogue: it is a debate, two clashing monologues. In some contexts such as scholarship and law, that often leads to truth. In the political context, however, it leads to nothing but more conflict.

Talk shows have been likened to the public square, but they are much more like therapeutic encounter sessions. What takes place is not the moral discourse on which democracy depends but the abreactions and peer solidarity on which group therapy depends. (For a fuller discussion of democracy and talk shows, see appendix 4.) The five men on *Donahue* are straw men, there to be knocked down by members of the audience or, if necessary, by Donahue himself. By participating in this symbolic battle either directly or vicariously, women can feel righteous without ever having to take seriously what the men are saying. (At the same time, though, men can feel justified in their alienation from women.) Participating in this symbolic battle, even vicariously, women are "empowered" to feel righteous without ever having to take seriously what the men are saying.

By the mid-1990s, talk shows were in trouble. Even Phil Donahue was off the air. So was his Canadian counterpart, Shirley Solomon, who made Donahue look intellectual and sophisticated by comparison.[35] The current situation is more complex than it was in the past. Donahue's successors – Oprah Winfrey, Sally Jessy Raphael, Montel Williams, Jenny Jones, and dozens of others – go marching on. Millions of people are still tuning in day after day, and new shows are still being developed. But society is more aware of problems. Politicians, in fact, sometimes denounce the genre.

Usually, they pick on shows that routinely feature titles such as "I Haven't Seen You Since Our One-night Stand," "Mothers Who Spy on the Their Teenage Daughters," "I Already Have a Boyfriend, but I'll Dump Him for You," "My Girlfriend Is a Man," "My Man Is a Pervert," and "My Life Is a Sexy Small-Town Soap Opera." Winfrey decided to elevate the tone of her show at the risk of losing some viewers. Other hosts began to fight back, and they were supported by at least some of the media mavens. A public furore developed over demands to clean up "trash TV." (By that, the politicians referred primarily to daytime talk shows and not the "daytime dramas" more commonly known as "soap operas"). Yet it is worth repeating that the problem singled out for debate was almost always sleaze, *not politics*. There were a few, very rare, exceptions.

Some late-night talk shows are considered more sophisticated than those that air during the day. *Politically Incorrect* is one of them. (For a discussion of "political correctness," see chapter 7.) It does not necessarily live up to its title, however, because the show's deck is often stacked against those who represent politically incorrect positions – that is, conservative or religious ones. Host Bill Maher does indeed see himself as a political maverick and likes to support controversial positions. But these are usually ones that could be described as radical individualism, libertarianism, or egalitarianism. His opinions sometimes coincide with those of the political left or centre, seldom with those of the political right.

To represent the right, he often chooses guests who represent extreme positions. They create good television, plenty of heated debates, but they seldom present serious threats to those who argue for moderate positions. These are straw people, set up only to be knocked down. Very often, they are religious fundamentalists. Their points of view are not ones that can be taken seriously, by the host, by other guests, or by viewers with liberal and secular points of view. Those who would present conservative or even religious positions in ways that could be taken seriously are seldom invited as guests.

Even worse, *Politically Incorrect* is organized in a way that undermines serious discussion of public controversies. Guests are not chosen for their expertise in the fields under discussion. Some are politicians, used to taking sides on controversial topics, certainly, but not necessarily on the basis of any knowledge. Most guests, by far, are merely celebrities. Their primary goal is to sound convincing or effective – or merely to sound off in the hope of garnering publicity. The resulting discussions are of no higher calibre than the kind of discussions that take place in bars or at office water-coolers. Participants on both sides spout opinions and take verbal pot-shots at each other. This display of emotion, presumably, is what entertains viewers. (In appendix 4, on talk shows and democracy, we discuss the focus on emotion at the expense of reason.) And no one, not even Maher, pretends that the talk show is about anything but entertainment.

Although few participants are stupid enough to attack women directly, the same is not true, unfortunately, in reverse. Ridiculing men is treated as an acceptable form of amusement. On one show devoted to the Clinton scandal, for instance, comedian French Stewart opined that men are "just souped-up monkeys."[36]

One genre that often, but by no means always, takes on misandric overtones is the television newsmagazine. The problem of journalistic bias – and, therefore, of manipulation – has been discussed many times from perspectives on both the right and the left. There is probably truth to complaints from both sides. When it comes to gender and relations between men and women, however, the bias usually favours women. It would be unthinkable for a journalist, except one willing to pay a high price in public hostility, to say anything that could be construed as unflattering or disadvantageous to women as a group. (Nowadays, the words of a token man are sometimes included, though not necessarily taken seriously.) But things like that are routinely said and written about men. And the context is often explicitly polemical, which is reflected in the endless series of shows and articles on the differences between men and women. At any rate, the mass media routinely ignore politically incorrect topics. (The Public Broadcasting System has been accused of focusing attention on liberal causes, for example, and ignoring conservative ones.) "Where are the stories on female marital violence," asks one journalist, "and the connection between abortion and breast cancer?"[37]

"The New Rules of Love," a special edition of the popular television newsmagazine 20/20,[38] consisted of four segments: Seduction, Second Shift, How to Argue, and Deborah Tannen. A brief description of each indicates the current state of popular discourse on gender.

If revealing the complexity underlying everyday life is a measure of journalistic success, the first segment is by far the most successful. John Stossel, the host, makes it clear from the beginning that it is primarily about rape. Where does seduction end and rape begin? Obviously, many men and women are confused. Most of the women interviewed declare emphatically that "no always means no." At least one woman, however, indicates that things are more complicated, that real life is far more ambiguous than either political theory or political rhetoric acknowledges. A lawyer who has both defended and prosecuted men for rape argues that men and women still play romantic or erotic "games," in spite of the dangers, and that they will probably continue doing so. Both men and women are still influenced by the idea, transmitted for centuries, that "nice girls don't" and "bad girls do." As a result, many women are reluctant to say "yes" without some coaxing. For the same reason, many men expect their girlfriends or wives to *want* some amorous coaxing. This, at any rate, is what previous generations have known as "seduction." Viewers are shown excerpts from popular movies such as *Gone with the Wind* in which "no" means "maybe" or even "yes." Not all men believe that seduction can be defined as a physical assault. Unfortunately, popular culture has convinced some people, both men and women, that it could be. Then too, some women now claim that even *verbal* coaxing constitutes rape. As Stossel points out, genuine confusion among men has not disappeared just because many women now declare that "no always means no." Reality is more complicated than political slogans. So far, so good.

In the second segment, Stossel discusses the fact that most men do less work around the house than women. The problem is defined like this: women feel not only tired from having to work both at the office and at home but also angry at the fact that their husbands work less at home than they do. A "typical" couple is interviewed. Because the husband spends a few hours commuting to work every day, he has less time to spend on chores in the early morning and early evening. Nevertheless, he does wash the dishes every night and cleans the entire house on weekends. In addition to preparing the children for school, his wife prepares meals every day and does the laundry on weekends. Observing that they go about their tasks very differently, Stossel discusses their conflict from both points of view. Viewers watch the husband placidly dusting off pictures in the living room and resting on the couch after turning the pillows and vacuuming. The wife, by contrast, is businesslike in organizing and distributing the tasks. She appears fanatical in the energy she personally devotes to her work. On one occasion she is shown furiously scraping what must have been microscopic traces of dirt from the underside of a refrigerator shelf. Men, by implication, are less fussy than women about the final results of their tasks. The implication is that men are dirtier than women.

Stossel speaks for the husband, and probably for many male viewers, when he asks why the wife really cares if her house is neat enough to pass military inspection. The focus of attention then shifts to her point of view. Why is her husband's performance so important to her? By not doing what she considers his fair share, she explains, he is saying in effect that he does not value or love her enough. In other words, this problem is intensely emotional for her, not merely practical or even moral. Men are wrong to do less work than their wives, and it is usually assumed that their behaviours can be explained entirely in purely moral terms. In that case, they are just selfish slobs. But are there additional factors that could explain their behaviour? If we are asked to consider the psychological needs of women, why not those of men as well? This woman is the domestic equivalent of a platoon sergeant, but Stossel fails to present her husband's point of view with much sympathy.

From that point of view, at any rate, men's position can be explained in terms other than pure selfishness. Many husbands might simply resent being dominated by their wives. No one likes to be "henpecked." In addition, men might resent being manipulated by the way in which this topic is generally discussed. Their own psychological needs are seldom even considered, let alone taken seriously. Neither Stossel nor anyone else on the show considers the possibility that doing housework presents a real problem, one that should be taken seriously, in connection with masculine identity. If women now work outside the home (formerly the distinctive sphere of men) and men now work inside the home (formerly the distinctive sphere of women), what can it mean to be a man? What is men's *distinctive* contribution to the family? Ironically, this situation presents women with an identity problem of their own. Just as it is often still assumed that husbands have primary responsibility for domestic income, it is often still assumed that wives have primary responsibility for domestic chores. It is for this reason that wives often find themselves in the position of having to order their husbands around. At home, it is usually women who dole out tasks, establish schedules for their completion, and set the standard for evaluation. Because few wives work for their husbands outside the home, however, the reverse is seldom true. Even Stossel points out that men who fail to measure up when it comes to domestic chores might be motivated by the psychological need to assert their dignity either as individuals or as men rather than simply by moral turpitude.

Stossel points out that couples often divorce because they do not know how to argue constructively. Of the problems in communication he lists, one is generally associated strictly with men: the tendency to remain silent, to withdraw from conflict. The other two could be associated with either men or women. Deborah Tannen is brought in to elaborate. She discusses the fact that men and women speak "different languages" and thus get into destructive fights. It quickly becomes clear, however, that the two modes of communication she identifies are not merely different. As we have noted, she implies that the mode of women is superior to that of men. Women use language to express caring and concern, to sustain relationships, and so forth, whereas men use language to express dominance or gain the upper hand. Although Tannen says that both men and women must learn to understand the other's use of language, she implies that most of the learning and changing must be done by men, not women. There is some truth to her observations of differences in the use of language by men and women. But she ignores the fact that women too must learn to speak what amounts to a "foreign" language – and that women have in fact done so very effectively not only in the business world but in the political world as well.

The point here is that each of the four segments is construed as a problem caused primarily by some deficiency of men, not women. Although Stossel attempts to insert some complexity, pointing out that there is another side to every question, the fact remains that the problems themselves are framed as the complaints of women. The complaints of men are expressed, to be sure, but mainly as *responses* that in no way set the tone for debate.

Misandric references slip by virtually unnoticed even on newsmagazine shows, a genre purporting to promote the objective standards of journalism (although it purports also to promote the subjective standards of advocacy journalism). This is possible now that misandry has become a feature of conventional wisdom, something taken for granted. Consider a segment on *PrimeTime Live* about AIDS.[39] While pregnant, Elizabeth Glaezer had been given a blood transfusion that left both her and the child infected. But Glaezer has fought back with the constant support of two close friends. Together they have established a foundation for research on pediatric AIDS. This story of courage and solidarity would surely be inspiring for all viewers. But Diane Sawyer thought it should be inspiring only for women: "Do you think three men friends would have done it this way?" she asks one of her guests. The answer is predictable. "No," says one of the friends with a laugh, "I think ... what's female about it is, first of all, I think, women approach problems differently than men and solving [sic] problems differently than men. I think that for women, as mothers, we come to it from a point of ... sensitivity and compassion." Morally, in other words, women are innately superior to men. (This particular section of dialogue, by the way, was featured in the promo before a commercial break.)

Only a few days earlier, the same kind of thing happened on another network. To conclude its featured series on gender, called "He and She," NBC's *Today* presented the upbeat authors of *Gender War, Gender Peace*, Elizabeth Herron and Aaron Kipnis.[40] During the interview, they are optimistic about the possibility for better communication. How? By assuming that men and women live in utterly different societies. From this, it follows that men and women should consider themselves ambassadors when sojourning in the alien society. To the extent that equality has been taken to mean similarity, they argue, it has been a mistake to focus attention on sexual equality. On the contrary, the focus of attention should be on the differences between men and women. One particular difference surfaces during the interview: although Kipnis emphasizes the role of culture in creating gender differences, Herron emphasizes the role of nature. For her, the differences are not only profound but inevitable. She claims nonetheless that difference and equality are compatible. This is certainly in keeping with rhetoric in some feminist circles. But does current reality support the hope that an emphasis on difference can sustain a belief in equality?

Judging from what could be seen on an earlier segment in this series, the possibility is very unlikely.

Several couples, presumably representing typical men and women, are interviewed. They discuss their perceptions of the opposite sex. One woman, Marna LoCastro, has the nerve to go on national television and proclaim the superiority of women in blatantly stereotypical ways: "I think that we're more sensitive. I think we're more emotional. I think we're more, more caring. I think we're more dependable than males. I do."[41] Her husband finds this amusing, or at least feels the need to appear amused. And neither Katie Couric nor Matt Lauer, the interviewers, finds her statements problematic. Clearly, in terms of gender, "equality" has become a virtually meaningless word. It would be tempting to argue that this mentality is the result of nothing more serious than public ignorance. But the fact is that this link between difference and *superiority* – instead of equality – has been prevalent among the most influential feminists for at least twenty years. Women might have believed in their own innate, or "racial," superiority no matter what their leaders said or did, it is true, but they might have been forced to challenge this belief had their leaders not made it publicly acceptable.

The situation had not changed by the late 1990s. One segment of *Dateline*, aired a week before Christmas in 1997, is called "Hit or Miss?"[42] The topic is advertising techniques used to address men and women. Stone Phillips introduces the segment by informing viewers not only that men and women think "very differently" but also that male viewers will not like what they are about to see and hear. The correspondent, Joshua Mankiewicz, interviews several of what he considers experts in the field: not neurologists, anthropologists, or even historians but advertisers. Their authority is based on the fact that they spend millions of dollars on market research. According to these experts, sales pitches directed towards men should be simple, direct, to the point. Men are too simple-minded, apparently, to understand the more complex, subtle, nuanced messages directed towards women. Messages to women are addressed to discriminating and imaginative individuals who appreciate opportunities to associate products with such elevated notions as "empowerment," not merely with such crude notions as sex. Messages to men are addressed to the generic slob. Throughout this segment, both interviewer and interviewees smirk repeatedly as if to say, "You already knew that men were primitive beasts. Now, we have proof!" The point here is not that market researchers are wrong about how contemporary American men and women respond to ads, but that contemporary American men and women do so at least partly because of how ads have *conditioned* them to respond.

One expert suggests that evolution might provide an explanation. Early women spent their time at a variety of tasks such as looking after children and gathering food: they had to think, he surmises, of many things at once. Early men, on the other hand, spent their time on only one task: hunting. They could not afford to be distracted. The implication is that women are smarter than men, capable of more sophisticated modes of thought. Never mind that hunting itself requires a variety of skills, complex planning, and so on. Never mind that men throughout history and throughout the world have consistently produced remarkably sophisticated thought – not only complex and subtle but also imaginative and intuitive – in forms such as philosophy and theology, music and poetry, mathematics and science. Why would a reputable newsmagazine ignore all this? Possibly because female viewers would likely approve the stereotypes that male viewers have long been conditioned to accept. This was the network's Christmas present, as it were, to women.

Viewers are asked to look down on men in televised fiction no less than non-fiction. In an interview on *Today*,"[43] Mark Harmon describes his role in *Reasonable Doubts* as that of "a cynical cop" and that of Marlee Matlin as "a cop who believes everyone is innocent till proven guilty." Pondering the people he deals with every day, Dicky (played by Harmon) says, "Wouldn't it be nice if all these guys just got together and killed each other off?" As usual, the man is associated with everything corrupt and sleazy and the woman – a victim of deafness, no less – with everything pure and idealistic. This is no accident. It conforms to a tried-and-true formula. The fact that Matlin is not only a woman but also a deaf woman, a victim of nature as well as a likely victim of men, makes it almost inevitable that viewers look to her as the source of inspiration and courage. The same is true of countless other series.

Among the last shows on television that we would expect to promote looking down on men, or any group of people, is *Masterpiece Theatre*. This show has been running for many years as a flagship of the Public Broadcasting System. As the name suggests, it is associated with high-quality drama based, as often as not, on literary classics. These productions are from Britain, a country renowned for its splendid theatrical tradition in general and, when it comes to television, for the British Broadcasting Corporation in particular. Some critics sniff that costume dramas such as *Upstairs Downstairs* really amount to nothing more than lavishly and exquisitely produced soap operas. For many years, however, no one pretended that *Masterpiece Theatre* offered more than good entertainment packaged with interesting historical commentary.

Recently, this has begun to change. More and more often, the chosen series has a distinctly political subtext. And it is almost always a feminist one.

In 1994, *Masterpiece Theatre* presented *The Rector's Wife*, based on a book by Joanna Trollope. Unlike many series, this one is set in contemporary England. The protagonist is Anna Bouverie. Like Gustave Flaubert's Emma Bovary, she is a middle-aged woman who lives in a provincial town and wonders why life is so frustrating. Like Emma, moreover, Anna could be described as self-indulgent. Unlike Emma, though, she is not *accused* of self-indulgence, but on the contrary, *applauded* for it. Most people nowadays would probably call it "self-empowerment." In fact, the whole point of this story is that Anna escapes from her inadequate husband.

Anna's hapless husband, too, could be accused, and is accused, of self-indulgence. In his case, though, it would now be called "sexism." Peter is a priest serving several rural parishes. In spite of his dogged efforts, it soon becomes clear that he is never going to achieve anything. Both he and Anna are understandably depressed by the "slammed doors, refusals, hierarchy, muddle, divisions, [and] loneliness" of parish work and diocesan politics. (Peter's failure is linked as much to the church's collective inadequacy, by the way, as to his personal inadequacy.) After twenty years of thankless work, Anna has lost her faith in both Peter and God – or, if not God, at least in the church. It all comes to a head when someone is chosen as archdeacon instead of Peter. After twenty years of selfless work, he succumbs to disappointment and bitterness. He and Anna quarrel over money.

Anna decides that their daughter should go to a private school. To pay for this, she finds a job at the local supermarket. And she refuses to quit when the girl is given a scholarship. Peter is outraged. This is partly because Anna has undermined his position in the community. Priests and their wives are hired as units; only one salary is paid, but both are expected to function as parish leaders by vocation. Once it becomes clear that Anna has no vocation, people come to the conclusion that she has betrayed them. By extension, they come to the conclusion that Peter has failed them. If he cannot sustain the faith of his own wife, how can he sustain theirs? Peter is outraged for another reason too. Anna's behaviour has undermined whatever remains of his own self-esteem. Anna takes a paying job, after all, because she cannot depend on him to make enough money. In any case, he asks her employer to fire her. Not surprisingly, this provokes Anna's outrage. And so it goes. Until …

Yes, Anna does exactly what Emma does. She has an affair. And why not? Is having an affair with another man, she wonders, "morally worse than having an affair with duty?" Some people would say it is. Before

you can say "feminism," at any rate, she finds her own satisfying answer.
What troubles her is not committing adultery per se, but the effect of
doing so on her troubled teenage son. But even that does not cause her
to reconsider. As it happens, not one but two men claim to have fallen
in love with her. The loser is a wealthy neighbour who might have taken
lessons in courtship from Boris Karloff. (When his housekeeper quits,
she tells him, "If I ever do marry, it will be either to a good woman or
a good book.") The winner is his younger brother, a clone of Daniel
Day-Lewis. After only a minor struggle, Anna decides to leave Peter. In
other words, she decides to reject patriarchal oppression.

Anna need not worry her newly liberated head about telling Peter
the bad news. He conveniently kills himself. The story ends in the
cemetery as Anna "talks" to Peter. Now that he is dead, she can forgive
him for not living up to her expectations. She walks away untroubled.
Now, presumably, Peter will understand her behaviour and forgive her.
Anyway, she forgives herself. That, apparently, is all that counts.

This story is politically effective, no doubt, but it is morally bank-
rupt. So Anna's life does not turn out to be as exciting and romantic
and fulfilling as she had hoped: anyone could sympathize with someone
in that position. But Peter's life is no better. At least some people could
sympathize with him. He too is the victim of a system that rewards
pretentiousness, condescension, artificiality, and even stupidity (represented rather well by his gung-ho replacement). In addition, his life is
intensely humiliating, not merely because of his wife's infidelity but
mainly because of his own sense of failure. A more sophisticated book
or movie would have encouraged people to feel sympathy for both
wife and husband. In this one, the husband has been turned into a
stereotypical patriarch who makes no effort whatsoever to consider
his wife's needs. Therefore, he *deserves* no sympathy. No wonder he
is killed off expediently as the apparently minor price to be paid for
his wife's freedom. Trollope makes it possible for Anna to avoid guilt,
in other words, for her own selfishness. Readers or viewers are clearly
expected to find this justifiable or even satisfying.

If either of these unattractive people is more to blame than the other,
it is surely Anna. Yes, she is unhappy. Yes, she has good reasons for
being unhappy. At issue is what she does about her unhappiness or, at
the very least, the way she does it. It is not as if she has no choices.
She has at least three of them. She could leave town with her family
and start over again in some other way of life. This probably would
not work. Peter's dedication to the church – to suffer for it, if necessary
– is deeply rooted in his sense of vocation, not his ambition for a career
(which is precisely why he could never succeed in a worldly church).
Failing that, Anna could simply leave him and make a life for herself

somewhere else. That would be hard for her, no doubt, but no harder than for millions of other people who feel trapped in loveless marriages. She would have the freedom to live as an independent woman, build a career, remarry, and take a lover. And Peter would have the support of his community. But Anna chooses another way, an easier way. She chooses to make a new life for herself but *without leaving*. Her choice, as she knows perfectly well, subjects Peter to ridicule and humiliation in the only world that means anything to him. That is what makes her selfishness inexcusable, not the mere fact of falling in love with a more exciting man. Feelings are obviously beyond our control.

Now the problem here is not so much that Anna lacks compassion for Peter or vice versa. The problem is that Trollope lacks compassion for him and the people – men – that he represents. Peter and Anna are fictional characters, not real people. To speculate about what they could have done as real people – which is to say, what we as readers or viewers would have done – is to bypass the underlying problem of what the author could have done. At issue is not why they act one way instead of another but why Trollope wanted them to do so. At issue, to put it another way, is the purpose of this book and the series it spawned. Like all other works of fiction, its purpose is to entertain. But works of "serious fiction" have additional purposes, which are expressed as "subtexts." And it is the subtext of this one that should, as postmodernist critics like to say, be "problematized."

As a work of fiction, it encourages comparison with other works of fiction, including the ones universally classified as great art. Consider the two most obvious parallels: Flaubert's *Madame Bovary* and Tolstoy's *Anna Karenina*. Both are about bored and frustrated wives whose search for happiness leads them to abandon their families. But the difference between either of those authors and Trollope is one of purpose and function, not merely of talent or virtuosity. Both Anna Karenina and Emma Bovary are tragic figures. Anna Bouverie, by contrast, is a role model. Both Flaubert and Tolstoy offer insight into the complexity and ambiguity of everyday life. Trollope offers only the "insight" that women can find no happiness with men, whether husbands (the man who rejects Anna) or lovers (the man she rejects). (The man who does win Anna has a very minor role. Because his character is undeveloped, the implication is that he provides Anna with sexual services but nothing else that might be understood as the foundation for a deep relationship.) Both Flaubert and Tolstoy wanted to unite men and women through compassion. Trollope wants to divide them through resentment. Both Flaubert and Tolstoy used their characters to explore the human condition in general and human nature in particular. Trollope uses hers to score political points for women.

Of all Tolstoy's novels, *Anna Karenina* offers the most obvious parallel to *The Rector's Wife*. It is true that Tolstoy's Anna is married to an ugly and dour man. Nevertheless, Alexis plays by the rules that both he and Anna accepted when they married. And he has good reasons for insisting that their son, Seryozha, should remain with him. But are these reasons good enough to separate the boy from his mother? As for Anna, she has good reasons for preferring the handsome and exciting Count Vronsky. But are these reasons good enough to justify abandoning not only her husband but her son? Like all human beings, both these characters are ambiguous combinations of good and evil, wisdom and folly. Tolstoy's novel is not a moralistic sermon or political tract in disguise. Anna's choice is wrong, certainly, but readers are not happy when she pays for her mistake. They are given no excuse to feel self-righteous at her expense. Sometimes, Tolstoy says, there are no satisfying solutions to the dilemmas of everyday life. No one can have it all. Everyone must make choices. And every choice comes with a price tag. In the end, Anna finds the price too high. But her suicide is a tragedy, not a punishment. It is a tragedy not only for her, by the way, but also for Seryozha.

And no, we are not taking a cheap shot at Trollope. She deliberately invites the obvious comparisons between her book and those of Tolstoy and Flaubert. Moreover, we are not even challenging expert opinion in the literary world. The most avant-garde critics these days would applaud Trollope's Anna precisely *because* of her political motivation. Their primary criterion for evaluating literature *is* politics, not aesthetics. If they allow the works of "dead white males" such as Tolstoy and Flaubert to remain within the "canon" of Western civilization at all, it is only on the understanding that the works of women such as Trollope are added as equally valuable "alternative voices."

Theoretically, condescension is not the same as sexism or any comparable "ism." It is possible to see other groups of people as inferior in some way but not hate them. Parents realize that children are inferior to adults in some ways but do not hate them. On the contrary, they love their children, at least initially, precisely because they are relatively helpless and dependent, physically and intellectually inferior. But, putting aside the unique dynamics of family life, the history of intergroup relations indicates a disturbing pattern that links not only condescension with contempt but also contempt with hatred. At the very best, condescension is linked with a sense of noblesse oblige and the resulting reinforcement of social and political hierarchies. It would make no moral sense, therefore, to trivialize the contempt shown for men routinely on both commercial and public television. Apart from anything else, it indicates that nothing has been learned from history.

CHAPTER FOUR

Bypassing Men:
Women Alone Together

I was raised to believe that if you had a child out of wedlock you were bad. Of course, I was also raised to believe a woman's place was in the home, segregation was good, and presidents never lied. Oh, it's so confusing.[1]

In the last chapter, we discussed "separate but unequal" from the perspective of "unequal." In this chapter, we do so from the perspective of "separate." There are limits to how separate from men women want to be, or can be, although that does not prevent some women from wishful thinking about pushing the limits. Within those limits, there is a wide range of possibilities. Andrea Dworkin wants as little contact as possible.[2] For her, the very act of heterosexual intercourse represents the invasion of female bodies. For her, every act of sex between men and women – and she includes not only consensual sex but also sex initiated by women – constitutes the rape of women. But most women love, or at least like, some men: sons, brothers, fathers, lovers, or whatever. Nonetheless, the bonds of "sisterhood" were heavily promoted in the 1990s, and not only because political gains would have been impossible without solidarity. That solidarity was reflected in popular culture. Among the more obvious examples, in music, were the Spice Girls, promoting "grrrl power," and the annual Lilith Fair, developed to celebrate the music of female artists.

There is nothing wrong with solidarity per se, but sometimes it has a lamentable by-product: withdrawal. In this case, that amounts to voluntary sexual segregation. The implication of many movies and television shows, for example, is that women do not or should not need men for any significant reason. Men are not necessarily evil, just superfluous. *Indifference* to men, not hostility, is encouraged, whether explicitly or implicitly. Why is that byproduct lamentable? Mainly because the idea that *any* group of people is superfluous should be recognized as inherently dehumanizing.

It was in this atmosphere that Vice-President Dan Quayle provoked a furore with his comments on single motherhood. Taking an indirect route, he referred to *Murphy Brown*, the highly rated sitcom about a successful journalist whose life is focused primarily on her career. In one episode, however, Murphy decides to have a baby.[3] This episode and its cultural context were described eloquently by Margaret Carlson:

When U.S. television viewers last saw Baby Brown's father, it was shortly after conception and well before birth. He's off now saving the rain forest, having opted out of Lamaze class and changing diapers. He may come back, but the show's premise is built around the notion that a woman who has made it in a man's world without one should be lionized for doing so alone through the "terrible twos" and beyond. The lack of a dad is not accidental but a running-joke opportunity. For the successful, glamorous woman who has everything: Now, live from Hollywood, your very own baby, father optional.[4]

According to Quayle, the scenario illustrated something significant about contemporary American life. The nation, he said in response, suffers from a "poverty of values" characterized by "indulgence and self-gratification ... glamorized casual sex and drug use ... It doesn't help matters when prime-time TV has Murphy Brown, a character who supposedly epitomizes today's intelligent, highly paid professional woman, mocking the importance of fathers by bearing a child alone and calling it just another 'life-style choice.'"[5] Not surprisingly, a hurricane of controversy swept over the nation during the days and weeks that followed. "On the night Murphy Brown became an unwed mother," according to Barbara Whitehead for an article in *Atlantic Monthly*, "34 million Americans tuned in, and CBS posted a 35 percent share of the audience. The show did not stir significant protest at the grass roots level and lost none of its advertisers. The actress Candice Bergen subsequently appeared on the cover of nearly every women's and news magazine in the country and received an honorary degree at the University of Pennsylvania as well as an Emmy award. The show's creator, Diane English, popped up in Hanes stocking ads. Judged by conventional measures of approval, Murphy Brown's motherhood was a hit at the box office."[6]

Many social commentators tried to trivialize all the fuss by suggesting that *Murphy Brown* was nothing more than a situation comedy. Obviously, they said derisively, Dan Quayle was too stupid to see the difference between reality and fiction. These critics, however, were often the very ones who complained most bitterly about the prevalence of violence in other fictional scenarios on television. How could they have it both ways? Either the impact of what appears on television is significant, or it is trivial. Scholars have always known that movies and television shows affect the culture that produces them. By the time of this episode, the critics knew that what people see on television can have a significant impact on the way almost everyone feels, thinks, and behaves. Otherwise, the people who produce commercial television, let alone commercials, would be out of business. The prevalence of violence on television is not the direct cause of actual violence, but the two could be related indirectly. The message is clear: our society considers violence not only inevitable but glamorous. At the very least, this desensitizes people to actual violence. It could also anaesthetize them and thus lead to passivity or apathy. Shows such as *Murphy Brown* are not the direct cause of single motherhood, either in the ghettoes or anywhere else. Nevertheless, they legitimate what many have already accepted in others or even decided to do for themselves. Few people, if any, have premarital sex after learning about it from sitcoms on television. But many feel no qualms about doing so, because, according to these shows, everyone's doin' it. And hey, if everyone's doin' it, how can it be wrong? In short, there is nothing trivial about popular culture. It is the folklore, the conventional wisdom, of an urban, industrial society. Shows such as *Murphy Brown* become popular by telling people what they want and expect to be told.

Among Quayle's critics were the entertainment industry's own writers, critics, producers, and performers. Even they often trivialized Quayle's comment by arguing that popular culture is pure entertainment and thus not to be taken seriously by culture critics. Yet on other occasions, they have protested vigorously when attacked for purveying nothing but pure entertainment. And they have a point. Almost all sitcoms – let alone crime shows, soap operas, and "dramedies" – have what are often called "relevant" plots and subplots, episodes that teach moral or political lessons of some kind. These lessons do not appear by accident. They are deliberately written for political purposes – almost invariably for politically correct ones.

Think of *The Golden Girls*. While being entertained, viewers are routinely taught about such timely subjects as health care for the elderly, drug dependency, homelessness, homosexuality, sexual harassment, suicide, unemployment, and marital infidelity. *Designing Women* is just as polemical: messages about gender and race, though sometimes confined to scattered jokes, occasionally fill entire episodes.[7] In the entertainment industry, only liars and hypocrites could claim to be shocked or amused that anyone would take the impact of their productions seriously.

Other critics from within the industry used a very different approach but reached precisely the same conclusion: that shows such as *Murphy Brown* were exempt from attack. According to Ken Tucker, these shows have the exalted status of art. And artists, as they have been defined in

Western societies ever since the nineteenth century, when bohemian painters rebelled against the moral and aesthetic standards of a bourgeois "academy," are supposedly responsible to and for no one but themselves. Tucker explains that "TV isn't an arm of social policy or government propaganda; it has no more responsibility to be upbeat and positive than do, say, poetry or the theatre."[8] *Murphy Brown* is nothing if not an upbeat portrayal of a career woman. Still, Tucker has a point.

As we saw all too often in the twentieth century, disaster has always followed attempts by the state to exploit cultural productions, whether elite or popular. But doing the opposite, abandoning society in the name of personal "authenticity," is surely no better. Why must we assume that those who give public expression to their ideas must do so with no consideration for the effects of these ideas on the public? At most times and in most places, art – we use the term broadly here – has functioned at least partly as a way of fostering communal cohesion by articulating commonly shared beliefs about the world. Neither the Hebrew poet-prophets nor the Greek philosopher-dramatists were always "upbeat," but neither were they indifferent to those around them. On the contrary, they were passionately involved in the collective search for truth, beauty, compassion, and whatever else confers dignity on human existence. Tucker's attitude would have been as incomprehensible to them as to the Chinese landscape painters or the Russian novelists. His position is based more than anything else on political expediency, carefully disguised as artistic sophistication.

As his critics were quick to point out, Quayle did make several mistakes. In the first place, he suggested that the Los Angeles riots were caused by the kind of mentality illustrated and promoted by *Murphy Brown*. This was an oversimplification. The show was extremely popular among Americans in general, it is true, but not among those who lived in the ghettoes and were involved in the riots. It ranked third among whites but only fifty-sixth among blacks. The protagonist was a white, middle-class, upwardly mobile yuppie. It is unlikely that many women from the lower classes, white or black, regarded her as a role model. (Many of those who belong to the gangs in ghettoes do not regard even black politicians, preachers, or other civic leaders as role models. These figures, they say, are so remote from their lives that they might just as well be white.) Of greatest interest here is precisely the impact of this show on the artistic and intellectual elite of our society, the people who control what is presented on television and thus set the tone for political debate. The social position of Murphy makes her far more culpable than a poor, uneducated woman. Viewers can assume that she has knowledge of and access to birth control. That even she chooses to have sex without "protection" indicates the depth of this problem.

Then too, Quayle neglected to point out that women in Murphy's position could, and often do, choose abortion instead of childbirth – especially when the fathers run out, as this one has, leaving mothers alone with their burdens. Many people would have agreed that having children outside of marriage, though more difficult, is a more desirable solution than abortion. Only those who argue that the "quality of life" is more important than life itself could have disagreed, and that would have pitted them against those who argue that any single woman, especially one in Murphy's position, should be able to provide her child with an adequate "quality of life." Had he been more charitable, in other words, Quayle could at least have provided support for millions of women whose value for life remains strong enough to motivate considerable sacrifice. Quayle's speech had an unnecessarily harsh and self-righteous tone. Too many who speak in the name of moral values, observed Meg Greenfield, "stint the values of charity, generosity and forgiveness that are so deeply etched in the Western spiritual tradition."[9] But the subject under discussion here is not Dan Quayle as a person any more than it is Murphy Brown as a "person." It is single parenthood in general and single motherhood in particular, because most single parents are mothers and are supported by a powerful political movement.

When Candice Bergen won an Emmy for her portrayal of Murphy Brown, she thanked Quayle. Everyone understood. But it was inevitable that the most symbolically significant response to Quayle would be made on the show itself, and so it was on the opening episode of *Murphy Brown* for the following season.[10] The day it aired, Bergen was interviewed on the network's morning talk show. According to her, the episode scheduled for that evening was going to "take the moral high road."[11] Viewers who tuned in discovered what that meant.

The controversy is mentioned very promptly in this new episode. On the evening news, Quayle makes his remark about *Murphy Brown* glamorizing single mothers. Well, in a way it does: after all, Murphy is a glamorous television journalist. In another and more important way, however, the show "naturalizes" single mothers. Like all single mothers, like all mothers, Murphy has to think about such mundane matters as burping, diapering, and toilet training. The clear implication is that single mothers, no matter how rich and famous, are just ordinary members of the community, not shocking or even glamorous anomalies. Dishevelled after spending a night with a cranky infant, at any rate, Murphy explains to a friend and colleague:

MURPHY: Glamorizing single motherhood? What planet is he on? Look at me, Frank. Am I glamorous? … I agonized over that decision. I … I didn't know if I could raise a kid by myself. I worried about what it would do to him. I

worried about what it would do to me. I didn't just wake up one morning and say, "Oh, gee, I can't get in for a facial, I might just as well have a baby."
FRANK: I don't blame you for being angry, but consider the source. I mean, this is the same guy who gave a speech at the United Negro College Fund and said, "What a waste it is to lose one's mind." [The audience applauds.] And then he spent the rest of his term showing the country exactly what he meant. Tomorrow, he's probably going to get his head stuck in his golf bag and you'll be old news. Murph, it's Dan Quayle. Forget about it.

Apparently, this personal attack on Quayle was the "moral high road." Quayle had attacked the idea of single motherhood as represented by a fictional character. Those responsible for this show, on the other hand, used their fictional character to attack a real person. In any case, the idea behind this ad hominem argument, used over and over again in connection with Quayle by late-night talk-show hosts such as Jay Leno and David Letterman, is that *whatever* Quayle says may be dismissed solely by virtue of who he is, without bothering to argue over the content of what he actually says.

The matter was not left here but was featured on two other occasions. Just before Murphy goes on the air in this episode with her formal response to the vice-president, for example, two other characters in the series discuss the problem:

CORKY: I was raised to believe that if you had a child out of wedlock you were bad. Of course, I was also raised to believe a woman's place was in the home, segregation was good, and presidents never lied. Oh, it's so confusing.
JIM: We live in confusing times, Corky. The White House criticizes Murphy for having a child while they're parading the Terminator around as a role model for young people.

Corky's "quandary" is taken seriously by Jim but implicitly ridiculed by the show. Its writers link opposition to single motherhood with three other positions that are supposedly conservative – that is, positions supposedly held by most or all conservative people. Once again, attention is shifted away from the positions themselves and towards those who hold them. But this is an attack on the immoral hypocrisy of conservatives, not merely their stupidity; those who oppose single motherhood on moral grounds can be opposed themselves, presumably, on moral grounds. And that strategy might work if it could be demonstrated that opposition to single motherhood were necessarily connected in some way with the other positions listed by Corky. But her argument is based on emotional associations, not logic.

Consider the three statements on the other side of Corky's "of course" and what is said to link them: Lying is universally condemned.

Segregation is universally condemned (in public, at any rate). The notion that mothers belong at home is more problematic. Unlike the statement about lying and even the one about segregation, *not* everyone would be willing to condemn this one out of hand. Even mothers who have business or professional careers often prefer to stay home for a few years to care for their children. There is nothing intrinsically wrong with the idea that women have a distinctive role to play in the home, in other words, only with the idea that women should be *forced* to stay home. But including that statement in this particular context is based on the clever assumption that fans of *Murphy Brown* will link it with the others, making an outright condemnation just as they do in connection with lying and segregation. Even if everyone could agree that these three things – lying, segregation, and women at home – were intrinsically evil, this would still not prove that opposition to single motherhood is evil. The only thing all four statements have in common, according to Corky, is an association with conservatism or what is perceived as conservatism by those who espouse liberalism. Corky's argument goes like this. The three allegedly conservative statements – that women belong in the home, that segregation is good, and that presidents never lie – are false. The other statement – that women should not have children out of wedlock – is conservative, and therefore is also false. (Viewers are expected to make a further association between conservatism per se and evil. In that case the deliberate propagation of lies is intended to keep women in their place.) What links all four statements is thus not logic but prejudice. Ironically, it is prejudice of precisely the same kind that conservatives often use against liberals.

Later on, the argument shifts again. Murphy actually discusses the sociological background of the controversy. She opens with a brief preamble: "Some might argue that attacking my status as a single mother was nothing more than a cynical bit of election year posturing. I prefer to give the vice-president the benefit of the doubt." But does she? By stating this popular argument as the introduction to her own, she gives it tacit approval even as she officially rejects it. In this way, her speech epitomizes a strategy characteristic of the entire episode. It is the accumulation of arguments, not the content of any one in particular, that counts.

Even some observers who disliked Quayle himself, criticizing him for lecturing self-righteously about "family values" but promising no legislation to help families in need, were willing to acknowledge that his words were timely. "If the message is that family disintegration and the dramatic rise of single-parent families are a major social disaster for this country," wrote John Leo, "then the message is clearly correct."[12] In Hollywood no less than Harlem, he pointed out, the pattern has been the same. Children are far more likely to lack one parent than they were in the past. According to the Census Bureau, the number of single-parent families has tripled since 1970.[13]

Quayle might have pointed out that Murphy rejected not only abortion but (in another episode) artificial insemination as well. Female characters on some other shows do not. They bypass relationships with men altogether in their efforts to become pregnant. In one episode of *Designing Women*, Mary Jo, successful and single, decides to heed her "biological clock" by resorting to artificial insemination.[14] Some of the other women find this disturbing at first, but they soon come to see her point of view. Mary Jo does not become pregnant on her first try, but the point has been made. Initiating a pregnancy is a "woman's choice" no less than aborting one.

The same approach is taken to its logical conclusion in an episode of *The Golden Girls*.[15] Becky, Blanche's daughter, arrives from out of town and announces that she has decided to visit the local sperm bank:

BECKY: I can't pass a carriage without looking in. I heard my biological clock ticking so loudly it was keeping me up at night. A baby should be doing that.
BLANCHE: But why don't you wait till you get married?
BECKY: I don't want to get married.

Blanche is horrified at first, but she relents by the end of the show. The sperm bank is a pleasant and tastefully decorated place of business filled with friendly and respectable citizens. If everyone's doin' it, what could be wrong? The episode might have been written as a promo for Single Mothers By Choice. That movement is based on two fundamental beliefs. In the first place, members believe that women have a "right" to bear children (or not to do so). This is why Becky tells Blanche, "What I am doing, Mother, is taking control of my life and having the family I need." Notice that her definition of "family," unlike that of a widow or a divorcée, clearly *excludes fathers*. Notice too the word "need." She does not merely want children: she needs them. As for the need of her children for a father, she does not even consider it. It is *her* need that counts. Members of the movement believe that a mother's love is all it takes to produce a healthy child. Fathers are luxuries at best and burdens at worst. Not one of the characters – not even Blanche, who opposes the procedure – considers the possibility that Becky's child would be at a serious disadvantage by not having a father.

The same thing occurs on *Maggie*, another sitcom. In an article about women in sitcoms on Lifetime Television, the network addressed specifically to women, Ken Tucker notes that "Tracy has been artificially inseminated, which would seem to leave her boyfriend, Grant

... with a limited role in the series, and the faster the show pushes the stolid Kelly out of the picture, the better ... In a better TV world, the boyfriend wouldn't exist and Tracy and Charlotte would be the couple having the baby."[16] Tucker does not raise the possibility that society as a whole could be at a serious disadvantage by not binding men securely to family life. The fact is that single-parent families are at a disadvantage.[17] From this, it follows that there is a moral distinction to be made between those who become single parents by circumstances such as death or divorce and those who do so by choice.

So much for the sitcoms. Now, consider the talk shows. On a *Donahue*[18] show about relations between men and women, everyone uses the rhetoric of equality. Both men and women say they believe in sexual equality, even though both claim that the other sex wants something more than equality. The problem is that no one has actually done any analysis. Although a few note that biological differences might interfere with equality, most assume that equality is simply a matter of moral and legal reform. No one notes that complete equality would mean not only drafting women into combat – not the same as allowing a few women to choose combat – but also finding ways for men to give birth.

When one man on the show condemns single motherhood by choice, which limits contact with the child's father to a few cells from a sperm bank, he meets with extreme hostility from the women. Giving birth and raising children clearly remain close to the heart of their identity. For men to do so would be a severe threat to women. What the women on this show want is the right, though not necessarily the duty, to do everything men do. But they do not want men to have the right to do everything they do – which means that they could never accept the idea of complete equality.

This topic is more complex than it might appear. Few people think about what might actually happen if complete equality were achieved, if we were to eliminate every vestige of gender as a cultural system. What we call "degendering" would mean the dissolution of *all* cultural differences between men and women and mitigate even biological ones. How, then, would either men or women as such form identity?

In the remote past, men made distinctive and valuable contributions to the community by virtue of their male bodies (apart from anything else). And we are not referring here to insemination. Male bodies in general are distinguished from female bodies in general by their comparative advantages of size, strength, and mobility. These were extremely useful for hunting, pushing iron ploughs, or wielding weapons in battle. Many people now find it hard to see why warfare was ever valued, but the fact is that most societies, including both men and women, have indeed valued it. Beginning with the rise of agriculture and city states, it was considered necessary for some people to defend the community from raiders and often desirable for them to raid other communities.

In the recent past, beginning with industrialization, the importance of male bodies has declined steeply. Machines and computers do much of the work that once required male bodies. The men with highest status now are precisely those who do not have to engage in physical labour. As a direct result, the biological basis of masculine identity has declined as well. This has left combat, unfortunately, as the *only* effective basis for masculine identity.[19] This explains, at least partly, the extraordinary resurgence of machismo in our society.

Machismo has been culturally supported by legal prohibitions on the conscription of women. Many women in our society might want the privilege of engaging in combat and the economic or political advantages that go with it, but very few want the *duty* of combat. This means that only men grow up with the expectation or possibility of being forced into combat and the need to develop appropriate psychological skills. By contrast, identity for women is still formed in connection with the one thing men cannot do: give birth. Combat has always been extremely dangerous, not only to society in general but to men in particular, but that was balanced throughout most of human history by the fact that childbirth was extremely dangerous for women. Because modern medicine has greatly diminished the danger formerly inherent in childbirth, that balance – both sexes being at risk of losing their lives for the community – is symbolically destroyed and, during wartime, *actually* destroyed as well.

In a fully degendered society, biological asymmetry would stand out more starkly than ever. Unless the technology of male gestation or an artificial womb[20] were developed – and feminists have already organized politically to prevent those "science-fiction" scenarios[21] – women as a class would retain both their biological identity and any cultural ones they choose. But men as a class would have neither one; biological identity would be ruled out on the grounds that women *can* do everything men can do (although men cannot yet do at least one thing women can do), and cultural identity would be ruled out on the grounds that women *should be encouraged* to do everything men do. This is not merely a theory, nor is it merely a matter of the existential angst felt by everyone. Social scientists have provided growing evidence that boys and men are experiencing many problems directly or indirectly related to identity.

In any case, degendering can never be the solution as long as men and women have different bodies. Taken to its logical conclusion, degendering would have to involve elimination of one sex. That very solution is sometimes implied in connection with men. One possible solution to the inevitable problem created by degendering might be called "regendering," retaining some sort of gender system but one in which men, like women, are encouraged to make a distinctive, necessary, and valued contribution to society (though not, we hope, through combat). But who can say how that would be worked out? It would require both sexes to give up something, of course. But neither, in all likelihood, would do that willingly.

The motif of bypassing men is exemplified by many movies made in the 1990s. Among them is *Waiting to Exhale* (Forest Whitaker, 1995). Though directed by a man, it was based on the novel by a woman, Terry McMillan. According to Karen De Witt of the *New York Times*,[22] this movie provided far more than casual entertainment for women. A front-page headline put it this way: "For Black Women, a Movie Stirs Breathless Excitement." And not only for black women – its story "seems to transcend the experiences of race and class." Apparently, women bought tickets in bulk. Why see it yourself or with only one or two friends? Groups of forty or fifty were not uncommon, according to De Witt. One woman bought out an entire showing. After screenings, moreover, women held informal discussion groups. The phenomenon, in short, was truly significant. No wonder De Witt points out that this movie was "the female equivalent of the Million Man March."

Exhale is the story of four friends: Savannah, Gloria, Bernadine, and Robin. "The only thing they seem to have in common," writes Owen Gleiberman, "is that they've been burned by men."[23] Savannah has a long-term, long-distance, relationship with a married man who has no intention of choosing either relationship over the other. Gloria has a husband, but he turns out to be gay. His flaw is not being gay, by the way, but being the wrong man for a straight woman. In any case, he leaves her to take care of their son on her own. Bernadine's husband dumps her after eleven years of marriage and two children, running off with a white woman. For good measure, he tells her suddenly and cruelly. Eventually, she meets another man, a civil rights lawyer, who seems much more suitable. In fact, he seems very sensitive, both emotionally and morally. He has no trouble seducing Bernadine. Trouble is, the guy is married. In fact, he is married to a woman dying of cancer! So much for moral sensitivity. Robin too attracts men who are less than satisfactory. One, for instance, is no good in bed. (When she pretends to have an orgasm, viewers go wild.) Later, he disses her at work and shows up with another woman. Her other men are no good at anything except lying blatantly and doing drugs. *Waiting* is not quite misandric. It escapes that rating on a technicality: at least one of the

minor male characters (there are no major male characters) is neither
evil nor inadequate. Marvin, Gloria's next-door neighbour, is a wid-
ower who seems to love her genuinely.

Even though *Exhale* as a whole cannot be called misandric, it does
contain a great deal of misandric material. Marvin notwithstanding,
the general message is clear: women do not need men. That point is
made both explicitly and implicitly. Metaphorically, the message is
given in visual terms. The movie both opens and closes with *women
alone and happy*. These two sequences are cinematic parentheses.
Sequences in between, all of which include men either explicitly or
implicitly, are to be interpreted in the context thus provided. Moreover,
the movie both opens and closes with women alone and happy *in the
desert*. To live in a world without men, it might seem at first glance,
is to live in a wilderness. But the emotional and spiritual thirst of
women can be satisfied, as at an oasis, through female solidarity – that
is, by rejecting men and the "civilized" world of men. This applies
even to the one friend who has found a good man. On New Year's
Eve, Gloria is celebrating with her female friends, so if Marvin is still
part of her life, it certainly is not a very important part. No matter
what men are like – inadequate, evil, or even adequate and good –
they are still irrelevant. Just in case anyone misses the message, the
same thing is stated in a less "subtle" way. Savannah's mother keeps
nagging her, "Every woman needs a man." Viewers respond by hissing.
But Savanah knows better and says so. Viewers respond with "That's
it, girl!" and applause. The two are reconciled after Savannah's mother
acknowledges the feminist perspective: "I just didn't want you to end
up like me."

But this movie does not focus only on women. It focuses on men
too – not on their needs, to be sure, but on their inadequacies.
Unsurprisingly, the movie has been accused of male bashing. Whitaker
denies the charge. But Angela Bassett, one of the stars, does not. To
point out the distinction between that movie and her more recent one,
How Stella Got Her Groove Back (Kevin Rodney Sullivan, 1998), she
acknowledges that, yes, "in *Exhale*, there was male bashing."[24] Many
women acknowledge it with pride. As one woman explained to a
reporter for the CBS *Evening News*, "I'm all for male bashing."[25]
Another common approach among defenders of *Exhale* is to point out
that the women are flawed no less than the men. And it is true that
the women are inadequate. They do make mistakes. But their mistakes
are not like those of the men. The men are at fault for not taking
women seriously. The women are at fault for not taking themselves
seriously. The men are too selfish. The women are too selfless. The
men do not love enough. The women "love too much." In short, the

men are cynical, which is a moral problem. The women are naive, which is merely a psychological problem. Viewers are not expected to forgive the men but clearly are expected to forgive the women, even though it could be argued that women are morally at fault by taking on lovers known to be married.

Another movie about women alone together is *How to Make an American Quilt* (Jocelyn Moorehouse, 1995). That theme was noticed on the set of *Quilt*, not only on the screen. Anne Bancroft recalls, "I walked into the rehearsal and it was the first time in my career where there were no men in the room. I thought I'd died and gone to heaven."[26] Presumably Bancroft is indicating her dislike only of the men in her profession. Even so, comparable remarks by men in any field would be greeted with self-righteous denunciations by thousands of outraged women. Bancroft's remark is quoted in an article by Karen Karbo, which is devoted exclusively to the almost total absence of men on the set of *Quilt*. The implicit idea is not so much that an all-female production is refreshing now and then but that all-female productions, defined as "no testosterone allowed,"[27] are inherently better than those involving men. *Quilt* is the allegedly glorious result, "a tender but resolutely unsentimental story about the life-changing loves of a group of quilters in a dusty central California town."[28]

Unsentimental? This movie is *based* on sentimentality, the belief that what really counts is not thinking but *feeling*. This gives rise to one sentimental cliché after another. No one, for example, speaks above a hush. The entire production is bathed in the soft light of hazy land-scapes. And consider the glorification of elderly women: these grand-mothers, no less hip than insightful, are symbols of earthy wisdom. But the wisdom is that of women, not of men. It is not only different but also better. The movie refrains from saying so explicitly. By now, that message should be clear to anyone who can place *Quilt* in its pop cultural context of other movies or sitcoms based on implicit misandry, let alone talk shows and magazines based on explicit misandry. The wisdom of men, if any such thing existed, would presumably be based on sterile reason. That of women, viewers are subtly encouraged to believe, is based on something far more powerful and benevolent, the primaeval instinct that supposedly guides women to be loving and caring and sharing and nurturing and so forth. With this in mind, female viewers may dive metaphorically into the joyous flow of life (just as one character dives literally into a river) and disregard the kind of considerations presented by a male-dominated society, which might make them think twice.

Quilt begins in Berkeley, where Finn, a grad student, is having a hard time trying to finish her dissertation on quilting (not by chance, a folk art associated with women). In addition, she is having a hard time accepting the idea of marriage, but Sam, a carpenter, is already designing their house. So she goes off to stay with her extended family, a rural group of quilters. In this idyllic setting, close to the good earth, that is, or to Mother Earth, several women tell Finn, in flashbacks, about decisive moments in their lives.

Finn's grandmother and great aunt, Hy and Glady Joe, are now enemies. (Being women, of course, they are *loving* enemies). Long ago, viewers see in a flashback, Hy had a one-night stand with Arthur, Glady Joe's husband. Meanwhile, her own husband was dying in the hospital. Then there is Em. She is now about to leave her husband, an artist who spends his time fooling around with his models. In the end, this lecherous guy spends at least some of his time painting portraits of his wife. He has really loved her all along. Sort of. But not to the extent of giving up his affairs with other women. Sophia is yet another disgruntled wife. Her mother advised her to marry almost anyone, but Sophia decided instead to become an Olympic diver. When a man came along and admired her skill, however, she married him. Smart woman, foolish choice. A salesman, he spends much of his time on the road. That leaves her with the kids. Eventually, the rotter just packs up and goes AWOL. Then there's Anna, once the housekeeper but now the quilting leader. (Being black, she can show that women are truly egalitarian.) Anna's family story goes back to the days just after slavery. An ancestor, following a crow, came to a cornfield and decided that her destiny was to marry the man standing there. They never did marry, but she became pregnant with his child. The destiny foretold by the crow was this daughter, she learned, not the man. Anna's own story is very similar. Her daughter, Finn, has had no man at all in her life. Well, she did once upon a time. In a flashback, viewers see her meet him at a restaurant in Paris and promptly decide that he is her soul mate. But wait – he is already married.

During Finn's visit, her problems escalate. Though he's been told not to intrude, Sam comes to visit her. Even worse, he has the audacity to discuss the possibility of having children. The result is a confrontation. Later on, Finn calls Sam, and a woman answers the phone. That gives Finn a good excuse to find a new lover of her own. Eventually, having tasted freedom, she goes back to Sam. But the choice is hers!

Underlying all this cliché-ridden sentimentality about "relationships" is the real foundation of *Quilt*: separatist misandry. It comes out in every story. Owen Gleiberman observes that the "moral of each story is the same: Men stink."[29] Of the few men who even appear, all are either evil (preventing women from achieving goals; cheating on them) or inadequate (more friendly than sexy; dying too soon). Sentimentality is merely a convenient mode, a form of presentation more likely to attract women than outright proselytizing. Nevertheless, Caryn James has this to say: "It's not quite as hard as it used to be to turn out a film by and about women. But to create one as eloquent, intelligent and *welcoming to men* [our emphasis] as 'How to Make an American Quilt' is still rare."[30] Rarer, obviously, than she imagines.

No one who has ever read Louisa May Alcott's *Little Women* or seen any of the earlier filmed versions should be surprised to learn that the latest filmed version (Gillian Armstrong, 1994) is based heavily on sentimentality. Its male characters are not evil, true – but they are inadequate. Anne Hollander has observed that all three filmed versions are products of their time. Even more than the first two (George Cukor, 1933; Mervyn LeRoy, 1949), Armstrong's has been adapted to suit the needs of contemporary viewers. That is, female viewers. It has little or nothing to do with its nineteenth-century setting.[31] Jo is "autonomous." So is her mother. In fact, she is "more of a feminist exemplar than she originally was."[32] Father, whose mature wisdom and moral integrity leave a deep impression on the novel's women, might as well not even have been part of this movie. Professor Bhaer is intense and romantic but also shy and withdrawn. He is adequate for Jo, the main character in this story, but only because he is unlikely to get in her way. Laurie, the boy next door, is more adequate in some ways. Not only sexy but extroverted and active as well, he has an inner life, or character, of his own. But that very fact makes him inadequate for Jo. The message is very clear: men are nice to have around but are otherwise irrelevant to strong and intelligent women.

Apart from anything else, *Fried Green Tomatoes* (Jon Avnet, 1992) is notable for its exquisite sensuality. Its very title evokes the texture, colour, taste, aroma – even the sound – of food. Before the movie actually begins, viewers can imagine the sputtering of fritters sizzling in hot spiced oil. Among the most memorable moments, however, are those created solely through cinematography. These include scenes that evoke the enervating moisture of rural Alabama: the muddy roads, rusting signs, and rotting wood, the cool moonlight of a summer night washing over the pearly flesh of two women bathing in a river, the sinister bleakness of a decaying mansion isolated in a setting of verdant fields, its peeling paint and collapsing columns betraying the character of its current owner. The underlying message, however, is not so beautiful.

Although two stories unfold, one set in the present and the other fifty years ago, they merge in the final sequence. One story focuses on Evelyn Couch, the supposedly maladjusted wife in a respectable marriage. The other focuses on Idgie Threadgoode, the supposedly maladjusted youngest daughter in a respectable family. From the very beginning, it is obvious that the two stories are linked metaphorically. Both women are troubled by crippling stereotypes of women.

When Evelyn visits an elderly relative in the Rose Hill Home, she and Ninny Threadgoode meet. Ninny says she is staying at the Home only because her companion, Mrs Otis, needs her there. Wolfing down one chocolate bar after another, Evelyn tells Ninny about her frustrating experience of everyday life. And Ninny tells her, in a series of lengthy flashbacks, about two women who endured and flourished in spite of their problems.

The flashback story begins in 1920. As a child, Idgie is a tomboy. She abhors the whole idea of putting on a dress to attend the wedding of her sister, Leona. She is consoled by Buddy, her favourite brother. He is a tall, slender, and handsome young man. He is charming, moreover, and sensitive. In short, he seems to be an ideal male specimen. After Idgie is ridiculed by a younger brother, Buddy climbs up to her tree house and reassures her. Soon after, Idgie goes along for a stroll with Buddy and Ruth, his fiancé. When Ruth's hat blows off, Buddy gallantly rushes after it. The one thing Buddy lacks, however, is common sense. Running along the railroad track, he catches his foot between the ties. As Idgie and Ruth watch, he is crushed to death by the oncoming train. Years later, Idgie is still bitter over this loss. Hoping to provide a healthy influence for her, Idgie's parents invite Ruth to spend the summer with them. It is Idgie, however, who exerts her influence on Ruth. At first, Idgie rejects her. Gradually, she helps Ruth realize that spontaneity is better than repression, adventure better than docility, and honesty better than respectability. Before turning completely into a protofeminist, however, Ruth marries one Frank Bennett. This, as Ninny tells Evelyn, is when "the trouble" started.

A brutal man, Frank beats Ruth black and blue. One day, Idgie sees evidence of this on Ruth's face. Although Ruth tells Idgie to say nothing about this to anyone, Idgie cannot forget what she has seen. Eventually, she returns with two helpers to rescue Ruth. When Frank returns suddenly and finds his wife packing, he slugs her. Idgie's helpers, her brother Julian along with a massive black man named Big George, indicate to Frank that he had better think twice about holding Ruth against her will. In response, he throws Ruth – by now, pregnant – down the stairs. As they leave the house, Idgie threatens Frank, "If you ever touch her again, I'll kill you."

The two women live together and start up a diner called the Whistle Stop Café. For a while, they are happy. Idgie is vaguely amused that Grady Kilgore, the local police chief, is romantically interested in her. Then Frank decides to claim his baby son (named, not coincidentally,

Buddy). At first, Frank is just a sinister figure lurking in the shadows. Then he shows up at the house. Before leaving, without the boy, he warns Ruth, "I'll be back." One night, he does come back. After belting Sipsey, Big George's mother, he runs off with Buddy Junior while Ruth and Idgie are out. Getting into his truck, he is "politely" stopped by Smokey Lonesome, an alcoholic drifter who hangs around the diner. At that moment, someone else attacks Frank from behind. Even though Frank's body is not found, a police officer from Georgia, where Frank and Ruth had lived, shows up to investigate his disappearance. Discovering that Idgie had threatened to kill Frank, Curtis Smoote sees her as an obvious suspect and, once the truck is found, arrests her for murder.

At first, it seems as if Idgie will be able to establish a good alibi. She had been acting in the "Town Follies" on the night in question. Between acts, Big George had come with news of Frank's return. Police Chief Grady advises her to frame Big George. Nevertheless, it was Sipsey who actually killed Frank with her frying pan. Realizing that a white jury would never acquit either a black man or a black woman, Idgie decides to stand trial herself. The case is thrown out of court, however, when the Reverend Herbert Scroggins – a self-righteous windbag for whom Idgie has never felt anything but contempt – lies in her favour. Swearing on what seems to be his personal Bible but is actually a copy of *Moby-Dick*, he tells the court that Idgie was at one of his three-day revival meetings.

In a brief epilogue, viewers learn what has become of these people in later years. At the age of eight or nine, Buddy Junior (like his namesake) has an accident on the tracks. He is mutilated but not killed. Without his arm but with Idgie as his surrogate father, Buddy seems to be growing up into a fine young man. This is due, no doubt, to the deep love surrounding him at home: that of Idgie, Ruth, and Sipsey. When Ruth dies of cancer, after some noble suffering, it becomes clear that the two remaining women love each other almost as much as both had loved Ruth.

Interspersed with segments of Ninny's story are segments of Evelyn's. After each episode of Ninny's, that of Evelyn's becomes more upbeat. Evelyn is unhappily married to Ed, a boring slob. She wants more out of life than she can get by keeping house for him but is afraid to ask for more. "I just feel so useless," she tells Ninny, "so powerless." Promptly diagnosing Evelyn's problem as "the change," her new friend advises her to "get out of the house and get a job." But Evelyn is not yet ready to take this advice. Some people single her out for abuse. A boy at the shopping mall – significantly, in the supermarket – pushes her aside, screaming "Screw you." Going out the door, he calls her a "bitch" and a "fat cow." Ed, on the other hand, hardly notices her. He comes home from work, takes his dinner into the living room, and settles down to watch the football game. Sometimes, he comments on how good her chicken is. His surname, Couch, describes him perfectly. Ed is a "couch potato."

Even in such unpromising circumstances, Evelyn tries heroically to save the marriage. First, she turns to a group promoting Marabelle Morgan's notion of the Total Woman. The leader burbles about the need for women to put "that magic spark" back into their marriages. Even as Evelyn imagines herself greeting Ed at the front door dressed only in Saran Wrap, she knows that he would respond by calling her crazy. A friend suggests that what they really need is an "assertiveness-training course for Southern women," something she regards as a contradiction in terms. With that in mind, nevertheless, Evelyn and her friend try a feminist group. According to its leader, women must regain their "own power as women," the source of their own "strength and ... separateness." Soon, Evelyn finds herself growing more assertive, more confident, and more furious. When two women take her parking space at the shopping mall, she rams their car six times in defiance.

Evelyn is learning to express her anger openly and defiantly. She begins by chopping down a wall in the house. Finally noticing the changes in her personality – it takes, almost literally, a sledgehammer – Ed comes home one day with flowers. By that time, Evelyn wants more than flowers. Learning that Ninny's old house at Whistle Stop has been torn down, leaving her with nowhere to live, she rebuilds the wall to make an extra room for her elderly friend. Ed is not amused. On her next visit to Rose Hills, she is shocked to find someone packing up Ninny's few possessions. Believing that her friend is dead, Evelyn falls into the arms of a black nurse and weeps (echoing an earlier scene with Idgie and Sipsey). But Ninny is not dead. Her companion, Mrs Otis, has died. Evelyn finds Ninny sitting sadly in front of what was her house for eighty-one years.

A very brief epilogue to this story links it with the other. Ninny and Ruth are at a cemetery nearby. There, Evelyn sees the tombstones of Ruth Jamison – she had reverted to her maiden name – and Buddy Threadgoode. On Ruth's she discovers a freshly written note. It is from Idgie – which is to say, from Ninny Threadgoode. As a good friend to the heroine of one story, Evelyn crosses the dividing line between that story and her own.

The three primary female characters are all both good and, in one way or another, heroic. As someone who cares for others – Ruth, Sipsey, and Buddy Junior at first, then Mrs Otis and Evelyn – Idgie/Ninny is associated with compassion. As a fiery rebel who overturns genteel standards of white womanhood, moreover, she is a heroine for female viewers. Ruth and Evelyn must learn, no matter how painfully, to rebel against patriarchal society and become autonomous. Not quite heroines, they are, however, role models. But Sipsey really is another heroine. Though not seen much onscreen, it is she who actually saves the day by killing Frank. Obviously, the solidarity of sisterhood transcends the boundaries of race and class. It transcends time too. By the time Evelyn has become Ninny's regular visitor and brings her some homemade fried green tomatoes, the elderly woman declares, "You couldn't be sweeter to me if you were my own daughter."

The solidarity of women even transcends the boundaries of sexual orientation. Though the movie never says so explicitly, it does imply that the relationship between Idgie and Ruth is based on something deeper than friendship. From the beginning, Idgie is presented as a tomboy. She cannot stand the idea of wearing a dress to her sister's wedding. Instead, she turns up wearing pants, suspenders, and a tie. Nothing changes with the passage of time. She demonstrates the kind of bravado associated with young men: reaching into a hive of swarming bees to collect honey for Ruth, she is doing what young men do when they want to impress their girlfriends. And she is more than casually interested in Ruth. How else can we explain Idgie's sense of rage and even betrayal when Ruth marries Frank? At that point, she has no way of knowing that Frank is a brutal monster. Nevertheless, she refuses to attend the wedding and can hardly bring herself to visit Ruth. Later on, the two not only work together but live together. Idgie continues wearing pants, playing poker, smoking, drinking whisky, and fighting – things conventionally associated at the time with men (or lesbians). At the trial, moreover, Ruth declares her love for Idgie in a way that could be interpreted in either platonic or erotic terms. Whatever the nature of their love for each other, the nature of their household is clearly that of a female oasis in a male desert. These women – that is, women in general – are autonomous. They neither want nor need men. This is made clear quite early. After her mother dies, Ruth sends a note to Idgie. It contains a page from the Book of Ruth. Because the father and his two sons have died and left the women alone, Ruth promises to leave her Edomite homeland and follow Naomi into the alien Israelite world. Because Frank represents death, Ruth leaves him behind and symbolically asks Idgie to join her in a new life.

There are no primary male characters in this movie. Of the secondary and tertiary ones, it could be said that (white) males are either evil or inadequate. Buddy is good, of course, but inadequate. His own foolishness, no matter how gallant, destroys him. Buddy Junior is equally good and equally inadequate. Foolishly playing around near the railroad tracks, he loses his arm. The same is true of Smokey Lonesome. He comes to Ruth's aid, but as a down-and-out alcoholic he can admire her only from a distance. Although we never meet Idgie's son, we are told about him. As a male in this cinematic world, Albert could be good, or lovable, but not without being inadequate; mentally retarded, he is dead by the age of thirty. Frank, on the other hand, is just plain evil. So is the sinister Curtis Smoote. Even though he is only doing his job, viewers know that his relentless pursuit of Idgie is based on a distortion of truth. Besides, his remarks to Big George are clearly racist.

In between are more ambiguous male characters. The police chief is willing to help Idgie, it is true, but only because of his lecherous interest in her. Moreover, his mentality is thoroughly racist. To help Idgie avoid arrest, he is willing to frame Big George. Grady complies with Idgie's plea to stop the Ku Klux Klan from lynching Big George, to be sure, but he makes not the slightest attempt to identify these men. Idgie hints that Grady himself is a member of the Klan. She has identified the "clodhopper" shoes under his costume. He has warned her, the owner of a respectable diner, that "some people don't like you servin' colored." Like Grady, the Reverend Scroggins is willing to help Idgie but for the wrong reasons. He lies to the court in her favour, but only because Ruth had bribed him with the promise of bringing Idgie to church. He is self-righteous to the core. No wonder Idgie tells Ruth, "I don't know what's worse, church or jail." Of the male characters, only Big George is unambiguously both good and adequate. His quiet strength translates into compassionate tenderness when he watches over Idgie after Buddy's death and into fierce defiance when he protects Ruth from Frank. But Big George is a black man. And black men are oppressed men. In effect, they are not men at all: exempt on political grounds from the critique levelled against white men, they are honorary women.

The worldview of *Tomatoes* is represented by two primary metaphors. Femaleness is cinematically associated with food. And food is associated, in turn, with "nurturance" and life itself. When Idgie visits Ruth and Frank for the first time, she brings a pie with her. When Idgie and Ruth jump onto a freight train, it is to throw cans of soup and vegetables to hungry squatters. Of particular symbolic importance is the scene in which Idgie is revealed as a "bee charmer." Free from stifling social conventions, she can be seen as an archetypal woman – fully integrated within the natural order, a personification of Mother Nature herself. (No wonder Grady tells his friends that no one can "tame" Idgie.) The bees do not attack her when she steals their honeycomb, because they recognize her as one of their own – which is to say, a female. Once Ruth understands this, she reaches into Idgie's pot, swirls the golden mess around, and licks her sticky fingers with delight. Viewers are reminded of poor Evelyn who, still a prisoner of social conventions, misunderstands the significance of food. Stuffing herself at every opportunity with equally sweet and sticky chocolate bars or doughnuts, she finds no joy in doing so. For women in this patriarchal society, the movie implies, food can become a neurotic obsession, a way of hiding from pain, say, or a way of rebelling against the unnatural standard of feminine beauty. Only when Evelyn, like Ruth, is ready to discard some of her stereotyped notions of femininity can food once again become a healthy source of natural vitality. In another scene, Ruth and Idgie play happily in the kitchen with food, daubing each other with squishy berries, dousing each other with snowy flour – and smearing Grady with gooey, suggestively fecal, chocolate icing. Messy play of this kind is usually associated with little boys, not girls. The episode visually reminds female viewers that they should do precisely what Idgie, as a tomboy, has done: appropriate the privileges denied them by a patriarchal society.

Over and over again throughout this movie, happy or hopeful sequences include verbal and visual references to food. These include advertisements for foods such as "fried green tomatoes served hot and spicy" plastered over a wall; Ninny telling Evelyn that what she misses most about being home is "the smell of coffee and bacon frying ... what I'd give for some fried green tomatoes"; party sandwiches and fancy cookies laid out in formal elegance for Leona's wedding; steaming berry pies and luscious fruit cobblers cooling on tables at the diner; baskets of ripe tomatoes and sacks heavy with produce in the shed where Idgie, Ruth, Sipsey, and Big George eagerly plan to barbecue Frank.

There is a dark side to this culinary metaphor – dark, that is, for men. Although girls have been expected to keep their hands clean at play, adult women have been expected to get their hands dirty in the kitchen. Food is their domain, the kitchen their sanctum. When a man invades it, therefore, he is either *attacked* with food, as Grady is, or he *becomes* food. Since Frank is killed at "hog-boiling time," it is easy to dispose of his body by reducing his skin to the soup du jour, his meat and bones to the blue plate special. Big George prepares dinner by slathering Frank's body with homemade barbecue sauce and then roasting it over an open fire next to the diner (though not in the diner itself – that is, the kitchen – which is the women's inner sanctum.) He serves it up with a smile to the hungry Smoote, who pronounces it the best barbecue he has ever tasted. Symbolically, it is food (femaleness) that brings life even out of death (maleness). It is with her frying pan that Sipsey kills Frank. And it is by chewing him up in a kind of reverse sacrament that the customers safely conceal Frank's body from the police.

Just as femaleness is conventionally associated with "nature," maleness is associated with "culture." In this case, it is associated specifically with machinery and technology. These in turn are associated with danger and death itself. Frank's truck, rusting and rotting as it is dredged out of the river, represents the corruption and evil of its male owner. But trains, often phallic symbols, are the primary images of maleness. Not one but two male characters are fatefully linked to the hard, cold steel of a railroad: Buddy is killed and Buddy Junior is mutilated by it. Every time a train appears, moreover, it is associated cinematically with something sinister in the sequence either directly before it or directly after it: Buddy's death, Frank spying on Ruth and Idgie from his truck, the Klan's arrival, Frank's death, the presence of Curtis Smoote, Buddy Junior's mutilation, and the announcement of Ruth's cancer. It is true that a train is the setting for one happy sequence: from a freight car, Idgie and Ruth toss canned goods to grateful squatters camped near the tracks. Viewers are aware, however, that these squatters have been put out of work or off their land because of the Depression. The train is thus associated with men in two conventional ways. It is symbolically linked not only with the unnatural quality of modern technology itself but also with the dehumanizing effect of technology on industrial civilization.

The movie is actually framed by the imagery of "man-made" death and destruction. It opens with a shot of Frank's truck being hoisted out of the river, followed directly by the opening credits superimposed on train tracks, and closes with a shot of train tracks. In between, spatially and temporally confined but morally and psychologically central, is the imagery of feminist defiance. Women dominate every sequence. The implication is that women live in an oasis of loving and caring surrounded by an oppressive and deadly wasteland created by men.

The feminist message of this movie, however, is not left to the discernment of imaginative or sophisticated viewers. The dialogue makes it perfectly clear that women must be prepared to overthrow the patriarchal order by whatever means necessary and live on their own. Utopia is to be sexually segregated, not integrated. When Ruth learns that Frank has been skulking around the house waiting to snatch the baby, she tells Idgie what has changed in her life. Before, she had no strength of her own: "All I could do was pray. If that bastard ever tries to take my child, I won't pray. I'll break his neck." Idgie has already demonstrated her courage and resourcefulness by challenging Frank and helping Ruth escape.

The story of Idgie and Ruth includes another reference to the current political world. After Ruth refuses to let him see Buddy Junior, Frank snarls, "You'd deny a father the right to see his own son?" This reminds viewers of a current political debate: some feminists would like the courts to acknowledge absolute primacy for mothers in custody suits on the grounds that fathers are not only unnecessary but untrustworthy as well. No wonder Idgie is shown playing baseball with Buddy Junior. After Ruth dies, the movie suggests, Idgie will be both mother *and* father to the boy.

By the end of *Tomatoes*, Evelyn – she is the surrogate for modern female viewers – has drawn the inevitable conclusions. Unhappy with the low-cholesterol meal she has prepared for him, Frank asks if she is trying to kill him. "If I was gonna kill you," she replies, "I'd use my hands." To make sure he fully understands the new rules, she adds a reference to herself as superwoman: "If you don't listen to reason, there's always Tawanda." Reporting to Ninny on her transformation, Evelyn declares: "Well, I got mad and it felt terrific ... I felt like I could beat the shit out of those punks." So terrific does she feel, in fact, that she is ready to attack men in general. She fantasizes about putting bombs in copies of *Playboy* and *Hustler*. "I'll take all the wife-beaters," she says, "and I'll machine-gun their genitals!" Even Ninny is concerned about this sudden and dramatic change when Evelyn fails to appear during visiting hours. "She has an urge to hit him on the head with a baseball bat" (in this case, perhaps, to destroy him with his own "phallus"), Ninny explains to the nurse. "That seems normal to me," replies the nurse. "You didn't kill Ed, did you?" asks a somewhat amused Ninny when Evelyn finally shows up. "Not yet," answers Evelyn with a smile.

The problem here is not that women will leave theatres and go on killing sprees. Everyone realizes that the dialogue is metaphorical. Nor is the problem a disproportionate reaction to husbands. Everyone realizes that marriages need to be shaken up once in a while or even dissolved. The problem is, as usual, the convincing presentation of a cinematic world – or the powerful reinforcement of a worldview already held by viewers – in which only women have a "right" to be angry. With that frame of reference, all women are implicitly proclaimed innocent victims and all men – all white men – either evil oppressors or inadequate burdens. To the extent that both women and men consciously or subconsciously adopt this worldview, the mutual hostility that now characterizes relations between the sexes will be exacerbated instead of questioned or healed. Justice is once again confused with revenge, albeit vicarious.

In some cases, there is no need even to speculate on a movie's message. The final scene of *Thelma and Louise* (Ridley Scott, 1991) makes that clear. Two women drive over a cliff rather than live in a world with men. No need to "deconstruct" this movie.[33] Its political perspective is made perfectly explicit by both the "courageous" screenwriter, Callie Khourie,[34] and its stars, Susan Sarandon and Geena Davis. The movie was considered notable for its writing in particular, and thus for its political message: Khourie won not only a Golden Globe from the Writers' Guild but also an Academy Award.[35] At issue here is not *whether* misandry is involved but *how* it is involved.

Thelma begins with a rather lengthy prologue. In the first scene, viewers are introduced to Louise, a waitress at a busy cafeteria somewhere in Arkansas. She calls Thelma to make final arrangements for their weekend fishing trip. Thelma is a suburban housewife unhappily married to Darryl, a boorish carpet salesman who treats everyone with surly contempt. In these circumstances, it is not surprising to find that Thelma is eager to get away for a few days. Instead of packing, she simply dumps the contents of her drawers into an open suitcase. Louise drives by to pick her up. Their first stop is a honky-tonk roadhouse catering to a "western" crowd. Eager to live it up, Thelma promptly orders a drink and convinces her more cautious friend to do the same. Thelma is ready for fun when Harlan, a notorious lecher, begins to flirt with her. After dancing, Thelma begins to feel sick and goes outside for some fresh air. Harlan follows her, and the movie implies that he will rape her. Fortunately, Louise reaches the car at just the right moment and pulls a gun on Harlan. He backs off but remains unrepentant. Louise shoots him in the heart, and he falls to the ground, oozing blood. Because Thelma had been seen dancing with Harlan, the two women realize that there is no point in reporting an attempted rape to the police. They are now fugitives.

In part one, they set off down the road in search of safety. Since they are running out of money, Louise stops at a motel and calls her boyfriend, Jim. He agrees to send her a few thousand dollars. Louise cannot tell him exactly where she is or why she needs the money, so she arranges to pick it up at a motel in Oklahoma City by identifying herself there as "Peaches." While Louise is using the phone, Thelma meets J.D., a handsome young man who asks for a lift. Though she finds him both sexy and sweet, Louise is in no mood to pick up a stranger. When they get to Oklahoma City, she is surprised to find Jim waiting there, in person, with the money. Later on, he proposes marriage. Louise reluctantly turns him down but agrees to spend the night with him. Meanwhile, Thelma prepares for bed in her own room. J.D. shows up, and she quickly decides to spend the night with him. Next morning, she leaves him alone in the room while she meets Louise for breakfast. Before they get back, J.D. runs off with the money. Now the women are out of money once more.

With Louise in a state of depression, Thelma takes charge. She robs a grocery store. By now, they are not only fugitives but also desperadoes. Having left the urban slums and rural farms far behind, they have reached the wilderness. On a lonely road, they are stopped by a police officer. Although they were driving above the speed limit, Thelma realizes that he must be after them for either robbery or murder. Taking charge again, she pulls a gun on him and locks him in the trunk of his car. They set off once more down the open road. Meanwhile, the police have gathered at Thelma's house. Thelma calls her husband, Darryl, but senses that the police are there and hangs up. Later on, Louise calls the house and speaks to Hal, the chief investigator. She stays on the tapped phone too long, and the police trace her call.

Part two begins when both Thelma and Louise fully realize the gulf that separates the present from the past. In spite of their problematic future, both women rejoice in the present. They quickly prove that they can initiate events instead of merely responding to crises. Their next encounter is with a sleazy trucker who has made lewd passes at them on several occasions. Feigning interest, they pull over and get out to meet him. Then they give him a lecture on sexist behaviour. When he responds angrily, they blow up his truck, laugh at his frantic screaming, and continue driving.

But time is not on their side. In part three, the chase speeds up. Thelma and Louise reach the Grand Canyon. Dozens of police cars arrive on the scene along with a helicopter. Hal pleads with the local state troopers not to shoot at the women. Thelma and Louise realize that they are surrounded on three sides. But Thelma decides that there is still one way out: "Let's continue on," she tells Louise. And so they do. Louise drives straight ahead, into the canyon. The movie ends with the car suspended in mid-air, cinematically frozen in the stillness of eternity, or paradise.

The climax comes when Thelma and Louise attain insight into the meaning of their lives both as individuals and as women. At this point, they have metaphorically come of age. As a coming-of-age story, *Thelma* is actually a secular variant of the conversion story so familiar from Christian stories of the saints and Protestant testimonials of the saved. Thelma and Louise discover truth on the open road just as St Paul did on the Damascus Road. This should not be surprising: the fact that many political movements are hostile to religion does not mean that they have no connection with religion. They are linked not only historically, in fact, but also functionally and psychologically. Like all forms of religion, they provide adherents with both personal and communal identity, and these are given public expression through both story and ritual. (Like some forms of religion, unfortunately, they provide adherents with a mentality that polarizes the human race into "good" and "evil" camps. More about that in due course.)

At any rate, Thelma and Louise realize that the old life (urban, technological, male-dominated) is dead, that the new life (rural, natural, female-dominated) is better no matter what the risks. "Something, like, crossed over in me, and I can't go back," says Thelma. Similarly, Louise says: "I'm awake, wide awake, everything looks different." They have seen the light. Better dead than alive as women in a man's world – in short, they are ready for martyrdom. For them, like countless martyrs before them, the road does not end at the cliff but in eternity. This is expressed both visually and musically. The movie does not end with mangled corpses, but in a single freeze-frame of the car in mid-air – no motion means no time, and no time means eternity – with a background of gospel music.

Martyrs are not merely victims of persecution. They are witnesses acclaimed as saints, or exemplary heroes, for the whole community. In this case, presumably, the police will learn something from their ultimate act of defiance. Hal will tell their story to the world through newspapers and television. More importantly, viewers in the real world, especially female viewers, will presumably be transformed or "converted" as well.

Thelma is somewhat unusual in that its protagonists, who metaphorically "come of age" or experience "conversion," are women.[36] But that in itself is not what makes this movie important. What does is the link it establishes between traditional coming of age and what feminists call "consciousness raising." In earlier movies, the insight finally attained by both male and female protagonists was usually information they had to assimilate in order to participate fully in a society based on commonly held assumptions about the way things are. The insight finally attained by the female protagonists of this one is information they must assimilate in order to participate fully in a community based on a systematic re-presentation of reality in order to achieve specific political goals. In this symbolic case, the new community consists of only two women.

Thelma is considered a cinematic landmark, and not only among critics and feminist leaders. This movie appeals to women. Millions of women. It does not, however, appeal to many men. Like only a few other movies since *The Birth of a Nation* (D.W. Griffith, 1915), which sparked racial unrest due to its glorification of the Ku Klux Klan, it became the source of a major public controversy. Called both a "betrayal of feminism" and "degrading to men," it was discussed on just about every talk show. Years after its debut, the movie's historical and cultural implications were still being discussed.[37]

In view of all this, it is worth quoting part of a review by novelist Alice Hoffman. According to her, this movie "has a courageous script, which takes stereotypes and boils them in a witch's cauldron, producing a film that goes beyond feminism into a sort of humanism rarely seen onscreen ... In spite of all the violence and sorrow, here was the thing about *Thelma and Louise*: They gave you hope for the future. They made you believe that women could fly."[38]

Nothing had changed by the late 1990s. *Polish Wedding* (Theresa Connelly, 1998) is about a young woman growing up in a blue-collar district of Detroit. Hala is very beautiful, but she is very flirtatious and manipulative as well – just like her mother, Jadzia. For years, Jadzia has been having an affair with a man named Roman. But when he finally invites her to accompany him on a trip to Paris, she declines. He means nothing to her. Neither does her husband. Bolek is a kind husband and doting father but an ineffectual one. When he discovers the affair with Roman, he does nothing. Jadzia began her affair, in fact, mainly because Bolek was so boring. Anyway, Hala soon attracts the neighbourhood's most handsome young man, Russell, a rookie policeman. She flirts with him to the point of removing her clothes but then changes her mind. Russell is inexperienced with women and fails to understand Hala's ambivalence about him and everyone else. At one point, he almost rapes her. Later on, when Hala becomes pregnant, Russell does not know what to do. He asks her to have an abortion, but she refuses. He considers leaving town. Eventually, after Hala's mother and brothers threaten him with violence, he decides to marry her.

No one in *Polish Wedding* is evil, but every male character is inadequate. Hala's henpecked brother is clearly unable to satisfy either his wife (for continuing to live at home) or his mother (for not encouraging his wife to have more children). The telling moment comes when Jadzia is asked about her religion. How can she go to church and be so pious without feeling the slightest remorse for being unfaithful to her husband? Because her real religion is not Catholicism at all, she says: it is the "religion of making love and having children and building homes" for their families. It is supposedly the religion of women and has little or nothing to do with that of men. When Hala is chosen to represent the Virgin Mary at a festival but turns out to be pregnant, Jadzia rescues her from the hostile crowd. Towards the end, Jadzia, her daughter, and her daughter-in-law sit in the kitchen and drink a toast to themselves. As in a critically acclaimed Dutch movie, *Antonia's Line* (Marleen Gorris,

1995), the clear implication – the clear message – is that they are "autonomous." These women have no need for men except as toys and sperm banks. In short, these women are modern equivalents of "the Goddess" under whose reign our remote ancestors are said by many feminists to have lived in paradise.[39]

Because no one could possibly mistake the misandric subtext of *Diabolique* (Jeremiah Chechik, 1996),[40] there is no point in offering a detailed analysis of it here. The story is about Guy, a sadistic and brutal man, Mia, his sweet and innocent but victimized wife, and Nicole, his acerbic and cynical but equally victimized lover. Nicole is not exactly an innocent victim. Posing as Mia's friend, she plots with her to kill Guy even though she is plotting with Guy at the same time to kill Mia. In the end, though, when all plans goes awry, she joins Mia in killing Guy. But why stop at two women acting in solidarity against evil men? Just in case anyone misses the message, a third woman is added. Shirley is a private detective with a chip on her shoulder, and it is ready to fall off every time the topic turns to men. When Mia admits feeling guilty for her unhappy marriage, Shirley says, "It's not your fault. Testosterone. They should put it in bombs." Later on, she says: "This guy gives a prick a bad name. What doesn't?" After investigating the case on her own, Shirley discovers that Nicole has been involved in Guy's disappearance. Then she watches as the two women, now truly acting in solidarity, drown Guy in a pool. Without a moment's hesitation, Shirley punches Mia in the face: "That'll make it easier to plead self-defense," she says.[40] Though primarily a comedy with noirish overtones, *Diabolique* makes the point we have been discussing in this chapter: women alone are entirely self-sufficient.

The goal of bypassing men does not necessarily imply segregation or apartheid, separate societies for women and men. For some feminists, it implies a utopia in which men are merely irrelevant to women. A literary example of this approach comes from the late 1990s. In *Ahab's Wife*,[41] Sena Jeter Naslund has rather self-consciously reversed motifs from Herman Melville's *Moby-Dick*. Captain Ahab's wife is peripheral in Melville's novel – Melville had virtually no female characters in his works and did not want women to read them – but she is central in this one.

Melville's work could be described as a story about a stereotypically masculine quest: fierce, neurotic, monomaniacal, and, in a word, macho. Naslund's could be described as one about a stereotypically feminine quest: peaceful, healthy, and benevolent. Ahab's worldview is based on conflict and power. His wife's worldview, according to Naslund, is based on harmony and justice. "Now," she keeps saying, "isn't this better?" Ahab is only one of her many husbands who meet unfortunate ends. They come and go. They make no difference to her. They are irrelevant. Nevertheless, Naslund adds the occasional misandric punch. She notes that men who kill whales, as Ahab does, truly hate the great oceanic Mother herself (and, by implication, terrestrial women as well). As one reviewer describes the heroine's point of view, "There, there. Such a fuss about a fish."[42]

It is worth noting here that Melville wrote a quasi-mythic novel about men precisely in order to counter what many men considered the feminized worldview of late-nineteenth-century America. Naslund has done the same thing in reverse: she has countered what feminists consider the masculinized worldview of late twentieth-century America. Even if Naslund's dichotomized perspective were justifiable, that would still leave her in the position of encouraging readers to move from one extreme to the other. Do we really want what this same reviewer calls a "glistening pink utopia"? "The book insists on happiness, sometimes to the exclusion of even the most generous reading of history. But why not? Men have got rich from their big harpoons and mythic beasts and improbable heroics. Don't women deserve their own fantastic voyages?"[43] In other words, don't women deserve an opportunity for revenge?

Bypassing men, like looking down on men and even laughing at men, is not necessarily misandric. In theory, it can be explained as merely creating "space" for women. The trouble is that it amounts on moral grounds to *segregation*. It could be argued that sexual segregation, unlike racial segregation, is voluntary rather than imposed. How, therefore, can it be challenged on moral grounds? The answer is ambiguous. At one time or another, we all feel more comfortable when surrounded by others of our own kind. That is about being home, about affirming identity. But these cultural productions represent a worldview, one in which the full humanity of half the population is denied. To be fully human in a moral sense is, apart from anything else, to make a distinctive, necessary and valued contribution to others. And that applies to groups no less than to individuals.[44] To say that women have no need for men, that they may therefore remain indifferent to men, is to deny a fundamental moral claim that all human beings have on others.

CHAPTER FIVE

Blaming Men:
A History of Their Own

MOM: Linda, the GIs should get the jobs. They've sacrificed a lot for us. They have families to support.
LINDA: Mother, if they can fire me, they can fire you too.
MOM: I'm head of the household.
LINDA: You're a woman.[1]

In the last three chapters, we discussed relatively "benign" sides of misandry in popular culture: laughing at men, looking down on them, and bypassing them. In this chapter and the next, we turn to a more malevolent side or, at least, a more obviously malevolent one.

By the 1990s, popular culture both reflected and propagated the conspiracy theory of history – a theory that had been adapted for feminism by academics, it is worth pointing out, operating within what many still assume is the "ivory tower" of elite culture. Like all other myths, this one tries to explain the way things are in terms of how things came to be that way. Given its importance, the "plot" is worth repeating once more: all of human history can be reduced to a titanic conspiracy of men usurping power from women, oppressing them, and – this is where popular culture comes in – covering up the ugly truth. In short, men are collectively or vicariously responsible for most or all of human suffering.

To understand how popular culture presents gender, we must understand that it projects the *present* – in this case, any notion of gender (or even, by implication, sex itself) that happens to be either fashionable or controversial right now – into the past as "history" and the future as "science fiction" or "speculative fiction." We argue in this chapter that evidence is often deliberately falsified to make political claims about gender.

One episode of the sci-fi show *Outer Limits*[2] is set in a rural matriarchy in the year 2055. Reigning over this paradise, Lithia, is the Goddess.

She rules through her wise women, or elders. Lithia is not only ruled but also inhabited only by women. After a cataclysmic "great war" and the ensuing "scourge," all the males have been wiped out. Women have managed to reproduce themselves due to vast stores of frozen sperm (although male infants die soon after birth.) On the one hand, life is hard. High technology is either unavailable or banned as a sinister work of men. Even electricity is strictly rationed. On the other hand, life is peaceful. And the women have found ways of satisfying their sexual needs without men. In fact, men are all but forgotten except in folk tales and history lessons for children. Little girls are told explicitly, in a stereotypically hushed and soothing female voice, that the old order was destroyed because of men: "The Goddess saw that the evil was gone and men were no more. And she unfurled the fingers of her hand. She made the sign of blessing upon the females, who now inherited the sea and the sky, the land and its bounty. And when the males of the earth had vanished, so, too, did wickedness and war and hatred. And the peace and glory of her kingdom was restored. And let us say, 'Praise Goddess,' … It was men who brought the war, and it was men who paid the ultimate price."

A few men, however, have been preserved cryogenically for experimental purposes. Thawed out, they are now being re-introduced on a trial basis. If they mend their ways, they might be given a second chance. One of them, a soldier named Jason Mercer, comes to a village and learns the truth about history but not about the experiment. The village elder, Hera, is immediately suspicious of him. She refers to him – a stranger, presumably, and a male – as someone "who worships destruction." Mercer tries to make himself useful in his distinctively male ways, but every time he does so, he ends up making things worse. As it happens, he is a very handsome young man. One of the women makes her admiration of his body obvious. When he responds, he unwittingly introduces new and disturbing feelings – heterosexuality and jealousy – to the women. Moreover, when a little girl wants to play with him, he lets her shoot his gun at a target. Even worse, he encourages the women to stand up for their rights by using their fair share of electricity (shared with other villages). That sets off a train of events that leads to the capture of one woman by a neighbouring village, a hostage crisis, and a killing. After that, it seems clear that the women have been right about men all along. Her suspicions vindicated, Hera declares: "We will never succumb to the devil's enticements. Males worship death, females life. Men destroy but women endure." When the children express sympathy for Mercer, she points out that "like most young men, he chooses to go to war." In other words, men *deserved* to be wiped off the face of the earth en masse. Mercer demands a second chance but is told that he has already had a second chance. Back to the freezer he goes. On the way, he screams at the women, "I want to help you ... I see someone in danger ... my instinct is to protect them, to be strong. It's who I am. I'm a soldier, a man."

This show makes several closely related points. First, men are innately violent and unfit for co-existence with women. As Hera puts it, they *chose* to go to war. (Apparently, forcing young men into combat by means of conscription was no longer necessary.) Just in case anyone misses the message, a male voice-over makes it clear: "The differences between men and women have been debated among philosophers since recorded history began. If indeed males are by their nature the aggressor, it is this quality that may one day be their undoing." Second, women are innately wise and good and just. "We do not steal, Major Mercer," snipes Hera. "We do not lie. We do not cheat." In other words, women alone are worthy of life. Third, the ultimate authority is a goddess. Never mind that her "compassion" consigns seven billion people to death. (Some of these were victims of war, both males and females, but the remaining males were killed off by the scourge as punishment for starting the war.) Some viewers, at least women, might find the notion of a female world enticing. But other viewers, including women, might be appalled by this particular feminist vision, a revenge fantasy in which the death of half the population is seen as a victory for women.

This episode of *Outer Limits* could be interpreted as a satire on current assumptions (in this case, those of some feminists). That would be in keeping with the observation that science fiction is usually intended to show what the world might look like if some of our ideas were taken to their logical conclusions. But the concluding voice-over makes that possibility unlikely. Every episode has a similar voice-over, after all, which seldom, if ever, suggests irony or questions the episode's stated message. Its function, on the contrary, is to make the message even more obvious. In this case, the narrator explicitly mentions the folly of men rather than women.

Movies have picked up similar themes. Set in "the recent future," *The Handmaid's Tale* (Volker Schlondörff, 1990) is based on Margaret Atwood's novel of the same name. The story is unimportant for our purpose here. What matters is the setting, which is intended as a warning: this, it says, could be our world.

Apart from the fact that the United States is now called the Republic of Gilead, nothing much is supposed to have changed. Some of the costumes are colour coded, but this place looks much like the world as we know it. Only one thing is different: these people have a "peculiar institution." As under the old slave system, one segment of the population is reduced to servility. In this case, it is fertile women. Following a revolution led by Christian fundamentalists, these stereo-typical conservatives have imposed a stern Old Testament worldview. The Old Testament, viewers are expected to "know," considered women nothing more than pieces of property to be used for breeding purposes. That is the premise of both Atwood and von Schlondörff. The moral here is that unless we challenge the conservative forces of our society, unless we rid ourselves of religious fundamentalism, we can expect the same sort of grim scenario to unfold before our eyes.

This scenario is cinematically associated with two of the most noto-riously evil regimes of modern history: the Old South and Nazi Germany. Crude allusions are made to both. The antebellum South was characterized by a strict hierarchy. The handmaid is thus warned about her low status even before she arrives at her new home. And just as slaves in the Big House looked down on field slaves, the black maids in the kitchen presented here look down on the new handmaid. More-over, the hymns sung over and over again are familiar from the ante-bellum period. When whites sang about a new life "by the river," they meant the Jordan River, which symbolically divides the present world from the next. When blacks sang the same song, they secretly referred to the Ohio River, which divided the slave states from the free states.

In case the connection with slavery is too obscure, viewers are clobbered with references to the Nazis. Running in terror through a forest in the opening sequence, three members of a family try to escape across the border. The wintry landscape and the military uniforms remind viewers of similar attempts by hapless racial outlaws during World War II. The father is shot and killed. The mother is arrested and sent to a detention centre for women. Like Jews on the way to Auschwitz, these women are stripped, sorted, and packed onto cattle cars. Using the biological symbol, an officer notes on the side of one car that it contains 116 females, just as ss officers once noted that their cattle guards contained so many "pieces" or "heads" of Jewish "cattle." As the train moves away from the platform, the women thrust their arms from openings near the roof and scream for help just as Jews did when their train left an *Umschlagplatz*. Thus Nazi Germany supplies the primary metaphor.

Unlike the Old South, Nazi Germany was obsessed not only with status, order, and control but with efficiency, sterility, and death itself. That is indicated in *Handmaid*, where massive infertility has been caused by sexual promiscuity and technological intervention. It is indicated also in the use of mise-en-scène. Food is handed out by officials wearing surgical gloves, say, and the new handmaids sleep in a relentlessly neat dorm. But Nazi Germany cannot easily be translated directly to the American scene. It is too alien for acceptance at face value, in spite of the fact that dissidents during the 1960s referred glibly to "Amerika" and compared black women with Jewish house-wives on their way to Auschwitz.

Consequently, the Nazi metaphor is mediated by that of the Old South, which is much closer to home; it can be seen as the American version of Nazi Germany. Yet *Handmaid* is an inadequate attempt at social commentary because it presents an extremely distorted view of both conservatism in general and fundamentalism in particular. More to the point here, it presents an extremely distorted view of the gender system.

Atwood calls her book "speculative fiction," which is a variant of science fiction, and that applies to the movie as well. Although it can be understood as a warning about the future, it can be understood also as a comment on the present. After all, the origin of Gilead must lie in its past. And that past, by implication, is our present. What is it about our society that might make or create a Gilead? The movie does not answer that question directly; viewers are expected to draw their own conclusions. Those who believe that our society sees women as less than fully human beings, which is what many feminists do believe, could interpret Gilead – in which women are seen as livestock – as its logical, though extreme, destiny. This would explain not only why *Handmaid* is set in "the recent future" but also why it has been advertised and acclaimed as a feminist production. It presents us with a picture of the world as experienced by women. And that is perfectly legitimate. But what, viewers might wonder, would the world of Gilead be like for *men*? Judging from other societies in which women are seen primarily as breeding machines, men would be seen primarily as war machines, as weapons. Indeed, viewers are told that Gilead is at war. Since the only males seen on city streets are soldiers, they can assume that all the young men are fighting. Unfortunately, no questions are raised about that.

Because this is a world controlled by men – even though women collaborate, they can be conveniently (but condescendingly) understood as the unwitting dupes of men – viewers are allowed to assume that men freely choose combat; viewers assume that, as in Lithia, they want to kill or be killed. But we should remember that even in Nazi Germany, the warrior society par excellence, very few young men greeted the outbreak of World War II with any enthusiasm. And whatever enthu-siasm they could muster faded along with hopes for a quick and easy victory. In fact, Nazi Germany, like the American Confederacy, depended on military conscription. Young men had to be drafted into combat.

Even then, many were shot for desertion. We should recall too that the dehumanization of young men in modern armies, even those of democratic societies, is the most obvious parallel for the dehumanization of young women in Gilead. American newsreels from World War II make this very clear. Recruits were processed like cattle. They were lined up, stripped, poked and prodded, classified, numbered, and sworn in. And this was accompanied by patriotic slogans no less contrived than those heard by the young women of Gilead. What happened to many of these soldiers of America in combat was at least as horrifying as anything that happens to the handmaids of Gilead. Many of them were mutilated, traumatized, or killed in battle.

Any society that expects to lose millions of soldiers in combat – and, if they fail to repel the enemy, millions of civilians in air raids as well – must find ways of replenishing the population. After wars, most people give themselves over happily to the generation of new life. And governments openly encourage this. The result is usually a "baby boom." But some societies are more preoccupied with demography than others. Social Darwinists believe that war is an essential feature of human evolution. The strongest and healthiest survive, and the unfit are weeded out. The Nazis openly glorified war in precisely those terms. But they also planned ahead.

Long before the outbreak of war, they began to prepare for the Aryan future. Their aims were twofold: to improve the racial stock, and to survive the depopulation of a coming war. Consequently, men were told that their highest calling was to die as soldiers for the *Reich*. And women were told that their highest calling was to produce more soldiers for the *Reich*. The two went hand in glove. Gradually, the Nazis decided to pursue their policy of eugenics more actively. Under the *Lebensborn* program, healthy young women were sent to stud farms in the countryside and made available for breeding purposes to officers of the racially elite ss. It is important to note that in Nazi Germany, a totalitarian state that serves as an implicit prototype of Gilead, these "handmaids" were *volunteers*. And even though their Christian parents were often secretly appalled, their Nazi sponsors were publicly delighted. These women had high status in official circles. During the war, when everyone else was deprived, they enjoyed food and medical care of the highest quality. (Even these measures, however, could not guarantee the survival of a pure race. By the end of the war, Nazi agents were scouring occupied countries in search of children who looked Aryan. These children were then taken from their parents and given to racially and politically pure families in Germany.) At no time did the Nazis force women to breed. Nevertheless, the ideal woman in Nazi Germany was a mother, just as the ideal man was a

soldier, and every opportunity was taken to promote both. This obsession, like that of eliminating Jews, took precedence even over the war
effort. Because the war economy incorporated slave labourers, it was
considered unnecessary to conscript German women for work in the
armament industries (something the British found necessary to do).

This parallel between the fate of men and women in totalitarian
societies is not accidental but inherent. As such, the former can hardly
be considered irrelevant in any work of art focused on the latter. In
fact, examining both simultaneously is necessary for any understanding
of these societies. Why, then, has the connection been made neither by
those who produced this movie nor by those who have reviewed it?
Probably, we suggest, because our society is now preoccupied with the
problems of women. And probably, in addition, because the belief that
men are expendable in war as resources of the state is still so pervasive
that it seems more like an unremarkable given of the natural order
than a shocking device of the cultural order. The most lamentable
failure of *Handmaid* is surely its failure to point out that any society
like Gilead would present horrific perils for both men and women. An
opportunity that might have been gained for dialogue between men
and women has thus been lost.

It is true that religious conservatives want to preserve the basic features of religious tradition. Apart from anything else, they want to
preserve the family as understood in theological terms. Outsiders often
imagine that this is due to the high value they place on antiquity itself,
being afraid of modernity. In that case, conservatives could be dismissed
rather easily as backward or retrogressive. But they value tradition as
something revealed by God, not merely as something old. They are
believers, not archaeologists. This movie asks viewers to believe that
Christian fundamentalists are motivated mainly by an urge to restore
the past. It could follow on the basis of pure logic that the more remote
that past, the better. Consequently, the leaders of Gilead restore not
only a biblical regime but also a specifically Old Testament one.[3]

Most religious and secular conservatives are profoundly committed
to a notion of family life that would exclude anything even remotely
resembling the "peculiar institution" of Gilead. It is precisely for their
hostility to moral permissiveness and social engineering, in fact, that
they are known. Religious conservatives stand staunchly, some would
say rigidly, for traditional monogamy and against the use of new
reproductive technologies. And it is the religious liberals who, along
with secular avant-gardists, argue for experimentation in the name of
greater freedom. The very idea of "situation ethics," for example, is
anathema to conservatives but de rigueur in many liberal circles. The
"peculiar institution" of Gilead could be justified very easily, in fact,

by recourse to situation ethics. On purely pragmatic grounds, it could be argued that the solution to infertility depends on "moral flexibility" of just this kind. In other words, the end (communal survival) justifies the means (exploiting women and destroying the sanctity of Christian marriage). The *only* segments of our society that would not find situation ethics acceptable are the conservative ones, whether Protestant, Catholic, or Jewish. For them, some things, including marital fidelity, are inherently good. Other things, including extra-marital relations, are inherently evil.

Those with power in Gilead are portrayed as cynical opportunists. Not one of them is portrayed as a true believer. They manipulate others without bothering to conceal their sneers and smirks. The obvious message is that the people being parodied, religious conservatives in our own society, are cynical opportunists. This position is arrogant, to say the least. By and large, moreover, it is false. It is true that some televangelists are dishonest and dishonourable, but the same thing could be said about individuals in any other community. Outsiders often assume that no intelligent or humanitarian person could possibly support a conservative worldview, which is to say, disagree with their own "progressive" ideas. It follows that those who promote conservative policies must be either cynical and exploitive (the televangelists) or ignorant and stupid (their supporters). Intolerance is characteristic of fundamentalism (though not necessarily of conservatism), which does indeed present a serious threat to any democracy – but not more so than many other worldviews.

Finally, it is worth noting that Gilead is a totalitarian state. The government intrudes on even the most intimate aspects of daily life. Why suggest, as this movie does, that a totalitarian revolution in America would be led by conservatives? The fact is that conservatives, and not only religious conservatives, are the very ones who most strongly oppose big government. They want less state regulation, not more. In this, it is true, they are joined by the libertarians. Politically, both are derived from what was in the nineteenth century called "liberalism." Both place a very high value on the individual. But the liberals of today have long since abandoned that philosophical tradition and moved towards socialism with its call for more and more government control.

At a superficial level, the rulers of Gilead sound like conservatives. At a deeper level, they are more like their opponents on the other side of the political continuum. Contemporary liberals and socialists would certainly oppose the vision of Gilead out of sheer compassion, but, ironically, they might not be able to do so very effectively. That is partly because they attach greater importance to the collectivity than to the individual, but it is also partly because they have adopted a distinctly utilitarian point of view. Conservatives, ironically, have often done the same thing. For example, they have seldom hesitated to conscript men for combat. In doing so, they have adopted the classic utilitarian argument (the greatest good for the greatest number of people) and the corollary (the end justifies the means) that often accompanies it (see chapter 8). That anomaly could be challenged on either liberal or conservative grounds, although many people would ignore it on practical grounds.

From all this, it can be concluded that *Handmaid* is a polemical diatribe in cinematic form. Explicitly, it attacks religious conservatives. These include but are not restricted to fundamentalists. Implicitly, it attacks all conservatives. These include but are not restricted to those at the political centre who support the family on purely secular grounds. But the nightmare of Gilead would follow from current trends on the left at least as consistently as from those on the right. Neither side is immune to totalitarian policies of one kind or another. To argue that danger lies only on one side does a disservice to the community. It prevents citizens from seeing the underlying dangers that lurk elsewhere on the political horizon – dangers that, if anything, lead more logically, albeit more insidiously, in the direction of Gilead. And, once again, it prevents the kind of dialogue badly needed in a society that already shows signs of succumbing to terminal polarization.

In some ways, *The Long Walk Home* (Richard Pearce, 1990) is unlike the other movies under discussion in this chapter. It is certainly one of the more sophisticated ones. At least one of its aims, to recall an early phase in the struggle of black Americans in the South for civil rights, is legitimate and even laudable. Its other aim, to promote a misandric view of gender, is another matter. With possible complaints in mind, the studio has kept that more or less out of sight until the very last sequence.

Part one begins at a bus stop in Montgomery, Alabama. Odessa, who works as a maid in the home of Miriam and Norman Thompson, stands in line with several other black women. When the bus arrives, each climbs in to pay, comes out again, marches to the rear door, and climbs in once more. After a long ride, Odessa reaches the suburban Thompson home and begins her chores in the kitchen. Then Miriam tells her to take the children to a local park for the day. As Odessa unpacks the picnic basket there, a white police officer notices her and tells her that only whites are allowed in the park. Odessa's explanation for returning home so early causes Miriam to lodge a complaint with the police department. Next day, the police officer delivers a formal apology to Odessa, the children, and Miriam.

Meanwhile, the local black community decides to protest the segregation of public transportation. Leaders ask black people to boycott the buses. Because most of the people who use and pay for the buses are black, they hope to force the city into abolishing segregation. Those who work in white homes will either have to walk or find other ways of getting to work every day. On the first day, Odessa is late for work. When she explains, Miriam offers to give her a lift twice a week on the way to do errands of her own. Miriam does not intend this as a political statement: helping Odessa is merely a way of ensuring the efficient management of her own home. She does not tell Norman, her husband, realizing that he would probably disapprove. Like her husband, her bridge group, and her guests at a party, Miriam is almost indifferent to the needs of black people and assumes that they will soon come to their senses and end the boycott. But it continues longer than anyone had thought possible. Miriam's friends discuss it idly over bridge. One woman says that she has nothing to worry about, because her maid has her own car. Later on, Miriam's dinner guests discuss it with greater irritation. As Odessa comes into the dining room to serve, one guest observes that the boycott started only because black people cannot be bothered to work. For a while, life continues as usual. One morning, because Norman is sick in bed, Miriam cannot leave to pick up Odessa. When Norman asks why Odessa is late, Miriam tells him what she has been doing. Norman is furious and forbids her to continue helping Odessa.

Part two begins with Miriam's rather sudden "conversion." When Odessa arrives, soaked after a long walk in the rain, Miriam tries to explain why Norman has forbidden her to offer any more lifts and why she has chosen to comply. But this conversation convinces Miriam that she has been dead wrong. She confronts him directly with an ultimatum: either she runs their home as she sees fit and without "help" from him, or she will "help" him by getting a job outside their home. He withdraws. The marriage is over, in effect, but a new life begins for Miriam. First, she agrees to provide lifts not only for Odessa but also for other black women on their way to work in white homes. And she asks them to sit in the front seat, not the back. Then, joining some northern white women from the nearby military base, she begins working full time for the cause.

Meanwhile, Odessa's world too has been changing. Martin Luther King addresses the community at a local church. Tired though she is, Odessa accompanies her husband and children to hear the great preacher. But the civil rights movement has only just begun. Racism is still openly approved, legally tolerated, and violently expressed. One day, Odessa's daughter has a bad scare. Breaking the boycott to see

her boyfriend, Selma is threatened on the bus by several white hooli-
gans. When they are all thrown off by a worried driver, she is attacked.
Fortunately, her younger brother has sensed danger, borrowed money
for a taxi, and come to her aid. He fails to rescue her, but the black
cab driver succeeds. They hurry back to their own part of town for
fear of reprisal.

Part three begins with Norman's "conversion" to the *white* cause.
Previously, he had been an indifferent spectator, vaguely sympathetic
to Odessa herself but decidedly unsympathetic to what he considered
the troublemakers she supported. His brother, Tunker, has seen the
implications much earlier. He understands that a victory by "uppity
negroes" would mean massive social, economic, and political changes.
After so many months of civic turmoil, and after the betrayal of his
own wife, Norman is convinced by Tunker to join the influential white
businessmen opposing the boycott. Tunker and his friends are really
middle-class vigilantes committed to ending the boycott by force.
Driving to a "stop" along one of the car-pool routes, one night, Tunker
tells Norman that Miriam has been driving one of the car pools on a
regular basis. When they arrive, Norman gets out and tries to take
Miriam away from what is obviously going to become a violent
confrontation. Then Tunker tries. Watching from a distance are Mary
Catherine, their daughter, and Odessa. Miriam walks back towards
them and away from Norman, Tunker, and the white mob. The movie
ends with the blacks holding hands and singing defiantly.

So what is the problem with this movie? The answer becomes clear
when a few more details are added to this outline of the story. Think
of what *Long Walk* says about the differences between men and
women. Think also of the fact that some late nineteenth-century
founders of modern feminism were racists. Ann Douglas[4] points out
that these women wanted votes for themselves but not necessarily for
black people – not even black women. (For a more detailed discussion
of this topic, see chapter 7.)

In *Long Walk*, every single black woman, without exception, is
good. And except for Selma, who soon realizes her mistake in taking
the bus to see her boyfriend, they are heroic as well. Every black man
is good too. It might be objected, therefore, that men and women are
treated equally in the black community. But even though black men
are good, they are inadequate. It is true that Odessa's husband is a
kind husband and father. Without saying so, nevertheless, he expects
her to do the cooking and cleaning after she has walked all the way
home from the suburbs. It is true that Odessa's son tries bravely to
rescue Selma, but he is unable to scare away her assailants. The cab
driver actually succeeds in doing so, but he runs away as soon as

possible to avoid further trouble with the whites. Even the heroic stature of Martin Luther King is minimized: because he can be heard but not seen, he is not really a character in the movie at all. In purely cinematic terms we are asked to believe that the civil rights movement was initiated, led, and fought for by black women, not by black women *and* men. Presumably, Odessa's husband and his friends were relaxing (or cowering) at home while the women took their places on the front line. Black women are good and heroic, in short, while black men are good but inadequate. With white people, the situation is different. Every single white man, without exception, is both evil and inadequate.

Some ambiguity exists when it comes to white women. Miriam and the northern women at the military base are not only good but also heroic. A few white women express overtly racist sentiments, but not one of them joins the mob even as an observer. Moreover, viewers are told that many others, as drivers, are actively helping blacks win the boycott. Viewers are asked to believe that the movement was actively supported by at least some white women, not some white women *and* men. Apparently, the northern men stationed at the military base all disapproved, like Norman, when their wives drove black people to work. Some viewers know that the historical events depicted were much more complicated. But a vast gulf separates our time from the 1950s. Since then, the civil rights movement has given way to the black power movement. Its particular political mentality (polarization between blacks and whites) has contributed, in turn, to misandric versions of feminism (polarization between women and men). Given the atmosphere prevalent today, it is easy either to forget history or to distort it for political purposes.

With this in mind, the message about gender in this movie is clear. The focus on women is not merely an attempt to add something that has been forgotten by many historians but is an attempt to *rewrite* history from a particular political perspective. Consider Miriam's "conversion." It is the climax of this story. The rest of the movie is a lengthy dénouement. But she is not "converted" to *new* ideas about race. In fact, as she explains to Odessa, she has long understood the futility of segregation. On a childhood trip to Portland, she observed children of both races swimming happily together in a public pool. So why has she tolerated segregation as an adult in the South? Because of her subservience to Norman!

As Norman's *wife*, Miriam considers it her duty to support him and even to justify his foolish opinions. "He just grew up with segregation," she explains. "Sometimes, he's a better husband than I am a wife." At this point, Miriam wants primarily to be a good wife. And, to the best of her ability, she is. Odessa knows better. "Is it who you are," she asks, "or who Mr Thompson wants you to be?" It is thus the problem of *gender*, not race, that actually "converts" Miriam into a heroine. She already understood the irrational nature of racism. Now, after linking it with sexism, she can do something about it. Once Miriam takes the frightening but decisive step of challenging Norman's authority, thus confirming her "rebirth" as a new woman, he moves out of the bedroom and out of her life. There will be no more "sleeping with the enemy" for Miriam. Considering the centrality of "consciousness raising" in the women's movement and "coming out" in the gay movement, it is surely no accident that *Long Walk* is accompanied by the voice-over narrative of Mary Catherine, Miriam's daughter. She recalls what her own generation would consider, in secular terms, a political coming of age.

The problem with this movie, then, is its misandric presupposition that racism is due to the hierarchical and patriarchal thinking of *men*, not to any flaws in human nature itself. Because Miriam's attitude towards race is merely a reflection of Norman's bigotry, because she is liberated from male bigotry and female submissiveness simultaneously, female viewers who identify themselves with her – and she is the protagonist – are conveniently let off the hook. Why should they be troubled by guilt when they can blame even their own racism on others? This is based on a common premise in misandric forms of feminism: that racism – like classism, heterosexism, ageism, and so forth – is a *byproduct* of the hierarchical thinking inherent in sexism. Which is to say, in men. In that case, the only way to eliminate racism is to eliminate misogyny. All of history is reduced to a primordial conspiracy of men against women, therefore, the ultimate source of all suffering and evil ascribed to men. To the extent that women are racist, including Miriam's friends, this movie clearly says that it is only because men made them that way.

If any further evidence of this misandric mentality is required, the concluding sequence provides it. Facing each other as enemies are not merely blacks and whites but black *women* (with a few white women) and white *men*. The movie ends, moreover, with the dramatic visual symbolism of female solidarity across racial and class lines. Because the black women are joined by Miriam and Mary Catherine, the movie makes it evident once again that sex, not race, is what ultimately polarizes humanity. In cinematic terms, what matters here is not that only two white females risk their reputations and even their lives to support the blacks but that not even one white male does. Apart from its obvious link with race, the opening sequence might be an unwitting but fitting visual commentary on the simplistic concluding one: the credits are displayed over scenes of Montgomery shot in black and white.

Mr and Mrs Bridge (James Ivory, 1990) is remarkable for the beauty of its cinematography. Unlike most misandric movies, it is distinguished from run-of-the-mill productions by restrained acting, subtle characterization, haunting music, and many other marks of fine craftsmanship. All the same, it qualifies for inclusion in this chapter. Because it is primarily a study of character – the movie is episodic, giving viewers glimpses of a woman's life over approximately ten years – the story itself can be told very simply.

India Bridge is the vaguely unhappy, undervalued, and frustrated wife of Walter Bridge. He is a quiet, dignified, and refined – but also stiff and formal – lawyer. They have three children: Ruth, Carolyn, and Douglas. All find ways of escaping the joyless atmosphere at home. India has two friends, Grace and Mabel, both seeking ways of expanding the limited horizons of their lives. But at the end of the movie, nothing has changed for India.

Of interest is not the way this story unfolds but the way these characters are revealed and, more specifically, the way two groups of characters – male and female – are used to suggest ways of thinking about their counterparts in the real world. That the story is primarily about women or told from the perspective of women is made clear in the prologue. In a silent, black-and-white home movie, women smile placidly as their children frolic on a summer afternoon at the swimming pool. No men appear. This is repeated as an epilogue. The movie is thus framed by the experience of women. Despite the title, therefore, *Mr and Mrs Bridge* is really about Mrs Bridge, not Mr Bridge. The title refers to the loss of her identity, along with her name, within marriage.

The female characters can be classified on a continuum from passive victims of men to active rebels against them. Despite occasional outbursts, India is a passive victim. The movie is about her half-conscious and unsuccessful search for meaning and fulfilment in what is presented as the materially comfortable but emotionally and spiritually empty world of upper-middle-class women who were rearing children in the 1930s and 1940s. It is about her emotional isolation both within the family and in the larger society beyond. India is gentle and kind. In one scene, her former art teacher, beset by hard times, comes to the back door selling subscriptions to *Doberman*, a magazine of interest only to the few people who, unlike India, actually own these vicious dogs. Surprising the salesman himself, she buys a subscription. But India is also a timid and inhibited housewife. Occasionally, she acknowledges her frustration in seemingly inappropriate outbursts of anger. When Douglas refuses to shave off his moustache, the rage accumulated over twenty years of marriage suddenly erupts.

Like the suburban housewives who suffered from what Betty Friedan called "the disease that has no name," India has no real understanding of the social forces that deny or ignore her full humanity. No wonder she tells her increasingly depressed friend, Grace, "Now, we really are awfully lucky, if you just think about it." But Grace would probably have agreed with Friedan, who said that wealthy women live in "comfortable concentration camps" (although Friedan, a political moderate, later regretted using such extreme imagery). Like Grace, India wants the freedom to express herself more fully. But Grace wants "too much" freedom. She is "punished" as a deviant, loses the will to carry on, and commits suicide. Unlike Grace, India is either unable or unwilling to kick over the traces. She is afraid of taking the risks that go along with freedom. In fact, she is conservative in even the most literal sense. Though wealthy, she almost "scolds" Ruth for throwing away a perfectly good comb that could be washed and used again. Symbolically, this scene identifies India with virtues such as thrift, frugality, and security. These make perfect sense in themselves, but they support the old order represented by Walter. They are anachronistic in the new world of change, adventure, progress, and emancipation represented by Ruth. Consequently, India is doomed to endure a life of futility and meaninglessness.

As ladies of leisure, India and her friends participate in activities of the local elite. They all show up at the opening of an exhibit at the modernistic art gallery. But India's understanding of art is minimal. She is thrilled in Paris when Walter buys her a painting, not an original but a copy of a rather sentimental portrayal by Chardin of a housewife preparing supper for her children. It is not a work of art that offers insight into the inherent contradictions generated by life in the modern world, the world she herself inhabits, but a symbol of the old order about which she herself is very ambivalent. India's lack of intellectual depth might be represented symbolically by the famous statue that she and Walter pass on their way through the Louvre: the Winged Victory of Samothrace, a woman without a head. But India's shallowness, the statue suggests, might not be innate. She too is a woman who has been damaged – that is, deprived of her head – by men.

India takes up painting along with her friends, although they rebel more actively than she does against their "oppression." As the women paint – the class consists entirely of women – India tells Grace that she votes the way Walter tells her to. Then the teacher comes over and tells Grace, "Keep at it, girl, we got something there." Grace is more sophisticated and insightful than India. She really does understand the problem afflicting her and other women of her class. But living a generation before Friedan, she finds no hope of changing the social order. As a result, she suffers consciously and acutely. "We do depend on them, don't we?" she replies sarcastically. By "them," she refers to paternalistic teachers who fail to respect their students as grown women, domineering husbands who fail to respect their wives as intelligent citizens, and men in general. Mabel too is more independent and intellectual than India. After class one day, she asks India to read a book by Thorstein Veblen on political and economic theory. India's two friends are already aware that as women they must make an effort to establish their own identities or find meaning in their own lives. Mabel succeeds by taking up new hobbies: painting, reading, and psychoanalysis. Grace fails by rebelling against social norms, both in public (causing a "scene" at the art gallery) and in private (kicking over the washing machine and flooding the basement). India neither succeeds nor fails. She resigns herself to a life of insignificance.

As potential rebels against patriarchy, Mabel and Grace represent a continuum among women. Mabel tries to use the system to her own advantage by exploiting whatever opportunities for personal growth her wealth and status provide. Grace tries to defeat the system by refusing to cooperate with the enemy. Viewers learn very little about these two women but are encouraged to fill in the missing details by referring to women from their own lives who live, or lived, under similar circumstances. For Mabel, painting, reading, and psychoanalysis could be activities on a par with playing bridge, hobbies to disguise the boredom and meaninglessness of everyday life. Theoretically, psychoanalysis could lead to a real breakthrough, and she might yet "find herself." There is something to be said for taking statements of this kind at face value. But it does not quite work, because viewers have no evidence that anything else in her life changes as a result. Psychoanalysis generally means passage through a lengthy period of intense emotional pain or, at the very least, turmoil. Mabel's breezy description of her sessions with Dr Sauer – "I am beginning to find out who I really am!" – suggest that for her the process has been tamed. From what viewers are shown, it could well be just one more diversion. If so, Mabel would be no different from millions of middle-class people in our own time who turn simultaneously to a variety of currently fashionable therapeutic movements – psychological, dietary, religious, and so forth – to relieve their anxiety, dull their pain, or pursue meaning.

For Grace, diversions are not enough to dull the pain. Trapped in a world that expects her to do nothing more than keep house and entertain dinner guests, she just stops doing what is expected of her. "I guess I'm the wrong kind of a wife for a banker," she says. While the others are partying at the museum, she goes out to her car for a smoke. After she returns to the party, someone discovers that her car is on fire. Symbolically, Grace is out of control. Her passion for life and freedom cannot be contained by the structures of society. Eventually, she gives up and dies, physically as well as emotionally, by overdosing on sleeping pills. She is defeated in the end, but her efforts to assert herself are valiant and even, in this context, heroic.

Less intellectual than Mabel and less proud than Grace, India follows neither path. She does not use the system to her best advantage, but she does not reject it either. She is neither well-adjusted enough to find happiness nor ill-adjusted enough to seek death. The implication is that her path is the one followed by most women, by ordinary women. As the movie concludes, she is trapped and alone in her car, snow gradually obscuring her view of the world outside. "Hello? Hello?" she calls. "Is anybody there?" According to the epilogue, Walter does get there, just in time to save her for many more years of dull but chronic pain. Presumably, they continue living together uneasily and unhappily as "two solitudes."

In view of this, it is clear that the name "Bridge" is used ironically. It is associated with maleness not only for the obvious reason that this is Walter's name, taken on by India through marriage, but also for some less obvious reasons – less obvious, that is, to those unfamiliar with misandric versions of feminism. Bridges are products of technology, which is often associated by feminists with maleness. Because bridges pass over land and water, moreover, they represent transcendence. And that too is often associated by feminists with maleness. (It refers to a preference for the abstract instead of the concrete and, in religious terms, for salvation in some other world instead of social and political justice in this world.) In any case, the movie suggests that no bridge could ever cross the chasm that separates Mr and Mrs Bridge or, by implication, between men and women. Mrs Bridge and her unliberated counterparts must try to find contentment playing bridge with each other.

India's daughters not only actively rebel but do so more or less successfully. They have no intention of being like their submissive mother. On the possibility of "staying home and raising kids in the suburbs," Ruth tells her father that it "was good enough for Mother, but it's not good enough for me." Walter says nothing to her about any contribution his wife might have made to his life. Explicitly rejecting the possibility of subservience to a man, Ruth sets out on her own quest for identity. When her boss's sexual advances make her uncomfortable, she decides to quit her job and go into acting. Walter is initially opposed to the idea. Then, possibly out of respect for her courage and ambition, he gives Ruth $1,000 to pursue her dream in

New York. No one consults India. Ruth consistently ignores her mother's letters containing earnest but outdated advice.

Carolyn, the younger daughter, has a more difficult time breaking away from the stultifying atmosphere at home. She arrives one day to announce her engagement. Her fiancé, Gil, is an ambitious lower-class man from out of town. Not being asked for her advice, India merely expresses muted anxiety and tells Carolyn to ask Walter. Much against his wishes, Carolyn marries Gil and discovers for herself that he is a lout. When she comes home after being beaten for not preparing his dinner on time, India tries to comfort her but observes that Carolyn herself might have caused the problem by not paying enough attention to her household responsibilities: "There are some things in marriage, dear, that every woman ..." Carolyn retorts that she, unlike India, refuses to be pushed around by a husband. Even though Carolyn is unsuccessful in her marriage, she is successful in a way that is far more important in this movie: being unlike her mother. Having found marriage unsatisfactory, she leaves with the intention of finding something better. In short, both daughters rebel. That alone is considered an accomplishment for women.

Two other female characters deserve comment. One is Harriet, the black housekeeper. When Walter takes her to get her husband out of jail, she tearfully tells her apparently unfeeling employer about the woes of living with a drug dealer, one who drinks too much. Another female victim of men is Julia, Walter's secretary. After work one night, she asks Walter to take her out for a drink. As they sit down, Walter asks if she has ever been to the Aztec Room. "Have I ever been here? I've never been anywhere," she replies. After a few minutes of small talk, she tells Walter that she came to work for him twenty years ago to the day. Walter as usual is emotionally inert. "I have given you the best years of my life," she says, "the very best years. It doesn't mean anything to you." Like India, Julia is taken for granted by Walter. But Julia wants more from him than appreciation of her typing skills. The implication is that she has wasted all these years loving Walter and hoping that he would eventually love her in return. The other woman in Walter's life, his wife, supplies additional evidence. She too feels undervalued. "No one can go through their whole life without some kind of appreciation," she tells him. She adds something that takes on more significance in view of Julia's situation: "Sometimes, I think you care more for your secretary than you do for me." Both women are Walter's victims, not from physical brutality or even mental cruelty, but from indifference. Walter knows a great deal but feels nothing.

The male characters in *Bridge* can be arranged on a continuum from inadequate to evil. Viewers learn almost nothing about them except the ways in which they victimize or fail the women in their lives. Carolyn's husband is clearly evil. Attracted by his charm, she failed to see his underlying potential for drunken violence. He beats her for not keeping house properly. The scene in which Carolyn tells her mother about his brutality is preceded by a shot of the full moon. The most obvious reason for this shot would be the association viewers are likely to make between Gil and the werewolves of folklore who turn into bloodthirsty beasts when the moon is full. "Then he tried to make it up to me," Carolyn says, "the way men always do ... it was so disgusting."

Dr Sauer, Mabel's psychoanalyst, is morally more ambiguous. He is the only man who actually expresses deep feelings, yet there is something vaguely disturbing about him. At a restaurant with Walter and some other men, he tells a lewd joke and suggests that there is something unhealthy about Walter for not laughing. From one point of view, that could be true. But from another, that of many feminist viewers, Sauer himself would be dismissed with contempt. His joke would be considered sexist, not merely lewd. Later on, Sauer buys flowers for his wife but is noticeably, suggestively, interested in the attractive saleswoman. From one point of view, again, this merely indicates that, unlike Walter, he has not neurotically repressed perfectly healthy sexual urges. From another point of view, though, his healthy attitude towards sex might not preclude a sexist attitude toward marriage. There is something sinister about this man, a sophisticated European who just happens to be living in, of all places, Kansas City. Walter is aware that psychoanalysts have often been accused of exploiting the neuroticism of elite society, preying on bored and wealthy women who have nothing more important to do with their lives than indulge in self-absorbed and neurotic fantasies. So, when India tells Walter that she wants to take Mabel's advice and begin psychoanalysis, he dismisses the idea with contempt.

Like his sisters, Douglas rebels against the dull and restricting atmosphere at home. He goes out with lower-class women, possibly prostitutes. Unlike his sisters, he rebels for purely selfish reasons. He is not a victim. He can hardly be bothered to acknowledge his mother's presence, let alone offer love, support, or even polite conversation. Driven by despair one night, she asks him why he keeps ignoring her: "You'd think I was poison or something." His sullen demeanour reveals his contempt for her. His insensitivity is most dramatically and painfully revealed as he becomes an Eagle Scout. At the ceremony, every boy stands next to his seated mother. When the boys are told to thank their "best friends" in the most appropriate way, Douglas just stands there while the other boys sit down and kiss their mothers. (For some reason, their fathers are considered insignificant. Walter and the others are seated separately in the back.) Why does Douglas feel this way towards his mother? No definitive answer is provided. He might simply consider his mother old-fashioned.

When India finds a magazine called *Strip Tease* in his room, she quickly hunts down a sex manual. Its title, *The Mysteries of Marriage*, suggests that she herself does not understand either sexual relations in general or the institution of marriage in particular – that is, the way in which marriage diminishes her – and is thus unfit to help her son grow up. Overcoming her embarrassment, she gives it to him. The boy sits there in angry silence. Later on, India bumps into him on the street with Pequita, a woman who is, to say the least, not of the Bridges' social class. Graciously, India pretends nothing is wrong and even feigns interest in his friend. That night, she timidly asks him why he goes around with "women like that." Douglas walks off in a huff. Not long afterward, he is seen necking with the same woman in a car. There is no cinematic evidence to suggest he is in love with her or that he has any intention of developing a "serious relationship" with her. Long before viewers learn from the epilogue that Douglas eventually marries and settles down to a respectable life in the suburbs, they know that he will discard Pequita. From the perspective of many feminists, therefore, Douglas is exploiting Pequita whether he gives her money in return or not. The obviously phallic chimney or tower that rises above them in the background is thus a cinematic comment. It amounts, almost literally, to an exclamation mark beside the behaviour not only of Douglas but also, by implication, of men in general.

From India's perspective, Douglas the man is no improvement over Douglas the boy. He returns from the war wearing a moustache. When she suggests he would look better without it, he makes no response. This time, the rage she has accumulated for years bursts out: "You're just like your father! Exactly!" For once, Douglas actually notices her pain. But instead of comforting her, he simply asks a question: "Who else should I be like, if not my father?" And that of course is the whole problem here: the son really is like the father. Douglas builds model airplanes and enjoys newsreels about the Royal Air Force defending Britain. One night, he goes up to the attic with his father to play with souvenirs from World War I. Walter refuses permission for Douglas to join the army and tells the boy that he himself was spared the necessity of killing anyone in battle. Nevertheless, the two dress up in military uniforms. The implication is that men have a perverse love of war, that men are either willing (Walter) or eager (Douglas) to ignore the risk of mutilation, suffering, guilt, and death to escape from the boredom and confinement of family life. Douglas goes to war. Eventually, he returns, marries, becomes a lawyer, and takes over his father's law office. In short, he inherits the legacy of his father and continues the patriarchal system.

Even though he is the primary antagonist, Walter is not presented as a demon. Unlike the villains of many other movies discussed in this book, he is still human. It is precisely due to this touch of subtlety that *Bridge* is artistically successful. As a lawyer, Walter is a man of probity. His sense of responsibility to the community, moreover, leads him to take on charity cases. When a disabled young man is refused adequate compensation, Walter decides to appeal the case. But Walter has a dark side. It is revealed in his private life, the subject of *Bridge*. As a respectable, successful, and conventional man of his time, he treats his wife with formal courtesy and protectiveness that are patronizing or even condescending. His attitude indicates an unspoken claim to authority. Troubled by his general indifference and ingratitude, India says, "You don't even know if I'm dead or alive … I'm getting a divorce." He sets her on his knee, comforting her as he would a little girl who occasionally demands attention. Worried about his heart condition, he discusses the matter with Douglas and warns the boy that his mother "must never know."

At his best, Walter buys presents for his wife – a painting, a car, flowers – in the sincere but misguided hope that he can satisfy all her needs by doing so and carefully plans to provide for her security after his death. At his worst, he ignores her. When she tries to begin an intellectual discussion with him, he is too busy listening to Nelson Eddy singing "Stouthearted Men" on the radio. And when India asks him for permission to begin psychoanalysis, he is amazed, unaware that she is troubled. India says that a psychoanalyst would be someone to talk to. He replies: "You can talk to me." India frowns and then sighs in despair. The same thing happens on many other occasions. In one extremely painful scene – strongly reminiscent of the one in which Douglas becomes an Eagle Scout – the special treat she has baked for Walter turns out to be inedible. Instead of saying something to release the tension and comfort his wife, Walter says nothing. After an awkward and accusing silence, he puts the cake aside and begins talking about something else. Learning that Grace has killed herself, India cries out in agony to Walter: "She was my best friend. I loved her!" He finishes his cocktail and goes over to comfort Grace's husband. (This heartlessness is represented medically as well as emotionally. Walter has a bad heart.) In one bizarre scene, Walter and India are eating dinner at their country club when the rapid approach of a tornado is announced. Everyone else hurries into the cellar, but Walter arrogantly insists on pretending that nothing unusual is happening. After repeated expressions of anxiety from India, he says: "I see no need to scurry

into a hole ... For twenty years, I've been telling you when something
will happen and when it will not. Now, have I ever been wrong?" As
the building is repeatedly shaken by to its foundation by the tornado,
yet another facile reference to the phallus, Grace observes to others in
the cellar, "She should just hit him over the head and leave."

India is a "woman with no head," but Walter is a man with no
heart. Yet at one time, Walter was emotionally alive. Standing inside
the steel cage of a bank vault as he explains the financial arrangements
he has made for her in case of his death, India asks him, "Do you love
me?" After a cool and indirect confirmation of love for her, she
continues: "Couldn't you *tell* me once in a while?" She reminds him
of the days when he was courting her, of the way he used to recite
quatrains from the *Rubayat* of Omar Khayam. Viewers might wonder
whether the passage of time has distorted India's memory of him, but
her words must be taken seriously as cinematic evidence. In that case,
something has profoundly changed him, turned him into a repressed
ghost of his former self.

Although Walter's goal in life is now "contentment" rather than
passion, he is not too repressed to experience the need for purely
sexual, physical release. He has little or no interest in his wife as a
person, but he has retained his interest in her as a sexual partner. On
one occasion, he tells Ruth, "I still feel great desire for your mother."
India seems to have no more interest in sex than Walter has in emotion,
but the marriage continues.

Being so dependent and vulnerable, India could never make a new
life for herself. Being so repressed and set in his ways, Walter could
never court another woman and start over again. A scene set in Paris,
though, suggests that Walter is willing to consider illicit sexual activities. Although he and his wife dutifully visit museums, the evocative
background music – the barcarole from Offenbach's *Gaieté Parisienne*
– suggests the hope of rekindling their romance. But after an evening
at the Moulin Rouge, where the whirling petticoats and acrobatic
kicking of the cancan dancers leave Walter actually licking his lips,
India is tired – too tired, at any rate, for sex. Walter is too self-
controlled to complain about it, but he is not too self-controlled to
have fantasies of finding another partner. He is next seen, later that
night, watching couples near a bridge. The implication is that he would
like very much to satisfy his own physical urges with another woman.
If he does not, it is because of dutiful conformity to the rules of
marriage, not willing loyalty to his wife.

It is in this sexual realm, moreover, that Walter's inadequacy takes
on sinister overtones. In one early scene, he plays Romeo to Ruth's
Juliet as they recite lines from Shakespeare's play. Looking down from

his bedroom window shortly afterward, he notices Ruth sunbathing on the lawn. She stretches out and adjusts her bra. Just then, India walks into the bedroom and Walter pounces on her. Clearly, he has turned to his wife for an acceptable release of sexual tension created by the unacceptable attraction he feels towards his daughter. This could explain, at least partially, his reaction to Ruth's discovery of her own sexuality. Late one night, he discovers Ruth on the living room floor with a man. He brutally hits her. Meeting at the Aztec Room for lunch the next day, they discuss her plans to get a job in New York. "I do worry," Walter tells her, "I worry a great deal." But Ruth says: "I don't trust you." Placing his hand over hers, he continues with a comment that has no obvious relation to what they have been talking about: "I still feel a great desire for your mother."

Thinly veiled incestuous desires could explain his hostile response to the suitor of his other daughter. Even though Gil eventually turns out to be a drunken lout, Walter could not have foreseen this. Gil resorts to open confrontation after Walter refuses to condone the marriage. He appears to be deeply in love with Carolyn. Even though he is poor, moreover, he is ambitious and willing to work hard. Because there is no obvious reason for Walter's intense hostility to him, viewers are encouraged to wonder if Walter's love for Carolyn, as for Ruth, is somehow sick.

Whatever the specific reasons for Walter's indifference towards his wife, the reason for his attitude towards women in general would today be understood as a form of misogyny. As presented in this movie, that is more often implicit than explicit. Very early, it becomes clear that Grace is not going to make it. She drinks too much. She loses control. In the end, Walter is utterly unable to understand what might have driven her to suicide or, for that matter, why India felt so close to her. For Walter, Grace is pathetic – self-absorbed and ungrateful, to be sure, but pathetic. And he makes it clear that his attitude towards her is linked with his attitude towards women in general. Thinking only of the material comforts provided by her husband, Walter opines, "He gave her everything a woman could want." Mabel, however, is not pathetic. She is dangerous. Walter would probably despise anyone who read such dangerous works as Thorstein Veblen's *Theory of the Leisure Class*. But that book is cinematically represented by a *woman*. A cinematic link is made between the socialist concern for oppressed workers and the feminist concern for oppressed women. At the same time, a link is made between feminine concern for the oppressed and masculine indifference towards them. Similarly, Walter would probably despise anyone who felt the need for a psychoanalyst. But this activity is cinematically represented, once again, by a woman. Walter's contempt for dangerous ideas and dangerous activities is thus cinematically linked to contempt for women. For Walter, Mabel represents much more than intellectual dilettantism, just as Grace represents much more than emotional instability. Both represent women seeking their own identities and, ultimately, their independence from men. Because he denies the legitimacy of their search, Walter can be classified as a sexist, albeit a genteel one.

But Walter's reactionary mentality has more than one modality. It is no accident that he opposes Marxism, which symbolically represents "progressive" movements in general. At the opening of an exhibit at the local art gallery, for example, Grace identifies capitalism as a source of suffering, including her own, and he contemptuously dismisses her. Even worse, he shows signs of racism. Although he occasionally thanks his black maid, Harriet, for bringing his drink, she is virtually invisible to him. And after she tells him that her nephew is hoping to attend Harvard, Walter complains to India that there are "plenty of good colored schools." The cinematic implication is that being patriarchal is necessarily related – as cause, effect, or both – to being racist, sexist, and bourgeois.

Bridge is by far the most sophisticated of the misandric movies discussed in this book, because the symbolic contrasts are subtle rather than stark. These attract sophisticated viewers, male and female, with the liberal and egalitarian sensibilities of feminists such as Betty Friedan. Beyond superficial first impressions of human complexity, however, the message is the same as all other misandric productions. Female characters are not heroic in this case, but they are all good, which is to say that they are innocent victims. Male characters are not psychotic or evil, on the other hand, but they are inadequate – every one of them. Given its relative subtlety, *Bridge* is all the more effective in convincing its relatively sophisticated viewers that men and women live in two isolated and conflicting solitudes.

By the 1990s, history was being rewritten on television every night of the week. That brings us to drama series – a category that includes prime-time soap operas.[5] Some drama series hide their political aims under a thin veneer of history or nostalgia. According to Richard Zoglin, there has been a shift of emphasis on shows set in the past. Previously, he argues, they

were mainly interested in using the past for its symbolic or mythic value. The Minnesota frontier of *Little House on the Prairie* and the Depression-era South of *The Waltons* were essentially the same locale: an all-American Everyplace, where ethical issues and family dramas could be worked out against an idealized backdrop, far from the messy moral ambiguities of modern days. In the new crop of nostalgia shows, by contrast, a particular period is re-created precisely and dwelt on lovingly. In a sense, these shows are *about* the past – a past, moreover, that most u.s. viewers personally remember (or, thanks to the media, think they remember). And though none of these eras are portrayed as totally idyllic, they give off a warm, comforting glow. Their problems seem more manageable when viewed in hindsight. We know how everything came out.[6]

Zoglin's analysis is flawed. Shows are often set in the past, but they are not necessarily *about* the past. On the contrary, they are about the *present*. But there is one difference between older and newer shows set in the past: newer ones project specific political movements onto the past, not merely universalistic questions about personal ethics or psychological development. ABC's *Homefront* was a soap opera set at the end of World War II, but it reflected the interests and attitudes of our own time. In the pilot episode,[7] Linda is planning to marry Mike when he comes back from the war. To her dismay, she learns that he has married an Italian woman. Then, she is fired from her job at the local plant. With the war over, the foreman explains, the plant must make room for returning GIs. Linda complains about all this to her mother:

LINDA: They fired me.
MOM: Oh honey, I'm sorry, but you knew it was coming.
LINDA: No I didn't.
MOM: Linda, the GIs should get the jobs. They've sacrificed a lot for us. They have families to support.
LINDA: Mother, if they can fire me, they can fire you too.
MOM: I'm the head of a household.
LINDA: You're a woman.

Linda's mother is clearly due for a comeuppance, according to modern feminist standards, so she too is fired the next day. In the meantime, Linda gets to the point about what is bothering her. Representing oppressed and unenlightened women before the advent of feminism, Mom suggests that Linda's anger is really due to disappointment at not being able to marry and start a family. "I'm not saying I didn't want to marry Mike," says Linda. "I'm not saying I don't want to have a family. I just think this isn't fair. That's it. That's all. It's just not fair for them to do this to me."

No, it was not fair that women, as such, were fired after the war. But it was also not fair that men, as such, were drafted into combat during the same war. In this pilot episode, no mention is made of the draft itself or the fact that the population as a whole, including women, saw nothing discriminatory in drafting men but not women. The implication is that injustice was done only to women. And no mention is made of a more practical matter. Having learned something from the Bonus Marchers of 1930, the government realized that men ordered to risk or even sacrifice their lives for the country were unlikely to remain submissive if they survived and found no reward – at the very least, to work at the jobs they had been forced to abandon.

Had the creators of this series taken history as seriously as they take current sexual politics, they would have presented an equally good argument for giving jobs to returning GIs. Instead, they put this argument into the mouths of three discredited characters: a naive mother, a flighty girlfriend who wants only to find a man to support her, and a racist factory foreman who grudgingly offers to take on the returning black soldier as a janitor. The point that really must be made here is that "two wrongs don't make a right." Yes, it was wrong to force women from their jobs. And yes, it was wrong to force men into combat. To oppose one must involve opposition to the other as well. The problem was not society's abuse of women but its abuse of both women *and* men. It is anachronistic to separate the two. From the beginning of the war, everyone knew that women were sought for work in the war industries for one reason only: to replace, temporarily, the men fighting overseas. Assuring the soldiers that they could expect, at the very least, to get their old jobs back in return for risking their lives was part of a social contract agreed to, albeit reluctantly, by the entire nation, including its women.

Christy, what could be called a "revisionist western," made its television debut in 1994. Like many made-for-television movies, it has a misandric tone. As Ken Tucker pointed out, "While [Kellie] Martin, [Tyne] Daly, and [Tess] Harper all represent strong, varied female images, the male characters tend to be either violent brutes or sensitive pretty-boys. *Christy* is obviously designed ... to cash in on the popularity of CBS's other frontierswoman series, the Jane Seymour vehicle, *Dr Quinn, Medicine Woman*, but it's not a cynical piece of work. Like *Dr Quinn*, the show suggests that it is women who are the harder-working and more civilizing inhabitants of this backwoods environment."[8] Not cynical? Well, selectively cynical – cynical when it comes to men but not women. Watching the pendulum swing back and forth, it is clear that revisionist history is not necessarily an improvement over the history being revised.

Although made-for-television movies are most notable in this context for their focus on women in jeopardy from men, some focus on women in control (despite opposition from men). For example, in *A Passion for Justice: The Hazel Brannon Smith Story*,[9] Jane Seymour plays the

crusading editor of a small-town newspaper in Mississippi during the
1950s. She is courageous and righteous. But every male character is
either inadequate (a husband who loses his job and provides no
substantial support) or evil (the racist sheriff, say, and the civic leader
who is supposedly her ally but, in the end, rejects her basic goal of
integration). The implication is that the civil rights movement was
supported primarily by women and opposed primarily by men. An
obvious cinematic counterpart is *The Long Walk Home.*

In 1995, *Masterpiece Theatre* presented *The Cinder Path*, based on
a novel by Catherine Cookson. This production, like *The Rector's
Wife*, is extremely disturbing and for the same reason. Charlie is the
son of a rich farmer in England just before World War I. He is a kind,
sensitive, and even beautiful young man. In one early scene, he cannot
bring himself to cut the throat of a pig. This earns him nothing but
contempt from both his father and Ginger, a farmhand of about
Charlie's age. Then too, Charlie cannot stomach the cruelty inflicted
by his father on the lower orders. When Ginger steals a book from
the library, his punishment is to crawl over a path of cinders. Charlie
is outraged. He cannot bear the thought of inflicting pain. At the same
time, he cannot bear the thought of disappointing anyone. It is clear
from the beginning that Charlie is willing to put up with almost
anything, no matter how much suffering is involved, to make others
like or at least accept him. But it never works. Kindness makes him
unacceptable. More specifically, it makes him unacceptable as a man.
Both Charlie's father and Ginger agree on one thing that transcends
their class differences: to be a *man* is to be selfish and ruthless.

But shame is not Charlie's only problem. Despite his looks, he is
unlucky in love. Victoria is the wealthy and beautiful but arrogant
daughter of a neighbouring farmer. For mutual gain, the two fathers
arrange to unite the families through marriage. Charlie, still hoping to
make his father proud of him, allows himself to be railroaded into
what anyone can see is an impossible marriage. The result is disaster.
Because Charlie is unable to consummate the union, and because
Victoria has never had any interest in him, she turns to other men.
But she has a younger sister who has long been hopelessly in love with
Charlie. Kind and supportive, Nellie would have been the ideal woman
for him. While Charlie is eaten alive by her sister, Nellie succumbs to
alcoholism and depression.

The main plot, however, revolves around Charlie's relationship with
Ginger. When Charlie sees his father killed by one of the farmhands,
he agrees to remain silent, partly because the man was trying to protect
his sister from being "taken" by the master. Ginger sees the same event
and uses his knowledge to blackmail Charlie. Eventually, Charlie

manages to throw Ginger off the farm, but viewers know – even if
Charlie does not – that they have not seen the last of this thug.

Charlie decides to leave Cambridge and run the farm. This, presumably, is the manly thing to do. For a while, it serves another purpose
as well: it gives him an excuse to stay out of the war. By 1916, the
British resort to conscription. Even though his class and education
would qualify him for a commission, Charlie is packed off to France
with all the other conscripts. (His sister is now forced to look after
the farm by herself.) As if things are not bad enough, Ginger turns out
to be his sergeant. Charlie endures his persecution stoically. And this
earns him respect, for the first time, from other men. Charlie's luck
seems to be changing. Maybe Charlie himself is changing. Now an
officer, the young man who ran away from the slaughter of a pig is
giving orders for the slaughter of other young men. He shows leader-
ship, risks his own life, and cares for his men.

Though he survives the war physically, Charlie is badly wounded
psychologically. Taking advantage of his condition, his sister tricks him
into signing away much of his inheritance. Still, the future looks
brighter than the past. For one thing, Charlie has finally stood up for
himself and divorced Victoria. Moreover, he has fallen in love with
Nellie. But Charlie has a secret about the war. When he tells Nellie,
she forgives him. But viewers (or readers) do not. That is the problem.

Cookson's main idea was to attack the class system. To do that, she
had to show that even members of the upper classes who *seem* good
are really bad. Either she herself or those who selected her book for
Masterpiece Theatre had another idea as well: to attack the gender
system. To do that, it must be shown that even men who *seem* good
are really bad. That is where Charlie's secret comes in. During the war,
Ginger shows up in his trench. Once again he has to address Charlie
as "sir." But even military rank cannot prevent Ginger from treating
Charlie with the contempt nourished by their years together on the
farm. The fact that Charlie is now an officer, snarls Ginger, has nothing
to do with ability. It has everything to do with class. Ginger threatens
to continue blackmailing him. And then, in the midst of enemy fire,
Ginger accuses him of being a loser. Charlie picks up his gun, pointing
it at his old enemy. Ginger smirks at someone he considers a born
coward. But this time he has gone too far: Charlie shoots him. Now,
presumably, he has become a man in his own naive eyes. At the same
time, presumably, he becomes a man in the eyes of viewers (or readers).
After all, he resorts to murder and gets away with it. He is no better
than his father, than Ginger, than any other male of any class.

The series concludes with a final commentary: "Am I the only one,"
asks the television host, "who feels sorry for Ginger?" Obviously not.

Otherwise, he would not ask this rhetorical question. Never mind that Ginger is ruled from beginning to end by lust for revenge on the *descendant* of someone who hurt him long ago. Even though Ginger treats his wife and children well, as we are told, he has two good reasons for treating Charlie so badly. For one thing, Ginger is a *man*. What more can you expect of a man? Besides, Charlie *deserves* punishment. He thinks he is better than other men. And that, the host tells viewers, is the message Cookson intended. But her message is not the only one men are going to hear. There are others. First, men who think that women are going to pin medals on them for being "sensitive" or "vulnerable" should think again. Second, men who accept the idea that they are innately brutal might just as well go on being brutal.

Any men who could identify with Charlie must have come away from this series feeling very angry. Among them, ironically, are precisely those men who are most eager to challenge the kind of masculinity that so troubles Charlie. These men have been *betrayed*. For once, they might have thought, someone was going to tell *their* story. Someone was going to acknowledge the pain of becoming a man, a decent man in spite of the social forces intended to prevent it. Instead, a tired old message is retold: even the best men are killers under the skin. Think of it: not one man in the entire production is worthy of anything but contempt. Some of the women are contemptible as well, but they are given the usual excuse – in a world created by men, even women can be less than perfect. This is not stated, but it is implied by the setting of violent struggles between classes and nations. Presumably, only men benefit from these struggles. Ergo, only men can be blamed for them. So Victoria, as a woman, can be forgiven for her selfishness. Even Ginger, as a member of the oppressed, or "feminized," class, can be forgiven for his macho brutality. But Charlie, it seems, cannot be forgiven for failing to see that all his attempts at decency are based on nothing more than self-righteous illusions.

The productions discussed in this chapter are *unambiguously* misandric. They cannot be dismissed by anyone with moral and intellectual integrity as "nothing more than entertainment." Once people accept the idea that men have been the historic source of evil, it does not take much imagination to go one step further and claim that men are the metaphysical source of evil. That brings us to the next chapter.

CHAPTER SIX

Dehumanizing Men:
From Bad Boys to Beasts

It's a case of serial sexual harassment: a dozen TV movies about women in jeopardy in the month of November alone. In NBC's "Deadly Medicine," a female pediatrician faces the loss of her practice, her family and her freedom when she's unjustly accused of murdering one of her infant patients. In ABC's "The Woman Who Sinned," a philandering housewife is falsely accused of bumping off her best friend, then chased around the house by the real killer. The messiest fate, however, awaits an innocent young dental hygienist in CBS's "In a Child's Name." She's beaten to death by her dentist husband, who tells the police – lying through his you-know-whats – that he caught her sexually abusing their baby.[1]

So far, we have tried to show that men are routinely trivialized in popular culture. It is time to up the ante by discussing the dehumanization of men in popular culture. In its most "benign" form, this involves the implication that men are evil, ontologically evil. To say that people do evil is merely to observe the reality of everyday life. Being human includes the ability and the need to choose between good and evil deeds.[2] To suggest that male human beings choose to do only evil, though, is to suggest that they *are* evil. Which is to say, less than fully human.

One newsmagazine show[3] tried to convince women that men, even those who *seem* friendly, are really subhuman. This was a documentary produced by the Canadian Broadcasting Corporation for its *Prime Time News*.[4] This "special report" is intended to deter sexual crimes. It focuses attention on Rick Acheson, who was convicted of sexual assault on two girls and sentenced to four months in prison. Later, he was convicted of raping a girl and sentenced to nine years. While on parole, he is alleged to have enlisted two girls as prostitutes. What to do with repeat offenders of this kind? According to one reviewer, John Haslett Cuff, this show "clarifies the debate and makes a strong case for either exterminating these brutes or at least keeping them locked up forever."⁵ Even Cuff, however, notices a characteristic problem in "documentaries" of this kind: "I have only one problem with the presentation of this story (a problem reinforced by the accompanying CBC publicity) and that is the idea that Acheson was an 'average Canadian boy next door ... raised in a normal family.'" Cuff identifies the problem correctly enough, but not the cause. He claims, "This is a pernicious fiction that news and documentary producers love to use (remember *The Trouble with Evan*) to enhance the thrill and mystery of their report, to give viewers a sense of participation ('Gosh, Martha, that could be our son')."

The real cause of this problem has nothing to do with sensationalism and everything to do with politics. To present Acheson as an "average Canadian boy" is, at worst, to suggest that *every* boy next door is a sexual predator. To be a normal man is to be "innately evil," a paradoxical term that could be rendered as "subhuman." More about that in due course. In the meantime, it is worth pointing out that the male rapists and murderers next door are *not* normal, even though they might appear to be.) They begin, as boys, with severe problems. According to the show itself, Acheson's childhood was not exactly normal. He was brought up in an institution with at least thirty children and considered "temperamentally difficult" from the time he arrived. Even as a teenager, he had begun posing as a police officer in order to molest girls. A cynical viewer would suspect that this show has made a strategic breakthrough by deliberately suggesting that everyman – every man – is a rapist just below the surface. Whether intentional or not, that is the effect.

Now, consider what those in the entertainment industry call "jeps" – made-for-television movies focused almost exclusively on women in jeopardy from men. Generating sympathy for women as plucky victims is big business. On *very* rare occasions, it is true, the villains are women. In *Dying to Love*,⁶ a lonely divorcé suffers at the hands of a malevolent woman who answers his ad in newspaper. In *Men Don't Tell*,⁷ the protagonist is a hapless husband who, beaten repeatedly by his wife, is ashamed to admit this to family, friends, or the police. (For some reason, these movies were broadcast by the same network during the same week.)

But when productions do cast women as villains, very often, feminist reviewers take the opportunity to excuse their behaviour. *Butterbox Babies,* a Canadian "fact-based" production, is about a Nova Scotian midwife, Lila Young, who takes in babies not wanted by their mothers. Unfortunately, she kills dozens of them and buries them in wooden butter boxes in her own backyard. The movie includes an indictment of the medical community. When Young botches a delivery, the mother dies. After the autopsy, doctors uncaringly toss the body into a cheap coffin and wash their hands, as it were, of the whole mess. "If Lila Young was reckless," opines Barbara Righton, "the medical community was uncaring and hypocritical." According to her, the incompetent midwife and the uncaring doctor are on the same moral level. But Young is more than incompetent. She is murderous. Nevertheless, Righton concludes her review by shifting attention away from this. "*Butterbox Babies* ... serves as a lasting indictment of a society that made Lila Young necessary."[8] Necessary? Since when is it "necessary" to murder babies? Was Young really just a victim? If we say that, then our society deserves to be condemned far more severely than for ostracizing unwed mothers.

Four of these fact-based stories, featuring female villains, were broadcast in the early spring of 1992. CBS's *Murder in New Hampshire*[9] is about a New England teacher who seduces a boy in her class and manipulates him into killing her husband. ABC's *Stay the Night*[10] is about a Georgia mother who steals her daughter's boyfriend and manipulates him into killing her husband. CBS's *In My Daughter's Name*[11] is about a rape victim's mom who takes the law into her own hands; and CBS's *A Woman Scorned: The Betty Broderick Story* is about a jealous woman who murders her ex-husband. But even these women are not portrayed unsympathetically. In the first place, their deviant behaviour is usually attributed very carefully to their own victimization. Ergo, presumably, it is not entirely their fault. Though not exactly innocent, they are still either victims (the seductive mother in *Stay the Night* is a victim of domestic violence; her daughter is raped by her father) or those who act on behalf of victims (the mother in *Daughter's Name* avenges her daughter's rape).

In an unusual about-face, CBS has admitted in effect that sympathy was inappropriately directed towards Betty Broderick in *A Woman Scorned*. The sequel, *Her Final Fury: Betty Broderick, the Last Chapter*,[12] was an attempt to make this clear. Meredith Baxter, who played Broderick in both movies, observed in an interview that she had originally had a great deal of sympathy for this woman who had put her husband through school, cared for their four children, and then discovered that she had been replaced by a younger woman.[13] Even though Baxter eventually had enough sense and courage to admit that she had been wrong, it is sobering to realize that she and millions of other women had believed otherwise. For them, Broderick, a manipulative woman who managed to get $16,000 a month from her ex, was the victim, not the person she coldly and deliberately murdered. These viewers had been comfortable with the notion that abandoning a wife might as well be a capital offence.

Then too, the deviant behaviour of female killers might be psychologically irrelevant to viewers. Evil women, such as the seductive mother in *Murder*, are still assertive women. No matter how inappropriate their choices, they nevertheless make choices. From the perspective of many viewers, nothing else really matters. Feminism, after all, is about autonomous choices for women (although almost all feminists would refrain from choosing murder).

In jeps, finally, the victims of evil women are very likely to be other women. Exceptions are made in *A Woman Scorned*[14] and *Murder in New Hampshire*. Nonetheless, *Stay the Night* is more characteristic of this sub-genre. The primary victim in *Stay the Night* is a man, but he is seen in only one or two brief sequences before being murdered. His wife plans the murder by manipulating her naive teenage lover into executing it for her. He is thus a secondary victim. But his mother is the one who seems to suffer most! Cinematically, therefore, she is the primary victim: the movie is about her. The boy is seen far less often than his mother, and when he is seen, it is difficult to sympathize with him. He is either too stupid to understand what is happening to him or too depraved even to consider the moral implications of what he has done. In prison, moreover, he seems concerned only about his lover. Not once does he talk about his own pain, except for missing her. Eventually, he tries to improve his circumstances by telling investigators that he was seduced and manipulated into murder, yet viewers are given no indication that he is suffering. Instead, they are told at the end that in real life he is productive and presumably happy in prison. The female villain is given at least some claim to sympathy, having been a victim of domestic violence and a helpless spectator at scenes of incest, but the male victim is *denied* much of his claim to sympathy, revealing little remorse for taking the life of someone else and little despair at the thought of spending the rest of his life in jail.

So, what about all these female victims? Journalists have commented on their prevalence in made-for-television movies. In an article for *Newsweek*, "Whip Me, Beat Me ... and Give Me Great Ratings: A Network Obsession with Women in Danger," Harry Waters observes: "It's a case of serial sexual harassment: a dozen TV movies about women in jeopardy in the month of November alone."[15] Richard Zoglin points out that to be presented as primary victims, female characters need not be the direct target of male villains:

Even when misfortune befalls others, it is the woman who seems to bear the burden. In ABC's *Stranger in the Family*, a teenager is stricken with amnesia after an auto accident. But the drama focuses on his mother (Teri Garr) and her efforts to recapture her "lost" son. In CBS's *My Son Johnny*, Rick Schroder

plays a small-time hood who has brutalized his younger brother from childhood. Again, Mom (Michelle Lee) is the star sufferer: she is forced to recognize
that she has raised a bad boy. Then there is the woman as surrogate victim.
In NBC's *She Says She's Innocent*, Katey Sagal is the mother of a teenager
wrongly accused of murdering a classmate. In one scene, Mom pays a consol-
ing visit to the dead girl's parents. "Your daughter murdered my baby!"
screams the mother in reply. "Now there's only one thing I'm living for, and
that is to watch you suffer!"[16]

Both daughters are innocent victims too. The list of movies like this
could go on and on. Almost any night of the week, viewers can watch
innocent but vulnerable women go through the following cycle: caring
diligently for their families and achieving their professional goals;
worrying patiently over some danger sign; suffering patiently or
screaming defiantly; fighting back with courage and intelligence; and
finally, overcoming their evil or psychotic male adversaries.

The vogue for movies about women in jeopardy began with a
theatrical release, *The Burning Bed* (Robert Greenwald, 1984). In that
movie, Farrah Fawcett plays a battered wife who eventually sets fire
to the gasoline-soaked bed of her sleeping husband. According to the
ratings, this movie was extremely successful. Not surprisingly, it
inspired many film imitators (and several cases of domestic violence in
real life too). Even so, it was only with the more recent proliferation
of both made-for-television movies and attempts to justify these generally shoddy and unimaginative productions as "fact based" or "relevant" that the "jeps" emerged as an identifiable genre comparable to
the notoriously cliché-ridden "disease-of-the-week" genre. Wrote
Harry Waters: "And of the approximately 250 [made-for-television
movies] set for this season, nearly half show women undergoing – and
overcoming – some form of physical or psychological mistreatment.
When network honchos listen to a movie pitch these days, the first
thing many say is 'Where's the jep?' (The second is '*More* jep!')"[17]

Almost by definition, jeps are about female victims (who become heroines) *and male villains*. Beginning on an ironic note, Waters explains:

Eager to enhance TV's reputation for fairness and balance, the purveyors of
jep portray contemporary men as homicidal husbands (ABC's "False Arrest"),
abusive lovers (NBC's "Wild Texas Wind"), alcoholic fathers (ABC's "Keeping
Secrets"), sadistic sons (CBS's "My Son Johnny"), psychotic doctors (ABC's
"Deadly Intentions"), sex-crazed hospital orderlies (CBS's "The Rape of
Dr Willis"), even diabolical college professors (CBS's "Victims of Love"). When
the genre's males aren't oppressing women directly, they're messing up their
children. Rape is a popular device. NBC's "A Mother's Justice" presents a

woman so obsessed with nabbing her daughter's rapist that she puts her own body on the line. Wrongful imprisonment is another. In CBS's "Locked Up: A Mother's Rage," a single mom gets framed by her drug-dealing boyfriend and, while serving time, learns that her three kids have fallen apart.[18]

According to Carole Lieberman, a psychiatrist and media consultant in Los Angeles, both men and women in the entertainment industry are responsible for pushing stereotypes of women at risk. Women, she observes, have created some of the scariest ones. "A lot of them feel anger toward other women in television who are getting more attention or who are more sexually desirable ... It's a clear example of *jalousie de femme.*" On the other hand, she believes that "as men feel more threatened about women gaining power in the TV workplace, putting women in jeopardy fulfils their sadistic fantasies about maintaining control."[19] According to Mark Harris, "It's tempting to read sexism and degradation into these plots, in which women are either agents of brutality or targets of violence. But what's going on here is less a media conspiracy than a product of two ineluctable forces: hungry audiences and hungry actresses."[20] Of importance here is not so much why these movies are produced but why they are so popular. Or, to put it another way, why they are so common.

Given the economics of commercial television, we must assume that these movies are watched and appreciated by a pool of viewers large enough to make money for the sponsors. Many of them are women. According to the Neilsen ratings, adult audiences on "typical" autumn evenings are about 58 per cent female. That figure rises to 61 per cent for dramas such as made-for-television movies. The result, according to Zoglin, is that "the vast majority of network movies and mini-series are aimed squarely at female viewers."[21] But precisely which women? Waters tries to answer this question by focusing attention on what these movies seem to be saying about women themselves. "What today's women want," he avers, "at least from their made-for-TV movies, is to watch other women suffer." Zoglin comes to the same conclusion. These movies, he continues, "put women in the time-tested role of victim."

But why would women want to see other women suffer? There are at least two explanations for the appeal of jeps to women. Both involve feminism, not masochism. The female characters who suffer on television are victims only at first. Inevitably, they turn into heroines. Waters notes that women like these movies because "the sufferer ultimately emerges victorious."[22] Similarly, Zoglin observes that these movies "focus on strong characters who, for all their troubles, triumph in the end. The dramas become parables of feminist self-realization."[23] But they are also parables of feminist misandry. What neither Waters nor Zoglin suspects is that the same viewers who want to see women as victims (as long as they end up healthy and happy) might want also to see men as victimizers (as long as they end up dead or in jail). What women enjoy watching is the confirmation of their attitudes towards both themselves and men. Women are good, they believe, and men evil. Whether consciously or subconsciously, these women have adopted as part of their identity a basic premise of misandric feminism. Not only are women the chief victims (and heroic icons) of society but men are their chief victimizers. Unless accompanied by an emphasis on the brutality of men, the emphasis on the suffering of women would be not only psychologically damaging to female viewers but politically meaningless to them as well. Watching the brutality of male characters night after night on prime-time television has a therapeutic value for many women. It provides a psychologically satisfying explanation for the cause of suffering. More than that, it provides a culturally accept- able source for suffering and evil. In short, it supplies an underlying order in the midst of apparent chaos. This popular re-presentation of reality makes possible – whether consciously or subconsciously, inten- tionally or unintentionally – the translation of misandry from an academic preoccupation to a mass movement. So much for the theory of female masochism.

Consider the problem of identity more closely. That women want to see female images of courage, endurance, and victory – or, at the very least, survival against the odds – should surprise no one: "If viewers indeed emulate what they see, few sights could be more salutary for women than that of gutsy, resourceful females figuratively untying themselves from the tracks."[24] And because many viewers are ready to emulate these heroines, a toll-free number for women's shel- ters, clinics, or support groups is almost always flashed onscreen after the closing credits. Obviously, these movies serve a real need. But whose need? And at what cost? Or whose cost?

Even observers who foresee a problem seldom identify it correctly. Mark Harris, for example, is sceptical of the idea "that the TV blood- bath represents a giant stride forward for feminism." Instead, "the format is rapidly heading toward ... well, overkill."[25] He is wrong on two counts. First, the format really does promote *misandric* feminism, even though that is not always obvious. And second, the result is more likely to be increased hostility from men, not mere boredom for viewers. According to Waters,

All that uplift ... comes at a potentially grim price. Studies have shown that heavy viewers of TV violence – and the jep genre reeks with it – overestimate the odds of being victimized in their own lives. "They inhabit an exaggerated mistrust of strangers, the urge to buy a new lock or a gun," says George Gerbner, dean emeritus of the Annenberg School for Communication. "I call it a 'mean-world syndrome.'" Such fears, Gerbner's studies have found, are especially acute among today's women viewers. While that's partly attributable to the rising rate of violence against women in real life, there's a more artificial explanation. For every female perpetrator of violence on TV, there are half again as many female victims. The possibility that jep films are helping to turn women into cringing paranoids doesn't faze Steve Krantz, the executive producer of "Deadly Intentions." "Though I hate the notion," says Krantz, "it's prototypical of women's role in society to see themselves as victims. So there's a high identification factor.[26]

To the extent that television movies "teach" viewers anything, they do so most effectively in noncognitive ways – which is to say, intuitively or subliminally. And the "lesson" is more likely to be about *identity* than morality.

Viewers identify themselves with the archetypal figures seen onscreen night after night just as their ancestors did when listening to folktales around the campfire or myths on sacred festivals. But – and this is extremely important – *male* viewers identify with male characters just as surely as female viewers do with female characters. Women are encouraged to identify with female characters in jeopardy from men, but men are encouraged to identify with male characters who *put* women in jeopardy. Even more problematic than female viewers, we suggest, are these male viewers.

At a time when virtually all positive sources of masculine identity have been sexually desegregated, some boys and men will inevitably turn to the remaining negative ones. Because traditional sources of identity for men have been severely undermined or even attacked by a society preoccupied almost exclusively with the needs and problems of women, many men are left with whatever sources happen to be supplied by popular culture. What the jeps say about men probably affects women directly, however, and men indirectly. The jeps are aimed at women. It is reasonable to suggest that what they say about men has at least some effect on the way female viewers see men. The jeps are not aimed at men. But because these made-for-television movies are heavily advertised, it is reasonable to suppose that many men are aware of them. Even men who are unaware, though, must still react to the expectations of women whose impressions of men are likely to have been shaped at least partly by the jeps (and the cinematic versions playing at local theatres).

Popular culture presents men in many roles, doing many desirable things. Men are often portrayed as heart surgeons, or crusading lawyers, for instance, but so are women. And if women can do these things as well or better than men, how can these images function as indicators of a *specifically masculine* identity? They did in the past, it is true, but they no longer do. What has taken their place? Whatever women do not want for themselves, and that amounts to the force of evil. It should not take too much imagination to realize that those who produce these movies and those who promote them as "realistic" and "socially relevant" are playing a dangerous game indeed. Characteristic of our times is the conclusion drawn by both Waters and Zoglin, nonetheless, who consider the effect only on women: "The real violence that the jep genre does to women," writes Waters, "is to patronize their intelligence. With its unyielding embrace of happy endings, it proclaims that women aren't mature or sophisticated enough to sit for anything more realistic."[27] The effect of this genre on men is considered irrelevant.

Movies distributed to theatres are no better in this respect. Some seem misogynistic and are attacked as such in the press, but they are more correctly classified as misandric. Movies *about* misogyny, for example, can *be* misandric if they suggest that all or most men are like their misogynistic protagonists. In *Foxfire* (Jud Taylor, 1996), a bunch of female teenagers beat up a male teacher, threaten a male student with a knife, hold up a father at gunpoint, shoot a man (albeit accidentally), and so on. What these incidents have in common is not the hostility of women towards men but that of men towards women, because most of these male victims had already been harassing or even trying to rape their female victimizers. Without actually saying so directly, this movie legitimates revenge and vigilantism. It implies that women are justified in seeing all men as harassers, rapists, molesters, or predators of one kind or another. But some movies are much more obviously misandric. Included among these would be *9 to 5* (Colin Higgins, 1980), *The Witches of Eastwick* (George Miller, 1987), *Something to Talk About* (Lasse Hallström, 1995), and *The First Wives Club* (Hugh Wilson, 1996).

Like *Thelma and Louise*, *Something to Talk About* was written by Calli Khourie. Not surprisingly, it is another "empowerment play," as the euphemism has it. The story is simple (and very, very common by now). After Grace's marriage to Eddie falls apart, she heads home to the family ranch. There, she encounters her dictatorial father, her self-effacing mother, and her armour-plated sister. The women are all

emotionally damaged victims, the men all emotionally damaging victimizers. The unsubtle message is that women should assert themselves,
externalize their pain, and inflict it on men. Grace does this by shoving
her knee into Eddie's groin. "Seems to you," writes Richard Schickel,
that "you've heard this song before? Yes. But it is very sweetly sung
here. Khouri writes characters, not tracts; dialogue, not bumper stick-
ers; and she has the good sense to let the men have their say – notably
Eddie, who makes Grace understand that ... distraction contributed
to his wanderlust."[28] That does not make him much less inadequate,
though, or the movie much less misandric. Schickel himself writes that
this movie, more than those that rely directly on ranting, is "perhaps
more intricately subversive in its assault on American patriarchy ...
[The movie] never lets its political correctness interfere with its delight
in human incorrectness."[29] Grace does give Eddie a second chance after
he repents for his sins. Well, that must comes as a relief to many
politically correct male viewers.

First Wives, adapted from a novel by Olivia Goldsmith, is very
similar. It is about three women, friends from school, who have helped
their husbands develop successful businesses. Each is dumped in middle
age. What to do? "This is not a revenge thing," says Goldie Hawn's
character. "This is about *justice*." The whole movie is about "justice,"
in fact, although that word is defined in a most peculiar way. "Armed
with that self-righteous, self-effacing semantic distinction," writes
Caren Weiner, "the three affluent middle-aged divorcées team up to
hit their exes where it hurts: in the wallet. The big bucks the movie
itself garnered – it grossed $105 million during its theatrical release
last fall – provided a high-impact pop-culture vindication of scorned
women and marked the coming-of-age of feminist comeuppance comedies, in which aggrieved heroines get mad, get even, and get laughs."[30]
Trouble is, getting even is *not* synonymous with getting justice. The
former is a psychological category. It is about feeling good. The latter
is a moral category. If the two always coincided, we would have no
need for courts.

At first sight, *Kids* (Larry Clark, 1995; written by Harmony Korine)
seems to be an indictment of society as a whole. If it is even remotely
realistic, then parents, academics, activists, and legislators should be
warned that the end of civilization as we know it is within sight. This
movie is extremely sophisticated. Entertaining it is not, but disturbing
it surely is.

These kids really are *kids*, physically no less than mentally and emotionally. The oldest looks approximately fourteen or fifteen, the youngest eleven. They are not merely empty. They are beyond empty. They

are human black holes. Just as some stars are so dense that they absorb light instead of giving it off, these kids are so empty that they absorb life instead of living it. They are zombies, really. In this way, they are quite different from their "elders," movie protagonists in their twenties. As depicted in the currently fashionable movies about "Generation x," those folks have the educational and financial resources to make worthwhile choices based on clear thinking; they are just too lazy or self-indulgent to do so. These kids lack any resources. As a result, they are amoral and asocial. Of interest to them is immediate gratification of the senses and nothing else. They do not suspect the existence of happiness in any deep or enduring sense. They cannot even recognize their own unhappiness unless confronted, as one of them is, with the immediate threat of death. That would require some ability to think. In this Pavlovian world, human beings are aware of their own existence only by responding to external stimuli. They gravitate towards anything that feels good at the moment: booze, dope, and sex. Tom Gliatto puts it this way: "The kids crawl from apartment to apartment, from cab to club, from indulgence to indulgence, depravity to depravity with lobotomized indifference, while rock music grumbles and blares on the soundtrack. Very depressing, yes. Yet even the most desensitized human being inevitably betrays some sign of inner life. These teenagers [however] are troll dolls, eyes like glass, on the road to hell. How can you be doomed and boring at the same time? *Kids* has been touted as shockingly empathetic, but it feels more like the work of a grownup having problems with his inner child."[31] But one character does betray a sign of inner life. More about that in a moment.

In spite of appearances, this movie is not cinéma vérité. The camera has not simply been placed on the street to record whatever passes by (although even that, as critics have pointed out, is not necessarily objective). This movie has a point of view. It is an interpretation of reality no less than any other. Apart from anything else, it says that teenage boys are more depraved than teenage girls (although it indicates that girls too are depraved). This claim might or might not be true. Viewers who agree, though, must rely on what they already believe on the basis of conventional wisdom. Viewers are manipulated on that basis.

Of all the characters, only one is depicted sympathetically – a girl, not a boy. But this movie is sophisticated. Even though all the girls are depicted as victims – the victims of boys – most are shown as willing participants in a "society" that victimizes girls. Still, Jenny is different. For one thing, she questions the promiscuity that her friends enjoy. She has had sexual intercourse, once, with the thoroughly base Telly. And it is she, of course, who turns out to be HIV positive. We have a reason for saying "of course": viewers would have been less likely to sympathize with the other girls, and not only because of their promiscuity. For one thing, the other girls are Hispanics; Jenny is the only "white" girl. The other girls are distinctly lower class, but Jenny, to judge from the way she speaks and dresses, comes from an upper-middle-class home and is probably destined for college. The net result is that viewers, including those most likely to examine the sociological implications of this movie, are set up to sympathize with Jenny. To some extent, they can sympathize with her friends as well. No one, however, can sympathize with Telly and the other boys.

Telly has not only dumped Jenny for other girls but also given her what amounts to a death sentence. At no point are viewers asked to consider the fact that Telly himself has the HIV virus, and the possibility that he got it from a girl. But even those viewers who do would be encouraged by the movie to argue that boys (represented by Telly) deserve it and girls (represented by Jenny) do not. In the end, Telly's friend Casper makes the misandric message of this movie clear. Even though Jenny is in a semi-comatose state, he has "sex" with her. He does not know, as viewers do, that she has HIV. That, presumably, is the ultimate revenge on boys. Rape becomes a capital offence.

According to one reviewer, "*Kids* may seem voyeuristic to some, it may eroticize young, shirtless males, *it may exclude girls' points-of-view* ..."[32] Yet the whole movie revolves around Jenny and *her* point of view. Another reviewer recognizes the movie's bias towards the girls: "The movie's female teenagers also have sharp tongues ... but they also arouse sympathy. Few films in recent memory have so clearly hammered home the vulnerability of young girls in this time of heightened sexual pressure and danger. Parents of daughters will be more than a little unsettled."[33] To be sure. But what about the parents of *sons*? What message does it give them? That their sons are vulnerable to lives of emptiness? That their sons are in danger from HIV? That their sons need a great deal of attention? Or that their sons are, well, innately evil and not worth worrying about?

It is true that the girls, except for Jenny, are delighted to talk about their sexual encounters in language little different from that of the boys. But their coarse talk is placed on a supposedly higher level than that of the boys. For one thing, at least some of the girls imply that they do not really enjoy sexual intercourse for its own sake; they demand the fantasy of romance in the form of lengthy foreplay. Others demand at least the pretence of emotional involvement in the form of statements about caring. The implication is that enjoying sex per se is dirty. Male. It can be made acceptable only in connection with "higher," female, things.

One or two girls make it clear that the real problem is practical, not emotional. In connection with the risk of pregnancy, it makes sense to hope for an enduring bond with the father. But being afraid of pregnancy or sexually transmitted diseases is based on *prudence*. Girls and women have always had good reasons for prudence when it comes to sex. Boys and men have not until recently. In fact, boys and men have always been carefully trained *not* to be prudent in *any* sphere of life. Otherwise, they would have been unwilling to take the risks necessary in combat or the other dangerous but necessary roles assigned to them. Prudence can be a virtue, but so can courage or even bravado. The point is that neither the boys nor the girls in this movie exist in a world that enables them to make moral choices. Both are motivated by pure self-interest. The girls want boys to behave in ways that could be described as morally responsible, but mainly because self-interest indicates that some activities might leave girls pregnant or infected. They demonstrate no sense of moral responsibility themselves. That would mean seeing life in terms of something other than hedonism. Neither the boys *nor* the girls see their lives in connection with a larger society. Neither the boys *nor* the girls are old enough to think seriously about marriage or families in addition to jobs or careers. And the impression left by this movie is that they never will be ready to do so. All the same, viewers are manipulated to feel sympathy for the girls but not for the boys. The girls are severely degraded humans. The boys are not humans at all.

No elaborate analysis is necessary to uncover the misandric core of *Dolores Claiborne* (Taylor Hackford, 1995), which is explicit. In keeping with its maritime setting, the predominant colour is blue. Not only is blue the colour of the mise-en-scène – the clothing worn by major characters, the buildings they inhabit, the sky above them, the sea – but a blue filter gives even warmer colours a blue tonality. This is in keeping with the atmosphere of coldness and foreboding. Flashbacks, on the other hand, have been filmed through a yellow filter. Ordinarily, that would indicate the warmth of nostalgia, but there is nothing warm or nostalgic about these flashbacks. Maybe the director's intention was to evoke a sense of irony.

The movie's prologue begins, as the epilogue concludes, with a shot of the sea. The camera gradually pans to a cliff. There, sprawling incongruously over the barren rocks, is an elegant mansion. Inside, a violent argument is taking place. Vera Donovan, owner of the house, is screaming at Dolores Claiborne, the housekeeper who has been looking after her. Suddenly, the struggle ends. Vera's crippled body is sent crashing down the stairs. Dolores passes Vera at the bottom and rushes into the kitchen. Finding a rolling pin, she returns to finish the job. But before she can do anything, someone enters the front door. What he sees is incriminating, to say the least: Dolores holding a weapon over the bloodied head of a corpse.

The story itself opens at an office in New York. Selena St George, a journalist, is working on a big story. Peter, her boss, fails to appreciate her efforts. In fact, he cuts out much of her most recent story. Their meeting is interrupted when she receives a newspaper clipping about her mother, sent anonymously by fax. Selena travels to Maine for the first time in fifteen years. Everyone in town knows her, partly because her mother has long been notorious as the chief suspect in a murder. John Mackey, the local prosecutor, is convinced that Dolores has struck again: first her husband, now her employer. Selena remembers how he intimidated her at the earlier hearing. Nothing in his attitude seems to have changed. For him, Dolores is just a statistic, the only murder suspect who got away from him. She will not, he tells himself, do so a second time. It was he who, spitefully, sent the fax about Dolores.

Because Dolores has not yet been arrested, she returns to her own home with Selena. For many years, she had been living at Vera's house. The house looks much like Dolores herself (whose name, by the way, means "sorrow"). It is ugly, old, worn, broken, decrepit. Mother and daughter spend much of their time fighting. Like John and everyone else in town, Selena believes that her mother murdered her father. She now believes that Dolores has murdered Vera too. Dolores denies both charges, but the evidence against her in this new case really does seem overwhelming. Hoping to continue on her story for the magazine and sick of rehashing the past with her mother, Selena decides to leave. When she calls Peter to make arrangements, he tells her that her story has been assigned instead to another woman.

Dolores did indeed kill her husband, and the implication is that he deserved to be murdered by his long-suffering wife. A lengthy flashback indicates that Joe is a boorish, drunken, violent lout. Dolores has no love for him but a great deal for Selena, saving up for the girl's education and putting every penny into a bank account held jointly with Joe. One day, she finds out that Joe has withdrawn the money and transferred it to his own account. She discovers that Joe has been raping Selena, moreover, which explains why the girl is so angry and remote. Dolores runs to Vera and begins to cry. Vera has been insensitive, but she takes some interest in this story. After all, she knows something about getting rid of husbands: a few years earlier, she murdered her own. Vera not only advises Dolores to kill Joe but even gives her the day off, so Dolores gets Joe drunk and provokes a fight. When he runs after her, she leads him over a hidden well. Joe falls in, of course, which is "death by misadventure" according to the law. But the result is not quite what Dolores had in mind. She is glad to be rid of Joe but not Selena; angry at Dolores for not having protected her from Joe, Selena finds it easy to blame her mother for his death. Yet somehow Selena can remember nothing about being raped (even though the act took place in the immediate past, not in early childhood). Dolores, now virtually a pauper, has no choice but to continue slaving away in the Big House for Vera.

When Selena is about to return to New York, Dolores gives her a tape recording of the whole story. Selena tells the prosecutor that his case is based on nothing more than circumstantial evidence. And she makes peace with her mother. The movie concludes with a short epilogue. Selena sets off on the ferry, once again separated from her mother. But now that makes no difference. She and Dolores have reconciled.

As a story, *Dolores* works quite well. And there is nothing wrong with a story about rape or incest. What should trouble us is the misandric subtext. Once again, every major female character is either a victim or a heroine or both (first one and then the other). Dolores has murdered, but only to protect Selena. She is nasty, but only because life has given her no reason to be nice. Even Vera, domineering and obsessive to the point of neuroticism, has a "good side." She is a bitch. She calls herself a bitch. But women are good or heroic in this cinematic world precisely *because* of their bitchiness, not in spite of it. The motif is stated explicitly on no fewer than four occasions. "Sometimes," says Dolores, "being a bitch is all a woman has to hold onto." For reasons of their own, both Vera and Selena repeat these words verbatim. On yet another occasion, Vera says the same thing in slightly different words: "Sometimes, you have to be a high-riding bitch to survive." Bitchery is not narrowly defined; it includes murder. "An accident," Vera tells Dolores, "can be an unhappy woman's best friend." (Exactly what her own husband did to deserve his fate viewers never learn; he appears on only one occasion and tries to ignore Vera, something that Dolores herself would like to do. No wonder the heroine is proud of being a bitch, so proud that she refrains from wiping the word, scrawled by some rowdy locals – boys, not surprisingly – from the front of her house. It is a badge of honour, not of shame, for all three female protagonists and thus for female viewers who identify themselves with them. Bitchery, viewers are told, is the result of victimization. Consequently, it is the ultimate source of solidarity among women. In spite of Vera's inadequacies as an employer, Selena makes it clear that "these two women loved each other." This means that Dolores would have had no reason to kill Vera. What they had in common was their discovery of what in this cinematic world amounts to a law of nature: as Vera says, "It's a depressingly masculine world that we live in."

Meanwhile, every male character is either a victimizer or a collaborator or both. Because this movie has not one major male character, the criteria must be applied to minor ones. Joe is a depraved villain. How did he come to be that way? No attempt is made to explain. Why bother even asking the question – he is a man. Peter is a worthless cad. The implication is that he has replaced Selena not only at the office but also in bed. John is a corrupt lawyer, more interested in his own reputation for winning cases than in justice. Keeping score is what counts for him. Inevitably, someone tells him, "John, this is your ball game." His only facial expression is a smirk. And the too-well-mannered bank manager, though seen for only a few seconds of screen time, is just as sinister. He could have contacted Dolores when Joe began withdrawing money from the joint account. It never occurred to him that Joe might be dishonest, even though most people would have taken one look at Joe and thrown him out of any respectable place of business, so he is surprised when Dolores asks, "It's because I'm a woman, isn't it?"

Dolores is what used to be called a "message picture." The story and characters exist not to stir the imagination but to impart a lesson. A sign on the ferry carrying Selena to and from the island, displayed prominently onscreen, does it concisely: "Report all your injuries." The implicit reference is to those injuries men inflict on women. More specifically, the reference is to domestic violence. In short, this movie promotes the "abuse excuse." Have we come to this? People who resort to murder under duress are to be pitied, yes, but surely not admired. The legal system should be reformed, if necessary, to help them, not scorned to encourage vigilantes.

Deceived (Damian Harris, 1991) is burdened with an excessively convoluted plot but nevertheless makes the same point. To women, it says the following: Watch out, for you never know what evil lurks beneath the surface of even the most charming man. Once again, this message might not be apparent at first. At one level, *Deceived* is simply a common thriller. At another level, however, it is a carefully constructed world in which men are psychopathic monsters and women their innocent but resourceful and eventually triumphant victims.

In the prologue, Adrienne Davis rushes down a crowded street in New York to meet Adam Lucas, her blind date. Little does she know just how blind she is. Waiting for Lucas, who never shows up, she notices a handsome young man sitting alone nearby. She tells the waiter to ask him if he is Lucas. But his name is Jack Saunders. Next day,

Jack appears at the museum where Adrienne works. He is a dealer in antiquities. After a few seconds of shop-talk, the two get down to the more important business of arranging a date. By that time, they are singing their favourite song, "Earth Angel," with its words that will prove prophetic: "I'm just a fool, a fool in love."

Fast-forward five years. Their daughter is having a birthday party. Mary and her father, like Adrienne and her husband, have the kind of relationships most feminists would consider ideal. Jack even offers to cook dinner, although he actually orders it from a restaurant. With their prestigious jobs in the art world, their domestic servant to take care of unpleasant tasks, and their happy sex lives, they clearly live in yuppie heaven. The trouble is, things are not what they seem.

Life at the museum takes a nasty turn when Thomas, one of the curators, is murdered. At the moment of his death, he had been testing the authenticity of an ancient Egyptian necklace bought from Jack. Not coincidentally, this (fake) antiquity is stolen at the same time. Life at home takes a nasty turn too when Adrienne begins to realize that Jack has lied to her about making a business trip to Boston. Her friend Charlotte mentions that she has just seen Jack in New York, at a lounge in the Chesterfield Hotel. And, going through his suit, Adrienne finds a candy marked "Chesterfield Hotel." When Jack returns, he brings her a negligee. Soon after, Adrienne is contacted by a New York boutique called Vogue Lingerie to say that Jack has left his credit card there. But Jack has an excuse for everything. He is insulted by Adrienne's insinuation that he has been having an affair and picks up his briefcase and storms out. It does not take viewers as long as Adrienne to put the pieces together. Searching Jack's briefcase for clues to explain his mysterious trip to "Boston," she fails to notice the necklace that falls out and lands in a dark corner. Clearly, it was Jack who killed Thomas in order to avoid exposure as the source of fake antiquities.

When viewers next see Jack, he is picking up a hitchhiker. The two drive off into the country during a snowstorm. Suddenly, the car lurches off the road, through a barrier, and down into a field where it explodes. After the funeral, Adrienne finds that she cannot collect any insurance because her husband's social security number belonged to someone who died years earlier. She decides to investigate. Jack had told her that he was from Nebraska. Relying only on that information and the date on which this other Jack Saunders had died, Adrienne finds that a Jack Saunders did indeed die in a Nebraska plane crash. But his picture is not that of her husband. On the back of *her* Jack's picture, however, she reads the words "John Garfield High School, Brooklyn, New York." She continues her search at the school board's archives. She finds the records there for Jack Saunders, but also the

high-school yearbook with a picture of her husband. His real name
was Frank Sullivan. Adrienne now visits Evelyn Saunders, the real
Jack's cousin. Evelyn tells Adrienne that she had been fond of Jack's
best friend, Frank, but that he had been an enigmatic loner. And since
Jack's death, she had heard nothing from Frank. Evelyn adds that
Frank came from an extremely poor, unhappy family. Later that night,
Evelyn calls Adrienne with a bit of information about the whereabouts
of Rosalie Sullivan, Frank's mother. Adrienne's subsequent visit with
Rosalie is depressing. An alcoholic living in extremely sad circumstances, she tells Adrienne that Frank was the worst thing that ever
happened to her, that he might just as well have been truly dead all
these years. Adrienne leaves her card with Rosalie in case she can do
something to help her.

But wait. Frank is alive and still trying to find the necklace! Night
after night, he lurks in the shadows, waiting, watching, searching. One
day, he murders the housekeeper, Lillian, so that he can continue his
search of the house. In the meantime, Adrienne has received a message
from Rosalie and rushes to her apartment. When she gets there, she
finds Frank instead. He has just murdered his mother and hidden her
body in the bedroom. After explaining his continued good health to
Adrienne, he tries to convince her that he still loves her. And he asks
her to give him the necklace: otherwise, he says, she and Mary will
be in danger from one Daniel Sherman, who originally sold it to the
museum. (Adrienne had already come across the name once before on
a business card in Frank's pocket. At the time, just before he left for
"Boston," Frank had explained the card as one of the many that
business associates continually gave him.) Adrienne agrees, but she has
no more knowledge of the necklace's location than Frank.

Desperate, she asks her daughter, Mary. The girl says she has given
it to a friend. Adrienne hurries to the friend's house and snatches the
necklace back. While searching for the necklace, however, she had
found something else in Frank's briefcase: an identity card with his
picture but the name and address of Daniel Sherman! Adrienne goes
there and finds Sherman's "wife" on the phone. While she waits
Adrienne notices a family photo album – the same one she has at
home. The woman tells Adrienne that the picture of Mary is a picture
of her husband's dead sister. At that moment, Frank calls and asks for
Adrienne. He arranges a meeting with her, promising to bring Mary
(now his hostage) if she brings the necklace for him. Back home that
evening, Adrienne takes the necklace along with a knife from the
kitchen drawer and waits in the dark for what she hopes will be her
last encounter with Frank. He comes. He tries to kiss her. She stabs
him. He chases her. He corners her. And then he conveniently falls

down an elevator shaft. It is worth noting that this sequence is marked by the ubiquitous presence of chains and bars. Only Frank's death delivers Adrienne from the prison of her married life.

The epilogue is brief. Adrienne is preparing to move. Mary finds the family photo album and asks why it has not yet been packed. Adrienne looks through the pictures and tells Mary to put it with her things.

Deceived has only one major male character: Adrienne's husband, Jack-Frank-Daniel. In this closed, or self-contained, cinematic world, he represents most (though not all) men. And he is either evil or psychotic (which amount to the same thing for many people). He describes himself as a kind of machine that cannot deviate from the sequence of actions programmed into him: "I never intended to hurt anyone. I always do what comes next, no matter how difficult it is." In spite of his charming exterior, this man is empty. He has no identity. Moreover, he has no conscience. Threatening to kill Adrienne, he tells her without the slightest hint of irony, "That's love too."

There are only a few minor male characters. Of these, the most important is Adrienne's colleague at the museum, Harvey Schwartz. And he is a very minor character – so minor, in fact, that his onscreen appearances amount to no more than a minute. Why, then, consider him even a minor character? Harvey does have a function in this movie. He is given a name and a few lines of dialogue precisely in order to indicate his inadequacy. As an additional male character, he might have offered Adrienne some encouragement, advice, or support during her ordeal. That he offers only the most perfunctory signs of sympathy, that she herself expects nothing more from him, says something symbolically important about the world established within this movie. Harvey is not aligned with malevolent forces, but he is not aligned with benevolent ones either. To the extent that he represents men – that is, all those men who are neither psychotic nor evil – he is disappointing, to say the least. Two other male characters are still more minor. Thomas is too inadequate even to stay alive. Adam Lucas exists only as the name of someone who never gets onscreen. The message is that even good men are not much good. Or, as Adrienne herself says, "Everything I believed in was a lie."

When it comes to women, the situation is reversed. As the only major female character, Adrienne represents female viewers. And she is the innocent victim. In the popular imagination, though not by any logical principle, being a victim is tantamount to being good. However, it is the peculiar genius of misandric movies to link victimization with heroism. As a woman, Adrienne is not only the object of terrorism by a man but *also* the subject who takes control over her own life. She relies on no *man* to survive. Instead, she relies on women.

Because the story is told from her point of view, she being the one who is deceived, the most important minor characters are those who provide whatever she wants or needs. Lillian, the housekeeper, is paid for her services. All the same, she enables Adrienne to maintain her job and look after her family. Charlotte, her friend and colleague, supplies Adrienne with important information inadvertently. Even so, it allows Adrienne to begin to unmask the villainy of her husband. Similarly, "Daniel Sherman's" wife unwittingly provides her with a missing piece of the puzzle that is her life. Evelyn Saunders and Rosalie Sullivan, on the other hand, explicitly agree to supply her with information. Rosalie, like Lillian, pays with her life for being Adrienne's helper. All of these female characters are warm, friendly, and healthy. (The one exception is Rosalie, but she has an excuse: her life has been blighted by poverty, alcoholism, and neglect by her husband and son.) Most of them are victims of men. Frank's "other wife" is the victim of a husband who commits bigamy. Evelyn is the victim of a friend or lover who dumps her. Lillian is the victim of an employer who kills her. Rosalie is the victim of a son who is ashamed of her, deserts her, and finally kills her. The message is that women must stick together in protecting themselves from men.

One object is the symbolic key to *Deceived*: a fake gold necklace from ancient Egypt. Anything might have been chosen as the item pursued. That this one was chosen, therefore, is of particular importance. All of its identifying features say something about Jack-Frank-Daniel, the man who seeks it so relentlessly. Because it is a *man* (the only major male character) who seeks the necklace, it is (the majority of) *men* who are cinematically linked to whatever it represents. And because it is a *woman* (the only major female character) who opposes him, it is (the majority of) *women* who are linked to whatever the opposite is in each case.

As a fake object, the necklace is a visual metaphor of the movie's title. It is a deception, an illusion. On a surface level, it is associated with the fraud who produced or commissioned it and tries to retrieve it. At a deeper level, it is associated with the "majority" of men represented by Frank-Jack-Daniel. The implication is that men, as such, are valued only by naive women who forget an old adage: All that glitters is not gold. Indirectly, this movie symbolically equates the necklace with patriarchy. Supposedly produced by and for men alone, the ornament is nothing more than a glitzy but worthless and even sinister artifact contrived by men to seduce and exploit women.

Then too, it is Egyptian. As one of the first great civilizations, a primary source of the classical civilization on which our own is founded, an early adversary of the biblical civilization on which our own is founded as well, ancient Egypt has retained its strong hold on the Western imagination. But its actual history is irrelevant here. All that matters is what it has come to signify, correctly or incorrectly, in the popular culture of our time. For one thing, ancient Egypt is popularly associated with the mummies, funerary art, the pyramids, and other tombs. Men too are thus indirectly associated with death. It is generally believed that the cult of the dead was accessible only to the wealthy members of noble and royal houses.[34] Men, therefore, are indirectly associated with social and economic stratification. Remember that Frank originally began his evil ways by running away from his lower-class background, taking up his dead friend's more genteel identity, and marrying upper-middle-class women.

Egypt is associated also with the mysterious hieroglyphs, the enigmatic Sphinx, and the partly ruined statues of pharaohs gazing serenely and impassively into eternity. Consequently, men are cinematically linked to everything that is exotic, alien, remote, and inscrutable.

Even those only vaguely familiar with the religion of ancient Egypt, moreover, usually know that it centred on Ra, the sun god. By implication, men are symbolically connected with transcendence, sky gods, and solar cults; women, however, are connected with immanence, earth goddesses, and nature cults.

The Bible – or, if not the Bible itself, then movies based on it such as *The Ten Commandments* (Cecil B. deMille, 1956) – is the ultimate source for our most powerful images of ancient Egypt. According to the Book of Exodus, Egypt was a civilization based on slavery, tyranny, and cruelty. In *Deceived*, men are cinematically associated with those very things. But Israel's unhappy sojourn ended with the destruction of Egypt. Adrienne's husband pursues a necklace and, like the Egyptians who pursued Israelites, is destroyed. The message is that those who worship false gods – men – will come to an equally unhappy end. But unlike the ancient Israelites, this movie suggests, modern women have no intention of waiting for God to intervene on their behalf.

The symbolic structure of this movie, then, can be summed up as follows. Men are associated with culture, transcendence, sky, death, afterlife, hierarchy, bondage, tyranny, and cruelty. Women, by implication, are associated with nature, immanence, earth, life, equality, freedom, justice, and kindness. It is with this worldview in mind that the epilogue can be seen as a perfect summation of the entire movie. Freed from her husband, Adrienne is left with Mary. Mother and daughter – together, happy, and victorious – are at the centre.

Like the other movies we have been discussing, *The Silence of the Lambs* (Jonathan Demme, 1991) could be described as a feminist "discourse" on male violence. Here is a brief synopsis of the story. Clarice Starling is an FBI cadet. She has been asked by her supervisor to investigate the case of a serial killer known as "Buffalo Bill." With this in mind, she visits a maximum-security prison for the criminally insane to consult the brilliant and charming but psychotic psychiatrist, Hannibal Lecter. His knowledge of the human mind and insight into the nature of evil provide the necessary clues in her search for Buffalo Bill. Eventually, both Starling and Lecter get what they want: respect for her and escape for him.

There are at least three ways in which this plot touches on gender. The primary plot focuses on Starling's relationships with two killers: Lecter from the beginning and Buffalo Bill towards the end. Both killers are unusual in their treatment of victims. Buffalo Bill skins his, possibly to clothe himself in their identity. Lecter eats his, possibly to incorporate their identities. Because Buffalo Bill kills only women, the subtext is violence against women. Because Lecter kills both men and women, however, the virulence of this subtext is somewhat mitigated.

A secondary plot focuses on Starling's relationships with her male colleagues. In one way or another, all of them present her with obstacles because of gender. Dr Chilton, the asylum official in charge of Lecter, is openly lascivious. Starling's supervisor is not, but he lacks confidence in her ability as a woman to move in for the kill. Most of the others look on as if she were a freak for trying this kind of work in the first place.

A tertiary plot involves Buffalo Bill's confusion over sexual identity. In *Sleeping with the Enemy* (discussed in chapter 7) Laura Burney becomes a man symbolically, first by disguising herself and later by taking on the autonomy sometimes considered characteristic of masculinity. In *Silence*, Buffalo Bill symbolically "becomes a woman," according to Lecter, through fantasies of being a transsexual. Taken together – and they can be taken together for reasons both internal (the transsexual motif of "putting on" the opposite sex) and external (opening within a week of each other and rating within the top five at the box office for five weeks in a row) – these plots indicate that it is legitimate and even meritorious for a woman to take on the attributes of a man but unacceptable and even pathological for a man to take on those of a woman. At least one of the underlying assumptions is that women have good reasons for envying men but men have no reason to envy women. It is for this reason that feminine men have always been persecuted more harshly than masculine women. This mentality is common, ironically, to women who believe that women are oppressed but not men and to men who believe that men are naturally superior to women.

Even though the critics have given it little or no attention, this last theme might be the most controversial and disturbing of all. Buffalo Bill actually appears only towards the end of the movie. All the same, he is the centre around which the plot revolves. Who or what is this bizarre creature who murders women, "silences" them by stuffing Asian pupae down their throats, and then flays them? The answer must involve pathology originating in some attitude specifically towards women. He is probably not a gay man, someone who is emotionally and erotically attracted to other men. In our society, it can be said that gay men neither believe themselves to be women nor want to be women. Their sexual identity is premised on attitudes towards men, not women. On the other hand, Buffalo Bill could be a transsexual, someone who believes himself to be a woman trapped in the body of a man. Then, too, he could be a transvestite, someone who pretends to be a woman by dressing in feminine clothing. This character is based on that of a man who wears not only women's clothing but also women's skins.

In one way or another, however, Buffalo Bill's problem is probably related to a hatred of women. That is why he finds gratification in torturing Catherine and other female victims. This might be based on anger at Mother or, as in the case of Marc Lépine, who murdered fourteen women at the University of Montreal before killing himself, at Father (projected onto Mother).[35] Yet it is expressed as a kind of distorted envy. Not only does he steal parts of their bodies but he also hides a characteristic part of his own in one telling sequence.

Whatever the origin of his illness, Buffalo Bill wants to be a woman, not a man. At the same time, most people assume that "it's a man's world." But if being a man is such a privilege, why do all these men feel envy and fear of women? Why, in fact, do they want to *be* women? So far, very few scholars have asked these questions. Those who think about men such as Buffalo Bill in purely moralistic terms see no need to consider factors other than the good or evil choices of individuals. Those who think about these men in purely psychological terms often see no need to consider factors other than the psychopathological aberrations of individuals. But even those who think about these men in social or cultural terms, including political ones, often succumb to reductionism. They merely replace individual reductionism with collective reductionism. It is true that some men in our society feel very hostile towards women and that this can be due to negative stereotypes of women. It is true that those who promote prejudice through these stereotypes are guilty for doing so. And it is true that those who respond to these stereotypes by deliberately harming women are guilty. But these conclusions fail to account for the complexity of reality. Not all stereotypes of women are negative. Even if they were, not all men hate women. Of those who are motivated by stereotypes to hate women, not all allow themselves to indulge in violence. And of those who do engage in violence, not all are truly able to control their destructive urges. Scholars who fail to consider these things assume that the behaviour of men can be explained totally in terms of their attitudes towards women. They seldom, if ever, ask what it is about being a *man*, what it is about being *masculine*, that causes so much anger and pain.

The immense popularity of this movie is due at least partly to the fact that it corresponds closely to widely perceived notions about gender. The title itself, *The Silence of the Lambs*, is based on a series of interconnected gender-related symbols. Starling tells Lecter about a traumatic experience from her childhood. Having been sent to live at an uncle's farm after her father was killed, she was awakened one morning by the sound of lambs screaming in the slaughterhouse. In Christianity, the archetypal innocent victim is the "lamb of God," or Christ. In misandric forms of feminism, women are the innocent victims of society. Moreover, these "lambs" are "silenced" by men. Which is why Buffalo Bill stuffs the throats of his female victims. Even after they are dead, he must "silence" the "lambs."

It is true that Starling had been close to one man. She tells Lecter that her father had been "her whole world." Nevertheless, even he was inadequate. In fact, he was killed. What could be more inadequate than death? Men can be classified along a continuum from evil and effective to good and ineffective. In a world of this kind, Starling succeeds in her task alone. She gets hardly any assistance, and even some resistance, from male colleagues.

Popular film is one front in the war over gender, and so it is not surprising that even animated features addressed primarily to children routinely dehumanize men. A frequent complaint of feminists has been that "traditional" fairy tales such as "Sleeping Beauty" and "Cinderella" have given boys an unfair advantage. The heroes are oriented to action; they make things happen. Heroines, on the other hand, are oriented to passivity; things happen to them. Why tell girls that young women should do nothing but sit around and wait for rich, handsome young men to rescue and marry them? Those who ask these questions have a point as long as they ask another question too: why tell boys that young men must continually risk life and limb to protect or merely to impress young women? The problem is not passivity itself, since all people – men and women – must be either passive or active in accordance with the circumstances. The problem is that passivity has been linked with dependency and dependency with femaleness. At the same time, "assertiveness" is linked with independence, or striving, and that with maleness. Some feminists argue that the problem is worse for their own sex than for the other. Having too little assertiveness can hinder girls and women from taking charge of their own lives, building careers for themselves, and so on. But there are two sides to this psychological coin. Having *too much* assertiveness can hinder boys from establishing deep and trusting relationships or even exploring their own emotional lives. For both sexes, the problem is how to find a balance between "being" and "doing." Moreover, assertiveness conditions men to take risks – at work, at play, or at war – that can undermine their health or kill them. All in all, there are some good reasons for dissatisfaction with the gender stereotypes associated with traditional fairy tales.

By the early 1990s, it was inevitable that any fairy tale adapted for the screen would be considerably revised. Unfortunately, the needs of boys are seldom considered in those revisions along with those of girls. An example of this problem is Disney's acclaimed animated feature, *Beauty and the Beast* (Gary Trousdale and Kirk Wise, 1991), in which maleness is associated, both metaphorically and literally, with beastliness. There is a reason why *Premiere* selected it as one of the ten movies that defined gender in the 1990s. As Elaine Showalter observes, it was "Disney's first feminist film."[36] According to her, the movie actually succeeds too well. She finds it "a distinct letdown when the Beast turns into a blue-eyed prince. In fact, the tamed, blow-dried Beast, with his limply wilting rose, is already a bit too gentle for my taste. In such female Gothic novels as *Jane Eyre*, the heroes always wind up castrated. BATB [*Beauty and the Beast*] is still the world of Disney, in which couples live happily ever after, but I bet there are nights when Beauty looks at her prince and misses the Beast who got away."[37]

In some ways, this movie is brilliant. Critics have been unanimous in praising the revival of Disney tradition: colourful animation, memorable tunes, humorous dialogue, and delightful minor characters. The latter – transmogrified versions of objects at the prince's cursed castle – include a teapot and teacup, a clock, an armoire, a feather duster, and a candlestick who sounds like Maurice Chevalier. Some episodes are clearly intended as entertainment for adult viewers with a knowledge of film history: the kaleidoscope of dancing flatware and chinaware recalls countless production numbers in *Forty-Second Street* and other musicals choreographed by Busby Berkeley. Gaston and his followers setting out with their torches to lynch the beast in his castle recall similarly self-righteous vigilantes in *Frankenstein*. Belle warbling on a mountaintop strewn with flowers might just as well be Maria trilling on top of an

Alp in *The Sound of Music*. As with earlier Disney classics, moreover, this one takes an innovative approach to the story itself.

Like most versions of the fable in English, Disney's is based on a translation of the 1756 text of Jeanne Marie (Madame le Prince) de Beaumont. That in turn was based on much earlier literary works and oral traditions.[38] Almost by definition, folklore is constantly changing; even written versions of oral traditions are in a constant state of flux. The mere fact that this movie deviates from the "original" story (but also from at least one other filmed version) is not, in itself, problematic. Very problematic, however, is the particular way in which it deviates.

Traditional versions feature a good and handsome prince who has been cursed by a wicked fairy. He has been turned outwardly into a terrifying wild beast, unable to resume his former appearance until a woman falls in love with him. One day, a merchant gets lost in the forest, approaches a castle in search of help, picks a rose in the garden, and is immediately taken prisoner by its angry owner, the Beast. After much pleading, the Beast agrees to let the merchant go home if he agrees to return with his daughter as a prisoner instead of himself. Because it was she who requested the rose and was thus responsible for her father's plight, the loving daughter, Beauty, agrees. Her life at the castle is not unpleasant. The Beast is an educated and refined gentleman who gives her every comfort she could possibly want. All he asks in return is that she meet him every evening for dinner. Time after time, he asks her to marry him. Despite a growing fondness for him, she always refuses. Finally, the Beast agrees to give Beauty what she wants most of all: one more week with her father, knowing that she might use her freedom to escape forever. And Beauty does exceed her week. Then she looks into a magic mirror given to her by the Beast. She sees him weeping and pining away for her. Realizing now that she truly loves him, despite his terrible appearance, she returns and agrees to marry him. Suddenly, the Beast returns to his original appearance and the two live happily ever after.

The Disney version's basic premise is entirely different: the prince had been selfish and was consequently punished justifiably by a *good* fairy. He is described in a voice-over as "spoiled, selfish, and unkind." A beautiful enchantress comes to the castle door disguised as an ugly old beggar woman. When the prince refuses to let her stay overnight at the price of one rose, she turns this emotional beast into a physical one. In other words, his new outward appearance corresponds to his inner self. The Beast has until his twenty-first birthday, until the enchanted rose petals begin falling, to remove the spell. To do that, he must not only be loved in spite of his outward ugliness (as in traditional versions) but also learn how to love in spite of his inward shallowness (unlike traditional versions).

The Disney version has altered the cast of characters as well. A new character has been added: Gaston, the village bully and braggart. Vain, ignorant, arrogant, and preposterously macho, Gaston excels at hunting, brawling, drinking, and spitting. To his entourage at the saloon, he brags: "I'm especially good at expectorating." He excels at sexism, too. "It's not right for a woman to read," he tells his pals. "As soon as a woman gets ideas ..." Later on, he smirks with satisfaction over a vision of marital bliss that includes "my little wife massaging my feet." Unfortunately for Belle (that is, Beauty), Gaston is her most ardent suitor. Tired of the way he preens, postures, and prances around town touting his own magnificence, she laments the fate of one forced to endure "this provincial life."

But adding Gaston is not the only alteration to the cast of characters. The Disney version eliminates Beauty's evil sisters. In traditional versions, they are vain, snobbish, stupid, selfish (and, of course, ugly). With good reason, they are envious of Beauty's effect on others, especially on men. Beauty has all the good qualities they lack. Her name thus refers to both body and soul. The sisters ask for expensive gifts when their father goes off on a business trip, but Beauty asks only for a rose. The sisters deliberately conspire against Beauty, moreover, using clever deception to delay her promised return to the Beast. In the end, they are punished. Only a very faint echo of these sisters can be seen in the Disney version: three simpering village girls who do nothing but drool over Gaston.³⁹ There is a reason for these changes – a political one.

The traditional cast of characters in filmed versions of the fable generally includes at least two major male characters. The father is good but inadequate.⁴⁰ The Beast is ugly but good. Sometimes, another male character is added. In *La Belle et la Bête* (Jean Cocteau, 1946), Avenant is introduced as Beauty's suitor. He is handsome but evil. In a sense, therefore, he is simply the Beast's other side. These two modalities of male beauty – goodness and handsomeness – finally merge once more when the spell is lifted and the prince reintegrates both. The traditional cast includes at least four major female characters too. Beauty is beautiful and good. Her two (or more) sisters are ugly and evil. So is the fairy who puts a spell on the prince. (Some variants, on the other hand, include good fairy queens, dream queens, and so forth.) It all adds up to a balanced picture of both sexes.

Now consider some striking contrasts presented by the Disney version. It has two major male characters. The Beast is ugly and *bad*.

Indeed, he is bad from the beginning, even before being zapped by the spell, and only gradually becomes good. Gaston is handsome, on the other hand, but also *bad*. The father has been reduced to a minor character. He is a scatter-brained, Rube Goldbergesque inventor who gets lost and lacks either the courage or the ingenuity to prevent his daughter from sacrificing herself. Like his traditional counterparts, he is good but *inadequate*. In short, not one male character is unambiguously exemplary! Taking this movie on its own cinematic terms, women have little to choose from. The major male characters, representing men in general, are evil in either the bestial or sexist sense.

Things are quite otherwise when it comes to female characters. There is only one major female character, and she is flawless. Apart from her physical charms, Belle is good. She feels compassion for the Beast. She is intelligent, being a "bookworm." She is ambitious, wanting "so much more" than anyone else in the village. She is heroic, risking her own life for that of her father and talking back to the Beast. Most important of all, she is liberated. Belle rejects the fate of peasant girls who swoon over sexist men, pray for offers of marriage, and then turn into housewives. Only one minor female character is worth mentioning: the teapot, who openly defies her master, the Beast, by organizing a dinner party for Belle. In short, not one female character is even ambiguously good, let alone evil! To the extent that this cinematic world symbolically represents the real world, therefore, it could be said that men are either evil or inadequate while women are either good or heroic. And yet, one politically correct reviewer opines sanctimoniously that "there's a generosity of spirit blowing through the movie."[41]

Here, then, is the message to girls: Watch out for men. For one thing, they are inadequate. Gaston is attractive in one way but unattractive in every other way, for instance, and Belle's father is good but incompetent. Even worse, appearances can be deceptive. The Beast looks like a monster on the outside but is tender on the inside (at least occasionally). On the other hand, he was once handsome on the outside but arrogant and selfish on the inside. Any woman who wants a man at all must try to transform the base material of maleness into something finer. To reinforce this message, Disney has made use of not-so-subtle psychoanalytical hints. Consider the threat of sexual violence represented by wolves – that is, rapists – terrorizing Belle on her night ride to the castle, and the log battering ram – or phallus – used by Gaston's men to storm the castle. No message is given to boys about any possible threat posed to men by women (and there are threats, even if these are unintended by or even unknown to women).[47] The Disney version thus falls clearly within the scope of misandric popular culture that dehumanizes men.

In traditional versions, the Beast is interesting and even appealing in his own right. Indeed, he is often more important than Beauty – not only to boys but to girls as well.[43] Despite its title, this new version is not about Beauty *and* the Beast: it is about Beauty alone. In other words, a story that had once been addressed to *both* girls and boys, helping each learn something different, is now addressed *only to girls*. Belle is obviously a feminist from late twentieth-century America projected as a "fairy tale" back to what looks more or less like eighteenth-century France. In itself, this might be fine; girls do need to see strong and competent female characters onscreen. The problem here is not what this movie does for girls but what it does *to boys*. Disney's cynical concession to the "needs" of young male viewers is the occasional depiction of wholesale violence. Brief but frequent episodes of brawling – among male characters, of course, not female ones – occur whenever Gaston is ticked off by his drinking buddies at the saloon. A more extended episode of choreographed violence occurs when Gaston's lynch mob attacks the castle. And the movie concludes, after residents of the castle return to human form, with a violent squabble between the clock and the candlestick.

According to traditional versions, the Beast is thoroughly human from the beginning. He just looks like a beast. He knows how to love but must learn how to *be loved*. A male counterpart to the female protagonist of "Sleeping Beauty," he must wait for someone to love him (as he really is). It is Beauty who must learn how to love. She discovers the difference between sexual attraction, for instance, and true love. Although physical beauty is only skin-deep, spiritual beauty is not. Or, to put it differently, she discovers that beauty is in the eye of the beholder. It is a matter not of the object seen but of the way it is seen.[44] Only when Beauty herself is transformed by maturity can she transform the Beast by "magic." And she transforms only his outward appearance, not his inner being.

We have come a long way in just a few years. Although Disney's horrid Beast finally turns into a sweet prince, he is just another patriarchal villain for most of the story, a "grouchy bison" who growls and snarls at everyone who fails to obey him instantly. Actually, he is nothing more than a depressed version of Gaston. Both are archetypal villains for feminists, because they are not merely evil but evil in a way that is specifically and stereotypically male, masculine, or both. Because only male characters are evil in this cinematic world, and because both major male characters are evil, maleness itself is identified with evil. No wonder the chorus emphatically agrees when Gaston's flunky sings, "Every guy here'd like to be you." It is true, once again, that the Beast turns good – but only *after* Belle goes into action. She transforms him both metaphorically and literally from a beast into a fully human being.

So the problem with men is not merely cultural, according to this movie, as it would have been if men had been represented only by the hypermasculine Gaston. It is also ontological, because Disney's Beast, unlike his prototypes, was *inhumane* (not ideally human) even before he became *inhuman* (not human at all). Men belong to some alien species, by implication, until women work on them. Like the Beast who slops his food all over the table, men are supposedly "mean, and coarse, and unrefined" until women civilize them. And even then, the effort can fail: Gaston, irremediable and unredeemable, is therefore trashed by being thrown off a parapet.

To be sure, this movie says something "positive" to girls. Femaleness confers not only autonomy but also superiority. But it says something very negative to boys. Maleness confers dependence and inferiority. That this movie aims to suit the needs of girls alone, and at the direct expense of boys, is made clear even in advertisements. The hideous beast has been reduced to a puffy white cloud pouting ineffectually behind his castle. Neither the disenchanted prince nor the disenchanting Gaston is anywhere to be seen. The story is not about them. They exist only to provide occasions documenting Belle's self-liberation. Gaston certainly does nothing to encourage her in this direction.

True, Gaston is important enough to be given a song. In it, however, he merely shows viewers why Belle has already decided, against popular opinion in the village, to reject him and everything he represents. Nor does the Beast contribute anything to her voyage of self-realization. It is not his surface appearance that prevents Belle from loving him, according to Disney, but his *actual behaviour.* Long before meeting him, in other words, Belle must have already discovered for herself the true meaning of love. No wonder the Beast is not even given a song. Neither is Belle's father; he, too, contributes nothing to her self-awareness. Because he is more like a child, Belle has already had to figure out for herself the importance of protecting and caring for others. If there is any message at all here for boys, it is that they are superfluous at best and contemptible at worst.

Until very recently, scholarly interpretations of "Beauty and the Beast" tended to be universalistic. In the early and mid-twentieth century, for example, most writers saw the story in psychoanalytical terms, whether Freudian or Jungian. It represented, according to Betsy Hearn, "personal dualities of light and dark, reality and fantasy, animal and spiritual, male and female, alienation and reconciliation."[45] By "personal dualities," she refers to the ambivalence inherent within *every* individual, not to the projection of negativity on to some *other* individual or class of individuals. The Disney version, by contrast, is not only particularistic but also dualistic. It addresses the needs of only one segment of society, namely women, and also projects all negativity onto men. In Cocteau's version, Beauty confronts the "animal" in *herself* when she confesses: "I am the monster, my Beast!" In Disney's, a similar metaphorical displacement of the "beast" occurs but in a radically different context. After Gaston ridicules the Beast, Belle protests: "*You're* the monster!" For Belle, unlike either Beauty or the Beast, the source of darkness is "out there," not "in here."

So how is all this an improvement over earlier forms of gender stereotyping? According to some, it is just a healthy "alternative." But a healthy alternative for whom? And what about an alternative to sexism of any kind? Do we really have to encourage further polarization between men and women? Do we really have to keep swinging from one side to the other on a political pendulum? Would it have been so difficult to produce a fairy tale that affirms both femaleness *and* maleness? Those who justify a form of prejudice in this way are covertly saying that the "other side" deserves what "our side" has had to put up with. This is revenge, as we have already noted, not justice.

Both *Beauty* and *Aladdin* (John Musker; Ron Clements, 1992) are self-conscious efforts to present overtly feminist heroines. When *The Lion King* (Roger Allers; Rob Minkoff, 1994) opened, nevertheless, feminists complained of its "sexism," not because it hurled abuse at women, to be sure, but because it did not present a feminist lioness. One outraged reader of *Entertainment Weekly* put it this way: "I'm glad Disney got its massive money machine tuned up for its most recent business venture, *The Lion King*. Maybe it can take a bit of that pile and *start* making movies that say something true and good about the American majority: that is, girls and women."[46] Some people are never satisfied.

In this chapter we have discussed the dehumanization of men. They have been turned metaphorically into beasts – that is, into subhuman creatures. But the process of dehumanization can be taken one step further. On a metaphysical level, after all, men can be demonized. In other words, they can be turned into distinctly satanic figures and thus associated with an eternal, cosmic source of evil. The addition of that metaphysical dimension brings us to the next chapter.

Demonizing Men:
The Devil Is a Man

The era of the cult of masculinity is now approaching its end. Its last days will be illumined by the flare-up of such a comprehensive violence and despair as the world has never seen. People of good will seek help on all sides for their declining society, but in vain. Any social reform imposed on our sick society has only value as a bondage for a gaping and putrefying wound. Only a complete destruction of society can heal this fatal disease. Only the fall of the three-thousand-year-old beast of male materialism will save humankind.[1]

At the height of her career, Marlene Dietrich starred in a movie called *The Devil Is a Woman* (Josef von Sternberg, 1935). Even though women were identified with temptation and Original Sin, they were seldom identified with an evil metaphysical force or being. The title of this movie was striking because it did precisely that. Even though men were sometimes "absolved" of Original Sin – never mind that, according to the Bible, Adam was just as guilty as Eve – men have been identified with an evil metaphysical force or being. Or, to put it another way, the Devil is a man[2] (although this tradition might be changing[3]). Humorous greeting cards, in fact, often feature male devils, which might reflect the traditional sexual hierarchy: women have no power of their own. The fact is that men no less than women (though in a different way) have traditionally been associated with the forces of evil.

But in our time, something has changed. Returning to the conspiracy theory of history, we focus specifically on its metaphysical connotations. Women have discarded the "biblical" belief that their sex alone is to blame for Original Sin but have done so by reversal instead of elimination. Relying on carefully chosen archaeologists,[4] feminist theologians (and their secular counterparts) have turned the traditional interpretation of Adam and Eve on its head: men inherit from the primaeval patriarchs not only the power stolen from women but also the supernatural (in effect) inclination to continue oppressing women.

Filtered down to the level of popular culture, this mentality is often given very stark form. Male characters are not merely foolish or inadequate. They are not merely selfish or immoral. They are *demonic* – that is, both less and more than human. They are less than human in moral stature but more than human in the power they wield. There is a distinctly metaphysical undertone. The men portrayed are either explicitly or implicitly motivated by something more sinister and more disturbing than mere malice, neurosis, or even psychosis.

Men are demonized directly by portraying either supernaturally evil beings (devils) or preternaturally evil aliens (extraterrestrial beings), but they are demonized indirectly as well. The sheer number of movies and television shows featuring hideously predatory men, many of whom act for reasons that *either are not or cannot be explained entirely or adequately to viewers in rational terms*, has its effect.

Sleeping with the Enemy (Joseph Ruben, 1991) is based on a novel by Nancy Price. Although almost any film reveals cultural assumptions about gender, this one is of great importance here for two reasons. It is explicitly about gender. And it has been enormously successful at the box office.[5] Whatever it says about gender, millions of people are either prepared to hear what sounds like a legitimate observation on daily life or want to hear what confirms their political convictions. Well, what does it say? To answer that question, we must consider the chain of associations conditioning its interpretation. The plot is extremely simple. Laura Burney lives in constant fear of being beaten by her husband, escapes from him, is followed by him, and finally triumphs over him.

As the movie opens, viewers see Laura standing on the beach at Cape Cod. In the crimson glow of a setting sun, gentle waves leave trails of foam at her feet, and graceful gulls flutter overhead before settling in for the night. Dressed comfortably in a sweatsuit of undyed cotton, her hair flowing in the breeze, Laura merges with sea, sand, and sky. In fact, she brings to mind Botticelli's famous painting of Venus rising from the primordial surf. She belongs here.

Into this idyllic scene comes Martin, her husband. He is dressed formally in a black suit and tie. He does not belong here. Although the conversation that ensues cannot be described in terms of overt conflict, it clearly involves some tension. Both are evasive, as if hiding something. In any case, the tension erupts into open conflict shortly afterward. Walking along the beach next morning, Martin comes across a stranger. This handsome young man, a neurologist recently arrived from Boston, is tinkering with his yacht. He has already noticed Laura. Because both men enjoy sailing, they discuss the possibility of doing so together. Martin remembers that Laura is afraid of the sea and cannot swim, but he decides to ask her anyway. When he gets back to the house, though, he immediately accuses her of having flirted with his new friend. In fact, he slugs her.

Although the forecast is for calm weather on the night of their voyage, a storm soon overtakes them. Not only have the meteorologists failed in their dependence on technology but the two men fail in the same way in losing control of the boat. Meanwhile, Laura disappears. Martin assumes that she has drowned. Later on, he finds out that she spent months at the YWCA learning how to swim and had, in fact, planned to escape from him by "dying" in this way. Anyway, she emerges from the water and runs back up to the sinister house. She quickly dresses and picks up her bag, packed long ago. Before leaving, though, she throws her wedding ring into the toilet. When Martin returns, his mood is one of rage rather than sadness. Picking up the sculptured portrait of an ancient Egyptian queen – significantly, her face has been broken and battered over the centuries – he flings it through the window. The prologue concludes with Martin screaming for revenge against the sea – that is, against the natural order.

Viewers next see Laura on a bus heading into the agricultural heartland of America. Sleepy after a night of terror, she lets her head fall onto the shoulder of a man sitting next to her. She sits up straight immediately without acknowledging his presence. Later on, after he has left the bus, an elderly woman sitting across the aisle offers her an apple. They begin a conversation. Laura explains that she has been visiting a "friend" whose husband beat her. With a knowing smile, the other woman asks how long she, Laura, had been married to this man. Though brief, the conversation lasts long enough for the woman to impart some sociological information on domestic violence aimed as much at viewers as Laura.

Finally, Laura arrives in Cedar Falls, a beautiful little Iowa town that embodies the nostalgic vision of American life in earlier, happier times. Her first task is to settle in at her new house. (Presumably, money is not a problem.) After some dusting and cleaning, she show-ers. Then, from her bedroom window, she notices Ben, her neighbour, watering his lawn, singing and dancing as he does so. Their eyes meet. She smiles. When they next meet, however, it is under strangely unpleasant circumstances. He catches her picking some apples from his tree and reminds her that this is against the law in Cedar Falls. She dumps the fruit on the ground and goes home. Later, he comes to her kitchen door with a load of apples and invites her over for dinner the next day, informing her that he is very fond of apple pie. They get to know and like each other quickly after that. Because Ben teaches theatre at the local college, he helps her find a job at the library.

But Laura's reason for choosing Cedar Falls is not its associations with Norman Rockwell's paintings or Frank Capra's movies about small-town America. Her aging mother lives in a nearby nursing home. Laura cannot visit her immediately, because she is afraid that this might somehow provide clues for Martin. Indeed, once Martin realizes that she is alive, having been contacted by one of her friends at the YWCA and having found her wedding ring in the toilet, he sets off to find information from her mother. He tracks the two of them down without much difficulty. In the meantime, Laura does visit her ailing mother, sneaking into the home disguised as a man. This episode, like the one on the bus, is notable for its expression of female solidarity in the face of evil men. Laura tells her mother that she has escaped from Martin. Her mother smiles knowingly – the implication is that she, like the woman on the bus, has learned something about domestic violence from her own experience – and comments on Laura's self-reliance: "There's nothing any man can say or do that'll take that away. You have yourself." That is the most obvious message in *Sleeping*. No wonder Laura's father is not even mentioned. Whether dead or "missing," he is no longer part of the family unit and would, in any case, be superfluous or irrelevant. (And if that were the deepest or underlying message, we would have discussed this movie in chapter 5.)

Eventually, Martin reappears. The movie ends after a Hitchcockian episode during which his presence in the house can be felt as he silently and invisibly stalks Laura from room to room. At one point, Ben comes to the door, but Laura, held at gunpoint by Martin, sends him away. Having been told about her past woes and her present worries, Ben senses that something is wrong. He breaks the door down only to be knocked unconscious by Martin. But the gun is knocked out of Martin's hand at the same time, and Laura picks it up. After taunting her to shoot him, he dares her to call the police instead. She does. But she tells the police to come because she has "just killed an intruder." On that note, she pulls the trigger. (For reasons that will become clear in a moment, it takes several shots to kill him.) After Martin sinks to the floor for the last time, Laura goes over to the barely conscious Ben and cradles him in her arms. She has saved the day. Women must never depend on men.

Finally, in a kind of momentary epilogue, the camera picks out a ring lying on the floor next to Martin's body. It is the one Laura had thrown into the toilet during her escape, the one Martin had worn on his own hand as a personal symbol of his continuing control over her.

As a public symbol of marriage, its isolation on the floor indicates that marriage, as an institution designed to control and exploit women, should be discouraged or even abolished.

Like other movies, *Sleeping* is based on the assumption that viewers will make specific symbolic associations. This obviates the need to express a point of view in direct, verbal terms. But the symbolic associations of this one are morally disturbing for several reasons. To understand these, we must first examine the primary symbolic contrasts, what Claude Lévi-Strauss called "binary oppositions," and place them in their political context within misandric feminism.

Consider the portrayal of men in this movie. Viewers learn nothing at all about Martin as a person. Unlike Laura, he betrays not a sign of the ambivalence or confusion that is characteristic of all human beings. What kind of childhood did he have? How did he get to be so obsessive-compulsive? Why has he become psychotic? Viewers never find out. Instead, Martin is cinematically identified with two stock figures, archetypes or abstractions, in Western folklore.

Through his house, he is associated with Frankenstein. If Martin did not design it himself, he obviously chose it to reflect his own personality. Modernist architecture is based heavily on the glorification of technology. One of its earliest advocates, Le Corbusier, once described a house as a "machine for living in." Martin himself is a machine. In this context, it is significant that viewers see him working at the computer in his office and working out on his exercise machine. With his arms and legs racing up and down like pistons, he looks like nothing so much as a steam engine. Once "plugged in" and set in motion, he acts with the impersonal, implacable, and irrational efficiency of a robot gone berserk, a modern and secular *golem*, a yuppified version of the creature made famous by Boris Karloff. No wonder the precision on which he depends is thrown off balance merely because Laura fails to hang the bathroom towels evenly. Martin is thus the embodied spirit of this place. He is the incarnation, so to speak, of technology as an almost transcendent force. (It could be argued that Laura represents the benevolent aspect of nature and Martin its malevolent side. But like the shark in *Jaws*, as both a character and a prop, he would still be a "killing machine.")

Significantly, moreover, Martin is cinematically associated with Satan himself – in Western folklore, remember, the Devil is almost always male – as he prowls the carnival in pursuit of Laura. Wearing a black cape with upturned collar, he is shown against a noticeably hellish background of glowing, swirling, flame-coloured lights. This explains why Laura has to shoot him several times. Martin has *superhuman* strength. From the perspective of "goddess" revivalism, which has been popular in some feminist circles for at least twenty years, the links between Frankenstein and Satan are clear. Both are male. Both are about control or power. And both are evil.

Bearded and dressed in funky jeans, Ben has the happy-go-lucky mentality of a latter-day hippie. This might make him attractive, in another movie, because the hippies rebelled against the dreary, competitive, conformist world of businessmen. In this movie, however, playfulness represents not the freedom associated with play among mature adults but the manipulative "games" associated with play among immature people. Entertaining Laura backstage at the college theatre, for example, Ben "creates" a swing and a snowstorm for her, then continues playing by covering her with various masks, hats, and costumes. He swings her body back and forth in dance. Symbolically, therefore, he is yet another man who controls her. Possibly because she has still not completed the learning process that will take her to maturity (and perhaps beyond men altogether), Laura finds his easy-going camaraderie amusing. But when he expresses more than casual interest in her, she balks. Meeting her after work one day, Ben asks her for a date. Angered by this "aggression," she replies: "What is it with men?" Female viewers are thus encouraged to see Ben, like Martin, not as a person (one man in particular) but as an abstraction (men in general).

These two men are binary opposites, two ends of a continuum. All men, this movie suggests, can be located somewhere on that continuum. Martin hates women. He is a victimizer. He is manipulative. He is efficient, like a machine. And he is evil, inexplicably and implacably evil. In effect, he is a *demon*. Ben, on the other hand, likes women.[6] He is a victim, moreover, ineffective. But he too is manipulative. Therefore though not evil, he is not exactly good either. Even if he were good, he would still be inadequate. At best, he is an entertaining playmate. When it comes down to effective action in the world, he is a loser, which explains why he manages to burn the pot roast, lovingly made for dinner with Laura, and why he decides to use the front door and is thus caught off guard by Martin. Because Laura ends up holding Ben in her arms, it is clear that he needs her more than she needs him. Unlike her, he remains damaged at the end. The message here is that even relatively good men are amusing luxuries at best and unnecessary burdens at worst.

There are other men in this movie, but they all fit somewhere on the continuum defined by Martin and Ben. In other words, they are less evil than Martin but less adequate than Ben. Some of these men appear only as visual images. During a parade in Cedar Falls, we see some Shriners rolling down the main street in cardboard airplanes and cars. They are not presented here as grown men doing valuable work for the community but, condescendingly, are presented as little boys playing with their toys – their technological toys. Being Shriners gives them a legitimate excuse to prance around in funny costumes and indulge themselves in childish fantasies. In short, they are trivialized. Once again, even good men are, in effect, not good enough to be taken seriously. The same thing applies to the presentation of Martin's friend, the yachtsman. For those familiar with sailing, it is obvious that he is incompetent. Not only does he not know enough to go ashore at the sign of an approaching storm, he does not know enough to stay at the helm in rough waters. No wonder he loses control of the boat and falls into the water. When at sea, this man is truly "at sea."

Even though his appearance onscreen is brief, one male character deserves special attention here. When Martin arrives in Cedar Falls and tries to locate Laura, he discovers that she has a friend or lover who teaches at the college. But he finds the wrong one. Held at gunpoint in his car, the man says: "You don't understand. I live with another man." This episode does nothing to advance the plot. Why has it been inserted? Probably to give *Sleeping* a politically correct defence. Just in case anyone gets the idea that this movie condemns *all* men as either evil or inadequate, something that those who produced it must have known would be likely to happen, the point is made that *some* men are exempt from attack. Like women, gay men are often classified as innocent victims of "the patriarchy," which makes them honorary women. Ergo, the producers believe they can feel safe from accusations of sexism.

As for the rest of mankind – in that gender-specific category would be included heterosexual men, the creators of evil technology, religion, and art – their legitimacy as participants in the social order is dubious, to say the least. Because Laura remains interested in Ben, the implication is that men who behave themselves might be tolerated as friends or even lovers (though not as husbands). But because Laura never expresses the slightest concern for the yachtsman who must spend the rest of his life feeling guilty for her "death," the implication is that men can simply be used to serve the practical, reproductive, or other needs of women. The message is once again that women are autonomous and indifferent to men.

Now, what about another symbolic opposition, that between the sea (or beach) and the house in Cape Cod? In the ancient Near East, the sea was associated with chaos and death. Here, it is associated with more benevolent aspects of the natural order – the womb and the origin of life – which makes it the house's binary opposite: nature, softness, and tranquillity versus culture, hardness, and tension. The beach is associated with Laura, moreover, and the house with Martin. Given the associations prevalent among feminists such as Marilyn French, especially in *Beyond Power*,[7] the beach represents not only femaleness but also authenticity, harmony, and goodness. The house represents not only maleness but also artifice, technology, and evil. Isolated on the beach, the house is an alien intrusion in both the landscape and the seascape. Characteristic of the modernist architecture associated with Ludwig Mies van der Rohe, it is cubic or rectangular (containing not a single curved line) and austere (decorated primarily in black and white). In another context, this house could well be experienced in a positive way. On a purely formal basis, it is characterized by elegance and clarity. There is nothing intrinsically wrong with clean lines, simple forms, or polished surfaces. Traditional Japanese architecture, based on similar aesthetic principles, is seldom described as arid, sterile, or dehumanizing. In this context, however, a building based on these principles takes on highly negative, even disturbing connotations. In fact, the house, including everything associated with it, is clearly a prison: on several occasions, Martin and Laura are seen from the outside through windows fronted by the bars of railings.

Another binary opposition is between Cape Cod and Cedar Falls. The former is presented in the prologue as an unreal world, neatly polarized between nature and culture. The latter is presented in the rest of the movie as a real world, an unstable but agreeable interaction between nature and culture. It is surely not accidental that Laura's new name of Sara Waters, Ben's surname of Woodward, and the town's name of Cedar Falls are all linked with nature: all are cultural creations with natural connotations. Nevertheless, Cedar Falls – set amid lush fields and verdant meadows, its quiet streets lined with shady trees and blossoming hedges, its inhabitants living in gracious old homes with wide front porches – is about as close to the American vision of paradise as any that Hollywood has ever created. The contrast between Cape Cod and Cedar Falls is dramatic even in purely chromatic terms. Cape Cod is almost monochromatic. It is visually and, by implication, emotionally cold, because the interior is virtually black and white and the exterior blue and white. (This lifeless and passionless atmosphere is highlighted by the brief appearance of a blood-red dress that Martin wants Laura to wear.) Cedar Falls, on the other hand, is polychromatic. It is visually and emotionally warm, because the colour of virtually every object – curtains, walls, chairs, tables – is in the range from yellow to red. Even blue or green objects such as trees and bushes are given a warm tonality through lighting. In the daytime, this serene and happy world is gilded by brilliant sunshine. At night, its snug houses and safe streets are bathed in the soft glow of amber lamps. The house in Cape Cod, moreover, is filled with avant-garde sculpture and other forms of art representing the elite culture associated in American folklore with European decadence. Unlike art deco, this kind of modernist architecture, inspired by the Bauhaus, was imported from Europe but never fully assimilated as part of the familiar American landscape. Cedar Falls, on the other hand, is filled with homey, folksy icons associated with the halcyon days of rural and small-town life in the late nineteenth and early twentieth centuries, which explains why the flag is flown there but not in Cape Cod.

But why glorify the patriarchal society of an earlier America? To answer this question, we must turn once again to misandric feminism. Considering the work of Mary Daly in books such as *Beyond God the Father*,[8] it becomes clear that the traditional ways promoted in this movie are those not of the recent past but of a remote past when the world was allegedly ruled by Wise Women in the name of a Great Goddess. And modern women, say some feminists, will rebuild that golden age on the ruins of patriarchy. Symbolically, Cedar Falls is the Garden revisited. If this metaphorical connection between the immediate past and the primaeval past still seems subtle, we should remember that America has long been seen as a once-and-future Eden, a new primaeval garden symbolically represented by farms on the frontier. This motif, expressed in movements such as agrarianism, populism, and regionalism, was part of a widespread worldview from the time of Jefferson until very recently.[9] So despite its beach, Cape Cod is an alienating world representing patriarchy (Martin) and Cedar Falls is a harmonious world representing matriarchy (Laura and the two wise old women).

In *Sleeping*, the sexual hierarchy has been reversed, not eliminated. Women once depended on men; now men depend on women. Women were once considered evil by association with nature, the fall from primaeval grace. Men are now considered evil by association with culture, the "fall" into historical patriarchy. It is hardly surprising, then, to find that *Sleeping* includes a revisionist rendering of the biblical story about Adam and Eve. This time it is not the woman who tempts the man by offering him an "apple" but the man who tempts – that is, seduces – the woman by offering her apples. Symbolically, moreover, Ben is not only the sinister male ancestor who is responsible for all suffering by women (thus confirming a worldview based on "us" versus "them") but also the angry male god who imposes an arbitrary law (thus confirming an ancient Christian misunderstanding of the Jewish Torah).[10] It is not merely the satanic side of transcendence that is rejected here, therefore, but the divine side as well. According to French, Daly, and their followers, both are characteristically male and intrinsically evil.

This blatant use, or misuse, of traditional religious imagery is consistent with the misandric premise and purpose of this movie. The mentality functions in many ways as a secular form of religion. Conversion, or "consciousness raising," is a major feature of life in some political circles. Viewers might be reminded immediately, in fact, of Christianity. Christian conversion is associated with baptismal immersion,[11] involving ritual passage through death and rebirth at the font. The baptismal water represents both death in the abyss and new life in the cosmic sea. Converts reach the latter only through the former. This symbolic pattern is based on at least two more ancient ones: Israel's mythic passage through death and rebirth at the Red Sea, and the world's passage through death and rebirth in the Flood. In *Sleeping*, these motifs, regenerative waters and protective arks, are cinematically linked. After leaving the boat, Laura "dies" in the sea to her old self and is "reborn," or "saved," on another "boat" (the bus) sailing across another "sea" (the fields of wheat swelling in golden waves). Clearly, female viewers are expected to undergo the kind of conversion experience suggested by this metaphor once they have grasped the "gospel" of feminism.

In conclusion, *Sleeping* is both parable, or art, and myth. To the extent that it subverts, or "deconstructs," a worldview, that of the established patriarchal order, it is parable. To the extent that it replaces this worldview with another, that of misandric feminism, it is myth. (We rely here on John Dominic Crossan's definitions of parable, which corresponds to the avant-garde definition of art, and of myth.)[12] Its evaluation as a myth is subjective. Some people like the worldview it expresses, and others do not. Its evaluation as art, however, is not quite so subjective. To the extent that subtlety and complexity are valued among artists, this movie cannot be considered good art. Perfectly reflecting its polemical aims, the opening and closing credits consist of white letters on a solid black ground. Like the movie's mentality, they are (literally as well as metaphorically) black and white. Domestic violence is an extremely serious social problem,[13] but its solution will not be found in simplistic thinking. By demonizing Martin instead of presenting him as a person whose psychopathology can be comprehended and possibly cured, by manipulating viewers so that they *want* Laura to pull the trigger, this movie offers encouragement to those who would build a new society on the basis of fear and revenge. On the contrary, the solution to domestic violence and many other problems will probably be found in our willingness to explore the psychological and moral complexity inherent in the human condition as it is experienced in everyday life by both men and women.

A Kiss before Dying (James Dearden, 1991) could have been called *Sleeping with the Enemy II*. Though slightly less obviously misandric, because it includes one or two male victims along with female ones, this movie makes precisely the same point: that no man can be trusted. And once again, its symbolic structure reflects a worldview profoundly influenced by an "us" versus "them" mentality.

The opening credits are superimposed on nightmarish views of an industrial smelter, with molten ore rushing like a volcanic lava flow into incandescent ingots. In the very brief prologue, a boy stares out of his bedroom window as trains of boxcars owned by the Carlsson Copper Company rush by on tracks just behind the house. Later on, it becomes obvious that both inferno and trains belong to the Carlsson Copper Company.

In part one, viewers are introduced to Dorothy Carlsson and Jonathan, her fiancé. Dorothy is the daughter of a wealthy entrepreneur who began as an immigrant. Her mother, reputed to have been unfaithful to him, committed suicide years earlier. So did her only brother. Jonathan's mother maintains a marginal existence selling real estate. His father, an accountant, left the family many years earlier. Neither Dorothy nor Jonathan is happy at home. Dorothy dislikes her controlling father, and Jonathan is impatient with his anxious mother. In any case, Jonathan is really after the wealth and power that would be within his grasp as Thor Carlsson's son-in-law. But his plans are disrupted when he learns that Dorothy is pregnant; he worries that Carlsson will disinherit her when he finds out that she, like her mother, has been less than respectable.

The story proper begins with a lecture on Nietzsche at the University of Pennsylvania. After class, Dorothy discusses her "mystery man" with a friend, Patricia Farren. Later, she and Jonathan appear at Philadelphia's city hall to get their marriage licence. Discovering that the office has closed for lunch, they go upstairs to the roof. Jonathan sits on a ledge overlooking a deep light well. When he places her on the ledge, she becomes anxious but remains trusting. Then, suddenly, he pushes her over. "It's all your own fault," he says. As he leaves the building, Jonathan mails what he knows will be interpreted as a suicide note from Dorothy to her father. Eliminating Dorothy has given Jonathan a chance to try again with her sister Ellen.

Ellen believes that her sister was murdered, but the note, along with a history of suicide in the family, suggests otherwise. Because her father is afraid of bad publicity, neither he nor the police in his pay pursue the matter further. Ellen decides to get away from her unhappy family by moving to New York. But Jonathan has his eye on her as the key to his future. Hitching a ride to New York, he learns that both parents of the car's driver, Jay Faraday, were killed in a Korean Air Lines tragedy. Faraday is alone. Seizing an ideal opportunity, Jonathan murders him and adopts his identity.

In New York, "Jay" finds a way to meet Ellen, who works at a shelter. Because Dorothy had never introduced him to her family, Ellen has no idea of any earlier connection between "Jay" and her sister. He is handsome, charming, playful, and apparently concerned with the fate of street people. In fact, he seems like the ideal man to both Ellen and Cathy, who works with her at the shelter. Meanwhile, Ellen remains unconvinced that Dorothy committed suicide and begins an investigation of her own. She discovers that a law student at the university had known Dorothy's "mystery man." Tommy Roussell offers to show her a picture of him in the yearbook. As she waits in the car for Tommy, Jay enters the apartment, murders him, and escapes.

Before long, Jay meets Thor Carlsson and impresses him as an attractive, ambitious young man who cares deeply not only about Ellen but about family life in general. Jay proposes to Ellen and she accepts. Following the wedding, they move into an apartment Carlsson has bought for them. As they unpack, Jay finds the shoes Dorothy wore on the day she was killed. Ellen has saved them either out of sentiment or in the hope that they might provide some clue to the mystery of her death. Jay burns them in the incinerator. But what really worries Ellen is a change she notices in Jay. Having accepted a job at Carlsson's company, he is becoming more and more like her father. He is distant, businesslike, absent, and, even worse, dependent on the older man. But Jay still wants the marriage to work, albeit for reasons that have nothing to do with love. When he misses a date with Ellen, therefore, he dutifully apologizes.

As part two begins, Jay's plans begin to unravel. Having discovered the name of Dorothy's "mystery man," Patricia tries to contact Ellen. But Jay overhears the message. To cover his tracks, he has to murder once more. After cutting up Patricia's body in her hotel bathroom, he stuffs the remains into a suitcase and dumps it into the river. When the police question Ellen, because her name had been found in Patricia's diary, he realizes that he must watch his wife very carefully. Soon after this fourth murder, something else goes wrong. An old friend from university runs into Jay at a bar and addresses him in front of Ellen as Jonathan Corliss – his real name. Really suspicious now, Ellen consults Corelli, an investigator who had previously shown no interest in the case. Once again, he seems either unable or unwilling to do anything. On her own, then, she goes to the university library and looks up Jay's real name in the yearbook. The picture is that of her husband. Now she knows that he was Dorothy's "mystery man," the man who may have caused her pregnancy and even her death.

The story concludes in part three. To learn more about Jay, Ellen visits his mother. Mrs Corliss lives, literally, on the other side of the tracks. She tells Ellen about the son she believes dead and then leaves for an appointment. Once the older woman is out of sight, Ellen breaks into the house and searches Jay's room. She finds a suitcase filled with newspaper clippings about the Carlsson family. In addition, she finds Dorothy's cigarette lighter. Because Jay has been following Ellen, he suddenly appears in the doorway. Ellen stabs him in the ensuing tussle and escapes through the window, followed by a wounded but desperate Jay. As they race across the railway tracks, he is overtaken by a train and crushed to death.

The epilogue is a rerun of the prologue: a boy who can now be identified as Jonathan stares out at the Carlsson trains.

Like many other misandric movies, this one opens with the presentation of background information. It takes the form of philosophy rather than the more common sociology, psychology, or criminology. Immediately following the opening credits and prologue, viewers are shown a university classroom (which offers a far more cinematically effective way of presenting technical information than adding it to dialogue). Introducing her lecture, thus introducing the premise underlying everything that follows, a professor discusses Nietzsche's notion of the amoral superman: "God is dead, declared Nietzsche. In his place, the amoral superman, his actions only limited by the strength or weakness of his own character." Continuing with a discussion of Dostoyevski's *Crime and Punishment*, about the murder of a woman by Raskolnikov, she asks the class about his failure. "Are there, in fact, inherent limitations on human behaviour built into man's spiritual programming?" In at least three ways, these few lines of dialogue establish the premise on which everything hangs: an inherent flaw in *man*.

In 1991, it was generally understood, certainly in the academic world of professors, that "man" referred to men, not women. As it happens, the two major male characters in the story that follows are, indeed, profoundly flawed. Similarly, it was generally understood, certainly in feminist circles, that the word "God" had a cultural context. In this case, it refers specifically to the god of Christianity. Those au courant with the latest political fashions, however, will immediately distinguish between the patriarchal male deity of Western tradition and the primaeval female deity – widely known as "the Goddess" – of "thealogical" revivalism. Both major male characters in this movie are associated with male supernatural beings, and both are sinister. Finally, the word "programming" is usually associated with computers and, in turn, with high technology in general. And that, or at least what would be considered high technology, is associated with maleness. Once again, the story that follows supports precisely the notion that men have an affinity for technology and are thus responsible for all the problems caused by it.

Jay's boyhood bedroom is filled with model cars and airplanes, for example, and he receives explicit approval from Carlsson after working on a major project that involves computerization. The copper industry is based on the use of technology, which is often said to "rape" the earth, a realm supposedly associated with femaleness. In one scene, Ellen and Cathy lie peacefully on the grass and watch Jay play baseball. As women, of course, they are literally close to the earth. As a man, Jay is metaphorically alienated from it. He walks or runs over it, swinging his (possibly phallic and certainly clublike) baseball bat.

Staring blankly out of his bedroom window at the passing trains, young Jonathan is an enigmatic and evocative figure. But he is not the only one of this kind in *Kiss*. Walking down the corridor to get their marriage licence, Dorothy and Jonathan come across a blind man walking in the opposite direction. This figure did not find his way onto the set by accident. He was placed there for a reason. The most obvious reference is to Dorothy's blindness; she is about to marry a man without knowing him or perceiving his intention of murdering her. But in that case, a blind *woman* would have been just as effective or even more so. Why choose a blind man? Possibly, to add the subtle suggestion that men as a group are blind. Unable to see beyond either his own psychotic delusions or his own selfish desires, Jonathan is about to murder someone. Blindness is a physical affliction, because part of the body does not function. To suggest that men are either pathologically or wilfully blind, therefore, is to suggest that men are *biologically* flawed. Whatever is wrong with men must be *innate*, even though the idea of being "wilfully blind" is no less oxymoronic than that of being "innately immoral," because being ignorant of what you already know makes no more sense than being guilty for doing what you cannot avoid.

Like the other movies we have examined, this one sharply polarizes men and women. Once again, all female characters, major and minor without exception, are good. As a good sister, Ellen is deeply troubled by Dorothy's death and refuses to rest until she discovers what happened to her. As a good daughter, she remains loyal to her mother's memory in spite of the publicity surrounding her divorce and suicide. And as a good citizen, she works at a shelter for street people instead of wasting her time among the idle rich. But Ellen is not merely a good human being. Sound intuition (possibly "female") provides her with the insight that Dorothy's death might not have been due to suicide. It is raw courage, however, that allows her to pursue the investigation on her own and also to cope effectively with Jay's sudden and final assault. The same is true of minor characters. Patricia, for example, is a good friend. After finding a photograph with Dorothy and her "mystery man" in the background, she remembers that Ellen had been looking for this information. Instead of contacting the police, she decides to contact Ellen directly. Cathy, too, is good. She works with Ellen at the shelter.

And once again, all male characters, without exception, are psychotic, immoral, or inadequate. Tommy Roussell is merely inadequate. Working as a clerk in the library, he seems diffident and generally anxious. He tells Ellen that he had a nervous breakdown shortly after graduation. Later on, he is unable to defend himself against Jay. Although that would have been extremely difficult for anyone in similar circumstances, in cinematic terms, it nevertheless represents his inadequacy. Investigator Corelli too is inadequate. When Ellen first meets him, he seems almost hostile to the idea of pursuing the case. With some justification, she accuses him of being in the pay of her father who wants to hush up the whole affair because the publicity might be bad for business. When she appeals to him again, he has quit the admittedly corrupt police force but is of no more use to her than before.

As a family man, Carlsson is inadequate to say the least. His reaction to Dorothy's death, after all, is not exactly sadness. When the police discover that she was pregnant, he tells his other daughter that Dorothy "was a whore like her mother." The implication is that she deserved nothing better than a horrifying death. When Jay comments on the suicide of Carlsson's wife, her daughter replies that he cannot imagine "what she went through for years with that man." Whether or not Carlsson actually drove his wife and son to suicide, the movie suggests that he lacked the ability to care deeply for them or any other human beings. He gives Ellen a wedding and an apartment, but she is troubled by the nagging suspicion that he has done so, as usual, merely to control her.

Carlsson is vaguely sinister, not merely inadequate. A symbolic key is provided by his name: Thor. In Scandinavian mythology, Thor is a son of Odin, the high god. As "the rampart of divine society," he represents the hierarchy itself and all the curses associated by misandric feminists with this "male" principle. He spends most of his time on journeys, hunting down monsters and giants to kill. But his colossal strength is often used selfishly and dishonourably, not on behalf of truth or justice. "Nothing restrains him," writes Georges Dumézil, "not even legal scruples: he does not recognize the promises and pledges that the other gods, even Odin, have imprudently made in his absence."[14] Furthermore, he is bloodthirsty. Disguising himself as the goddess Freya, he seduces Thrym, the giant who stole his magical hammer. In the presence of his older sister, Thrym proudly displays the hammer. Thor promptly picks it up and "gaily massacres the brother, the sister, and all who get in his way."[15]

But Thor is primarily a storm god and therefore most often associated with thunder and lightning. In *Kiss*, though, Thor Carlsson is visually linked directly to the subterranean world of rock and metal and fire, not the celestial world of cloud and wind and rain. Thus it is interesting to note, as Dumézil points out, that Mars, the Roman god of war, and Vulcan, the Roman god of fire and metal-working, were Thor's counterparts in the classical world.[16] Carlsson's use of fire is associated in this movie not only with Thor's use of lightning as a weapon but also with Vulcan's use of fire to forge tools or weapons and Mars's use of them in war. Given the intricate symbolic structure, these mythological links are clearly intended by the director (but it would make no difference, in any case, if they were not).

Even viewers who know nothing of the mythological origin of the visual images respond at some level of consciousness to properties either inherent in or associated with them. Carlsson is thus a "merchant of death" representing the titanic forces associated with the technology required by both heavy industry and war. That these forces are associated in this particular movie with malevolence rather than benevolence is clear to at least some viewers from the juxtaposition, through montage, of the two opening sequences: molten ore flowing in an open-hearth furnace and boxcars rolling across the horizon. Alone, the ore suggests the fire and brimstone of hell as imagined for centuries in art and folklore. In combination with the boxcars, it suggests the flames of a crematorium at a Nazi death camp fed by freight trains loaded with victims from all over Europe. One of the trains passes under a metal gate with the words "Carlsson Copper Company" arching overhead. An almost identical gate at Auschwitz warned all who entered that *Arbeit macht frei*. The association is most fitting when we recall that the extermination camps were run like factories.

Jay and Carlsson are the only two important male characters. In the self-contained cinematic world of *Kiss*, they represent men in general. And the unmistakable implication is that Jay is just like his highly respectable father-in-law, not a rare psychological or moral deviant. He is a younger version of Carlsson, less polished and more impatient. The two are linked not only through marriage, remember, but through friendship and business as well. Carlsson's corrupt policy of buying off the Philadelphia police department is matched by Jay's corrupt policy of lying to anyone who could be of use to him. And Carlsson's cold and calculating response to the death of his daughter is matched by Jay's cold and calculated willingness to kill anyone who gets in his way. The only significant difference between the two is that Carlsson has not, to the knowledge of viewers, actually resorted to outright murder in his pursuit of wealth and power.

Jay is unambiguously sinister, but the cause of this remains ambiguous. In both prologue and epilogue, he stares out of the window with a blank expression on his face. Viewers can thus project anything onto this face, just as earlier viewers were able to project a wide range of emotions onto the blank expression of Greta Garbo as she sailed towards an unknown destiny in the final scene of *Queen Christina*. Having observed his life as an adult, viewers are left with at least two possible conclusions. Consumed by dreams of wealth and power represented by the trains rushing past his impoverished world, the boy turns into an ambitious but selfish man. Or, devastated by the sudden loss of his father, the boy turns into a charming but psychotic man. The only difference is that the former approach evaluates him by moral standards and the latter by psychological ones. There is nothing in the movie that requires either interpretation. Some reviewers refer to Jay as a "maniac" or "psychopath."[17] Even though they do evil things, these people are considered technically sick, not immoral, because they are driven by destructive urges beyond their control. Their behaviour is thus amoral, not immoral. Having failed to internalize the moral standards of society, they are incapable of making moral choices in the first place. Although they are often intelligent and rational,[18] they are emotionally isolated and incapable of empathy or compassion. For this reason, they often appear to be "normal" but are really dangerous.

The movie allows viewers to explain Jay's behaviour in terms of psychological deviance, but it prefers to do so in terms of *moral* deviance. He seems to take no particular pleasure, for example, in the act of murder itself; it is merely a means to some other end. He tells Ellen that he killed Dorothy and the others simply because they were ruining his plans. But whether he behaves as he does because he is sick and *cannot* do otherwise, or because he is immoral and *will* not do otherwise, he is dangerous and must be eliminated. Either way, his behaviour can be explained in causal terms familiar to most viewers. Some emotionally or materially deprived children really do become antisocial in later life, though other deprived children do not and some very fortunate children do.

But what if Jay is both psychotic *and* immoral? This would make no sense in logical terms, as we have already noted, because moral agency depends on free will. Yet it would make a great deal of sense in political terms, because it is easier to mobilize political resentment against those considered immoral than against those considered merely sick. In fact, it makes sense even in theological terms. Jay is symbolically linked with someone who is both driven to evil *and* guilty for evil. This is done in purely visual terms. When Jay burns Dorothy's shoes, his face is lit from below by the flames of the incinerator. In the eerie glow, he looks like everyone's image of Satan himself. Cinematically, he has become the metaphysical adversary of God. He is someone who revels in doing evil for its own sake, as an end in itself, and not merely as a way of achieving something else. Theologically, even the most sinful people are normally differentiated from Satan just as the most holy ones are distinguished from God. When theology takes on dualistic overtones, however, the former distinction is "forgotten." Specific groups of people – Jews, witches, infidels, heretics – are identified as agents of Satan and thus classified as *willing* participants in the metaphysical realm of evil.

Jay is linked with both Satan and Carlsson. He is a personification of both evil, therefore, *and* masculinity. Thor Carlsson is linked directly with Thor, the Scandinavian god of storms and wars. And Thor is linked indirectly with two Roman gods, Vulcan and Mars. Completing the symbolic circle, Vulcan is linked with Satan: both are male, and both preside over infernal underworlds. At a time when industry and technology are blamed by many for most of the world's major problems, both represent the principle of evil.[19] The expected conclusion is obvious. Men behave like Jay or Carlsson not only because of a biological flaw (being male) but also because of a moral flaw (choosing to dominate, exploit, and destroy). In short, this movie allows misandric viewers to have their cake and eat it. Men behave as they do, it suggests, because they are incarnations of evil.

Among the slickest and most effective cinematic demonizations of men is *Cape Fear* (Martin Scorsese, 1991). In a brief prologue, viewers meet the two main male characters. Max Cady is a convicted rapist, Sam Bowden his former lawyer. Instead of defending his client, Sam "buried" evidence that the plaintiff had been promiscuous. As a result, Sam lost his own case and his client spent fourteen years in jail. Cady has this in mind as he leaves prison.

To get his revenge, he decides to terrorize Sam. When Sam and his family go to a movie, Cady finds a seat just in front of them and makes his presence known to Sam by laughing raucously. Next day, Sam spots Cady in a car across the street. On another occasion, Cady has the waiter inform Sam that his lunch has been prepaid. Outside the restaurant, the two meet for the first time in fourteen years. Sam tries to buy Cady off, but Cady wants revenge, not money. His campaign of terrorism heats up. When he brutally rapes Sam's latest lover, Lori Davis, Sam takes it as a signal of what is to come. Cady then begins to harass the family by "revealing" himself to Sam's wife, Leigh, and their teenaged daughter, Danielle.

After Leigh sees a stranger sitting on the fence outside her window, Sam tells her about Cady. He suggests in addition that Cady probably killed their dog. When Lori calls Sam from the hospital, Leigh overhears the conversation, and she concludes that Sam has been having

an affair with Lori. During the ensuing argument, Sam warns Leigh
that Cady might already be planning to murder her and even Danielle.
Cady does drive by to return the dog's leash, in fact, and thus meets
both mother and daughter. Later on, Danielle receives a call from him,
posing as her new drama teacher at school. Next day in the empty
theatre, he convinces her to be more adventurous and "adult" by
allowing him to fondle her.

By this time, Sam has consulted the police and found that no
protection will be offered to his family. He resorts to Claude Kersek,
a private detective who advises him to hire three thugs and give Cady
a "hospital job." But Cady gets the better of all three. Sam realizes
that a final solution is necessary. He and Kersek plan to murder Cady.
They lie in wait for him after Sam pretends to leave Leigh and Danielle
unprotected while he is on a business trip. Once again, Cady survives.
He manages to kill Kersek and escape.

Desperate for a safe place to hide, Sam and his family drive to Cape
Fear where they rent a houseboat. Cady, however, has hidden underneath the car. As the boat glides downstream, he suddenly appears and
attacks Sam. But he does not kill him: for revenge to be complete, Sam
must first be made to watch while he rapes Leigh and Danielle. For a
moment, though, it looks as if the family will escape: Danielle sets him
on fire with gasoline and he dives into the water. Before long, nevertheless, he climbs back on to the boat. By now, a storm is tossing the
boat in all directions. In the midst of the confusion, Leigh and Danielle
jump into the river and swim ashore. The two men are now left alone
on the sinking boat. Because Sam has chained Cady's foot to a post,
Cady finally meets his end as the boat breaks apart on the rocks. Sam
swims to safety.

A brief epilogue on the riverbank shows the two women huddled
together for mutual support. Sam pulls himself out of the water and
locates them but remains apart. In a voice-over, Danielle tells viewers
that her life has been irrevocably changed by these events.

All major female characters are good. They are victims and thus
associated with innocence. Lori is not innocent in the traditional sense;
she knows that Sam is a married man and continues seeing him,
although she refrains from sleeping with him. She deliberately invites
Cady into her bed, but she has no way of knowing that he is going
to beat her and even bite her viciously. Lying in the hospital, horribly
injured, she is very much the innocent victim. Her only mistake has
been to believe that women should have the same sexual freedom as
men. This makes her innocence all the more poignant, at least to female
viewers. It makes her a symbol of liberated women in general, victims
of a continuing double standard. Leigh and Danielle are symbols of

more traditional women. Leigh has a career in commercial art. Viewers see her working at home, nonetheless, not in an office outside the home. And she clearly believes in the traditional notion of monogamy. She is a victim not only of the brutal Cady, therefore, but of the unfaithful Sam as well.

It might be argued that *Cape Fear* is misogynistic because the women are passive and subordinate to the men. Leigh and Danielle react to what men do but initiate no action themselves. Even Lori, who seduces Cady, is ultimately the victim of a cultural system supposedly established by and for only men. On the other hand, women are the focus of all action by men. The implication is that the behaviour of men can be explained adequately in terms of their feelings about women and described adequately in terms of what they do or do not do to women. Attributing such an exclusively androcentric mentality to men – all men in the cinematic world of this movie – is itself the product of a profoundly gynocentric mentality. In other words, the androcentric structure of the movie is not a tell-tale sign of lingering misogyny among those who produced it – this would be very unlikely at a time when the political spotlight is focused on movies that are explicitly about the increasingly problematic relations between men and women. On the contrary, it is a clever device used to reinforce the misandric belief that "men have only one thing on their minds." The central theme of *Cape Fear* is that violence against women is caused by a cultural order created by men obsessed with women. This means that men are neurotic or, at the very least, emotionally incompetent. But the women are only "extras" to be exploited, property to be stolen, or animals to be slaughtered. This means that men are evil, too.

All major male characters are either inadequate or evil. Sam is both. He is unable to protect his family from Cady. In fact, he is unable to protect himself. As Cady beats the hired thugs to a pulp, Sam cowers behind a garbage can. He came to gloat but is left to cringe. He is a coward in the most obvious and fundamental sense. Moreover, he is inadequate as a lawyer. By "burying" that file on the woman who brought Cady to trial, he violated the fundamental premise of the legal system, that everyone must be given the best defence possible. (Whether that should include the right to attack the alleged victim in court is another matter.)

Cady correctly points out that a lawyer who subverts the law has no right to expect protection under the same law. Lawyers have always known that they can find themselves with the burden of having to defend people they believe are guilty. Nevertheless, there are compelling reasons for insisting that everyone brought to trial be given the best defence possible. Our legal system is based partly on the moral insight that it is better for a few guilty people to go free than for even one innocent person to be punished. Consequently, the accused are presumed innocent unless proven guilty beyond the shadow of a doubt. And our political system is based partly on the practical insight that officials must not only seek justice but be seen doing so. As a result, the burden of proof is on the powerful state, not the vulnerable individual.

But Sam had indeed taken the law into his own hands. It is ironic, therefore, to hear him refuse Kersek's advice to intimidate Cady by means of hired muscle: "I can't operate outside the law. The law's my business." Later on, he is willing not only to intimidate Cady but to murder him. Although he makes plans to protect himself and his family in this way, he once again takes the law into his own hands. In other words, he becomes a vigilante. But he does so in defence of a woman, and so it might be argued that Sam is good instead of evil. "Naive" would be a better way to describe him, even in that context. Sam is a rich lawyer, part of the patriarchal evil that eventually drives him to vigilantism. What he should have done, the movie implies, was to cooperate with those working to reform the legal system in favour of women. Instead of secretly hiding evidence that a rape victim was promiscuous, he should have openly protested the legality of using that information. Instead of helping only one victim attain justice, he would then have helped many. Because the law itself is attacked here as a corrupt and patriarchal institution, this movie focuses more attention on Sam's inadequacy or incompetence than on his evil. But he has betrayed his wife; that is unambiguously evil as long as viewers assume that monogamy is one traditional moral standard that should remain unquestioned.

Cady is the archetypal villain. His evil, however, has distinctly metaphysical connotations. Because he continually quotes verses from the Bible, viewers are encouraged to identify him with the traditional theological imagery of evil. But the imagery used in *Cape Fear* is much more specific than that. Satan makes a notable appearance in the Old Testament, the only one, arranging with God to test Job by punishing him without cause. Cady himself refers to the book "between Esther and Psalms," which is the Book of Job. But he sees himself as Job, not surprisingly, the innocent victim par excellence; viewers are encouraged in a variety of cinematic ways to identify him with Satan, the evil adversary par excellence. In that case, Sam would represent Job. Like so many other commentaries on biblical texts, this one takes liberties with the story in order to make a point. Satan tempts Job, through innocent suffering, to reject God. Unlike Job, Sam really does succumb in the end to the temptation. He resorts to violence. In the Bible, God dismisses with contempt the idea that Job's suffering is caused by his own sin. Sam, on the other hand, really has brought the suffering on himself.

But Cady's association with the supernatural is by no means based entirely on the Book of Job. Like Rasputin – that villain of almost superhuman strength who died only after being stabbed, shot, strangled, and drowned – Cady is virtually indestructible. He is relentlessly, implacably, ontologically, and even metaphysically evil. In the river, with spray cascading over his head, he laughs and sings in ultimate triumph, not defeat. Now, as throughout the movie, he has transcended the natural order just as he has transcended the cultural. He emerges with renewed energy after every assault, in other words, just as he uses the philosophy he read in jail to reject morality. Far from being destroyed by the storm, he *is* the storm. Plunging into the abyss, Cady merges with archetypal symbols of chaos: the sea, the underworld, the whirlwind.

Marxists and feminists have long argued that movies are never "just entertainment," that they are never politically or ideologically "innocent," that they send "messages" to viewers about the way things are, can be, or should be. That is certainly correct about most movies, perhaps even about all of them, but the very same point of view would surely apply to misandric movies no less than to misogynistic ones. It would certainly apply to this one. *Cape Fear* is a sophisticated attack on patriarchal society, which according to this movie is rotten to the core. It is beyond redemption. But several institutions are singled out for particular attention.

The most obvious attack is on those charged with protecting society. The police force is hopelessly inadequate, offering no real protection Sam's family. The implication is that police departments, run largely by and supposedly for men, consider measures to ensure the physical safety of women and children a nuisance at best and irrelevant at worst.

At the root of this problem is the patriarchal family, an even more fundamental institution. Long before Cady's release from jail, Sam's family has become "dysfunctional." He is clearly alienated and isolated from both his wife and his daughter. The reason for Leigh's anger is obviously his extramarital affairs. The reason for Danielle's anger is slightly less obvious. Although she rebels against both of her parents, as adolescents always do in one way or another, she resents her father more than her mother. She shrinks from Sam in revulsion – a physical loathing – when he comes to her bedroom and discusses Cady's attempt to seduce her. Perhaps the father has tried to seduce his own daughter.

More subtle is an attack on the school. It cannot protect girls such as Danielle from the sexual perversity of adult men. In the most obvious cinematic sense, Cady has no difficulty invading the school premises and impersonating a teacher. But the problem goes much deeper than a lack of security guards. Because the school has generally failed to offer students a cohesive, challenging, and durable worldview, many teenagers see it as anachronistic or even oppressive. They want nothing more than to escape from or rebel against this extension of the family. As a result, they are left to the mercy of social and cultural forces that seem exciting but are in fact sinister. We would point out, though, that the school, as a mediator of culture, fails to provide both girls *and* boys with the kind of enduring principles that would protect them from social and sexual anarchy. The same system fails to offer boys what they need to become mature and fulfilled adults – unless we assume that cultural chaos actually works in their interest on the grounds that men are innately immoral. But this would be a contradiction in terms, as we have noted, in view of the fact that morality, by definition, always involves choice.

The school, however, is a mediator only of external cultural forces. In this case, it is presented as the mediator of art and, more specifically, of patriarchal literature and drama. Cady easily seduces Danielle with the lure of Henry Miller's *Sexus*.[20] Miller has been condemned by feminists for obsessing over male potency and female masochism. Even though his work is not part of any high school curriculum, his paean to sexual liberation represents what passes in our society for adult sophistication. This explains its appeal to teenaged girls such as Danielle. Women who fall for it land up, like Lori Davis, the victims of men. Unlike earlier feminists, many in the 1990s began questioning the notion that women should adopt "the male model" of sexuality or anything else. Essentialists, those who believe that there is some "essence" to femaleness and to maleness, have argued that women are fundamentally different from (as we showed in chapter 5, that almost invariably means superior to) men. What women really want in relationships is emotional intimacy, they say, not physical sport. In that case, the search for sexual pleasure is not only dangerous for women but also unnatural. What women really need is not a single moral standard but a new double standard, one that works in their own interest.

In *Cape Fear*, a scathing attack is levelled against patriarchal law. During the past twenty years, feminists have repeatedly attacked the legal system for allowing a woman's past to be used as evidence in defence of alleged rapists or, to put it another way, for discouraging women from filing charges against rapists. But the law oppresses women, according to this movie, because it is ultimately derived from, and legitimated by, a *religion* that oppresses women. For Cady, justice is established according to the letter of the law instead of its spirit. He could have escaped punishment for rape on a technicality. This is why Cady sincerely believes himself a victim and that this denial of justice legitimates his revenge. No wonder he tells Sam, "You are guilty of betraying your fellow man." He means men as a class, not the human race.

On his arm is a tattooed verse, "Vengeance is in mine heart," from Isaiah. On his back, moreover, is a tattoo depicting the scales of justice.

On one side is a Bible and on the other a sword. Clearly, Cady sees himself as an agent or counterpart of ancient Israel's righteous male deity. Apart from anything else, therefore, *Cape Fear* perpetuates the old notion of Judaism as a "religion of law" to be carefully distinguished from Christianity, the supposedly superior "religion of love." Cady represents a Christian stereotype of the Old Testament God, the wrathful and vengeful Father. But where is the New Testament God? Where is the loving and forgiving Son? He is absent. In view of the fact that Christians have traditionally thought about the Old Testament primarily in terms of the New, viewers might conclude that Christ is absent for a reason. Very likely, it reflects the conviction among many secular feminists that Christianity is just another version of patriarchal religion. It is a more damaging one, perhaps, because it presents the insidious illusion of improvement over the earlier version. In order to expose the underlying reality of *all* patriarchal religion and *all* the institutions derived from it, Christianity is ignored. Well, not quite ignored: along the road to Cape Fear are crosses with the words "Where will you be in eternity?" This might be a visual indictment of Christian otherworldliness. If so, the implied response is another question: "Where are you now?" Translation: What are you doing to liberate women from tyranny in the present world order?

Given the political premises of this movie, the epilogue has a fitting message. Just before the closing credits, Sam and his family emerge from what amounts to the primordial ooze. Stripped naked in the water, they are no longer encumbered by the dirty and torn fabric of culture. They will have to abandon our civilization, rotten to its patriarchal core, and start over again. In fact, their new beginning is visually related to the primaeval Beginning. Squatting on the shore, inscrutably surveying his new world, Sam has become ... an ape.

Viewers might recall that Cady too has been associated with the subhuman world. When Danielle meets him at school and asks who he is, he replies: "Maybe I'm the big bad wolf." In a kind of reverse baptism, the rushing waters have washed away his innocence and revealed his underlying pollution. Without his surface appearance as a human being, his ontological reality as a subhuman being can be seen. Now that the veneer of culture has been removed, in other words, he can be seen for all that he, like every other man, has ever been: a male primate biologically driven to dominate females in the troop. This brief sequence is almost entirely silent, because the characters have reverted to a prelinguistic stage of the evolutionary hierarchy.

Only at the very end, in a voice-over from the *future*, does the use of language resume. In misandric feminism, language itself is a very important example of male corruption. Not surprisingly, therefore, it is used here by a woman to describe the gradual and painful reassertion of her humanity. When Leigh and Danielle emerge from the river, they embrace and caress each other. In purely cinematic terms, female solidarity directly follows immersion. The flowing waters have washed away their pollution and restored their underlying innocence. The surface appearance of psychological deformity, due to conscious or unconscious cooperation with patriarchal institutions, has been replaced with the ontological reality of their autonomy and wholeness. The story concludes for women with a symbolic blessing, hope for a better future. But it concludes for men with a symbolic curse, relegation to the scrap heap of history. According to Owen Gleiberman of *Entertainment Weekly*, nevertheless, *Cape Fear* is a "humanistic thriller."[21]

Before concluding this discussion, we should mention briefly the earlier version of *Cape Fear* (J. Lee Thompson, 1962). Thirty years before the remake, there was no such thing as misandric feminism. This does not mean, however, that problems such as rape were ignored. It just means that they were not interpreted in the same political framework. The earlier version makes no attempt to disguise that Cady is predatory in a specifically sexual way. He has been raping a woman when Sam overhears and comes to her aid. The woman starts screaming for help, which brings the police. And that, in turn, drives Cady "berserk." He attacks the woman once more, brutally enough for her recovery to require a month in the hospital. For that, he pays with eight years in jail. He blames Sam simply for leading to his arrest. (In the more recent version, he blames Sam for withholding evidence on moral grounds, thus losing the case for his own client and supporting the larger political subtext of male infidelity.) Moreover, the 1962 version makes no attempt to disguise the no-win situation of rape victims. Cady rapes a prostitute. (In the remake he rapes Sam's mistress). "There's no need to take a beating like this lying down," says the police officer. "A man like that has no right to walk around free … You've got the law on your side, why don't you use it?" But the woman explicitly refuses to bring charges against him for fear of both Cady's eventual revenge and the damaging notoriety that would accompany a trial.

In the earlier version, Cady is unambiguously evil, but Sam is unambiguously good. Yet that duality is not given polarizing connotations, because good and evil are both characteristics of the *same group*. The former is not projected onto one group of human beings, per se, and the latter onto another. Dualism is avoided precisely because Sam's benevolence matches Cady's malevolence. No doubt is cast on Sam's credibility as a husband, nor is doubt cast on him as a lawyer. Even though he uses his influence with the police to persecute Cady, trying to get rid of him by locking him up on dubious charges such as lewdness or vagrancy, the threat posed by Cady to innocent citizens – that is, to Sam's wife and daughter – is so obvious that viewers cannot help siding with Sam. In fact, recent legal changes make this clear. Those who merely threaten others may now indeed be arrested and detained even before they commit crimes. The cinematic world presented by this earlier version of *Cape Fear* makes no link, therefore, between maleness and either good or evil. Men are presented as human beings, neither angelic nor demonic ones.

It should by now be clear that current popular culture does more than merely ridicule or trivialize men, more than merely encourage indifference or contempt for men, more even than dehumanize men, although any of these things would be bad enough. It goes further to demonize men. And, in doing so, it encourages the profound polarization of society or even of the cosmos. How did we get to this point? Like misogyny, misandry is about hatred, not anger. And hatred is seldom, if ever, a grassroots movement. It is a culturally propagated movement, albeit one that feeds on the inchoate fears and hostilities of the masses. We turn in the next chapter to the political and academic sources of misandry.

CHAPTER EIGHT

Making the World Safe for Ideology: The Roots of Misandry

We live today, at the end of the twentieth century, in a world increasingly polarized, between light and dark, between "them" and "us," between women and men, with nuclear war looming as the most terrible form of potential collective destruction, but with group violence occurring all over the world, always with one justification or another. In a time of dislocation, the Manichean view – we, the "good," versus them, the "bad" – is, though comfortable, also false and dangerous. False, as I myself know, remembering a little girl who wanted a gun and a brother who did not; a father who could never kill a deer and a hunting brother who does not see the sport in war. Dangerous because this simplistic view depends on rigid notions of what men and women are in relation to war and of war itself as an absolute contrast to peace.[1]

The hope ... was that patriarchal society would change into a liberal-democratic society in which both men and women could retain their individual identities. Instead, we have leap-frogged into the group society and decided that the favored group of the moment is the female. Now we are attempting to make female instincts, reactions and behavior normative for all members of society.[2]

Postmodernism is the ultimate antithesis of the Enlightenment. The difference between the two can be expressed roughly as follows: Enlightenment thinkers believed we can know everything, and radical postmodernists believe we can know nothing. The philosophical postmodernists, a rebel crew milling beneath the black flag of anarchy, challenge the very foundations of science and traditional philosophy. Reality, the radicals among them propose, is a state constructed by the mind. In the exaggerated version of this constructivism one can discern no "real" reality, no objective truths external to mental activity, only prevailing versions disseminated by ruling social groups. Nor can ethics be firmly grounded, given that each society creates its own codes for the benefit of equivalent oppressive forces ... Scientists, held responsible for what they say, have not found postmodernism useful. The postmodernist posture toward science, in turn, is one of subversion ... The scientific culture is viewed as just another way of knowing, and, moreover, a mental posture contrived mostly by European and American white males. One is tempted to place postmodernism in history's curiosity cabinet, alongside theosophy and transcendental idealism, but it has seeped by now into the mainstream of the social sciences and the humanities.[3]

Americans, still believing in the isolationist Monroe Doctrine, were not eager to join the European struggle in World War I. When it became clear that American interests were involved, the case for war had to be argued. Why fight in a foreign war? Because, Americans were told, this war was different from most others. It was not merely about territory or power. It was about protecting the peaceful American way of life from aggressive powers that would destroy it. This was a "war to end war." The irony of waging war to end war was not lost on everyone. Then too, this was a war that would "make the world safe for democracy." But despite even the best of intentions, the war did nothing of the kind. On the contrary, it made another war almost inevitable. Instead of being an instrument to bring about reconciliation, the Versailles Treaty turned out to be an instrument of revenge (mainly on the part of France). Ignoring the pleas of President Woodrow Wilson, the United States never did join the League of Nations. Even if it had, that would not have done much to prevent the rise of fascism[4] and the advent of World War II. Why mention this here? Because many other conflicts fought in the name of high ideals have led to the overthrow of those very ideals (and, sometimes, even to their replacement with opposing ones). That, we argue, is a factor in the cultural war waged by one influential branch of feminism.

In this chapter, we examine the roots of misandry. After discussing ideology in general and feminist ideology in particular, we turn to the strategies used by feminist ideologues in promoting their misandric worldview. They use three main ones: what critics call "political correctness," what academics call "deconstruction," and what we call "fronts." In this way, they hope to make the world safe for feminist ideology.

It is commonly believed that feminism has always been about equality. Actually, that is not quite true. Some feminists have indeed been truly devoted to the notion of equality. Others have applied it selectively. That was certainly the case among many feminists of the late nineteenth and early twentieth centuries.[5] Although they used the rhetoric of equality to achieve their goals for women,[6] they did not necessarily follow the logic of equality to its conclusion. Women were equal to

men, yes. But blacks, for example – even black women – were not
necessarily equal to whites. The principle of equality, in short, was
severely compromised by that of hierarchy. As Ann Douglas points
out, white American suffragists of the late nineteenth and early twentieth centuries were anything but eager to secure the vote for black
women. In fact, "white women won the vote by playing to the nation's
anti-Negro sentiments"[7]:

The suffragists promised to make the Negro's disenfranchisement permanent.
Frances Willard dedicated herself to suffrage as well as to temperance – *woman*
suffrage, of course, not Negro suffrage. In the late 1880s, she made a tour of
the South that moved her to offer her "pity" to white Southerners, saddled
with the "immeasurable" problem of "the colored race," a debased and unre-
strained race, to Willard's mind, "multiply[ing] like the locusts of Egypt,"
whose male members were mainly, it seemed, rapists looking for white victims,
"menac[ing]" the safety of women, of childhood, of the home." For her part,
[Carrie Chapman] Catt confessed publicly that the North had acted unwisely
in legislating "the indiscriminate enfranchisement of the Negro in 1868" during
the carpetbagger days of Reconstruction; now that Negroes were beginning to
migrate in increasing numbers to Northern cities, Northerners like herself, she
said, could understand, share, and even further the South's anti-Negro suffrage
position. After all, as another suffrage spokeswoman pointed out, "there are
more white women who can read and write than [there are] Negro voters."
Women, once enfranchised, would end what Catt called "rule by illiteracy"
and "insure immediate and durable white supremacy, honestly attained," as
the Southern suffragist Belle Kearney boldly put it in 1903.[8]

Not all American suffragists were racists. Jane Addams joined the
NAACP and fought to integrate Chicago's schools. But even she supported Theodore Roosevelt's Progressive Party when it called for
woman suffrage but rejected Negro rights. And not many of her colleagues would have thought twice about that. In 1870, Elizabeth Cady
Stanton and Susan B. Anthony refused to lobby for the Fifteenth
Amendment. They did so on the grounds that this would give Negro
men the vote but not (white) women. Like many other white women,
Stanton saw black men as rapists. She predicted "fearful outrages on
womanhood" if they were enfranchised. By 1867, both Cady and Stanton
joined forces with a Democrat who supported woman suffrage. George
Train's motto was "Women first, and Negro last."[9] In 1899, the
National Suffrage Convention refused to endorse the pleas of black
members to abolish Jim Crow cars on railroads. In 1913, black suffragists were asked not to participate in a Washington parade. In 1919,
a delegation from the Colored Negro Women's Clubs was "politely but

firmly" denied membership in the National American Women's Suffrage Association. Correctly or incorrectly, W.E.B. Du Bois came to the conclusion that "the negro race has suffered more from the antipathy and narrowness of [white] women both North and South than from any single source."[10] At any rate, this dirty little secret is no longer a secret. When Carrie Chapman Catt's alma mater, Iowa State University, decided to name a building after her, the result was protest. Catt is defended by those who argue that her behaviour should be understood within its "context," a degree of historical objectivity that would never be granted to men with a record of racism. Others disagree. "Morality and people treating people with dignity," said one protester, "are not things that are bound by time. They're basic principles."[11]

There are those who would try to blame white men for the racism of white women, even white feminists. Women were merely products of their culture, they would argue, and that culture was "male dominated." But Douglas points out that the racism of white suffragists was not merely a passive reflection of what men were thinking and saying:

NAWSA's racism was an almost inevitable corollary to its credo of feminine essentialism. Historically speaking, essentialism of gender and essentialism of race or nation have gone hand in hand. The one set of prejudices seems to attract and require the confirmation of the other. Put another way, one might say that once a group of people starts thinking of themselves as innately qualified for power, it's pretty hard to stop. Why not exalt your race as well as your gender? You've already junked the hard thinking of self-criticism for the aggressively blind pleasures of narcissistic flight. Hitler's Nazi Party, with its fanatical insistence on Aryan blood purity and ultra-masculinity, is the most extreme and notorious example of interlocked gender-and-race essentialism, and African and African-American art was as distasteful to the Third Reich as Jewish art. When Catt wrote, "American women who know the history of their country will always resent the fact that American men chose to enfranchise Negroes fresh from slavery before enfranchising American wives and mothers," she was suggesting to her readers that "Negroes" were somehow not "American men" or "American wives and mothers." White suffragists excluded black women from the meetings and their thoughts because black women weren't, to their minds, truly "women." "Women" are – need it be said? – *white* women.[12]

Black suffragists, notes Douglas, seldom succumbed to sexist essentialism. That made them unlike white suffragists, who often declared that women were superior to men. Black women saw black men as their equals, at least in suffering. (Whether they succumbed to racial essentialism is another matter.) And black men saw them in the same way. Once black men got the vote, in fact, they devoted themselves to getting it for black women as well. But this does not mean that black women were inherently better, either morally or intellectually, than their white sisters. "Once full-blown gender essentialism became a cultural possibility for black women," writes Douglas, "if only for a tiny handful of them, it proved as irresistible as it has always been to privileged white women. One thinks of the moments of self-aggrandizing sentimentalism, of near-worship of the black woman as life force in the work of contemporary black writers like Alice Walker, Gloria Naylor, and Maya Angelou, and of similar moments in the various television productions of Angelou's 'spiritual daughter,' the television talk-show host Oprah Winfrey."[13]

White women were not more racist than white men, but they were not less racist either. This problem re-emerged in the late 1930s and early 1940s, when a "mothers' movement" of right-wing women mobilized anti-Semitic and even pro-Nazi sentiment to agitate against America's involvement in World War II.[14] There would be no need to say so, the annals of history being filled with racists of all kinds, except for the fact that so many feminists today have neglected to read their own history. They truly believe that the suffragists, being not only women but also feminists, would have been virtually incapable of anything as malevolent as racism. That belief would be naive in any context. What should make anyone suspicious of it in this context is the fact that so many early feminists made this claim on their own behalf. The suffragist victory came about not despite the racism of white feminists, moreover, but at least partly because of it. So, American feminists cannot look to the suffragists for confirmation of their belief that women are morally or intellectually superior to men.

Both mentalities, the one based on equality and the one based on superiority, have survived to our own time. Both movements have appealed to the shared values on which society rests. Egalitarianism has been refined. When feminists talk about equality these days, they are careful to include racial and every other kind of equality, although they hardly ever acknowledge the contradictions tolerated by their predecessors and their non-egalitarian contemporaries. Advocates use the rhetoric of sameness, believing that men and women are interchangeable in almost every way. In many ways, they are like those who advanced the cause of civil rights for blacks. What could be called "superiority feminism," on the other hand, has remained unchanged. As Elizabeth Kaye puts it in a discussion of women trying to make it in Washington today, "contrary to popular wisdom, women did not enter the political fray because they wanted to be equal to men. They entered that fray in the belief that they were better, a misapprehension that would demonstrate how much easier it is to judge a game that you don't play."[15] If this book were about feminism, we would have to mention both kinds of feminism at all times. But because this book is about the misandric fallout from feminism, its focus is on superiority feminism.

Advocates of superiority feminism now use the rhetoric of *difference* instead of superiority. This is more acceptable in a democracy. Originally, liberals referred to "pluralism." Eventually, postmodernists began referring to "diversity." The result was the same: a glorification of difference. The trouble is that the word "difference" often takes on the connotation of either superiority or inferiority. In connection with their own difference from men, feminists often imply not merely that women are different from men but that they are superior to men.[16] They focus attention not on the ways in which men and women are alike but on the ways in which they are unlike. The rhetoric of equality remained dominant among feminists during the 1960s and 1970s, but it was overtaken by the rhetoric of difference in the 1980s. A similar (and related) transition can be seen in the prior shift from the rhetoric of racial equality and integration to that of black superiority and separatism.[17]

Misandry is a characteristic product of superiority feminism, which, for reasons that will be clear in a moment, is what we call "ideological feminism" (or "feminist ideology"). We are concerned primarily with this particular branch of feminism. Many people assume that it is marginal. Our careful look at feminism in popular culture should indicate that this is by no means the case. On the contrary, many positions of ideological feminism have become mainstream, part of almost everyone's cultural baggage (although their origin is not always stated or even known). In some cases, these have passed into the category of conventional wisdom. The burden of proof, in other words, has shifted from those who propose these positions to those who question them.

The word "ideology" can be used in several ways. In popular usage, it refers to any school of thought, point of view, philosophy, worldview, set of "ideas," or whatever. In academic circles, the word is defined much more carefully. Academics use it in two ways, actually, both of them pejorative.

For Marxists, the word "ideology"[18] refers to carefully concealed assumptions that most people leave unexamined. As a result, unverified or unverifiable assumptions make the way things are *seem* to be the way things have always been, should be, and even must be. In other words, real change is both pointless and impossible. These hidden assumptions amount to "false consciousness," invented and propagated by members of a ruling class through a symbolic and institutional "superstructure" in order to perpetuate their own power and privilege. The masses are, in effect, prevented from understanding their own reality and thus from rebelling against it. All of history, in short, is reduced to a titanic conspiracy. Ideology is "their" sinister plot designed to perpetuate hegemony over "us." For some feminists, all this applies to gender no less (or even more) than to economics. They want to abolish culturally propagated notions of masculinity and femininity, believing that these are insidious notions subconsciously carried, as it were, by both men and women, and thus bring down "the patriarchy."

But the use made of what Marxists have understood as "ideology" has given rise to another, though related, definition. According to that definition, used in this book, it refers to *any* systematic re-presentation of reality in order to achieve specific social, economic, or political goals. This amounts to establishing a new worldview after "our" righteous unmasking or subversion of "their" sinister plot (even though the word "ideology," with all its negative connotations, is used only by outsiders). The names of those identified with good and evil change from one ideology to another, of course, but the polarization remains. According to this definition, the word "ideology" can refer not only to movements on the political right, such as nationalism or racism, but also to those on the political left. In that case, Marxism itself is an ideology. (It is an ideology according to the first definition as well, ironically, because Marx himself made several unverifiable and dubious assumptions about both human nature and history.) Of greatest interest here is not Marxism itself but the ideological branch of feminism derived partly from it.

Before discussing that case in particular, we present the following discussion of ideology in general and the problems it creates. We have isolated nine characteristics that, when all or several occur together, can be considered defining features of ideology: dualism; essentialism; hierarchy; collectivism; utopianism; selective cynicism; revolutionism; consequentialism; and quasi-religiosity.

By far the most important feature of ideology is *dualism*, which we have mentioned so far only in passing. Because most other features of ideology are inherent in dualism, it could be considered the sine qua non, the defining feature, of ideology. It is a mentality, a way of perceiving reality and organizing it as a symbolic system.

The word "dualism" is often misunderstood. Like "ideology," it can be used in two quite different and even contradictory ways. Sometimes, it refers to what should be called "duality." In this sense, it indicates merely the presence of two things – usually forces, aspects, or principles

– that can coexist in a state of perfect harmony or balance. Worldviews based on duality usually involve at least an attempt to see the relation between two seemingly opposed things in terms of complementarity. Even when asymmetry between the two prevails, each is considered good and necessary in some relation to the other. An obvious example of this would be the Chinese notion of *tao* as a state of equilibrium between two cosmic principles, the *yin* and the *yang*.[19] At other times, the word "dualism" refers to a way of thinking based on the belief that two forces or principles – these are almost always identified with good and evil – are locked in a titanic war from which one must emerge victorious by marginalizing or even annihilating the other. We use the word in this second sense, because that is the one that prevails in Western thought (non-Western thought being beyond the scope of this book).

Those who hold dualistic worldviews internalize the source of good and identify it with themselves but externalize the source of evil and identify it with some *other* group of human beings. "We" are good, in short, and "you" or "they" are evil. Because the latter embody some cosmic force or principle, they are considered *inherently* evil. Their evil is not merely the result of historical circumstances or personal idio-syncrasies but of something essential to the very fabric of their being, something that is transmitted from one generation to another regardless of variation among individuals. Not only do the "others" look or sound different, but they *are* different. In fact, they are ontologically or even metaphysically different.[20] We argue here that all ideologies of both the right and the left are inherently dualistic. As a result, they distort reality, target specific groups of human beings as the source of suffering and evil, and thus encourage polarization. In short, they promote *hatred*. (That word too is problematic and will be discussed more fully in due course. We use it in connection with a culturally propagated attitude, not a personal and ephemeral emotion such as intense dislike.)

Religious dualism has been translated into secular terms in the modern world. Marxists, for instance, want to expose the hidden assumptions or contradictions of capitalism and show that they were creations of the cultural order, not givens of the natural order. To do this, they must show that the ruling classes propagate these assumptions in order to perpetuate their wealth and power. What this amounts to is a conspiracy of the rich and powerful (or "privileged") against the poor and powerless (or "oppressed"). Marxism is about destroying the conspiracy by exposing it to the light of day. Explicitly or implicitly, Marxists maintain that the world is divided into two categorically different groups. Even though they maintain that it is culture, not biology, that makes the classes different, they still say that evil is linked with one and good with the other. Justice is the triumph of the powerless over the powerful, of the good over the wicked.

Nationalists have done precisely the same thing. The Nazis, for example, saw all of history in terms of a Darwinian struggle for survival of the fittest. They themselves, of course, were supposedly the fittest. They were the master race, the *Übermenschen*. In theory, the Jews were a subhuman race, the *Untermenschen*, and therefore unfit for survival. In fact, however, the Jews were considered *too* fit for survival. Like the Germans themselves, many Nazis suspected, the Jews were a kind of master race, but theirs was allied with the forces of evil rather than good. In Nazi ideology, there was no more room in the world for both Aryans and Jews than there was in Marxist ideology for both a proletariat and a bourgeoisie.

Closely related to dualism, representing the other side of that coin, is a second characteristic of ideology: the celebration of some essence that people share with others of their own kind. *Essentialism* is dualism from a different perspective. The thrust of dualism is negation of a collective other. That of essentialism is affirmation of a collective self. Dualism focuses attention on the innate evil of "them," in short, and essentialism focuses attention on the corresponding innate goodness of "us." (The words "innate" and "inherent" are close in meaning, but the former can have a specifically biological connotation.) Within every dualist, not surprisingly, is an essentialist.

Essentialism is particularly (though not exclusively) characteristic of ideologies on the right, those that originated in romanticism rather than the Enlightenment. The romantics glorified whatever made communities distinctive. They used the rhetoric of blood, race, ancestral land, national spirit, and so on. No matter how assimilated Jews might have seemed, for example, they could never become Germans. They could speak German without the slightest flaw. They could fight proudly for the Kaiser. They could even become Catholics or Protestants. But they could never become Germans. Something about their Jewish essence, no matter how mysterious or difficult to describe, prevented them from absorbing the German essence. Even worse, said the Nazis, the former contaminated the latter. Consequently, it was not enough merely to marginalize or segregate Jews: they had to be exterminated.

By virtue of both dualism and essentialism, ideologies are likely to involve *hierarchy* as well. Hierarchy is the logical conclusion of dualism and essentialism. Once people have been reduced to groups with inherent characteristics, it is extremely tempting to prefer one's own group and its characteristics to other groups and theirs. The result is a ranking system, with "us" at the top and "them" at the bottom. "We" are always better in some very important way than "they" are.[21]

Despite the egalitarian rhetoric of Marxism, the workers are inherently superior to members or supporters of the bourgeoisie (let alone the feudal aristocracy). In theory, it could be argued, this is not true dualism. Workers are not innately superior to other members of society. Only those who reject "false consciousness" are superior. Members of the bourgeoisie are not innately inferior to workers. Only those who fail to see the light are inferior. In practice, however, all this amounts to hierarchy. That is because the hierarchy can be transcended only after the Revolution, when the workers triumph and the bourgeoisie disappears. Even after the Revolution, steps are sometimes taken to *make* it disappear. After decades of Stalinism, including the wholesale murder of anyone associated with the bourgeoisie during the *ancien régime*, Soviet citizens were obliged to document their "class background," or proletarian ancestry.

We have already noted that the Nazis saw themselves as the fittest for survival. But all forms of nationalism, including much less sinister ones, are based implicitly or explicitly on the idea that "we" are not merely different from but in some sense superior to "them." This is what makes nationalism distinct from patriotism.

Because of their dualistic worldviews, all ideologies frown on individualism. Instead, they promote *collectivism*. At stake are not the destinies, interests, needs, or rights of individuals but those of the group, class, nation, race, or sex. Consequently, ideologies are often promoted by stereotyping their enemies. The fact that some individuals do not fit the group pattern makes little or no difference. Exceptions are anomalies to be explained away as mutations, accidents, idiosyncrasies, even unusual virtue. The point is not that all of "them" think or act in a particular way but that most do. By avoiding universal claims that are obviously unverifiable, advocates believe they can avoid accusations of prejudice and sometimes even claim to be "moderate" by comparison with those who make still more outlandish claims. But prejudice is still prejudice. Individuals are still judged, either negatively or positively, in terms of qualities alleged to be typical of whatever group they have been assigned to. In spite of the claim that our society is founded too heavily on individual rights, collectivism is on the rise.

From the beginning, Marxism focused attention away from individuals with their personal needs and towards the group. The latter was identified not with the nation, however, but with the proletarians of all nations. This was not merely a rhetorical device: it was understood that the individual meant very little in the larger scheme of things.

Individual proletarians were expected to sacrifice themselves for the greater good of the international proletariat. Workers of the world were asked to unite, to fight and possibly even die for the cause. In communist states, not surprisingly, individual rights were not taken very seriously. On the contrary, they were derided as bourgeois illusions. It was with this in mind, at least in theory, that Stalin forced the collectivization of Soviet agriculture, starving millions of peasants in the process. In the West too, Marxism asked people to lose themselves as individuals in the movement. In response, they formed "collectives" or "communes" of one kind or another.

Collectivism is just as deeply embedded in ideologies of the right. Nationalism, by definition, is about the nation and its ethnically defined people, not the state and its legally defined citizens. Although the Nazis maintained private property, they made sure that almost all institutions – women's clubs, business associations, student organizations, religious networks, and so on – were united under various government agencies and formally supervised. And they made sure that the rights of individuals or even families never took precedence over those of the *Volk*. Hitler encouraged children to spy on their parents, for example, and to report them for listening to foreign broadcasts or even making jokes about him. Like the Marxist May Day celebrations, the Nuremberg Party Rallies expressed collectivism in the most direct possible way: hundreds of thousands of people organized visually as a single organism. Marching in carefully choreographed processions, uniformed individuals were reduced to the level of cogs in the state machine – even though the impersonal nature of modern bureaucracies was one of the problems National Socialism was supposed to solve.

Utopianism, seeking an earthly paradise, has always been controversial.[22] As Marx pointed out, it can discourage people from dreaming passively of otherworldly rewards instead of actively struggling for their own class goals, which is why he called religion an "opiate of the people." As Norman Cohn has pointed out, on the other hand, utopianism has also given rise to radical revolutionary movements.[23] And many of them, including some based on Marxism, have proven highly destructive. At least three notions of the terrestrial paradise, all of them highly problematic, are currently vying for popularity.

Neo-conservatives look back with nostalgia to a paradise of the recent past. Whatever the benefits our parents and grandparents enjoyed, however, both men and women suffered in ways either like or unlike those familiar to us. If they were so happy, after all, why are we now going through such painful communal convulsions? Surely the seeds of at least some current discontent or strife were sown back in the good old days.

Neo-romantics, on the other hand, look back with nostalgia to some paradise of the *remote* past (mediaeval, ancient, prehistoric, or whatever). But can we assume that there was ever a golden age of perfect peace and harmony? If our primaeval ancestors were so happy, why was there a worldwide revolution to establish patriarchies? At issue, moreover, are not only the desirability of restoring paradise of one kind or the other but also the *possibility* of doing so. In fact, it would be impossible. We cannot turn back the clock any more than King Canute could turn back the waves; gradually or suddenly, circumstances keep changing. What was possible when human societies consisted of a few dozen people foraging for nuts, berries, and small animals is no longer possible in societies that consist of a few hundred million people. Even if we wanted to live once again in the rural intimacy of small bands, we could no longer do so. We can learn much from the past, but we cannot restore it.

Neo-utopians, by contrast, imagine that a paradisal state of affairs can be brought about in the *future*. At its best, utopianism has been linked to the anarchism of a few people who go off into the wilderness and experiment among themselves. At its worst, utopianism has been linked to the totalitarianism of party cadres who impose their vision of society on everyone through social engineering. Of interest here is the latter. Although planning and legislation can be useful ways of improving the conditions under which people live, neither can bring about perfection. That is because neither can eradicate finitude, or imperfection, which is a defining feature of the human condition. The history of the twentieth century, unfortunately, is littered with the stories of those who tried to ignore this. In their attempts to establish an ideal of purity or perfection, no matter how noble in theory, they caused human suffering on a colossal scale.

The danger of trying to create paradise is if anything even greater than that of trying to restore it. Utopianism encourages the claim of "true believers" to know what is best for others. They can do so explicitly, which is the route of both religious and secular ideologies. Or they can do so implicitly, which is the route of secular ideologies masquerading as "pluralism." Consequently, they are willing to compel participation by the masses "for their own good" – which is precisely what happened in both Nazi Germany and the Soviet Union. In America, on the other hand, utopianism was linked at first to an eschatological millenarianism according to which the Kingdom would arrive very soon but not be of this world.[24] This led, say theological

critics, to a passive retreat from worldly affairs. Since the late nineteenth century, however, utopianism has more often been linked to a
secular pragmatism according to which the golden age will be built
gradually but within the present world order. But that has led, say
theological critics, to naive optimism. When elements of both utopianism and pragmatism combine, however, the result is potentially far
more dangerous: a belief that the new order will be brought about not
only very soon but also within the present world order. Which is to
say, in spite of human finitude.

Cynicism is often confused with pessimism. As it has come to be
understood in our time,[25] cynicism refers to the belief that all people
are really scoundrels beneath the surface. Pessimism refers merely to
the lack of hope. Both are generally considered unattractive but for
different reasons. Cynicism is usually challenged on moral grounds
because it leads to opportunism. If everyone is so horrible, from this
point of view, then morality is nothing more than a pretty veneer. Even
worse, it allows some people to pretend that they are better than
others. Why not admit that life is just a struggle for selfish pleasure?
Pessimism, on the other hand, is usually challenged on psychological
grounds. With a sense of foreboding instead of hope, healthy living is
impossible. Pessimism is also challenged directly or indirectly on moral
grounds, because of its effect on the community. No community can
endure if too many people succumb to despair, especially if doing so
leads in turn to cynicism. But that does not necessarily happen. Pessimism can lead to a wide range of emotions: frustration, anger, anxiety,
sadness, and so forth. In short, cynicism and pessimism are two
different things. Of importance here is the fact that ideologies are
inherently cynical worldviews, not pessimistic ones.[26]

Why, in any case, are some people attracted to what most would
consider unattractive? For one thing, cynicism seems to replace the
apparent disorder prevalent in everyday life with order. Suffering
exists for a reason. No matter how well they hide it, people are rotten.
When applied universally, this school of thought has an intellectual
integrity that commands grudging respect. Evil lurks within the
hidden recesses of our own hearts just as it does in the hearts of
others. But ideologies do not apply cynicism universally. And this,
more than anything else, explains their appeal. Ideologies apply cynicism very *selectively*. "We" are okay. Only "they" must be watched
carefully for telltale signs of wickedness.

This critique of cynicism applies not only to Marxism, which is no
longer so fashionable on campus, but also to every academic derivative
such as "literary and cultural studies that consist essentially in

unmasking every event and every text as a shield for or a response to patriarchy and racism."[27] It applies also to ideologies on the right. The Nazis believed that every act or utterance of Jews, no matter how innocuous on the surface, was sinister. They never applied the same cynicism to their own people. (Many ordinary Germans, however, did. Berliners, in particular, were known both before and during the Nazi period for a cynical wit that they applied to everyone, without exception.)

We turn now to *revolutionism*. According to Marx,[28] "false consciousness," the illusions fostered by bourgeois culture, must be exposed before the revolution can begin. This will occur, he believed, as soon as members of the proletariat think carefully about their circumstances. When they do, they will realize that their labour is the true means of production and therefore that they are being exploited by the bourgeoisie. They will then choose new principles such as distributive justice by which to live, overthrow capitalism, and create a new society.

Hitler said much the same thing. The revolution he fostered would begin as soon as Germans realized that they were being exploited by Jews. To facilitate that realization, the Nazis, like their communist counterparts, produced officially sponsored forms of art and "agitprop." But the Nazis are seldom associated today with revolution. That is partly because they came to power legally, not through violence (although they had used violence systematically long before 1933 to terrorize rival political parties and would continue using it to terrorize dissidents and Jews until 1945). Then too, the New Order was aborted after only twelve years. Finally, many revolutions – the French Revolution, say, or the Russian – were heavily influenced by leftist philosophies. Some scholars have referred to the Nazi takeover of Germany, therefore, as a "conservative revolution."[29] But that is highly debatable. Hitler did bring about a revolution, but it was not exactly a conservative one.

The Nazis wanted a massive upheaval, but they did not want to scare away potential supporters. And among the most important of those were German industrialists. Like the two earlier German revolutions, Lutheranism and romanticism, this was to be a spiritual one. Nevertheless, it would abolish parliamentary democracy and revert to mediaeval "corporatism" as the organizing principle of society. The Nazis wanted to reassure people that their lives would be enhanced but not changed beyond recognition. Private property would be maintained along with a bourgeoisie. At the same time, the economy would be reformed along socialist lines. The Nazis opposed both communism, in short, and capitalism as it had come to be understood in liberal democracies.

The past that the Nazis wanted to restore was not that of the immediate and familiar past. Had Hitler been conservative in the usual sense of that word, he would have restored the monarchy, left the churches alone, maintained Wilhelmine standards of sexual morality, encouraged children to obey their parents, and so on. But he was not conservative. His party was radical – so radical, in fact, that many Germans failed to take it seriously until it was too late. As soon as he came to power, Hitler made it clear that he would release Germany from the shackles of the Versailles Treaty, liberal democracy, bourgeois morality, Jewish "domination," and even Christian morality. Every aspect of society would be questioned, including the most basic notions of morality such as the Golden Rule, and, if necessary, changed.[30] The New Germany and the New Order in Europe were not continuations of the status quo except in the most superficial sense.[31]

One school of ethics is called *consequentialism*. It emphasizes the consequences of behaviour rather than behaviour itself. Acts are right or wrong, in other words, depending on whether the consequences are desirable or undesirable. Other schools disagree. The topic has been debated for centuries, with most philosophers, ethicists, and theologians agreeing that extremism either way is undesirable. The point here is that ideology relies on consequentialism. To be more specific, it relies on the belief – in many cases, it amounts to an assumption – that ends can justify means. When this assumption is questioned, the response is often that "it depends on which ends." The implication is that if the end suits our own needs, or the needs of those who happen to have our sympathy, any means to achieve it can be justified.

This is hardly a new idea. It probably goes back to the dawn of human history. For one reason or another, people have always felt the need to justify behaviour that would under most circumstances be considered morally unacceptable. Those who believe that ends cannot justify means, therefore, have usually acknowledged at least one exception. A very few pacifist communities notwithstanding, societies have always acknowledged the legitimacy or even the necessity of killing in self-defence. And the problem for philosophers, theologians, and ethicists has always been the fact that people want to extend this principle in dubious ways. With that in mind, "self-defence" can be taken to mean many things. It can mean protecting yourself, your family, your community, or your nation. It can mean protection against predatory animals, invading armies, or economic hardship. Likewise, "killing" can be extended analogically to include almost any preventive measure from physical assault to verbal assault.

The problem can be solved only by insisting that some forms of behaviour are *inherently* wrong. That is the solution of secular communities that rely on some form of natural law and religious ones that rely on divine revelation (but also, in some cases, on natural law). Behaviour must not be declared good simply because the goal is noble, even though guilt can be mitigated depending on the circumstances (that is, the actual choices available). Otherwise, almost anything can be justified in the name of some allegedly greater good. Slavery is an obvious example.

This problem has been around for a long time. But it has become especially pervasive in modern times, because so few people are prepared to challenge two ways of thinking. One, characteristic of highly industrialized and bureaucratic societies, is based on a popularized and distorted combination of pragmatism and utilitarianism. Almost any form of behaviour, by the state or by private citizens, might be acceptable if it effectively and expediently achieves "the greatest good for the greatest number of people." The other way of thinking, characteristic of both dynamic and decaying societies, is based on the idea that change or flexibility is an end in itself. Almost any kind of behaviour might be acceptable depending on the "context." In neither case is there a bottom line. It is easier than ever before, then, to justify hurting people, whether by killing them or abolishing their rights or simply refusing to hear their side of the story, in the name of some ideological utopia.

There is surely no need to do more than illustrate briefly how this mentality was prevalent among both Marxists and Nazis. The Marxists preached universal brotherhood (among the proletariat), but they preached also the necessity of violence. Revolution was the legitimate means towards a desirable end, that of the "classless society." The Nazi approach was even more direct. They openly despised peace and glorified war. The latter was a means to an end – more *Lebensraum* for the *Volk*, say, or survival of the fittest. But it was an end in itself too. War was an institution that continually proved the innate superiority of the master race.

Ideologies are *quasi-religious* worldviews (or "secular religions").[32] Mircea Eliade and many other scholars have commented on the obvious parallels between traditional forms of religion and secular ideologies on both the left and the right.[33] These parallels are most obvious when ideologies are associated with the state: public parades on special days, public monuments focusing attention on heroic founders and fighters, public buildings festooned with slogans or exhortations, and so on. We are all familiar with images of mass rallies in the Soviet Union, Nazi

Germany, Maoist China, and elsewhere. A parallel only slightly less obvious, from a distance in space or time, is the use of "scriptural" texts such as *Das Kapital, Mein Kampf*, or Chairman Mao's "little red book."

Even when ideologies lack full state support, however, they often function as surrogate religions for the members of ideological communities. The esprit de corps of early Marxist "collectives," for example, can hardly be exaggerated, especially in contexts of official persecution or public disfavour. But the parallels between secular ideology and religion go much deeper:

[I]t is clear that the author of the *Communist Manifesto* takes up and carries on one of the great eschatological myths of the Middle Eastern and Mediterranean world, namely: the redemptive part to be played by the Just (the "elect," the "anointed," the "innocent," the "missioners" in our own days by the proletariat), whose sufferings are invoked to change the ontological status of the world. In fact, Marx's classless society, and the consequent disappearance of all historical tensions, find their most exact precedent in the myth of the Golden Age, which, according to a number of traditions, lies at the beginning and end of History. Marx has enriched this venerable myth with a truly messianic Judaeo-Christian ideology; on the one hand, by the prophetic and soteriological function he ascribes to the proletariat; and on the other, by the final struggle between Good and Evil, which may well be compared with the apocalyptic conflict between Christ and Antichrist, ending in the decisive victory of the former.[34]

Another parallel between religion and secular ideologies (or secular religions)[35] is less obvious, but it is the most important of all in purely practical terms. The advocates of secular ideologies, like their counterparts in fundamentalist religions, refine their positions and develop ready-made answers for every challenge encountered in debate. This reinforces the basic worldview and becomes a closed circle of meaning. There is a standard response to every anticipated challenge.

Having discussed ideology in general, we suggest that all of its characteristic features show up in an influential form of feminism. Up to this point, we have referred to it as "misandric feminism" or "superiority feminism." From now on, we will refer to "ideological feminism." The qualifying word includes all the others that might be used – not only misandric feminism or superiority feminism but also radical feminism, militant feminism, dualistic feminism, essentialist feminism, hierarchical feminism, gender feminism, and so on.) At the outset, we note that ideological feminism is a marriage of the two major intellectual traditions of Western culture over the past two hundred years: the

Enlightenment, here represented by Marxism, and romanticism, represented by nationalism.

It was the *Enlightenment*, via Georg Wilhelm Hegel, that produced Marxism. Feminism is what Arthur Marwick calls "Marxisant," by which he means "a broad metaphysical view about history and about how society works, derived from Marxism."[36] Feminists are more interested in gender than economic class, but gender has precisely the same *function* in feminism as class has in Marxism. In short, the names have been changed but not the ideology. The ruling class is identified not merely with the bourgeoisie in general but with the *male* bourgeoisie in particular – now known, however, as "the patriarchy."

Romanticism, in the form of essentialism, was added to the Marxist foundation of ideological feminism. (The irony of this collusion is that, because the romantics had rebelled against rationalism, they had rebelled also against the very mentality that eventually generated Marxism.) Romantics, especially nationalists, have always argued for the centrality of innate, or biologically based, characteristics. Those of their own groups are always superior, not surprisingly, and those of other groups are always inferior – even demonic. Directly or indirectly, many ideological feminists have repeatedly argued that women are psychologically, morally, spiritually, intellectually, and biologically superior to men.[37] This was more explicitly expressed in the late nineteenth century and early twentieth than it was again until the 1980s. That mentality is now pervasive – not only in academic circles but in popular culture as well, where it will no doubt endure far longer. Though usually classified as a leftist movement, ideological feminism has close ties with ideologies of both the right (not modern conservative movements but those based on national or ethnic identity) and the left.

Central to all ideologies, as we say, is *dualism*. Like Marxists, ideological feminists identify a "class" that is inherently hostile, one that has forged a universal conspiracy to dominate, exploit, and oppress. The class of men is privileged and, virtually by definition, evil. The class of women, on the other hand, is underprivileged and, virtually by definition, good. Justice, therefore, is the triumph of women over men. The old sexual hierarchy has been stood on its proverbial head, not transformed. Not all feminists are dualistic, and thus ideological, but some of the most brilliant, innovative, and influential ones are.

Consider the following dualistic passage from Mary Daly, among the most fashionable feminist critics of Christian theology: "The weapons of Wonderlusting women are the Labryses/double axes of our own Wild wisdom and wit, which cut through the mazes of man-made mystification, breaking the mindbindings of master-minded double-think ... Recognizing that deep damage has been inflicted upon consciousness under phallocracy's myths and institutions, we continue to Name patriarchy as the perverted paradigm and source of other social evils."[38]

Naomi Goldenberg, among many others, has made dualism more accessible to rank and file feminists: "I only hope that a feminist rhetoric based in the body inspires theories that value life more than has a patriarchal rhetoric based in the mind."[39] This is just an upside-down version of the classic body-mind or matter-spirit dualism that is endemic in Western thought, only now it is the mind or spirit associated with maleness that is evil, not the body or matter associated with femaleness. It is profoundly anti-intellectual too, even though Goldenberg herself teaches at a university.

To the extent that feminists indulge in dualistic thinking – whether in the context of socialism, communitarianism, or some other philosophical tradition – they can be considered ideological. Their way of thinking

is centred on women's oppression, based variously on sex, or on women's marginal membership in a capitalist economy, or on some amalgam ... By sharp contrast, the naturalist position put forward by the right draws on widely varied sources of data having to do with heredity ... Most disturbingly from our perspective, both the leftist feminists and the naturalist feminists are deeply deterministic. The feminists' oppressors, whether economic or personal, seem so powerful and ubiquitous as to be impervious to attack, while the forces of biology suffused through the cultures of man that the naturalists emphasize similarly resist transformation. Flesh and blood persons vanish altogether in these treatments, to be replaced by one-dimensional figures, child-bearers or maintainers of the economic order. Males and females emerge only as programmed antagonists or biologically bonded partners, not as persons with at least some common dilemmas. Those multifaceted individuals whose aspirations are so important to liberalism are much distrusted by both Left and Right. Men and women will become what the genes – or the economy – would have them be, not what they might prefer.[40]

From the perspective of feminists on the right, feminism is trying to subvert the natural order by taking women out of the home. From that of those on the left, of course, feminism is trying to restore it by overcoming a cultural order based on the historic tyranny of men.

The fact that some feminists have adopted a dualistic worldview and given it full expression as an ideology says less about women than it does about a way of thinking that might, lamentably, be endemic and pervasive in our culture (although it has functional equivalents in many other cultures). The name given to the source of evil varies from one time or place to another, but the basic mentality remains unchanged. (Despite the long tradition of monotheism, in fact, it could be argued that dualism is the "original sin" of Western civilization.) The problem addressed here is not feminism as an expression of concern for women, but feminism as an ideology.[41]

The rhetoric of feminist *essentialism* is more insidious than that of dualism. It often sounds like nothing more dangerous than promoting collective self-esteem or, at worst, collective self-righteousness. In theory, it is possible to love your own community without hating others. In fact, it seldom works that way. It certainly has not worked that way in connection with men and women. Feminists have accused men, with good reason, of essentialism (worshipping themselves) no less than dualism (hating women). But it works both ways: until the recent advent of scholars such as Ann Douglas, few egalitarian feminists "remembered" that many of their suffragist forerunners in the late nineteenth and early twentieth century were essentialists, not egalitarians.

Essentialism is today most evident in the lesbian attack on heterosexuality. That connection is not always obvious, however, or even consciously understood by women. Looking down on sexual behaviour – including both heterosexuality and homosexuality – has a long history in our society. At the moment, many heterosexual women have come to the conclusion that men who display their erotic interest in women are sexist. Most of these women see nothing wrong in theory with the heterosexuality of men. They have boyfriends and husbands. Nevertheless, they are often extremely ambivalent about male heterosexuality. They like it when it satisfies their own erotic needs, but dislike it in a wider cultural context, because this involves the "objectification" of female bodies. Feminists assert that women are fully human beings, not merely objects that give pleasure to men. They deplore a wide range of phenomena, therefore, although they differ among themselves over precisely which ones: prostitution and pornography (whether violent or merely erotic), sexual harassment, and behaviours once associated with nothing more sinister than inept seduction (whistles on the street, say, or leering construction workers). Women are surely justified in wanting men to see them *not only* as erotic objects. The problem is that some feminists now object to objectification itself. They see it not merely as one necessary factor in every erotic activity (whether vicarious or actual) but as the prelude (whether direct or indirect) to violence. But eroticism of any kind, by definition, involves sensual attraction to the body – its appearance, smell, taste – as an object. If it were correct to consider objectification inherently both male and wrong – even though many women, including those who read *Cosmopolitan* or watch *Sex and the City*, acknowledge their own objectification of men – then what would we have to say about the natural order that has produced human biology?

The problem here is not mere prudery but a virtual revival of puritanical attitudes towards sexuality (minus their theological context). Sexuality, including heterosexuality, is considered not merely unaesthetic or embarrassing but also sinister. The reason, however, is new. Sexuality does not represent innate human sinfulness nowadays but innate male wickedness. The essentialist premise works both ways. Male sexuality is innately evil, but female sexuality is innately good. Given that premise, it follows logically that the best solution would be homosexuality. For women to express their sexuality appropriately, in some ultimate sense that few heterosexual women consciously think about, would mean doing so in a lesbian context. That is the ultimate logic of this mentality, even though it is seldom noticed except by lesbians.[42]

All too often, the rhetoric of difference turns into that of *hierarchy*.[43] Why has hierarchy been so pervasive in discussion of gender since the 1980s? One answer is found in the historical lineage of feminist ideology, which, as we have noted, is a variant of Marxism. Instead of transcending the old class hierarchy, Marxism merely reversed it. Instead of being ruled by a bourgeoisie, the new "classless society" would consist only of "workers." But in the meantime, before the revolution, members of the proletariat may consider themselves morally superior to those of the bourgeoisie. Likewise, the new genderless society will consist only of women and male converts to feminism. In the meantime, women may consider themselves morally superior to men.

But the continuing prevalence of hierarchy has another explanation. Hierarchy is likely to follow from essentialism when combined with dualism. If a group of people has some inner essence, after all, then it must be defined by one or more distinctive characteristics. What are the distinctive characteristics of women? To answer that question, feminists had to find contrasting or even opposing characteristics that defined the inner essence of men. By the late nineteenth century, many women had come to believe that they were superior to men: more caring, more spiritual, more earthbound, more life-affirming, more relational, more benevolent, and so on. By the late twentieth century, additional designations had been added: women were said to be more eco-conscious, more right-brained, or whatever. Dualism offers both moral and cosmic dimensions within which to "celebrate" the "differences" that define women's "essential" nature and, not incidentally, to condemn those that define men's "essential" nature.

One peculiar feature of our society at the cusp of a new millennium indirectly supports the new hierarchy. The prevalence of pop psychology, with its emphasis on "self-esteem" and "self-help," has allowed people, not only individuals but communities as well, to rationalize in therapeutic terms their feelings of superiority. Women will be able to "empower" themselves only by defining, or redefining, their essence. And if that means defining themselves as superior to men, as some explicitly or implicitly suggest, then so be it.

From the beginning, feminists have relied on *collectivism*, often in the form of "collectives." Grass-roots groups were established for the purpose of "consciousness raising," exposing the false consciousness of domesticated women – mothers, wives, daughters – in a patriarchal society. These groups have never been isolated, moreover. Inspired by feminist writings, they have been linked by feminist networks at various organizational levels. This has enabled them to translate the new consciousness into political activism. The personal, feminists have always maintained, is political. All of this contributed to the solidarity of women, leading to the establishment of institutions such as the National Organization for Women, the Feminist International Network of Resistance to Reproductive and Genetic Engineering, and many other political action committees. Some feminists have supported and contributed to a trend in jurisprudence called communitarianism, which emphasizes *group* rights over individual ones. To some extent, collectivism is a mentality that has disadvantages for women themselves. In the interest of women as a collectivity, the needs or interests of women as individuals may be sacrificed.[44]

The other side of this collectivist coin is separatism, moving as far away from men and their institutions as possible. These feminists want "a room of their own" for women, as Virginia Woolf put it. On college campuses, this has meant the establishment of not only women's studies programs but also women's centres, women's unions, rape crisis centres, and so on. In theological circles, this has been called "womanspace" or "womanchurch." Unfortunately, recognition of the need for separate space is not extended to men. That lapse in egalitarianism is usually explained by the claim that every space is dominated by men; why, then, should they demand additional spaces? But that claim is dubious. Once, there were truly segregated spaces for men, the most obvious being clubs, schools, armies, and sports teams. That is no longer the case (except for professional sports teams). Besides, women demand that the state pay for all-girl sports teams along with integrated ones but often reject the very idea of all-boy teams along with integrated ones.[45]

Ideological feminists promote a *utopian* vision of society. Like the Marxist version, it is defined in purely secular terms as a classless society attainable on earth and within history. And in both cases, the advent of this classless society coincides with a radical transformation of human nature.[46]

Some ideological feminists like to describe this visionary society in terms of sexual equality – social, economic, legal, and political – to be brought about by reforming the patriarchal order. To institute that kind of world would take more than the reform of patriarchy, however, which is by (their) definition utterly devoid of value. Patriarchy would have to be destroyed through revolution before any new society could be built on the ruins.

The new order would have room for every conceivable perspective, in short, *except* that of men. What place men might have – or even want to have – in a world based explicitly on ideological feminism (or "feminine values" or "women's spirituality") is another matter. The fact is that this new order would be anything but egalitarian. It would merely substitute some form of matriarchy, though possibly one based on an attitude of noblesse oblige towards men, for patriarchy. Precisely what are the "values" supposedly unique to women? They are usually discussed in connection with freedom from the constraints imposed by patriarchy. Women seek "power for," Marilyn French and others have claimed, not "power over." They reject, presumably, anything to do with systems of control or domination. Ironically, their own program involves precisely that. The world they describe is one in which citizens, at least male citizens, are carefully controlled and duly punished for deviation from the norm prescribed by ideological feminists. This is a world that can be achieved only by social engineering on a colossal scale.

Other ideological feminists describe utopia in frankly religious terms – neo-pagan ones for the most part, occasionally with a thin veneer of Christian or Jewish imagery to legitimate them. These women hope to restore a lost golden age under the aegis of a Great Goddess, a paradise that was destroyed by evil patriarchal gods and their male supporters. It does not take much imagination to see that this myth is merely the reversal of an ancient one. In short, Original Sin is blamed on Adam (and men, his "followers"), not Eve (and women, her "followers"). Salvation is to come through a new Eve, therefore, not a new Adam such as Christ. The new Eden would be a paradise for women – but would it be a paradise for the entire community, for men as well as women? Probably not. Some women might say that the new order would benefit men whether they like it or not, that it would be "for their own good." But they could do so only by relying on the same condescending and patronising mentality – noblesse oblige – that they themselves have come to resent from men.

Cynicism is applied by feminist ideologues only to men, not to women. Given the dualistic nature of ideologies, this is hardly surprising. Even though many believe that a few men can "convert" to feminism, some suspect or believe that there is something innately alien or sinister about even these men, something that prevents any man from ever participating fully with the elect in "womanspace." Although feminists have to acknowledge the obvious fact that women can act badly as individuals, they have usually explained this away (until very recently, at any rate) as the lamentable and inevitable result of a social order controlled by men. Women do not go wrong of their own accord, in other words, but only because they are "forced" to do so by men. Moreover, these feminists do not acknowledge that women might be implicated as women in anything that is wrong with the world.

Ideological feminists want *revolution*, but they see no need for military tactics. Feminists of all stripes have found much more effective ways of producing radical social, economic, and political change in democratic societies – that is, societies in which public order relies on public opinion. To change public opinion, they have exploited debates over major public events such as the confirmation hearing of Clarence Thomas, the trial of O.J. Simpson, and so on. Then too, they have relied on the fact that many men consider shame, as they have for countless generations, a "fate worse than death." In other words, men – especially political, religious, and other leaders – can be manipulated easily through fear of public humiliation for feeling "threatened" by women.

Ideological feminists want more than change, as we say, or reform. They want the old order swept away entirely, root and branch, to be replaced by a new one. Daly, for instance, furiously attacks all traditional forms of religion as inherently patriarchal and thus thoroughly and irremediably evil. She considers all Jewish and Christian feminists nothing more than "roboticized tokens."[47] Why try to reform old religions when you can create new ones? Daly can be accused of many ugly things, including sexism, but not of naiveté or duplicity. Believing the Roman Catholic Church hopelessly corrupted by patriarchy, she did what honest dissenters have always done: she left the church.

But not all ideological feminists would be willing to destroy current institutions and start over from scratch. Most by far do not. They realize that it is much easier, and probably much more effective in the long run, to do so indirectly and from inside than directly from outside. They want to change the meanings attached to institutions or traditions, to substitute a new social and cultural order without undergoing the trauma of doing away with the political order.[48] They want to pour new wine, as it were, into old wineskins. In this way, they are unlike revolutionaries of the old left and even, in most cases, the New Left. In fact, the less said about revolution (especially in the United States, which has not yet forgotten the hysteria that accompanied McCarthyism), the greater their chances of success.

We turn now to feminist *consequentialism*. Like Marxists and nationalists, ideological feminists believe that the end of creating a new order justifies whatever means that might involve. Feminists, as we say, seldom refer to violence as a justifiable means. They refer instead to law reform. That certainly does not sound morally problematic, not when you consider the alternative of violence, but it can be highly problematic on closer examination. The laws proposed are intended to serve the needs of women, for one thing, not those of men. Whether these new laws can effectively and appropriately serve the needs of society as a whole, therefore, is a moot point. Besides, changing public consciousness is not necessarily as innocent as getting people to discard their old prejudices. Very often, it involves getting them to replace the old prejudices with new ones. In this case, that often means presenting men as worthy of nothing but ridicule and contempt. That this often boils down to prejudice, not merely disapproval of this or that individual man, can be seen almost any day of the week on television, at the movies, in newspapers and magazines.[49]

In view of all this, it is fair to say that ideological feminism, like other political ideologies, functions in many ways as a *religion*. Consider the public reaction to Princess Diana's death.[50] Diana, widely perceived as the victim of a patriarchal institution who gradually triumphed over it, had been strongly associated with feminism. When she died, many people began to think of her not merely as an "icon" but as a "saint." Observers could hardly avoid the religious connotations of what went on during the week between her death and her funeral: pilgrimages to London and later to her grave, makeshift shrines with offerings, prayers addressed directly to her (not only for her), and so on. This "cult" was not necessarily focused exclusively on Diana. Nor was it associated exclusively with feminists. Nevertheless, both Diana in particular and ideological feminism in general are clearly linked with something that bears more than a vague resemblance to religion.

Several observers have noticed more obvious ways in which feminist ideology is quasi-religious in nature. "What Mary Daly is doing," writes David Sexton, "is creating a religion, founding a church of elect women – 'nag-gnostics' – which is why she refers to herself as a 'scribe.' These women are said to enjoy 'Elemental powers of Geomancy, Aeromancy, Hydromancy, Pyromancy,' and to have metamorphosed into another species – 'in her Self-transcending dimensions, each woman may be compared to angels' ... [O]nce feminism is made the exclusive means of interpreting the world, it is inevitable that it should present itself as a religion. We should be grateful to Mary Daly for showing us what it would look like."[51]

In discussing the identity crisis of feminism,[52] Wendy Kaminer refers to Camille Paglia's dictum that contemporary feminism is a new kind of religion. "But if [Paglia's] metaphor begs to be qualified, it offers a nugget of truth. Feminists choose among competing denominations with varying degrees of passion, and belief. What is gospel to one feminist is a working hypothesis to another. Still, like every other ideology and 'ism' – feudalism, capitalism, communism, Freudianism, and so on – feminism is for some women a kind of revelation. Insights into the dynamics of sexual violence are turned into a metaphysic. Like people in recovery who see addiction lurking in all our desires, innumerable feminists see men's oppression of women in all our personal and social relations. Sometimes the pristine earnestness of this theology is unrelenting. Feminism lacks a sense of black humor."[53] Elsewhere, Kaminer observes that

in some feminist circles it is heresy to suggest that there are degrees of suffering and oppression, which need to be kept in perspective. It is heresy to suggest that being raped by your date may not be as traumatic or terrifying as being raped by a stranger who breaks into your bedroom in the middle of the night. It is heresy to suggest that a woman who has to listen to her colleagues tell stupid sexist jokes has a lesser grievance than a woman who is physically accosted by her supervisor. It is heresy, in general, to question the testimony of self-proclaimed victims of date rape or harassment, as it is heresy in a twelve-step group to question claims of abuse. All claims of suffering are sacred and presumed to be absolutely true. It is a primary article of faith among many feminists that women don't lie about rape ever: they lack the dishonesty gene.[54]

Like both religious fundamentalism and Marxism, feminist ideology seems to have an answer for every challenge. At no point after conversion are women forced or even encouraged by ideological feminists to question their presuppositions or analysis. Nor do they force women to question their own behaviour or take responsibility for it.

Because feminist ideology has created a closed system of meaning, it resembles religion in yet another way. Like sectarian churches, which are often characterized by both fundamentalism and dualism, it relies on a profound distinction between insiders (the elect, who have seen the light) and outsiders (the "world," with its heathens, which must be either converted or shunned). This applies not only to men but also, ironically, to some women as well.

Having discussed the definition and origin of feminist ideology, we turn now to the strategies used by feminist ideologues to promote their misandric worldview. They use three main ones: what critics call "political correctness," what academics call "deconstruction," and what we call "fronts."

For the past fifteen or twenty years, "political correctness" has been used as a derogatory term. That, we believe, is as it should be. Originally, however, the term was taken very seriously by Maoists and Marxists to indicate compliance with doctrinal orthodoxy. If they and their ideological peers now find the pejorative use of this term tiresome, they have only themselves to blame. It has come to mean not only compliance with doctrinal orthodoxy but also the smugness and self-righteousness that so often accompany it.

Defenders sometimes admit that the ugly connotations are often well founded, but they argue that the basic concept is nevertheless useful. The basic concept, they say, is "sensitivity." It is a matter of courtesy to avoid offending people. What could possibly be wrong with that? Well, nothing. And some people might indeed have nothing else in mind. Unfortunately, that definition of political correctness does not account for the phenomenon in all, or even most, cases. Something else is involved. And a brief look at courtesy and etiquette shows what it is.

Courtesy can be understood as an attitude of respect towards others and etiquette as the formalization of courtesy, the rules of conduct that people are expected to follow even if they do not actually feel respect towards others. In addition, however, etiquette can foster genuine respect. The rules of etiquette should not necessarily, therefore, be dismissed as empty conventions. No society could endure very long without some form of etiquette. For a few decades in the twentieth century, many people in our society thought otherwise. Drawing directly or indirectly on a misunderstanding of Freudian theory, they believed that personal "authenticity" was more important than conventional politeness. By the late 1980s, that naive belief was no longer tenable. Too many people were complaining that everyday life had become contaminated by coarseness, self-indulgence, and outright aggression.

But there was another reason for reappraising the vogue for "letting it all hang out." To put it very simply, that reappraisal was seen as an ideal strategy by "women and minorities" for building "self-esteem." They wanted protection from the "epithets" hurled at them by their "oppressors," because the damage caused by "verbal abuse," some said, was as serious as that of violence. And they wanted that protection to be codified in both the laws governing society as a whole and the in-house rules governing particular institutions. They got what they wanted. Notorious exceptions notwithstanding, white people are indeed reluctant to use the "N word" or its equivalents – possibly because they now have more respect for black people than they once did, and possibly because the price of public bigotry is higher than they are willing to pay. Our point here is that there is no direct cause-and-effect relation between that change and political correctness. Moreover, as we will explain in a moment, new forms of racism have replaced the older ones.

Even so, it could be argued that the world is better off because bigots are silenced. At the very least, people are forced to think about the way they use language and, therefore, their attitudes towards others. Unfortunately, that is not the only result. Because this form of etiquette has been so closely identified with specific groups, it has been hopelessly compromised by political expediency: hence the term "political correctness." Far from fostering genuine courtesy, it actually fosters nothing more than outward signs of respect for those deemed on political grounds to be worthy of them. Not all human beings, in other words, are deemed worthy. The term "political correctness" has thus come to imply not only smugness and self-righteousness but hypocrisy as well. Unlike etiquette, which fosters harmony, political correctness fosters disharmony and even polarization. It pits "us" against "them" in the most direct way by introducing a double standard. "We" deserve" to have our feelings protected. "They" deserve nothing but contempt in the forms of public ridicule and public attack.

What all this amounts to is a very convenient way of silencing potential enemies. Some people are given permission to say anything they want about their real or perceived enemies; the latter are not given permission to respond in kind or even to defend themselves. And we are not talking about defending behaviour: we are talking about defending identity. It is now unthinkable for people, especially public figures, to ridicule or attack women. (Those who do are quickly punished in one way or another.) But it is considered perfectly respectable for women to ridicule or attack men. By responding to slurs on their cultural and even biological identity, men place themselves in the untenable position of defending "the patriarchy." (Moreover, they open themselves to the shameful accusation of being "afraid of women.") They are silenced just as effectively as women were once silenced. The atmosphere established by political correctness, a term now applied not only to speech but also to causes, provides an ideal opportunity, in short, for feminist ideologues. They can say whatever they want – no matter how preposterous, outrageous, hypocritical, or even overtly hateful – and still be taken seriously by everyone (at least in public) as people who have a "right" to make their "voices" heard.

Human nature has not changed since the advent of political correctness. The ugly part, for men and other groups not considered worthy of public respect or even self-respect, has merely gone underground.

For at least twenty years, "deconstruction" has been de rigueur among academics in the humanities. Books and articles that make use of it are instantly recognizable by the mechanical, almost ritualistic, overuse of fashionable jargon: "discourse" or preferably "discourses," "inscribe" or preferably "reinscribe," "construction" or preferably "social construction," along with a host of other words such as "text," "contextuality," and "intertextuality."

Deconstruction has become the technique of choice among feminist ideologues. In a way, it is simply a new word for critical analysis. But critical analysis has always been central to scholarship, so what is the difference between older forms and this new one? That question is easy to answer. The primary purpose of deconstruction is to score political points, not to establish truth. (More in due course about the deconstructionist notion of truth per se.) Practitioners deconstruct this or that worldview not merely to point out the inherent flaws in any way of thinking but in order to *replace* one with another – that is, with their own.[55]

Defining deconstruction can be a problem. Many deconstructionists[56] – and these include Jacques Derrida, the movement's founding father – claim that defining deconstruction is impossible.[57] (For some background on Derrida, see appendix 5.) There can be no fixed meaning to any word, they claim, because language (let alone literature and philosophy) consists of rhetorical devices, such as metaphor, whose meaning drifts. Nevertheless, they use the word "deconstruction." They claim that it is a method of interpretation. More specifically, it is the method they use to attack "logocentrism" – another term that is seldom defined. According to John Ellis,[58] "logocentrism" is merely a new word for the older "essentialism," a way of thinking in which words refer directly to real objects in the external world or to real concepts existing independently of language. This is ostensibly what deconstructionists want to attack. Because all meaning is subjective, derived, mediated, or indirect, they focus attention on language itself: on the "text," whether a book, a movie, a philosophy, an institution, or anything else.

Yet even the "text" is never an objective reality. It is inherently unstable, they argue, for three reasons. All of its words, symbols, or ideas are interdependent.[59] They contain "surpluses" of meaning conveyed through metaphors or other symbolic devices. They have only "traces" of meaning in the present, because their implications and repercussions will be fully known only at some time in the future.[60] These notions are usually summed up in the notion of "play." Words "play" against each other in the present and into the future.

When attention shifts from text to reader, even more interpretations become possible. "Texts" are read by many people. They can never know precisely what was originally intended. Moreover, they bring their own experience and interests – politically vested interests – with them. After a while, they might come to understand the "text" differently. Derrida refers, therefore, to an infinite number of possible interpretations. The lack of objectivity and the infinity of meanings are two sides of the same coin. Popularizers of his method take it a step further. Because they lack any external authority, not even a stable "text," readers are autonomous. They can thus read whatever they like into a "text." In short (and this is most important) they can understand it in any way they like – which is to say, in any way they find politically expedient.

Deconstruction's epistemological relativism clearly opens the door to moral relativism. How can there be objective meanings on which to base morality when there is only a "play of meaning"? If one interpretation is no better and no worse than any other, one moral system is no better and no worse than any other. To this, many deconstructionists have a standard reply. Because their way of thinking acknowledges all views, it is inclusive, tolerant, and pluralistic. And democracies presumably depend on these things to function properly. This claim, therefore, must be taken seriously. But what precisely does it mean?

According to Ellis, deconstruction's attack on logocentrism, objectivity, and certainty of knowledge can include any claim to truth, revelation, tradition, origin, ethnocentrism, common sense, received opinion, reason – or, in a word, "presence." He observes that "deconstruction performs an operation that is variously described as undermining, subverting, exposing, undoing, transgressing, or demystifying. It performs that operation on phenomena variously thought of as traditional ideas, traditional limits, traditional logic, authoritative readings, privileged readings, illusions of objectivity, mastery or consensus, the referential meaning of a text, or simply what the text asserts or says."[61] Nevertheless, deconstruction needs this supposed naiveté: "Since deconstruction wants to show that the text says the opposite (or also says the opposite) of what it seems to say or is traditionally thought to say, the traditional version is the reference point that deconstruction needs both during and *after* it has done its work in order to exist."[62]

Deconstructionists use several strategies to "interrogate" those "texts" considered suspect. They grossly generalize the viewpoints of critics to make them seem simple and naive, indulging in passionate denunciations peppered with phrases such as "put into question" or "problematize." They deny that "texts" can be understood through reason or logic. They claim to be using a "new logic" that is based on *none* of the following: either-or, both-and, neither-nor. At the same time, they claim that this new logic does not totally abandon these after all.[63] When all else fails, they accuse critics of being reductive by trying to define deconstruction in the first place. And then they claim that they are being misunderstood!

Whatever the strategy selected, deconstructive rhetoric is provocative and moralistic but also bombastic. Almost invariably, it is couched in amusing or clever slogans – these carry "essentially an emotional, not a logical or theoretical, message," according to Ellis[64] – and sweeping claims. What they consider naive positions are called "privileged" or "hegemonic," which is to say, evil. Overcoming these, they believe, is a moral duty. In these ways, deconstructionists are primed "to strike an attitude, to rally a movement, or to intimidate an opposition."[65] Encounters with the critics are more like performances than debates, albeit ones that create the illusion of intellectual confrontation.[66] In each case, the deconstructionist "supplies a polar opposite to be set beside the naive beliefs with which the argument began."[67] This in turn creates the sense of being revolutionary. For obvious reasons, these reversals are more attractive in some ideological circles than others. "Doubtless ... deconstruction has gained some credibility from those particular situations where specific perspectives have been neglected; in the deconstructive rhetoric of the marginal becoming central and of subverting the distinction between the two, feminists have seen support for their sense that female voices have been neglected; the same is true of Marxists with regard to voices from outside the political and social elite."[68]

But deconstruction is not merely trite for reminding us of the obvious fact that we can never completely overcome the subjective element in verbal communication. It is absurd, because deconstruction itself would be impossible if language were truly so inadequate. Why, then, is deconstruction de rigueur in the academic world? According to Ellis, the reason is to be sought primarily in psychology: "To oppose a particular tradition or viewpoint with a particular alternative program is to set out a real position; but to announce simply an indiscriminate and unspecified opposition to any tradition in general and none in particular, *with no particular alternative in mind* in any given case, is not to take a position at all but only to gain rather too easily acquired feelings of iconoclastic superiority."[69] In other words, pretentious people like deconstruction – they have no particular beliefs, yet want to appear as if that makes them superior. The deconstructionists *are* pretentious, but for a reason that escapes even Ellis. The fact is that most of them do have beliefs and do have alternatives in mind, even though they do not articulate them as deconstructionists per se. And these are nearly always ideological alternatives.

Deconstructionists, especially those associated with feminism and "cultural studies," are almost always affiliated with ideological movements. There might be those who approach deconstructive theory in the pure spirit of intellectual play or philosophical inquiry; if so, they are few. In any case, they are not the people under discussion. We are discussing those who use deconstructive theory to promote their own political interests. The point here – and it underlies everything that follows – is that it might be naive to call these people deconstructionists in the first place. Put simply, we are not convinced they actually *believe* in the infinity of meanings or the absence of a centre proclaimed by deconstructive theory.[70] Ellis assumes the sincerity of deconstructionists.[71] We do not. These people are not dumb. They know very well, for example, that by using jargon they are not "demystifying" but, on the contrary, remystifying. They know very well that, taken to its logical conclusion, deconstruction would deconstruct itself. If no "text" can be said to mean anything definitively, all being informed by the prejudices of their authors and distorted by the interpretations of their readers, that would surely be true of their own theories and works. Precisely for this reason, they prefer to attack the theories of others.

We thus conclude that they knowingly refrain from *doing* what they *say* they are doing or intend to do. In spite of appearances, these people are not relativists or nihilists, nor are they merely playing intellectual games. If taken at face value, deconstruction is self-defeating. No society can exist without establishing order through culture. No culture can exist without selecting some possibilities and rejecting others – that is, without a "centre." But deconstruction is hardly ever *taken* at face value. More often, it is the means to an end, not an end in itself.[72] Because the end is defined ideologically, and because a characteristic feature of secular ideologies is the belief that ends justify means, deconstructionists feel free to use deconstruction as a way of legitimating their attacks on competing worldviews but conveniently stop short when it comes to applying the same logic to their own "texts" or their own ideologies.

We do not accuse these deconstructionists of stupidity, of misunderstanding the obvious implications of their own theories. We accuse them of intellectual dishonesty, deliberately using a dubious theory in order to undermine their adversaries and thus achieve their own political goals.[73] We can think of no other way to explain the immense popularity among highly educated and highly sophisticated people of a theory that, on its own, is trivial at best and absurd at worst. It is important to remember that deconstruction is a movement with a life of its own. It cannot be defended adequately merely by referring to the sophisticated and virtually sacrosanct work of its founder. People use deconstruction for their own purposes, no matter what Derrida actually thought or said.

Once again, it is possible that some people sincerely believe in deconstructive theory. Nothing inherent in it requires ideology. As we say, though, most of those who use and promote deconstruction do so precisely in order to promote their own ideologies. We point as evidence to the fact that deconstructive books and articles usually *support* currently fashionable ideologies. And they are written by people who are passionately devoted to the kind of social and political changes advocated by those ideologies. They do not write from the neutral perspective of sceptics – those who doubt everything. On the contrary, they write from the normative perspective of those who clearly believe that some ways of thinking are good or true and others are evil or false. Reversing rather than eliminating the hierarchy of values is the true goal of their deconstruction.[74] In short, we suggest that many people identified with deconstruction are really ideologues masquerading as deconstructionists for reasons of political expediency. Put simply, deconstruction is a tool used to justify attitudes and proposals that could not be justified in any other way. This is why we have discussed it here in connection with feminist ideology.

Deconstruction is used to attack not only conservatism but also modernism, which is the reason those who call themselves "postmodernists" favour this technique. Why attack modernism? Because they see it not merely as a rival ideology but as the ultimate one. Modernism, they believe, is responsible for the perpetuation of both bourgeois and patriarchal oppression. Like Marxism, modernism originated in the eighteenth-century Enlightenment. Its characteristic products, science and technology, are based on rationalism in general and empiricism in particular. But for feminist ideologues – in this way, they are unlike Marxists – rationalism is inherently contaminated. They associate reason, by which they mean mechanistic logic, with the essence of maleness. And they associate emotion, by which they mean "feeling" or "caring," with the essence of femaleness. (Never mind that they do so in the context of academic institutions that are supposedly based on the use of reason or that that this mentality undermines the status of women at universities and supports the stereotype of women as irrational beings.)

Consequently, feminist ideologues draw heavily on the romantic reaction against Enlightenment thought, even though they use the latter too, especially in the form of Marxism, for some purposes. Not surprisingly, they focus attention on these classic hallmarks of romanticism: intense subjectivity, emotionalism, pseudo-mystical ways of knowing, tribalism, and nostalgia for a lost golden age. These form the very essence, as it were, of postmodernism. So, postmodernism is not only a reaction against modernism, as its name indicates, but also the latest incarnation of romanticism. By deconstructing an alleged belief in perfect objectivity, postmodernists – including feminist ideologues – attack, or at least undermine, everything produced not only by modernism in general but by men in particular (although they sometimes find it politically expedient to make exceptions for non-white or non-heterosexual or non-Western men).

The ideological rhetoric of feminism is not palatable to all women, so a "front" is required. By that we mean rhetoric that is generally considered respectable and can therefore be used to conceal ideas and goals that would otherwise be considered unacceptable. Ideologues routinely use fashionable rhetoric but without following through on its inner logic. As we have already observed, they fill old wineskins with new wine. The words are familiar to almost everyone, yes, but not the implications or interpretations intended by this or that ideologue.

Not entirely by chance, the rise of feminism was paralleled in Canada and the United States by the rise of a political rhetoric that made an ideal front: that of "pluralism," "diversity," and "multiculturalism." Instead of the traditional political rhetoric of unity, advocates substituted the rhetoric of *difference*. They celebrated ethnic and sexual or other particularities, not human universals. And with that came "identity politics." The concepts of equality, democracy, and tolerance have provided the bridge between the old rhetoric and the new. All groups deserve equal respect, do they not?[75] Because these beliefs lie at the very heart of collective identity, no one can argue with them (at least not in public). In short, they create the perfect front for ideology of one kind or another.

What has feminism to do with pluralism, diversity, and multiculturalism? Feminists often attack critics for assuming that feminism is a single, homogeneous movement. They argue that there are many "feminisms"; they tolerate various, and sometimes opposing, schools of feminism. Moreover, they use the rhetoric of postmodernism to defend the resulting chaos. Feminism is good, they say, precisely because of its "inclusivity" and "multivocality." One result is a refusal, mainly for political reasons, to challenge those forms of feminism that might be considered undesirable or irresponsible. Under attack, the ranks close. In this sense, feminism has indeed been a single, homogenous, movement (although there are signs of change).[76] It can be challenged from within but not from without. Moreover, all feminists must have at least a few things in common; otherwise, there could be no political movement, and the term would be either meaningless or unintelligible.

It is worth noting that all these trendy words – "pluralism," "diversity," "multiculturalism," and the rest – are not inherent in democracy. And that might be unimportant in countries with homogeneous populations. But in Canada and the United States, society would fall apart without some way of uniting everyone in a larger whole. As the Americans put it, e pluribus unum. Tolerance is not merely a virtue: it is a necessity. No movement in a democratic society can hope for success unless it can make use of these concepts. Even movements that are ambivalent about them must articulate their programs in this lingua franca, no matter how blatant the contradictions. Marxists often found it difficult to do so, because they were linked with totalitarian regimes in other parts of the world. Feminists, on the other hand, are seldom suspected of promoting goals that might be incompatible with the rhetoric of democracy. The burden is on critics of ideological feminists, therefore, to support any claim that feminist rhetoric is not necessarily what it seems.

To sum up, although there are important differences between one school of feminism and another,[77] the ideological nature of some is disguised by notions such as pluralism, diversity, and multiculturalism – notions that, if analysed and applied consistently, would not support many of the claims made by feminist ideologues. All this jive talk about difference and pluralism conceals something very important: underlying it is an ideology derived from Marxism and romanticism but with class or nation replaced by gender as the central concept. The feminist take on pluralism and even equality, as we have shown elsewhere, is often nothing more than a convenient, though not always consciously intended, front for a gynocentric and even misandric ideology. Why bother with a front? Because people seldom acknowledge their own theories and programs as ideology, which has always had negative connotations.

But there are more specific fronts for feminist ideology. Two are of particular interest here: reform as a front for revolution, and anger as a front for hatred. Take the example of reform: virtually all Canadians and Americans today accept the idea that reforms – suffrage, education, work in the public sphere – have been necessary to improve the lives of women. Acceptance of reform for women is by now a foregone conclusion. But it is sometimes hard to distinguish between reformist and revolutionist rhetoric. Not all women acknowledge or even understand the revolutionary implications of what ideological feminists advocate in the name of reform.

Many Jewish and Christian feminists believe that they are trying to restore lost features of their traditions, not to destroy those traditions. But the fact is that some proposed changes cannot be legitimated by tradition, no matter how liberal the interpretation, without destroying its historical or intellectual integrity. That is what happens when feminists advocate the worship of a female deity but still claim to be Jews or Christians. They say that their goal is merely "inclusion." But to be included on their terms, in many cases, would mean abandoning the most fundamental features of Western monotheism: the rejection of female deities and the insistence on a single deity that transcends both femaleness *and* maleness. (The latter is a fundamental tenet of both Jewish and Christian theology, by the way, despite the popular tendency to use masculine imagery.) Because the truth would be obvious to everyone, they find ways of disguising it.

Consider the use of "Sophia" in the rhetoric of Christian feminists. Some defend it as a mere attribute, a feminine one, of God; others acknowledge it as a code word representing "the Goddess." That is the subtext. As a result, women are encouraged to identify themselves with the godhead. The end once again justifies the means. Like Marxists, these feminists want to infiltrate religious organizations, to use them as fronts. They want to change every institution or tradition from within.

Now take the example of anger as a front for hatred. Many people use the word "hatred" as a synonym for "intense anger" or "intense dislike." This popular interpretation is evident in a comic strip. A little girl tells her brother "I hate you! I always hated you! And I always will hate you!" She is rebuked by her mother for using such "harsh language." Finally, the girl turns to her brother and corrects herself: "I dislike you. I always disliked you. I always will dislike you!"[78] But "hate" is *not* merely a harsh version of "dislike." It is something quite different, though not necessarily unrelated. Some extremely important distinctions can be made between the two terms.

Anger is an emotion. Hatred is a worldview.[79] Anger is a response to either individuals or groups. Hatred is a response to groups. Anger is transient, because the experience of everyday life, even if only on a purely physiological level, soon provokes other emotional responses.

Hatred is enduring (and this is important) because it is sustained and promoted by culture, primarily as beliefs passed from one generation to the next. In modern societies, these beliefs – prejudicial beliefs, or negative stereotypes[80] – are transmitted through both popular and elite culture. It is true that anger can *lead* to hatred, but then it is no longer anger but has become something else. A way of feeling has become a way of thinking. Besides, the origin of hatred does not excuse it. As a psychological mechanism, anger itself is often a perfectly healthy response to people. No one could survive a lifetime of psychological and physical threats without being able to experience anger. As a cultural mechanism, on the other hand, hatred – we include here both forms of sexism, misandry and misogyny – is a highly inappropriate response to people. When enough people deliberately perpetuate their anger, whether originally due to malice or fear, it is institutionalized as hatred. What had been morally neutral, because emotions involve no choices and can thus be neither good nor bad, is no longer morally neutral. It is evil.

This is why people who hate seldom acknowledge doing so, not even to themselves. That would be tantamount to acknowledging that they too participate in evil. And that would be very difficult. They instead rationalize hatred away by calling it something else. Usually, they call it righteous or at least justifiable "anger." Sometimes, they simply deny the connection between what they think and how they behave. Sally Jessy Raphael once introduced a guest on her show as someone who was "proud to be a racist." Ruth Jackson was indeed proud of her racism: for her, racism meant "to love your own people, your own race." It meant defending your own race against those threatening it. With this in mind, she described Jews as the "offsprings [sic] of Satan, Lucifer." But Raphael did not let the matter rest there. "Do you feel," she asked, that "you are full of hate?" And Jackson replied, quite sincerely in all likelihood: "No, I don't feel I'm full of hate ... I don't hate the black race. I don't hate the Chinese."[81]

Raphael's racist guests were unsophisticated. But no matter how beguiling its presentation, no matter how sophisticated its attempted legitimation, hatred is still a brutal and primitive response to the problems that confront us. One form hatred takes is racism, but that is by no means the only form. What is true of racism is true also of sexism. No one, not even a victim, is immune to hatred. (Even gays and lesbians, surely the victims of hatred themselves, are beginning to confront the fact that members of their own communities have expressed open hostility toward bisexuals.[82]) How could it be otherwise? Hatred is made possible by ignorance, but it is actually caused by fear. Neither victimizers nor their victims can claim a good enough reason for hatred, because hatred is *inherently* wrong; both victims *and* victimizers, on the other hand, might have good reasons (though not necessarily the ones outsiders expect) for their fear. There are often several steps between primary experience of fear and the secondary one of hatred. These might include the teaching of contempt and the institutionalization of hatred. The original cause, however, might be forgotten in the process. That is why political correctness can never solve the problem of hatred. Those who hate can be taught that their targets are inappropriate and even that hatred itself is inappropriate, but they cannot be taught to ignore the fear that generated their hatred in the first place. Unless the underlying cause of this fear is correctly identified, taken seriously, and effectively addressed, they will consciously or subconsciously seek one group or another as the target of hatred.[83]

Men in our time in fact have good reason to fear that feminist ideology leaves them with no basis whatsoever for a healthy identity. A fundamental premise of feminism is that women can do, and should do, everything that men do. That leaves precisely nothing on which to base masculine identity except for those immoral things that women, unlike men, are allegedly immune to. In other words, men can make no distinctive, necessary, and valued contribution to society, *as men* (although they can make personal contributions as individuals). Better a negative identity, perhaps, than no identity at all. If women say that they are evil, some boys and men think, then so be it. No wonder Annette Insdorf, director of undergraduate film studies at Columbia University, has thought about the impact (you should excuse the expression) of *Fight Club* (David Fincher, 1999): "I am worried about young males. What bothers me is that the body is rendered as an object upon which pain can and should be inflicted."[84]

But even a well-founded fear such as loss of identity among men is no excuse for hatred of women. Men must not be excused for converting fear into hatred. Similarly, women must not be excused for ignoring that fear, much less for converting their own well-founded fear into hatred of men. Women have been allowed to explore the causes of their fear and take action to eliminate its causes. Men, unfortunately, have not. So far, both men and women have paid the price for this folly.

Among the most obvious expressions of hatred is the desire for revenge. It is a lamentable sign of the times, to take only one example, that the 1994–95 edition of *Books in Print* listed many titles under the word "revenge." One of these entries was discussed on talk shows: *Sweet Revenge: The Wicked Delights of Getting Even,*[85] by Regina Barreca, a professor of English and feminist theory at the University of Connecticut. Everyone knows that the desire for revenge is a universal feature of human existence. Barreca felt a need to say so, nevertheless, and at great length. Her book is a characteristic product of a society in which pop psychology has replaced moral principles, in which whatever feels good *is* good (read: therapeutic).

To be sure, Barreca explicitly condones only "wholesome revenge." By this, she refers to forms that teach lessons but do no permanent harm. "Revenge, as a concept, can oblige us to explain – to others, but more importantly, to ourselves – what we need and want from the world,"[86] she argues. For her, this supposedly profound insight turns revenge from a sign of moral shame to a sign of emotional health. It is worth noting that she devotes a whole chapter to one particular realm of revenge: "Just Like a Woman: Distinctive Feminine Revenge," in which she discusses *Thelma and Louise.*

The ideological aspect of her book becomes clear at the end. Because it restores "balance," she implies, revenge is not only emotionally useful but – and this is what counts most of all – socially and politically useful as well: "Balance ... can only be achieved if everyone has access to power ... The world being what it is, revenge flickers on our screen, fills up our pages, and lights bonfires in our imagination."[87] On the assumption that women have no power (even though there are many different kinds of power, some of which are held primarily by women), Barreca maintains they are justified in exacting revenge from men. But the mentality of fighting fire with fire is a long way from that of doing unto others as you would have them do unto you. Emotional manipulation is no longer something to avoid on moral grounds. On the contrary, it is something to cultivate on psychological and political grounds. Which is why Barreca calls one chapter "How Sweet It Is."

Of course revenge feels emotionally satisfying. So do many other things that most people would even now find repugnant. The only question is whether revenge can be considered morally acceptable. If everything that felt right *were* right, there would be no need for morality at all. Precisely because of the simple – but nevertheless profound – insight that some feelings are inherently destructive, human beings in every society have found it necessary to establish moral and legal codes. The desire for revenge is the desire to see other people suffer, to feel good at the expense of others. This is not the same as justice, which involves not only the legal requirement that wrongs be made right, usually through restitution or recompense, but also the moral requirement of reconciliation. It is true that legal justice involves punishment. But legal punishment is administered by the community – the state, the tribe, the clan, or whatever – not by those personally involved, those whose personal desire for revenge takes precedence over the restoration of order and discouragement of further disorder.

Barreca has chosen to foster a mentality that poisons relations between men and women or any other groups locked in cycles of hatred and retaliation. Barreca is part of the problem, therefore, not the solution. The very best that can be said of her approach is that it can have a temporarily therapeutic effect on those who take revenge. As everyone knows, those on the receiving end seldom respond in helpful ways. The fact is that shame or humiliation do not and cannot provide the kind of foundation on which harmony is based. As an indication of how far we have moved from recognition of common sense, let alone moral awareness, note that Barreca's book is published by an establishment called "Harmony Books."

In a 1990 article on the victims' rights movement, "Getting Even: The Role of the Victim," Jeffrie Murphy[88] argues that our society has for too long placed love and forgiveness at the "centre" of what could be called our "moral and legal discourses." To rectify this egregious situation, he suggests that we consider instead giving the "privileged" position to hatred and revenge. (Even Murphy does not follow the deconstructive strategy of attacking all "privileged" positions, which just goes to show that postmodernism is by no means the only way of thinking that promotes social and political fragmentation.) There is nothing new about hatred and revenge. What *is* new is the fact that many people no longer feel any need to legitimate them, but on the contrary now place the burden of proof on those who give moral and legal primacy to love and forgiveness. Clearly, we can no longer take for granted even the most fundamental ideals of our society, or of any society. Everything will have to be argued all over again from scratch. In short, we will have to re-invent the moral wheel.

It will not do, therefore, to dismiss ideological feminists as members of a radical fringe group of no consequence in public life. To the extent that democracy is only as good as the moral fibre of its voters, that it can be maintained on the basis only of constant vigilance, and that all ideologies constitute inherent threats to democracy by denying value to specific groups of citizens, ideological feminists must be taken very seriously.

In this chapter we have argued that the roots of misandry in popular culture can be found in the misandry of elite culture. Ideological feminists are usually, though not always, academics. (See appendix 6 for a case study, Kaja Silverman's film theory.) Just as the influence of feminist ideology was peaking in elite culture during the 1990s, at any rate, so was the influence of misandry in popular culture. This was no coincidence. But precisely how has the former become so deeply embedded in the latter, so deeply that it is taken for granted? So deeply that, for all intents and purposes, it is invisible? We turn to these questions in the next chapter.

CHAPTER NINE

Conclusion

Men and women are really angry at each other ... We don't know how
to live together, don't trust each other. Men are feeling displaced; women
are angry.[1]

The signature slogan of *Star Trek*, the original series on television, had
a mission "to boldly go where no *man* has gone before." Twenty-five
years on, the mission proclaimed in *Star Trek* movies was "to boldly
go where no *one* has gone before."

It is hard to believe that an industry as conscious of public opinion
as the entertainment industry would allow other products to be advertised in what is now called "sexist language." Nevertheless, *The
Shadow* (Russell Mulcahy, 1994) was marketed with just that kind of
language. Its slogan could have been: "Who knows what evil lurks in
the heart of anyone?" Instead, the paradigm used decades earlier was
retained: "Who knows what evil lurks in the hearts of men?" By 1994,
"men" could mean only *male* people, not people in general and
certainly not female people. No wonder Jim Mullen of *Entertainment
Weekly* made an overtly sexist joke about it: "*The Shadow*: 'Who
knows what evil lurks in the hearts of men?' Anyone who's ever dated
one."[2] Did feminists complain that women were excluded or even that
men were mocked? If any did, their letters to the editor were not
published. Listen to the promo for *Wolf* (Mike Nichols, 1994): "In
every man, there are two men: one who learns to be civilized by day
and one who longs to be savage by night."[3] Once again, the reference
is to male people, not people in general and certainly not female
people. Since the 1980s, misandry in one form of another has become
pervasive in popular culture. The promos for many movies leave no
room for misinterpretation about the existence and public acceptability
of misandry.

We cannot get into the minds of other people and declare that misogyny no longer exists. But whatever the level of misogyny in private

life, it shows up less and less in public life, including popular culture. And when it does, the perps are promptly hauled before the court of public opinion and punished. The same does not happen in connection with misandry. It is seldom even recognized, let alone challenged.

But many readers might object, okay, so misandry is pervasive in popular culture – but misogyny was once even more pervasive. Why get all upset? We do not claim that all of the artifacts and productions of popular culture are misandric. Some are neither misandric nor misogynistic. (There is more to human existence than gender.) Even so, many *are* misandric. Our immediate goal in this book has been the rather modest one of describing a phenomenon or, to be more precise, the link between two phenomena: pop cultural misandry and ideological feminism.

It is not enough merely to point out a few isolated cases of blatant misandry. Those would amount to nothing more than, well, a few isolated cases, but dozens of examples cannot be brushed aside so easily. In this book, we have presented a massive array of pop cultural misandric artifacts and productions: movies, television shows, comic strips, greeting cards, and so on. It is not enough, moreover, merely to examine the most blatant examples of misandry. Those are usually obvious to everyone, whether or not they generate any concern. To achieve our goal, we have done two things that are seldom done. First we have examined enough cases of misandry in popular culture to establish a pattern, one that cultural observers – film and television critics, social scientists, feminists, journalists – should feel both intellectually and morally obliged to account for. Second, we have analysed these artifacts and productions at a level that is both deep and subtle enough to provoke questions – psychological, philosophical, theological, political, and moral – about what is going on below the apparently innocuous surface of everyday life. That, we hope, will set the stage for additional research on the condition of men in our society.

Our ultimate goal, however, is to help reverse the current polarization of men and women[4] by laying the foundation for a new social contract between the sexes – one that takes seriously the distinctive needs and problems of both sexes. But that is far beyond the scope of this volume.

We are still left with several questions. How did we get from misandry in elite culture to misandry in popular culture? Why do so many people who see pop cultural misandry nevertheless try to ignore it, trivialize it, excuse it, or even justify it? And what is likely to happen as a result?

Ideological feminists have not chosen to create an ivory tower for themselves. One of their basic goals, after all, is cultural revolution.

Consequently, they seek specific ways of propagating their theories and implementing them. We have already discussed the use of fronts: "political correctness" as a front for genuine etiquette, "reform" for revolution, and "anger" for hatred. But they use many other strategies too. One which we can do no more than mention here is infiltration. That is an ugly word, especially because of its association with communism and anti-communism in the not-so-distant past. Even worse, it is a dangerous word suggesting an organized conspiracy. We have no evidence of that, at least not on a massive scale (although the like-minded have always found ways of linking up with each other). Trouble is, there might not be a better word to describe this complex phenomenon. Like the word "revolution," the word "infiltration" is used here in connection with something much more subtle and sophisticated than secretly organizing cadres to overthrow existing institutions. Whether by design or by default, the result is highly placed feminist ideologues in almost every institution.

Ideologically motivated professors, for example, indoctrinate new generations of young women (and young men, too, if possible) at universities. Ideologically motivated members of the helping professions counsel their clients, ostensibly for strictly therapeutic purposes, to adopt ideological perspectives. Some establish their status, moreover, by publishing research. And they have used the mechanisms at their disposal, not surprisingly, to promote their worldview with all its practical and moral implications. That is to say, they have expanded their grass-roots collectives into larger networks for political mobilization. If this can be called infiltration, so be it.

With that linguistic problem in mind, we pause here to comment on a very complex and subtle phenomenon, one that is easily – and, from the ideological point of view, fortunately – misunderstood. Most people, both women and men, are unaware of strategies intended to produce cultural revolution. They think in terms of cultural reform. Their goal is to improve the political status and economic situation of women by correcting an androcentric worldview. They sincerely approve of the women's movement in general and its stated goal of improving society in the name of equality and democracy. And that is as it should be. But they are not the only ones who use the word "reform." So do ideological feminists. And both groups agree on many points, which often makes it hard to see where they disagree. This is where two very different phenomena converge: the mainstream desire for reform and the ideological rhetoric of reform. The process of translating the former into the latter, so to speak, is seldom visible. Even when it is, many people are conditioned by their belief in tolerance and pluralism to overlook what they believe is a lapse in judgment or an excess of zeal. Whatever the specific intentions of individuals, and whatever their organizational links with other individuals, the result has been the direct and indirect influence of ideological feminism in every significant institution.

Many would be shocked to realize how profoundly their own thinking has been influenced by ideology, the influence being so subtle that it would hardly seem possible. Even if the direct line of influence seems unclear, one thing really should be evident from the pervasive misandry of popular culture: a major change in our society that must be accounted for. Either directly or indirectly, ideological feminism has resulted in the teaching of contempt for men. And a lot of well-meaning citizens, both female and male (though for different reasons), have been swept in with the tide of fashion or convention even if not of hatred. Those involved in the entertainment industry, whether ideologically motivated or not, popularize the resulting misandry in movies, say, or sitcoms. Journalists, whether ideologically motivated or not, popularize it through the talk shows and newsmagazine shows. All find it profitable to comment on "women's issues," especially sensational cases that occasionally monopolize public attention. The final step is taken once again within the context of elite culture. Politicians, whether ideologically motivated or not, advocate legislation based on the resulting popular opinion. Even Supreme Court justices are by no means immune to popular opinion.

By now, the worldview of ideological feminism, including its misandry, has taken on a life of its own. Popular culture reflects feminist assumptions that are pervasive and deeply rooted in our society. (The process works both ways, actually, because popular culture not only reflects cultural assumptions but also shapes them.) The teaching of contempt, moreover, is financially lucrative. Misandry sells. Sometimes, as in the case of *Masterpiece Theatre*, it earns prestige as well as money.

Both men and women often fail to see misandry as a problem, because sexism has been defined exclusively in terms of misogyny. They find what they are looking for. And they do not find what they are not looking for. Everyone would admit to seeing examples of misandry now and then, but many or most people fail to see the pattern. After decades of relentless searching for every vestige of misogyny, it can be very difficult to accept even the possibility of misandry as a significant counterpart to misogyny.[5] Even when it appears in its most blatant forms, in fact, misandry is often *mistaken for misogyny.*

Consider *In the Company of Men* (Neil LaBute, 1996). Because the main character and his sidekick victimize a woman, many viewers have complained that this movie is misogynistic. Because the main character truly hates *everyone*, on the other hand, it could be described more appropriately as misanthropic. Just because a movie is *about* misogny, after all, does not mean that it is misogynistic. At the moment, in fact, depicting misogyny is far more likely to be an indictment of it than a justification of it. In this movie, one male character is evil and the other inadequate. The main female character is a virtuous victim and heroine. According to the criteria outlined in chapter 1, therefore, *Company* is described most appropriately as *misandric*. The mere fact that so many women react to it with anger – and to the world of men supposedly represented by its male characters – indicates that its primary effect (as distinct, at least in theory, from its aim) was to incite misandry rather than misogyny. Male viewers are expected to identify themselves with characters presented as the villains. Female viewers are expected to identify themselves with a character eulogized as movie's victim and heroine.

Here is the story. Howie and Chad are two junior executives sent out by their company to some remote midwestern branch office for a six-week job. Both are frustrated and angry, having recently lost not only promotions but girlfriends. But the two could hardly be more different. Howie is a typical loser, bland in both appearance and manner, lacking self-confidence, and almost completely passive. Chad, on the other hand, is an impossibly handsome young man endowed with boundless self-confidence and an incredibly dynamic personality supported by a high level of physical and psychic energy. His presence is electrifying. For obvious reasons he dominates, controls, and manipulates Howie, along with everyone else, and convinces Howie to join him in taking revenge. Because revenge against the company is too dangerous, they settle for revenge against women. They will find the most vulnerable woman around, court her simultaneously, and then dump her. Christine, the woman they select, happens to be ethereally beautiful and deeply sensitive. She is also deaf, and thus not likely to have seen much action in the way of dating. Everything goes according to plan. Howie woos her first. Then, turning on his considerable charm, Chad showers Christine with flowers and eventually seduces her. In love with Chad, she has to break up with Howie. And Howie, unfortunately, has actually fallen in love with her.

So where is the controversy in all this? It could be argued that *Company* is a feminist movie, which should make it immune to explicit attack. Look, it says, see how horrible men are to women. But this movie is not about a misogynist. It is about a *misanthrope*. Chad hates women, but he hates men as well, including his friend Howie. He says as much, explicitly, about virtually every man at the office. He humiliates a younger man by demanding that he pull down his pants and demonstrate that he literally has the "balls" for his job. Chad's main goal at this moment in his life is to hurt *Howie*. Chad has planned his "revenge" primarily with him in mind, not a woman. Chad's girlfriend, he later admits, had never dumped him; he had used that lie as an excuse to entice Howie into morally unacceptable behaviour. When Howie finally asks him why, Chad responds nonchalantly: "Because I could." This is followed by a revealing question. "How does it feel to hurt someone?" he asks Howie.

Unlike some misanthropes who make exceptions for individuals, Chad has contempt for everyone; he is incapable of love for anyone. His behaviour is not analogous, therefore, to that of men (or women) who grow tired of this or that partner and move on to another. Breaking up is always difficult, and someone always gets hurt. But Chad does not merely grow tired of Christine or find someone else he likes better. He is not merely insensitive or cowardly, or even immoral. He is amoral, which makes him a psychopath. Lacking the capacity for empathy, he is incapable of being a moral agent, but he is capable of doing evil. The whole point of his affair with Christine, even before meeting her, is to make someone suffer. If women identify Chad as an ordinary or "average" man, they have not only misunderstood the movie but also succumbed themselves to the very sexism they attribute to Chad.

Howie, on the other hand, really is hopelessly confused and ordinary. But he, not Chad, is the protagonist. Male viewers are expected to identify with him, not Chad. In fact, they have no choice: it is impossible on both philosophical and psychological grounds to identify with a character defined exclusively in connection with evil. Not even Hitler thought of himself as evil, after all; on the contrary, he thought of himself as heroically good. Howie does go along with Chad's plan, after some surprise and hesitation, but he has enough humanity – he is a real person, unlike Chad – to realize that Christine is someone he could genuinely love and to feel genuine remorse for hurting her.

But even though *Company* itself is neither misandric nor misogynistic, many of its critics and viewers really do succumb to misandry. Critics often fail to see the misanthropy, blinded by the possibility that *women* might find doing so offensive. Or they see nothing wrong with misandry in view of the assumption that men somehow deserve prejudice. The implication is that Chad and Howie represent men in general and Christine women in general. Richard Corliss notes that "the most interesting part of the film comes after it's over. That's when the real knives come out. At the Sundance Film Festival, where this pitch-black comedy was an award winner, [director Neil] LaBute was widely rebuked by the sensitivity patrol. After a Manhattan screening, a male publicist was punched. Well, he was a guy. Probably deserved it."[6] Corliss reports that the star playing Chad, Aaron Eckhart, had mentioned the desire of some women to slap or punch him. Controversy began even before the release of *Company.* "Quite simply," writes Colin Brown, "distributors were scared of offending the female audience with such a naked exhibition of male piggery."[7]

Forgotten or ignored, though, was what should have been obvious to everyone not blinded by feminist politics. By implying that all men are evil and all women are their innocent victims – who nevertheless get even in the end! – the critics, unlike those responsible for the movie, really are misandric. Controversy increased, not surprisingly, once the movie was released. Tom Bernard puts it this way: "Women love the movie. It shows men behaving badly, and women feel like a fly on the wall watching the things men do."[8] Corliss points out that "[w]omen can take a peek at – and, if they wish, confirm their suspicions of – that dangerous and perplexing house pest, the modern middle-class male."[9]

In the late 1990s, what some people called "frat-boy humour" became extremely common both in movies and on television. Think of the cinematic "comedies" associated with Jim Carrey, say, or Adam Sandler, or television shows such as *Men Behaving Badly, Beavis and Butt-head,* or *South Park.* All of these productions are based on the premise that men are morons, vulgar morons, who enjoy nothing more than jokes about feces and vomit or about women used as sexual toys. It could be argued, and has been argued, that, well, men *like* this stuff. These movies and shows do make money. Ergo, critics argue, the basic premise must be correct. One critic has written about the spate of shows featuring this kind of humour. By the late 1990s, these included *The Man Show, Happy Hour,* and *The X Show.* All were attacked as misogynistic. But these shows are *about* misogyny. The joke is always on misogynistic men, not the women who are their victims. To the extent that they represent men as a class, which they do, the shows themselves would be more accurately called misandric. Due to the cultural preoccupation with misogyny, their inherent misandry simply disappears from view.

Something very similar happened when *All in the Family* made its debut thirty years earlier. At first, people were shocked that any network would be allowed to broadcast such a hatefully "sexist" and "racist" show. One of the main characters spends most of his time making overtly bigoted remarks. But the joke is on Archie Bunker himself, not on those he stereotypes or attacks. Viewers laugh at him, not with him (even though their condescension towards him is mixed with pity). Or, to put it another way, they identify with women represented by his saintly wife, Edith, or blacks represented by his long-suffering neighbours, the Jeffersons. In fact, this show is now widely considered to have broken new ground in the struggle against racism and sexism. Nothing has changed. In *The Fighting Fitzgeralds*, Archie has been resurrected as the bigoted patriarch of a lower-middle-class family; the joke is still on male viewers who are too stupid to realize that all men are being relentlessly ridiculed. According to Ken Tucker, television executives "are wise enough to see that there's a vacuum on TV that's waiting to be filled" and that they "can't resist trying to cash in on a predictable trend."[10] The question, however, is precisely whose vacuum is waiting to be filled: That of men who need more misogynistic jokes? Or that of women who need more misandric ones? Shows that depict women in the grip of lust and filled with contempt for men, such as *Sex in the City*, are seldom attacked as misandric. On the contrary, they are lauded as sophisticated "commentaries" on the dating scene.

A more recent example of cinematic misandry, disguised as comedy, is *What Planet Are You From?* (Mike Nichols, 2000). Taking a direct cue from John Gray's bestselling book, *Men Are from Mars, Women Are from Venus*,[11] viewers are asked to believe that there is a planet inhabited only by males. One of them is sent on a mission to earth, his goal to mate with a female and thus ensure the reproduction of his kind. Once established here as a banker, albeit one with a penis that hums, Harold reveals himself (by implication, every male) as a primitive, though friendly, barbarian. He has no idea of how to please a woman and resorts to the most stereotypically gauche and offensive approaches. "The character is a walking send-up of the long-out-of-date macho-caveman pickup artist," writes Owen Gleiberman.[12] Moreover, says Gleiberman, Harold is cynical. "He doesn't believe a thing he says – his 'seductive' patter is all just a means to an end – but then, that's the wormy operating principle of so many lotharios: Tell a woman not what you think but what you think she wants to hear. The movie capitalizes quite smartly, on [actor Garry] Shandling's blasé solipsism – the lack of feeling he radiates toward anything but his own immediate goals." His friend at the bank is even worse. He takes Harold to an AA meeting, even though neither is an alcoholic, in order to hit on vulnerable women. Eventually, Harold meets a woman who likes him, unaccountably, in spite of everything. They land up together, of course, but only after she teaches him how to behave as a human being – which is to say, after she tames the male beast in him.

Given this atmosphere, it is no wonder feminist icon Germaine Greer could finish up the twentieth century with yet another book on misogyny. In *The Whole Woman*,[12] she opines that all men hate some women at some times in their lives (as if all women do not hate some men at some times in their lives). This, she implies, is proof of universal misogyny. Against all evidence to the contrary, moreover, she claims that our society considers misogyny normal and acceptable. No one, she claims – that is, no man – thinks twice when women are ridiculed, brutalized, or killed. Clearly, she herself does not think twice when men are ridiculed, brutalized, or killed. In fact, she gives no evidence of thinking about men at all except as a class of oppressors.

Although not all women approve of everything said by feminists or even identify themselves as feminists, most have consciously or unconsciously absorbed the "secular myth" of ideological feminism[14] (secular, as we say, because its traditional biblical setting and explicit theological context have been replaced with those considered more in line with "scientific" evidence and more useful for political purposes). One version emphasizes the attitudes formed and transmitted by culture. In the beginning, men and women lived happily in a paradise that was, paradoxically, both egalitarian and female dominated. At the moment, men and women live unhappily in a male-dominated dystopia. In the (near) future, women will re-establish the original paradise and welcome any men who can be taught or forced to mend their ways. Another version emphasizes not merely culture (which can be changed) but nature itself (which cannot). Men are "innately evil," in effect, because of "testosterone poisoning," a genetic propensity to brutality, violence, selfishness, or whatever.[15]

This point of view, in one version or the other, became extremely widespread in the 1990s. We refer not only to its acknowledged status as a politically correct version of truth but also to its unacknowledged but powerful status as conventional wisdom. By "conventional wisdom," we refer to assumptions about the way things are that few people, female or male, bother to question or even think about – which is to say, "ideology" in the sense used by Marx and his followers.

There have probably always been feminists who have recognized misandry and been troubled by it. It flies in the face of everything feminists have learned from the experience of women and everything that some feminists claim about the innate decency of women. But it is worth pointing out that this extraordinary phenomenon, the dehumanization of half the population, has gone almost unnoticed not only by the reviewers and journalists who work for the mass media but also by the critics and theorists who write for academic journals. Despite the vaunted capacity of women for empathy, only a few feminist publications, albeit ones of profound moral significance, have so far expressed sympathy for men in general, except as a way of encouraging men to believe that feminism is in their own interest.[16]

Until very recently, moreover, the few feminists who dared to speak out against misandry were usually declared to be enemies of feminism, or even enemies of women, and thus effectively silenced. Most feminists deny misandry. When challenged, which happens occasionally, they use three strategies: excusing it, justifying it, or trivializing it.

Women who try to excuse misandry acknowledge it as a moral problem. They do not approve of it, but they are willing to tolerate it, at least for the time being. There are several characteristic excuses.

One of them is based on psychology. It is a lamentable but inevitable fact, some observe, that most women see nothing wrong with attacks on men, masculinity, or even maleness itself. People always find it hard to feel sympathy for those they consider privileged (although that did not prevent many women from feeling sympathy for the unhappily married Princess of Wales, who had access to privilege and status beyond the wildest dreams of most women or men). It is even harder for people to feel sympathy for those they consider rivals or enemies.[17]

Another excuse is based on expediency. It is a lamentable but inevitable fact, some say, that many women succumb to misandry. However, when feeling endangered, people tend to close ranks. In a more secure future, maybe women will address the problem of misandry. Maybe, or maybe not.

Underlying all excuses for misandry is the tenacious belief that men have "all the power." Resistance to men's studies, for instance, is often based on the belief that only victims are worthy of study. The response among female academics is often as follows: "Oh, please. Something like 90 per cent of the world's resources are owned and operated by 3 per cent of the population, all of whom are white males."[18] Never mind that this 3 per cent is a tiny fraction of the *male* population, even of the white male population. The underlying assumption, in any case, is that men cannot be damaged by misandry. Anyone who complains should "take it like a man." These women seldom take seriously forms of power other than physical, political, or economic power. The fact that many men do not have godlike power in any of these realms, something anyone can observe merely by walking down the street or watching the nightly news, makes no difference. Neither does the fact that not even physical, political, or economic power can generate emotional invincibility (assuming that this would be a good thing). They see men as a "class," in any case, not as individuals or even as a class with a "diversity" of "voices." Rendering women either unwilling or unable to see men as fully human beings, as people who can indeed be hurt both individually and collectively, might well be the single most serious flaw in feminism. If men are truly vulnerable in any way, after all, then they can surely be expected either to fight back or to withdraw sullenly when threatened at a fundamental level. And the level of identity is about as fundamental as you can get.

Women who *trivialize* misandry belong in a second category, probably the most popular one (although they could be included in the first category on the grounds that the easiest way to excuse misandry is to argue that it is a trivial phenomenon.) They sometimes acknowledge misandry as a moral problem but not a serious one. They are willing to tolerate it, therefore, though not necessarily to encourage it.

Both unsophisticated women and ideological feminists are likely to say, for different reasons, that pop cultural misandry is ephemeral and trivial; lapses in good taste, common sense, or even common decency may be excused. But they would never tolerate that argument in connection with pop cultural misogyny: feminists have argued very effectively that there can be no such thing as taking that too seriously. In fact, they have made popular culture one of the chief battlegrounds in their struggle for women.

The world presented in movies or on television, they continue, is merely a fantasy world. Well, yes, but it is also a self-contained and often convincing simulation of the real world. Indeed, movies fail at the box office and shows fail in the ratings when they do not convince viewers of a likeness between the fantasy world and the real one, when they do not encourage the willing suspension of disbelief. With both this and their own intellectual or political interests in mind, those who create these productions carefully select features of everyday life that they consider significant and reject others that they consider insignificant. Virtually nothing of the real world that appears onscreen, in theatres or at home, is there by accident. Similarly, virtually nothing of the real world that "disappears" onscreen is absent by accident. In other words, movies and shows are never direct transcriptions of reality; they are always interpretations of reality. What would otherwise be dry theories of interest only to academics become powerfully evocative experiences of interest, if made with skill, to all viewers. They are secular myths. Their moral value, therefore, depends more on what *kind* of secular myth than on their correlation with empirical information that can be verified by historians or social scientists. It could be argued that misandric movies such as those discussed in this book are either immoral or unhealthy, for instance, because they encourage people to stereotype men as evil, psychotic, or, at best, inadequate. The same argument would apply to movies that stereotype other groups of people, including women. But moral consistency is not always a high priority among critics or, for that matter, the population at large.

When criticized for their silence in the face of misandry, at any rate, these women usually argue that only "radical" feminists on the "lunatic fringe" could ever be found guilty of hatred. Others argue that misandry might have been common in the past – in the 1980s, say – but is no longer.[19] Maybe they actually believe that. We have been told for decades that women are innately "nurturant" beings and thus virtually immune to hating. Women who do hate must therefore be rare anomalies, either the crazed victims of a male-dominated society or the crazed victims of some psychological or physiological disorder. Theory notwithstanding, the evidence presented to everyone in everyday life indicates that women are no less capable of prejudice and hatred than men.

Women who try to *justify* misandry are in an entirely different category. They do not acknowledge it as a moral problem, but on the contrary see it as a moral and practical duty. Thus, they are willing not merely to tolerate it but also to encourage it.

Some women try to justify misandry as a legitimate "choice" for women, a "voice" for those who have been "silenced." Expressing anger is useful, they believe, as one feature of collective therapy for women. But they make the dubious assumption that misandry is about anger, not hatred. Even feminists who disapprove of Andrea Dworkin's misandric claim that any act of sexual intercourse with men amounts to rape, for example, often defend her as someone who "pushes the boundaries" and thus promotes the cause of women (albeit in a way that embarrasses some of them).

In its most sophisticated form, this attempt at justification is couched in terms of postmodernism. Once that became de rigueur among feminists, they could argue that man-hating was merely one example of the "diversity" or "pluralism" within feminism. According to one variant of this strategy, misandry is not aimed at all men but only at those with "privileged" status: rich men, white men, or any other group of elite men. Yet the distinction is often more theoretical and politically correct than practical, because they go on to argue that all men benefit from the behaviour of those few. Implicit, therefore, is the belief that all men are intentionally or unintentionally the enemies of women and therefore legitimate targets of attack in popular culture.

Other women try to justify misandry on the purely practical grounds of political expediency. Even passive sympathy with men in connection with misandry would be tantamount to sympathy for the enemy or even, as one feminist put it in when her university was considering the establishment of a men's studies program, sympathy for Nazis.[20] Whether in connection with movies and talk shows or greeting cards and comic strips, moreover, misandry is seen as a legitimate attack on those who foster misogyny. That is fighting fire with fire. They are not troubled by the moral non sequitur. The continued existence of misogyny has nothing whatever to do with the existence of misandry, after all – not unless two wrongs make a right. To those who point out that misogyny is being fought directly through legislation and indirectly through the manipulation of public opinion, some would reply that it persists in the form of a "glass ceiling" (even though the explanation of that problem does not necessarily involve misogyny[21]) or that it persists in non-Western countries and in non-Western subcultures within the West. Once again, though, what has one thing got to do with the other? How does the existence of misogyny justify misandry, whether in our society or any other?

Still other women try to justify misandry with something far more sinister in mind: revenge. They argue that negative stereotypes of men are long overdue, because negative stereotypes of women have been around for so long. If that argument is to be taken seriously on moral grounds, those who use it would have to demonstrate that revenge is synonymous, or at least compatible, with justice. But if negative stereotyping is wrong when applied to women, how can it be right when applied to men? Is there nothing *inherently* wrong with promoting contempt or hatred for an entire group of people? If not, then things are right or wrong only when it is politically expedient to say so. In addition, advocates of this approach would have to demonstrate on purely pragmatic grounds that it is likely to bring about the desired results. The practical problem with revenge, of course, is that it quickly becomes a vicious circle. Once it is accepted as a legitimate political device, there is no way to prevent or terminate vendettas. And the current state of relations between men and women could well be described in precisely that way.

Underlying all of these attempts to justify misandry is a fundamental problem. Morality and practicality sometimes seem incompatible. Some women believe that feeling or expressing concern for men as the victims of misandry would mean indulging in a luxury that women cannot afford – this despite the vaunted capacity of women for compassion. But since when is compassion like money? Must it be carefully budgeted by reserving it for one's own people? Must we avoid squandering it on those judged "undeserving" for one reason or another? The fact is, nevertheless, that the more compassion is "spent," the more there is to go around.

Other women believe that taking any problem of men seriously would mean taking a non-feminist point of view. In fact, it would mean taking men seriously as they see themselves, as people. The worldview of ideological feminism, like that of every other religion or movement, is all inclusive; nothing is beyond its purview. From that perspective, it would seem that men can be understood best through its lens. The trouble is that this form of feminism has no philosophical or moral framework for the notion that women, like men, can succumb to sexism or that men, like women, can be seriously damaged by hatred.[22] To the extent that feminists refuse to focus much attention on their own gains (mainly because doing so would undermine their call for continuing political action), and to the extent that they refuse to acknowledge the problems of men (including misandry as the intentional or unintentional fallout from ideological feminism), they are morally implicated in the problem. That perspective leaves women largely unaccountable for their own behaviour.

Now, what about the reactions of *men* to misandry? Ironically, many ordinary men have a vested interest in *not* seeing the pervasive misandry of everyday life. Misandry, no matter how trite it might seem on the surface, is an attack on men. Even worse, from a traditionally masculine point of view, it is an attack from the perspective of women (though not necessarily by women). To acknowledge being under attack is to acknowledge vulnerability. And to acknowledge vulnerability, for many men in our society, is to deny their own manhood, even if doing so would be in their own best interest. Being a man, they have been taught, means being in control, not necessarily of others but certainly of themselves and their own fate. These are often the men who find it easier to hide behind macho posturing than to admit being threatened by women (or by other men presumably acting on behalf of women).

Many men, therefore, find that acknowledging the problem of rampant misandry is too painful. Some ignore it. That usually happens at a subconscious level. Other men, though, deny it. That happens on a conscious level among those who are sincerely motivated by the need to ensure justice for women, not merely by the pressure of political correctness. (Some of these men, unfortunately, actually believe that men are morally responsible for most or all of women's problems.) This could mean internalizing a negative identity, which would be both neurotic and self-destructive. But "male feminists" have discovered a way of getting around that problem: they maintain their self-respect not as members of a group (men) but as *individuals* at its *expense* (as what could be called "honorary women"). They expect nothing from other men, but they do expect to be rewarded by women for being politically correct. Not many men are impressed by the self-righteousness inherent in that position. They are alienated not only from feminists in general, therefore, but from "male feminists" in particular (even though many of them believe that men are morally obliged to help create a more egalitarian society).

Most men, however, are probably too confused to take a position specifically on misandry. They are aware at some level of consciousness that something is wrong, but they are not equipped to identify or analyse it. Even the few men who really are equipped to do so often find it difficult to say anything in public. The taboo on male vulnerability is not only experienced internally, remember, but also enforced externally. Men who admit to feeling vulnerable are attacked as cowards, and by no group more effectively than women. The ability to shame men has always been among the most useful of women's weapons. In this case, men are shamed into silence, a form of abuse that few women today would tolerate.

What is happening to men as a result of this massive assault on their identity?[23] How do men feel about being portrayed over and over again as psychotic or sinister thugs? What does it mean for a group of people to be identified as a class of victimizers? We will not know the full effect of all this misandry for many years. Given the predictable results of unleashing institutionalized anger against identifiable target groups (which is hatred) and the unpredictable results of manipulating collective guilt (which would be either destruction or self-destruction), this is a questionable method for pursuing social change, to say the least.

In the meantime, one thing is certain: attacking the identity of any group of human beings per se is an extremely dangerous experiment. People are not like rats in a laboratory. They cannot be manipulated conveniently and safely with fairly predictable results. Misandry could convince some men to seek new sources of identity. To be effective, however, these would have to be chosen by men, not dictated by women. At issue here is identity, in short, not sociology.

It should be obvious that most men consciously or unconsciously resent misandry. That is because all people resent having their identity undermined or attacked. Less obvious, perhaps, is the fact that misandry can backfire on women. What if men feel the need to reassert their identity as men? Ironically, misandry could encourage other men to reassert their identity as macho aggressors. Since our society tolerates a high level of hostility towards men *as such*, why be surprised when they resort to misogyny? That, after all, is a major feature of machismo. And it is surely no accident that the resurgence of machismo in the 1980s – consider movies such as *Rambo: First Blood II* (George Cosmatos, 1985) and *Top Gun* (Tony Scott, 1986), which suddenly ended two decades of glorifying the mentality of those men who had rejected both Vietnam and Wall Street – coincided with the flowering of ideological feminism. This particular response to misandry is clear. If men are told over and over again that they are not only brutal subhumans in general but also hostile to women in particular, they are likely to say, "So be it." Whatever their own inclinations, they realize that even a negative identity is better than no identity at all. Thus, when women think about misandry in popular culture, they should consider the danger of self-fulfilling prophecies. What goes around, according to the old saying, comes around. Or, for those who prefer biblical allusions, whoever sows the wind shall reap the whirlwind.

That possibility is often denied by those who view misandry as a political weapon to fight misogyny. They argue that the immediate result might be polarization but the eventual result will be reconciliation. In other words, the end justifies the means. But if polarization can bring about changes for the better, it can also bring about changes for the worse. How do we know that polarization will give rise to reconciliation? We do not. At the moment, things are moving in the opposite direction.

At any rate, the possibilities for mutual understanding between women and men did not increase in the 1990s. On the contrary, they diminished. Women such as Andrea Dworkin openly advocated that women become vigilantes and murder the men who afflict them.[24] If any of this indicates the shape of things to come – and much of the material we have analysed might have been produced by Dworkin herself – those who hope for healing and reconciliation have every reason to look ahead with foreboding. The popular culture of misandry had a life of its own in 2000. Ideological feminists had to make only occasional appearances to ensure that it stayed that way.

At no time of the year has this been more obvious than on Valentine's Day. The day that supposedly celebrates (heterosexual) love was hijacked. According to Donna Laframboise, "V" no longer stood for valentines but – you guessed it – for violence against women, or, "vagina, anti-violence [against women], and victory."[25] The process began in 1998 when celebrities such as Glenn Close, Calista Flockhart, Whoopi Goldberg, Winona Ryder, Susan Sarandon, and Lily Tomlin used the day to capture headlines and raise $100,000 for cash-starved centres for battered women. It did not take long for the idea to travel from a few elite feminists to the universities and from there to the larger community. Only two years later, V-Day events had spread to more than 150 American colleges and a few Canadian ones as well. Featured in the V-Day promo of 2000 was *The Vagina Monologues*, Eve Ensler's hit play. It was sponsored in Canada by The Body Shop, a well-established retailer of "natural" lotions and soaps, in the hope of appearing to be "with it" in the female or feminist world. But an ideological play was not enough; leaving the theatre, people were handed copies of the play with comments by Gloria Steinem, along with pamphlets on violence against women.

These days, however, there are a few feminist dissidents around. In the United States, Christina Hoff Sommers called the play "silly and pathetic" and V-Day a day that "will further embarrass, abase and discredit the sad remnants of American feminism."[26] Referring to the pamphlet's statistics on violence against women,[27] she pointed out that, according to the u.s. Bureau of Justice, only 1 per cent of emergency-room visits are related to ongoing abuse. The Canadian statistics, too, have been hotly debated. Because these originated with a 1993 study by Statistics Canada, that is very disturbing. Journalists such as Laframboise have pointed out, along with academic critics such as John Fekete, that the study "surveyed only women, didn't ask about violence they had experienced at the hands of females and defined minor pushing, shoving and grabbing as violence."[28] Other critics noted the rampant misandry in *Vagina*: Camille Paglia pointed to "a poisonously anti-male subtext."[29] A Canadian organizer, Taryn McCormick, disputing that assessment, called the play "hilariously funny and not about male bashing at all."[30] In doing so, however, she tacitly acknowledged the widespread perception that this play is indeed an example of male bashing. Laframboise pointed out that "while sexual transgressions by men are portrayed harshly, the play presents the seduction of a 13-year-old girl by an adult lesbian in a positive light."[31]

Does the very fact that critiques of feminism are now reported mean that we have reached a turning point? Or does the fact that events such as "V-Day" can be so easily engineered and propagated from websites or universities mean that misandric popular culture is alive and well?

Whatever their attitudes towards the male population in general, most women will continue to have powerful ties to at least a few males. Some women will try to exclude all males from their lives except fathers, brothers, husbands, lovers, or close friends. A few will withdraw even from these. Only lesbians are actually in a position to exclude men whenever possible (which is not to say that most lesbians would want to do that). Excluding any group of people is now considered a reactionary step, a form of segregation, in the context of democratic societies. Political convictions notwithstanding, few women would ignore the psychological needs of their own *sons*. Even today, mothers seriously consider the distinctive needs and problems of boys they themselves have brought into the world. At issue is not merely the destructive effect these boys could have on the world but the destructive effect the world could have *on them*. It is one thing to teach them that women are worthy of respect. It is another thing to teach them that men are worthy of nothing but pity at best and contempt at worst. Much damage has already been done, damage not only to men, which might not matter very much to some feminists, but to women as well. As a direct result, it will take decades to sort out the feminist wheat from the chaff, let alone to create a spirit of genuine reciprocity between men and women. We will discuss these very controversial matters in another volume.

In the end, our society will have to find ways of solving the pervasive problem of dualism. We have defined it as a way of thinking, a worldview, a mentality, one that is confined neither to feminists nor to any other group. All individuals can choose, ultimately, whether or not to promote hatred against others. No group of people is either immune or enslaved to this way of thinking. That applies equally to Christians and Jews, Israelis and Arabs, Hindus and Muslims, gay people and straight people, capitalists and socialists, blacks and whites, men and women. Consequently, no group of people should be considered either innately good or inherently evil. Some feminists agree. Others do not. In any case, we do not argue that feminists, even ideological feminists, invented dualism. Astonishingly, some of them seem utterly unaware that this chief characteristic of ideology is a fundamental feature of their own thinking. The evil of dualism, they argue in all seriousness, is characteristic of male thinking. That very statement, ironically, is an excellent example of dualism! It is worth noting here, moreover, that among the most dualistic feminists are *men* who acquire their own sense of self-esteem, or self-righteousness, by isolating themselves from *other* men. "It is not we who cause all the problems," they say, "but those others."

The problem is an *idea*, once again, not the existence of ideologues as people or groups of people. We do not believe in some cosmic, eternal, or even ancient struggle between "us" and "them," the forces of "light" and "darkness." At the same time, though, we recognize a paradox of the human condition: that even good ideas can become bad ones if carried to extremes. There are limits to everything. We do not need to tolerate dangerous ideas, for example. On the contrary, we need to identify them and argue with those who promote them. Otherwise, we would be in the absurd position of having to tolerate intolerance. As Arvind Sharma points out, that would mean the destruction of tolerance itself:

The intolerable and the intolerant can only be tolerated to the point where they do not endanger the existence of the very system which ensures tolerance … On the one hand, if a religion or a political system only tolerates conformity, then what does its tolerance consist of? It is hardly a virtue to tolerate the pleasant or the acceptable. It is precisely by tolerating what would normally not be tolerated that tolerance becomes a virtue. Yet, on the other hand, if this tolerance of deviance from the norm itself leads to the destruction of the very system which renders such tolerance possible, then obviously such self-destructive tolerance will be self-defeating. This dilemma can only be resolved by seeing the limits of tolerance at that point beyond which tolerance would subvert the very system which makes it possible.[32]

This problem was exemplified by the situation in Germany during the 1920s and 1930s. The Weimar constitution was the most liberal in Europe. Among those who benefited from this liberality, unfortunately, were the Nazis. They used the freedom given to them by the state to destroy it. They used the tolerance promoted by society to destroy it. Few were able to see in time that tolerance can exist only if intolerance can be opposed, not tolerated. If dualism is a destructive way of thinking, and if ideology is profoundly dualistic, then refusing to oppose it would be folly. It is important to oppose misogyny and the androcentric worldview that generates it,[33] but it is equally important to oppose misandry and the gynocentric worldview that generates it. What should be opposed are not women or those who want to improve the condition of women (the same being said for men), but those who do so by turning men into symbols of evil (or vice versa).

Fostered by political correctness, misandry was the characteristic pattern of the 1990s. At first, it was actively promoted in academic and political circles as justifiable "anger" or a way of "pushing the boundaries." And this tendency, directly promoted on talk shows and either directly or indirectly in other genres of popular culture, quickly went mainstream. Popular culture both mediated and fostered the teaching of contempt for men. This was now the establishment. Androcentrism, often accompanied by misogyny, did not cease to exist but generally went underground (although it probably declined too, because many men really did take seriously the message that an androcentric world was unjust to women). It surfaced only in the music of very alienated subcultures, among individual men who "forgot" the new rules, and in some traditional or isolated communities. To the extent that gynocentrism and androcentrism can be described as worldviews, then the dominant worldview of this period, at least in public, was clearly gynocentrism. The fact that it has a dark underside has been ignored, excused, and trivialized. The revolution has been successful, as Marxists would say, because the new values are now so firmly embedded in everyday life that we can hardly see them, let alone challenge them. That is why we have written this book.

Quasi-Misandric Movies

Our intention is to argue not that every movie of the 1990s was misandric or even that most were (apart from any other factor, it would have been impossible for us to see every movie made during that decade) but only that misandry was characteristic of many. Our interpretations do allow for ambiguity. Excluded from the discussion in the main text of this book, therefore, are movies that show traces or even heavy doses of misandry but, on purely technical grounds, escape classification as misandric. Also excluded are movies that have blatantly misandric subtexts but focus greater attention on other subtexts. Their raison d'être, in other words, is not the promotion of misandry.

First, not all movies with feminist subtexts are even quasi-misandric. We are concerned in this book only with those that have subtexts based on *ideological* feminism. The effect, though, can be almost as egregious. In *V.I. Warshawski* (Jeff Kanew, 1991), every male character is either evil or inadequate, but so is the female protagonist. Misandry is clearly present, to be sure, but so is misogyny; this movie is misanthropic, therefore, but not dualist and thus sexist. Consequently, its worldview is not ideological (see chapter 7). As the protagonist, Warshawski is good, not evil, and heroic, not inadequate. Paradoxically, however, she is also sexist. She openly promotes negative stereotypes of men. Viewers are asked to conclude, therefore, that being good and being sexist are quite compatible in women.

Taken to its logical if lamentable conclusion, equality is understood here as equality in coarseness, brutality, and evil. The underlying message is that women will never be liberated until they have asserted the "right" to be just as contemptible as men (the underlying *assumption* being that everyone, male or female, has some "right" to indulge in sexism). This is a far cry from anything Betty Friedan, the apostle of gender equality, would have tolerated. Most feminist theoreticians who use the idiom of equality would prefer to argue that women should be able to participate equally with men in public life, not in crime or prejudice. But that is a moral and intellectual refinement not required by the sheer logic of equality. To the extent that this genre meets the emotional needs of women, it is because they consider equality of any kind, including brutality and exploitation, a form of "empowerment." Because the focus of attention is on women, though, it is *their* freedom to indulge in sexism that dominates. Thus the misogynistic remarks of male characters are mocked, but the misandric remarks of female characters are applauded.

The spectacle of critics falling all over themselves in an effort to be politically correct is never an edifying one, but a new low was reached with their efforts to canonize[1] *The Piano* (Jane Campion, 1993). Bewitched, evidently, by the "best film in a long, long time," one critic, John Griffin, has written that "nobody was prepared for the rooted power, the craft, the magic of The Piano. It left even the thumbsup crew speechless. Giving [Jane] Campion the Palme d'Or for best film at Cannes, and [Holly] Hunter the honours for best actress, were well-intentioned gestures but somehow too feeble. Keys to the town of Cannes might have been more appropriate. Or, come next Oscar night, maybe a special trophy for restoring faith in film."[2] Elsewhere, Griffin gushes over Hunter's "supernatural performance." Almost as favourably impressed by *Piano*, Geoff Pevere gives it superb rating: nine out of ten. Maybe Orson Welles and Ingmar Bergman should make room in the pantheon of great directors for Jane Campion.

Critical acclaim does not necessarily translate into popular demand, but it has in this case. *Piano* serves the current need of many women (and some men) for movies that promote not only strong female characters but also feminism of one school or another. According to the hypesters – clearly, they "protest too much" – this is *not* feminist "propaganda." Campion herself has said that her intention in directing and writing *Piano* was to adopt a "feminine perspective."[3] And if by that she had referred to a story focused exclusively on a female protagonist, as was the case in what used to be called "women's pictures," there would be no problem. But Campion has been evasive. The movie itself, in fact, shows clear evidence of bad faith. And for evidence, think of the ending, which has no connection with anything that precedes it. The ending is, in a word, dishonest. More about that in a moment. First, here is the story.

Campion's female protagonist is Ada, the victim of an arranged marriage, a practice not uncommon in nineteenth-century Britain. Accordingly, she and her daughter by an earlier liaison are packed off to the New Zealand bush. But the marriage gets off to a bad start. Stewart, Ada's husband, refuses to bring her piano from the landing beach to his shack in the highlands. Because Ada is mute, this amounts to a personal violation; the piano, viewers soon learn, is part of her. It is her voice. By abandoning the piano, in other words, Stewart abandons her. He "silences" her. But wait – things get worse. Attracted to Ada, Stewart's employee, Baines, decides to make use of this situation. He buys the piano from Stewart and arranges to take "lessons" from Ada. No one asks Ada, whose piano it is. But she submits. She wants her voice back, even if she has to pay for it, one ebony key at a time, with sexual favours. Eventually, even Baines realizes that he has turned Ada into a prostitute and decides to give the piano back to her without asking for full "payment." But he still wants her. And Ada wants him, because Baines, having treated her as a mere thing, now treats her as a fully human being. He wants her love and respect, not her submission. Stewart, meanwhile, is deceptively wimpy. He keeps hoping that she will want intimacy with him. He meekly asks her to sleep with him and goes off with his tail between his legs when she refuses.

Enraged when he discovers her affair with Baines, Stewart tries to rape her and then chops off her finger. That is to say, he removes her ability to "speak" through the piano. The "marriage," clearly, is over. Ada sails off with Baines and the piano. As their canoe glides across the stormy sea, Ada suddenly decides that she must rid herself of the piano. The Maori rowers toss it overboard. Tangled in the rope that had held it in place, Ada is pulled overboard as well. Is this an accident? Or is it suicide? It hardly matters. What does matter is that Ada's life has been destroyed by the primary institution of marriage. The story actually ends at this point: either with Ada, anchored to the piano, being sucked down into the abyss, or with Ada, having freed herself by removing a clunky Victorian boot, floating triumphantly back to the surface.

Water is heavily laden with symbolic associations. As the sea, it represents chaos and death. Drowning, Ada represents the female victim of a patriarchal society. Water is associated in addition with that internal sea, the womb, and thus with the origin of life. Visibly at peace for the first time as she hovers above the sunken piano, she has returned to the bosom of "mother nature." In the sacrament of baptism, moreover, water represents resurrection. Struggling free from her literal and figurative bonds, Ada rises as the archetypal heroine of all feminists.

A preposterously contrived ending, though, has been tacked on so that the protagonist lives happily ever after in a world not much different from the one she has escaped. Ada merely lands up in some other town. By now, she is respectably married to Baines, teaching piano with the aid of an artificial finger and learning to speak verbally. Why is this ending so contrived? Because it makes no sense of everything that has gone before. Only those who have never seen a soap opera, a talk show, or even read a newspaper could fail to realize, at some level of consciousness, that Campion has used Ada's story as a metaphor. No wonder Owen Gleiberman comments as follows on the scene in which Stewart attacks Ada: "It's a shockingly brutal moment that seems to come echoing through a chasm of feminist despair. This, Campion seems to be saying, is what men have always done to women, and what some men always will."[4] Only those who are incredibly naive can fail to realize that encoded within *every* current movie about relations between men and women is a political "message," whether overt or covert, profeminist or antifeminist, intentional or otherwise.

How else to explain the striking correspondence between the image of Ada and that of women promoted by many feminists? For them, as Gleiberman points out, her story is that of all women in an oppressive, patriarchal society that "silences" women. (Never mind that the same society silences men in other ways.) For them, her story is that of all women who are treated as the possessions of their husbands. (Never mind that men are treated as possessions by the state.) For them, indeed, marriage itself is an evil institution that must be destroyed or escaped in order for women to be fully human and find their "voices." And that is exactly what happens in this movie. Not all viewers make connections at a conscious level between what they see on the screen and what they read in countless books and magazines or see on countless talk shows and sitcoms. Even so, the social and political context in which we all live these days ensures that these connections are indeed made at a subliminal level.

So why does Ada end up married once more? The answer might well involve some political and economic expediency. For one thing, the happy ending makes an ideological message easier to swallow. In other words, it makes better results possible at the box office. Then too, it allows Campion to answer the charge, made often enough to require an answer, of having produced feminist indoctrination "Look," she can say, "Ada remarries. What's everyone complaining about? If Ada affirms anything, it's the bourgeois and patriarchal order." That answer would be deceptive.

The Book of Job has a very similar denouement. That story is about the inexplicable suffering of an innocent man. The answer is experiential, not philosophical: God's holy presence in the midst of suffering no less than of joy. There is not much to be said after God appears to Job in a theophany. Nevertheless, an epilogue has been tacked on. After taking everything away from Job, God gives everything back to him! And Job, with his new family and new riches, lives happily ever after. This conclusion drains what goes before of its gritty power. It represents the kind of "pie in the sky" religion that comforts those who maintain conventional standards of piety but bewilders and enrages those who suffer and die without recompense in this world. Similarly, *Piano* would be much more virulent, politically, without its artificially happy ending. On the other hand, it would be less effective, politically, because fewer people would want to see it in the first place.

In *theory* then, *Piano* is not quite misandric. Stewart is both inadequate and evil. But Baines is more ambiguous. On the one hand, he is somewhat inadequate. On the other hand, he takes Ada away with him, and he has pressured her into having sex with him. This constitutes rape in some feminist circles of our time, not merely prostitution, but he does repent. However, he repents. So much for the male characters. There is only one major female character, and she is not only a victim but also a heroine and, by the standards of those feminists who see nothing wrong in violating the vows that support an evil patriarchal institution, virtuous as well. (Imagine, however, if Stewart had been the one to indulge in an affair. He would be denounced as a faithless, two-timing "womanizer.") A third criterion for diagnosing misandry, therefore, can be discerned in productions that implicitly reinforce specific political convictions – in this case, the conviction would be that marriage is a patriarchal trap for women – even though they explicitly deny this on technical grounds by superimposing a conclusion so isolated from everything else that, for all intents and purposes, it has no effect.

How can we understand Gleiberman's paean to this "brooding romantic melodrama of almost classical grandeur"?[5] His statement is a matter of taste. But another statement, that "Campion views all her characters with a compassion bordering on grace, a humanity ... as dark, quiet, and enveloping as the ocean,"[6] is no longer a matter of taste. It is a matter of observation. And he is wrong. What compassion does she extend to poor Stewart? And Griffin fails to see what is right in front of his eyes. "There are no bad characters in the film,"[7] he writes. Since when are attempted rape and mutilation not the work of a bad character? Baines is let off the hook, it is true, but only because he has "gone native." Campion's dualism has not one focus, you see, but two: men versus women and European versus Maori. Stewart represents "civilized" societies and Baines "primitive" ones. (So what if the Maori, with what Griffin calls their "casual, carnal grace,"[8] were actually warlike? And so what if these noble savages, "who celebrated their physicality and physical impulses," once practised cannibalism?)

As usual these days, everything ugly and brutal and sick and patriarchal is exemplified by the dirty old Victorians. Trussed up in costumes unsuited to the primaeval bush, these respectable Europeans are at this distance safe targets of ridicule. Baines "goes native" and Ada falls in love with him, even though she remains too repressed by her upgringing, or oppressed, to go as far as he does. Decorated with facial tattoos by his Maori friends, Baines offers an explicit critique of Western society. So, unlike Stewart, Baines supposedly deserves at least some compassion from Campion. He is a man, but he is associated with an oppressed class. Like all men, he is innately bad; his natural first impulse is to exploit Ada, as an object, for his own gratification. Yet unlike most men, Baines is not quite beyond redemption. Contact with a liberated woman, one who defies the authority of a patriarchal order, liberates him as well.

The protagonist of *Paris Trout* (Stephen Gyllenhaal, 1991) is a southern redneck who reneges on insurance payments to a black customer. When the creditor makes it clear that he intends to collect, Trout decides to intimidate him. But intimidation quickly turns to murder. With an accomplice, Paris shoots the man's mother and little sister, Rosie. Miraculously, the mother eventually recovers from multiple wounds, but Rosie dies. Racist that he is, Paris has not taken seriously the possibility that a new day has dawned in the

South and that he can be brought to trial for murder. "Things'll be how they were," he says complacently. But the prosecutor has other ideas.

Paris's behaviour at home is not much better. He treats Hanna, his wife, with contempt and brutality. One scene says it all. "Get me a drink from the store," he commands, "and clean up what spilled." After opening the bottle for him, Hanna gets down on her hands and knees to scrub the mess he had made on the floor. Then he slugs her and rapes her with the bottle. As a former schoolteacher, Hanna is neither a redneck nor a racist (which should make viewers wonder why she married Paris in the first place). In fact, she attends Rosie's funeral. After that, Paris fears that she will betray him to the police and on one occasion tries to strangle her in the bathtub. Finally, she moves out of the house to live with his reluctant lawyer, Seagraves.

Paris is found guilty but given a very light sentence. For some reason, he is released from custody before being taken to prison. In that time, he brings his invalid mother home, totally paralysed, and shoots her. Then he waits for Hanna and tries to shoot her too. But Seagraves gets there first and is killed almost as an afterthought. Finally, Paris puts the gun in his own mouth and pulls the trigger. Hardly anyone attends his funeral, but the entire town turns out for that of Seagraves.

Paris Trout is about racism in the postwar South. A clear link is made, however, between the racism and sexism – but only the sexism of men. Paris rapes Hanna after she goes to Rosie's funeral, a public affront to his dignity as a white man. "Tell that to the niggers," he screams at her. Four of his intended victims are either black, female, or both, including his wife, a child, a mother, and his own mother. Only one, by chance, is a white man. By implication, it is no accident that the hatred and brutality of Paris extend equally to both blacks and women. That someone whose mentality is warped by prejudice should hate more than one group is hardly surprising; this is often the case. It certainly was the case in the South at that time. Because the local haters are mainly white men, however, the implication is that women were (and are, because this movie is addressed to viewers in our own time) generally immune to prejudice, both racial and sexual. At the very least, the implied assertion should require some explanation. It is not self-evident from history. (In 1939, only a few years before the period in which this movie is set, the Daughters of the American Revolution denied the black singer Marian Anderson permission to perform at their Constitution Hall.) As in so many other misandric movies and other pop cultural productions, the basis for it lies in the notions that racism and sexism are both forms of hierarchical thinking and that hierarchical thinking is "male." Ergo, sexism is just another form of racism, and both are just modalities of a mentality characteristic of men, not women.

One woman in *Paris Trout* really is racist: the white nurse assigned to care for Rosie cannot bring herself even to touch the child. After doing so, she immediately washes away the pollution. But this nurse is a very minor character;

the phenomenon she represents, therefore, is cinematically declared to be of very minor significance. If women ever do succumb to prejudice, some feminists claim, it is only because they have been infected by the virus of a patriarchal culture. In other words, women are innocent whether they hate or not.

Balancing the one racist white woman in this movie, there is a good white man (apart from the prosecutor, who is seldom seen). Largely because of Seagraves, the cinematic world retains a complexity that most viewers know from the world of everyday life. As a result, *Paris Trout* cannot be classified as a misandric movie. Seagraves is a hero. He dies in place of Hanna. But even he is tainted! Looking at snapshots of Rosie's horribly wounded body, he calmly munches his sandwich. This brief scene has no cinematic purpose if not to show that Seagraves is emotionally unaffected by the grisly sight of a murdered black girl. Then too, Seagraves is rather cynical about the possibility of honest relationships. In an early meeting with Hanna, he notes "the polite lying that makes cohabitation possible." Something more sinister is revealed in another scene. During the trial, Seagraves comes to tell Hanna that he has misgivings about defending her husband. Hanna begins to discuss her life with Paris. After she tells him how Paris raped her, Seagraves admits that he is aroused by the idea of using a bottle. In other words, he is aroused by the idea of raping her.

Unlike so many popular movies, *The Hand That Rocks the Cradle* (Curtis Hanson, 1992) is about a *woman* who terrorizes a family. Technically, therefore, it cannot be classified as misandric. Even so, it has distinctly misandric overtones.

Meet the Bartels, a yuppie family living comfortably in Seattle. Claire is a bright, capable woman who works part-time at the botanical gardens. Michael, her husband, is a handsome, sensitive, and successful genetic engineer. They have a young daughter, Emma, and now Claire is pregnant again. So far, so good. But a routine examination by her gynecologist, Victor Mott, proves very disturbing. In fact, she accuses him of molesting her. The scandal that follows drives Mott to suicide. Because the estate is sued by several other women who filed similar charges, no money is left for his pregnant wife, Peyton. The trauma of losing both her home and her husband brings on a miscarriage. In the emergency room, doctors remove her uterus. What to do? Peyton comes up with a satisfying answer: revenge.

Claire lands up in much better shape. After recovering from the trauma, she has her baby, Joe. But taking care of a family is not enough for her. She decides to build a greenhouse and grow strawberries, possibly for commercial purposes. Fortunately, she and Michael can afford to hire servants. One of these is a handyman named Solomon, a gentle but mentally retarded black man from the Better Day Society. In addition, they need a nanny to look after the children. Carefully manipulated by Peyton, Claire meets her on the street, invites her home for dinner, likes her immediately, and hires her without so much as a request for one reference.

Peyton "Flanders" promptly ingratiates herself with the family. In her own mind, Michael and the children "belong" to her. For a while, everything goes according to plan. Claire likes her because she seems both pleasant and efficient. Peyton "finds" Claire's red earring just in the nick of time in the baby's mouth just in the nick of time, for example – having put it there herself. Michael likes her, because she is charming and attractive. Putting on some of Claire's preferred perfume, Peyton has no trouble attracting his attention. Emma likes Peyton, because she is more accessible than her mother. Encouraging the little girl to tell secrets, Peyton learns that a boy at school has been bullying her. She goes to the schoolyard and intimidates the boy. "Leave Emma alone," she warns him in front of the other boys while Emma smiles smugly. "If you don't, I'm gonna rip your fuckin' head off." Even the baby likes Peyton, who gets up every night at three o'clock, goes upstairs to the nursery, and secretly nurses him. Claire notices after a while that the baby refuses her own nursing. At first she dismisses the problem, but then things begin to go wrong.

After Michael completes a lengthy proposal for the Environmental Protection Agency, Claire offers to mail it for him. Peyton steals it and tears it up. When Michael blames Claire, her shock and guilt provoke an asthma attack. Michael tells her not to worry about it, but she does. Just beneath the surface, she is also angry at Peyton, and disappointed. And this is only the beginning.

Solomon is Peyton's next target. On a stepladder painting the house one day, he looks in the window and sees her nursing the baby. Somehow, even Solomon realizes that something is amiss. "Don't fuck with me, retard," she threatens. "My version of the story will be better than yours." Nevertheless, she leaves nothing to chance. She tells Claire quite nonchalantly that Solomon has been touching Emma in inappropriate ways. Claire at first, disregards this accusation. But Peyton has plans for Solomon. Soon after, she arranges for Claire to find Emma's underpants in Solomon's tool cart. Believing the worst, Claire attacks him physically and fires him. Emma herself, unable to understand why her mother is so angry at Solomon, turns more and more to Peyton for comfort and friendship.

Peyton appears at Michael's office one day and suggests that he give Claire a surprise birthday party. Michael likes the idea and decides to ask Marlene, a family friend, to help. Before leaving, Peyton cleverly asks him not to tell Marlene who thought of the idea for fear that this would lead to competition for Claire's friendship. Michael, naive and slightly infatuated, agrees. He and Marlene plan the party over lunch. She forgets her cigarette lighter, and he puts it in his pocket. On the day of the party, Claire finds it and, after another attack of asthma, has a tantrum in the kitchen. Guests hiding in the living room listen as she screams: "You son of a bitch! You're fucking Marlene!" Having been accused of adultery in public, Marlene walks out.

So far Claire has alienated Michael, Emma, Joe, and Marlene. Beginning by now to suspect that Peyton might be responsible for this onslaught of problems, she suggests to Michael that they go away for a while and stipulates that the vacation should include "just the family," not Peyton.

Unlike Claire and Michael, Marlene has always been suspicious of Peyton; when they first met, Marlene had noticed Marty, her husband, ogling Peyton. But then, Marlene is a shrewd businesswoman. As a real-estate agent, she routinely looks through pictures of houses for sale and notices that one shows a wind chime exactly like the one Peyton had given to Claire. This house had belonged to the notorious Dr Mott. Marlene runs to the library and checks newspaper pictures of the Mott funeral. And there she is: Peyton Flanders is really Peyton Mott. This explains why so many unpleasant things have been happening to Claire. Putting aside any residual resentment over what had happened at the party, Marlene speeds across town to warn her friend. So certain is she of danger, in fact, that she calls Claire on the way over. Peyton answers the phone, unfortunately, and Marlene makes no effort to conceal her hostility. By the time she arrives, Peyton is ready for her. Having already rigged the glass panels in the greenhouse with the intention of killing Claire, Peyton directs Marlene to the greenhouse. Marlene is slashed to death by a shower of broken glass as soon as she enters.

When Claire finds the body, she has another asthma attack. This time, because Peyton has hidden her medication, she almost dies. It is only after she returns from the hospital that she finds a note written by Marlene. Why, she wonders, would Marlene have asked her to call on urgent business? She goes to Marlene's office and asks what Marlene had been doing before she left for the last time. On her desk Claire finds a photo of the Mott house. Pretending to be a potential buyer, she asks to see it. In the nursery she finds the same decorative frieze that Peyton has added to Joe's nursery. Claire understands. Tires screeching, she rushes home. She finds Michael and Peyton preparing dinner. Before Michael figures out what is going on, she slugs Peyton. "Michael," coos Peyton, "tell her about us." But the game is over. "Call the police," says Claire. Michael foolishly replies, "Claire, calm down." Now, Peyton exposes her true self: "I'll just go get my baby." Michael finally gets the idea and tells Peyton to leave without even packing.

Afraid to stay in the house, Michael and Claire decide to go away for a few days. After Claire and Emma go upstairs to pack, Michael suddenly hears music from Peyton's room in the basement. As if he had never seen an Alfred Hitchcock movie, he goes down to investigate. Peyton is waiting for him, of course, in the shadows. Before he can say, "What are you doing here?" she belts him. The impact throws him down the stairs, knocking him unconscious and breaking his legs. By now, even Emma knows that her beloved nanny is a psychopath. She fetches the baby and hides him in a cupboard. Meanwhile, Peyton runs into Claire and Solomon up in the attic. Unlike her loyal but now lame husband,

Claire is able to defend herself even in the midst of yet another asthma attack! Solomon stands by and comforts Emma. "When your husband makes love," laughs Peyton, "it's my face he sees. When your baby is hungry, it's my breast that feeds him." In the ensuing struggle, Claire throws her obviously insane adversary onto the floor, across the room, and out the window.

According to Gleiberman, *Hand* "trades on the most retrograde images of women imaginable; they're either '90s Doris Days or murderous destroyers. The climax descends into pure demagoguery, becoming a kind of pro-wrestling match between good and evil homemakers. There's no denying the movie gets a rise out of us, but it does so by mining the fears within our hokiest prejudices."[9] That is one point of view. It is by no means the only possible one. Compare the three major female characters: Peyton, Claire, and Marlene.

Peyton is the villain of *Hand*, to be sure, but notably unlike the male villains of misandric movies. In *Sleeping with the Enemy* and *A Kiss before Dying*, the villains are enigmatic and alien. No real attempt is made to explain the origin of their psychopathological behaviour. They might as well represent some other species, some dark force of nature, some demonic being, utterly and eerily "other." In short, they are men. How different they are from the villain of this movie. In *Hand*, a considerable effort – it consumes nine very expensive minutes of screen time, including a horrifying scene in the operating room – has been made to show precisely what *caused* Peyton's behaviour. She was not born evil. She was born into an evil or uncaring world. Nothing suggests that she is biologically, ontologically, or metaphysically associated with evil. On the contrary, the movie suggests that Peyton is really good. Too good! It is the profound desire for a child to love that drives her to usurp someone else's after losing her own. Even her implacable desire for revenge is presented as somehow "understandable." Unlike the villains in *Sleeping* and *Kiss*, moreover, Peyton is clearly out of touch with reality. The male villains know precisely what they are doing and why. Peyton does not. "It's okay, Emma," she says after whacking Claire, "Mommy's here." Soon after, she warns Solomon: "You give me my baby or I'll bash your skull in." She really believes that Michael and the children "belong" to her, that she can take on Claire's identity by wearing her perfume and bracelet, by nursing her child. She can no longer distinguish between right and wrong. Because she is a victim herself, her guilt is mitigated. In fact, because she is not a competent moral agent at all, her guilt is removed entirely! Peyton is clearly supposed to inspire a complex emotional response in viewers, certainly in female viewers: sympathy and fear, empathy and revulsion, admiration and pity, not merely moral condemnation.

Peyton is a heroine, in fact, not a villain. But her heroism is not the standard kind, which evokes public acclaim by a community. Nor is it the anti-heroic kind, which challenges a community on moral grounds. Hers is a tragic heroism, all the same, doomed by the very act of struggling to achieve her ideal. But for the grace of God, a female viewer might think, there go I. Given her distorted view of reality, the fact remains that Peyton displays at least one thing – wanting to be a mother – that is generally considered extremely admirable in women. All feminists would agree that her autonomy, at least, is admirable. After telling Emma that she never had a mother, Peyton explains, "I had to take care of myself." Not surprisingly, she stops at nothing to get what she wants and needs, what she believes to be hers by right. She sets her own goals and relies on no one, certainly not on any man, to achieve them. Viewers cannot love her, but they can respect her.

During the Depression, many movies encouraged viewers to admire and even to envy similar hero-villains. Consider *Little Caesar* (Mervyn Leroy, 1930), say, and *The Public Enemy* (William Wellman, 1931). These gangsters represented at least temporary victory over an economic system that was obviously not working for most people. It should come as no surprise to learn that many female viewers identify themselves with Peyton. What drives her over the brink is a problem that, according to this movie, potentially threatens any woman, whether stable or unstable: the exploitation and brutality of men. Few would act out their anger and grief as Peyton does, but many might do so vicariously and perhaps subconsciously. Peyton thus fulfils not merely one criterion but *both* criteria identifying female characters in misandric movies: even though she victimizes others, she is nonetheless an innocent victim; and even though she behaves immorally, she nonetheless behaves heroically.

Marlene and Peyton are alike in some ways, but their similarities reveal underlying differences. Both represent undesirable extremes. Peyton is too "female," being driven solely by maternal obsessions. Marlene is too "male," being driven solely by material obsessions and career aspirations. Neither woman corresponds to the popular ideal of "having it all." Both sacrifice something vital, but not the same thing. Peyton's identity is based exclusively on her status as wife and mother. When she loses these, she loses her identity and tries to find it once more by seducing Michael and the children. Marlene's identity, on the other hand, is based exclusively on her status as a successful career woman. "These days," she tells Claire, "a woman can feel like a failure unless she brings in $50,000 a year and still makes time for blow jobs and homemade lasagna." She is very attractive, sensually dressed, immaculately groomed, and stylishly coiffed, yet her manner is cynical and harsh. After a colleague brings her some information, she asks him: "What're you waiting for, a tip?" Accustomed to open confrontation, she displays the bravado and foolhardiness of many men. When Peyton agrees to give Claire a message, Marlene cannot resist the urge to reveal that she is on to Peyton by snarling, "Sure you will." Finally, Marlene likes to take control of things. When Peyton suggests that Marlene might like to help out with the party for Claire, Michael laughs: "Help out? She'd take over."

Like Peyton, Marlene is virtually alone, but not for the same reason. Before the trauma that unhinged her, Peyton might have been able to sustain durable relationships. Even after the trauma, she forms what seems to be a primal relationship with the baby. But Marlene does not appear to have what it takes to form any strong relationship. Her intimidating behaviour at the office indicates that she has few if any supporters there. Her quasi-friendship with Claire is at least partly due to the fact that she grew up with Michael, was once his lover, and possibly still has designs on him. It does not take much to convince Claire that Marlene has been sleeping with him. From what viewers see of Marty, moreover, it seems clear that Marlene might just as well have no husband. And she neither has nor wants children.

Like Peyton, Marlene is "punished," but for the opposite reason. Her death can be seen as a symbolic warning to women who believe they can find happiness by choosing a career instead of a family. Feminists who oppose this message should remember that the death of Peyton, an obsessively maternal woman, can be seen as a symbolic warning to women who make the *opposite* choice.

This brings us to Claire. Some critics say that *Hand* subverts feminism, because its protagonist – its role model for women – prefers to work at home rather than at an office. If so, the movie must be interpreted as a warning to those who identify themselves with Claire instead of Marlene. But another point of view is possible. *Hand* might subvert feminism, ironically, because Claire actually does work outside the home – that is, in her greenhouse – and is therefore made to look selfish and negligent, like someone who truly deserves a Peyton. But this interpretation is facile.

As someone who has volunteered her services at the botanical gardens for seven years and hires someone to look after her children, Claire might seem anachronistic to many feminists. But her position is not entirely antithetical to feminism. She relies on her husband's domestic assistance, or at least on his ability to pay for domestic help. But when push comes to shove, literally, she is quite able to fend for herself. Michael is a luxury, not a necessity. Claire relies less on him, evidently with good reason, than on herself. Claire has personal autonomy. She demands her own private space, both literally and figuratively. She not only dominates the home, administering its staff as she would an office, but a place beyond the home as well. Claire is the happy medium, according to this movie, the woman who has the best of both worlds, the woman who "has it all." Preferring her to Marlene might worry those feminists who insist on the need of women for more choices – by that, they almost always mean the choice of a career outside the home – but probably not the majority of women. They would rather not have to make that choice in the first place. They want to do both.

We cannot see into the mind of screenwriter Amanda Silver. Nonetheless, judging from what is presented, it seems reasonable to conclude that she intended to reinforce the branch of feminism according to which women, represented by Claire, are innately given to "nurturing." Claire works both outside the home and inside it. The greenhouse is literally outside the house but metaphorically an extension of it. In other words, Claire turns the larger world into a symbolic home. Like the nursery, the greenhouse is devoted to the "nurture" of living things (in fact, greenhouses are often *called* "nurseries"). And for some feminists, especially the followers of Carol Gilligan, that says something *positive* about women.

Women like Claire realize that their "different voice," as women, can be heard, should be heard, everywhere: in the home, in the greenhouse, in the schoolyard, in the business world, and so on. Neither Peyton nor Marlene realizes this. Peyton knows that she has a "different voice," but unfortunately believes that it can be heard only by her own "children." This leads directly to her downfall. Instead of trying to express her female "voice" in some other way, she tries to steal the children of someone else. Marlene, on the other hand, is unaware that she has a "different voice" and speaks and acts in ways stereotypically associated with men. And this leads directly to her downfall. By confronting Peyton with what she has discovered and brusquely indicating her intention of telling Claire, Marlene makes her own demise almost inevitable. Only Claire is a fully mature woman, one who corresponds to Gilligan's ideal. Far from indicating that the only healthy and happy women are those who take care of children, therefore, *Hand* indicates that healthy and happy women like Claire are "nurturant" whether they take care of children, plants, offices, or anything else.

It could be argued that the sets, for example, would have been used to better advantage if those who produced *Hand* were consciously intending to make a political point. Considering Claire's way of life, it is not surprising to find her associated with a traditional set: the house. And, considering Marlene's way of life, it is not surprising to find her associated with a very modern one: the office. In view of the fact that Peyton's way of life is more traditional than either, however, the modern sets associated with her, the Mott house and the hospital, are "anomalous." On the other hand, the sets representing Peyton *highlight* her status as an outsider, out of her element in the modern world.[10]

At least one reviewer, Richard Schickel, has noted yet another subtext in *Hand*. "It wants to be something more than a one-weekend stand for slasher-movie fans," writes Schickel. "Shrewdly conceived, soberly paced, squeamish about gore, it wants to get its true audience, people very like the Bartels, muttering into their Chardonnay about how this particular movie got them to thinking. And about how it just may be the first movie to combine, however tentatively, the seemingly antithetical conventions of feminism and horror."[11] Well, there is nothing antithetical about horror and feminism. In fact, horror seems to be an ideal vehicle for the propagation of misandric feminism. Far from being the first to combine horror and feminism, *Hand* is merely a successor to *Sleeping with the Enemy, Silence of the Lambs, A Kiss before Dying, Cape Fear*, and many, many others.

Like all misandric movies, this one really does aim, consciously in some ways and unconsciously in others, "to get them thinking." But thinking about what? We suggest that viewers think about at least four things corresponding to four levels of consciousness. At a superficial (fully conscious) level, men and women – mothers and fathers – are encouraged to think about the potential dangers of handing the care of their children over to others.

At a slightly less superficial, but still conscious, level, men and women – but especially women – are encouraged to think about the psychological stress of women who choose to work full-time either at home or outside the home. At a deeper, and only partially conscious, level, men and women – but, once again, especially women – are encouraged to think about the ultimate autonomy and power of women. The only contenders for power in this cinematic world are the two who actually rock cradles, Claire and Peyton. In the end, Claire is triumphant, literally standing upright. Michael is defeated, literally prone and metaphorically "buried" below ground in the basement.

At the deepest, and completely subconscious, level, women – those, at any rate, who are sensitive to the evocative world of symbolic associations – are encouraged to think about a worldview in which men are ultimately and collectively (though not always immediately or individually) responsible for all evil and suffering. That worldview is both "profoundly simplistic," so to speak, and profoundly immoral. What appeals to many people, nevertheless, is its emotionally satisfying explanation for the apparent chaos they encounter in everyday life. It would be a grave mistake, a dangerous oversight, to trivialize *Hand* or any of the other movies discussed in this book. What they lack in moral depth and intellectual rigour, they make up for in emotional power and political effectiveness.

All the female characters, including Peyton, are innocent victims *and* heroines. In the most direct sense, Marlene, Claire, and even little Emma are all innocent victims of Peyton. But in a more indirect sense – and this is very important – they are all innocent victims of Peyton's husband, Dr Mott. Peyton too is his innocent victim, even though she considers herself the victim of Claire. But *Hand* clearly suggests that even though women are not free from problems in a world run by men, they are clearly able to *handle* these problems on their own. All of *Hand*'s female characters prove heroic in one way or another. Peyton attempts to rectify the wrong done to her. Marlene attempts to warn Claire of impending danger. Claire defends herself and her family. And Emma saves the baby by hiding him and locking Peyton out. It is worth noting that both Claire and Peyton appropriate what could be considered phallic devices. Peyton attacks Claire and Michael with a shovel. Later on, she attacks Claire with a crowbar. And Claire defends herself with a long knife, as if thrusting and parrying her sword in a sixteenth-century duel. Ultimately, it could be argued, heroism means never having to say, "I need you." Being autonomous, the female characters have little or no need for men. Both Peyton and Marlene act as they see fit. But Claire proves equally autonomous when the chips are down. While Michael lies uselessly on the basement floor, she does what has to be done. Even little Emma knows enough to grab Joe and bring him to safety.

So what does *Hand* say about men? True to misandric form, the male characters are either inadequate or evil. Marty, seen for only a few seconds as he ogles Peyton, is at best inadequate. Solomon is good but inadequate; like baby Joe, he is mentally incompetent. Michael too is good but inadequate. In a crunch, he flops on the floor, literally paralysed. And Dr Mott is unambiguously evil. What makes him so sinister is the fact that his outward respectability (as a male physician on whom women depend) hides his inward depravity (as a male beast for whom women are pieces of meat). The same is true of the physicians who operate on Peyton during her miscarriage. In a hideously gory scene, heavily laden with political overtones, they butcher the woman and remove her uterus. The "emergency hysterectomy" is seen as an unnecessary invasion by a man of a woman's body. The prologue thus corresponds perfectly to a current feminist critique of "patriarchal medicine." Yes, the movie suggests, Peyton is bad, but only because her husband and his colleagues *made* her bad. Even when women are bad, in other words, they can still blame men. The appearance of this motif even in a movie that apparently *rejects* a major plank in most feminist platforms – the need of women for economic autonomy – indicates just how pervasive the misandric mentality has become.

The Misandric Week on Television

The problem under discussion here is by no means confined to the occasional made-for-television movie or sitcom. Day after day, viewers are exposed, either intentionally or unintentionally, to the idea that women are a class of innocent victims and men a class of evil victimizers. This can be seen from a cursory glance at almost any edition of TV *Guide*.

The surveys that follow are by no means complete. Excluded are programs in five categories: (1) Shows dealing with either male evil or male inadequacy that are not indicated as such in TV *Guide*. Even though rape, domestic violence, and sexual harassment are staple fare on the soaps,[1] for example, daily plot summaries are not provided. The same is true, obviously, of daily news broadcasts. (2) Shows that normally feature misandry but not during the particular week surveyed. The popularity of *Designing Women*, for example, is based partly on routine mockery or trivialization of men. On any given week, however, the theme of male stupidity or evil might be reduced from explicit feature to implicit subtext. The whole point of *Home Improvement*, on the other hand, is mockery or trivialization of men. No episode, therefore, is free of it. (3) Movies that depict male hostility towards women but were made in earlier eras. A good example would be *Psycho* (Alfred Hitchcock, 1960). It has become famous for the shower scene in which a crazed serial killer slashes a young woman to death. But it was made at a time when this theme was neither intended nor perceived as a political indictment of men, as such. There is no reason to assume that broadcasting movies of this kind today is politically motivated. (4) Segments from news-magazine shows and talk shows that focus generally on feminist political strategies or feminist leaders rather than specifically on feminist theories about men. During the week of 18 January 1992, for example, Gloria Steinem was interviewed frequently in connection with the publication of her new book. This book is primarily about Steinem's personal life, not her attitudes towards men, although these were implicit throughout the interviews and occasionally surfaced as the rather glib one-liners for which she has become famous. (5) Shows that feature topics often assumed to be associated only with male offenders, such as incest or domestic violence, but that include at least passing references to female offenders as well.

Although we refer to the "misandric week" on television, we do not argue that every show listed here was *intended* as misandric fare. On the contrary, most shows were intended solely to entertain the public and turn a profit for the sponsors. Of great importance is the fact that misandry is so pervasive and so deeply rooted in our culture that few people among either those who create television shows or those who watch them are even aware of it. This is precisely what many feminists have said about misogyny on television, although some have gone further by arguing either implicitly or explicitly that misogyny is due not to ignorance or even stupidity but to hatred and thus to evil.

In any case, what might or might not have motivated the creators of these shows is irrelevant. What matters is the effect that these shows have on viewers. Day after day, week after week, month after month, viewers are presented with a worldview in which men are either inadequate or evil. This very problem, in reverse, was serious enough to mobilize women in self-defence. To a great extent, they have been successful. Mistakes are still made, but these remnants of misogyny on television are greeted with public outrage. We argue that misandry on television is now an even more serious problem than misogyny – not because misandry is worse than misogyny on moral grounds but merely because misandry has yet to be acknowledged and challenged.

Without further ado, then, consider the evidence on its own terms. Here are the listings of television programs for several "misandric weeks" at the beginning, the middle, and the end of the 1990s.

The scheduled programming for the week of 25 April to 1 May 1992[2] was not necessarily typical, but it was characteristic.[3] According to the listing of shows for that week and whatever information was provided about them, at least eighteen shows were explicitly about either the affliction of women by men (male evil) or about the superiority of women to men (male inadequacy).

Saturday, 25 April: The misandric week begins with *Unsolved Mysteries*, which includes one segment on "the 1989 assault and murder in Louisiana of a 26-year-old Milwaukee woman [and one on] the 1991 kidnapping of an Austin, Texas woman at a car wash."[4] Half an hour, later the movie on First Choice is *Mr Frost*, about "a serial killer who has an attraction/repulsion effect on his attending [female] psychiatrist."[5]

Sunday, 26 April: John Leonard's weekly sermon on *Sunday Morning* is based on *Miss Rose White*, an NBC movie set in the late 1940s, to be shown that evening. He takes the opportunity to warn viewers of the danger inherent in nostalgia: failing to see the present as an opportunity for changing the future. Nevertheless, Leonard promotes the production because underlying the nostalgic setting is a feminist theme. This movie is primarily about the destructive effects of a man who had been not only too proud (explicitly as a man) to accept help in getting his wife and daughter out of Nazi Europe but also too emotionally inept (implicitly as a man) to provide his other daughter with the love she needed. In the afternoon, First Choice presents *Switch* (discussed in chapter 2), about a man punished for his attitude towards women by being reincarnated as a woman. This is followed immediately by another movie, *Flatliners*, about four medical students who induce near-death experiences. The three male students have bad experiences, but the only female student has a good one. The movie on CBS that evening is *Honor Thy Mother.* A son, hoping to inherit a fortune, brutally attacks his sleeping parents. His mother, who survives, then defends him against the accusation of murder. Meanwhile, NBC presents *Miss Rose White* and ABC presents the first part of *Stay the Night* (discussed in chapter 6).

Monday, 27 April: This afternoon the rerun of *Night Court* is about Christine being sexually harassed by her boss. In the early evening, *Star Trek: The Next Generation* is about a female-dominated planet, Angel One, on which women consider men their physical and intellectual inferiors. The aim is to satirize male-dominated societies. On *The Golden Girls*, Dorothy convinces a hardhearted father to forgive his unwed daughter for being pregnant. On *Blossom*, "Joey learns about sexual politics on the job."⁶ ABC broadcasts the concluding part of *Stay the Night.*

Tuesday, 28 April: A segment on *This Morning* is on female candidates in current elections and why they expect to win over male incumbents. NBC's *Today*, meanwhile, features Patricia Bowman, the woman who accused William Smith Kennedy of rape. These are followed immediately by a *Donahue* show about sexual harassment and rape, a *Sally Jessy Raphael* show about a woman held hostage by a madman (repeated in the afternoon), and a *Montel* show on rape. That evening, the moral lesson on *Full House* is about "Michelle's best friend [who] backs off when he's hassled for being friends with a girl, and Michelle ... [herself, who] concludes [falsely] that it's better to be a boy."⁷ On *Home Improvement*, "Tim advises Al [ignorantly] ... on just how sensitive a man should be when Al gets nervous about a new woman in his life."⁸

Wednesday, 29 April: Joyce Carol Oates is interviewed on *Today* in connection with her new book about Mary Jo Kopechne, the long-ago victim of Ted Kennedy. *Good Morning America* includes one segment on Lynn Yaekel's hopes for electoral victory over Arlen Specter, the senator who challenged Anita Hill during the Thomas/Hill hearing, and one on fathers who molest their children, the resulting estrangement, and so forth. This morning's instalment of *Montel* is about violence against women in rock music. Late in the afternoon, a rerun of *Golden Girls* is about Blanche, whose "psychology professor ... makes a pass, and makes it clear that unless she obliges, she'll never pass the course."⁹ In prime time, PBS presents *Priorities*, a phone-in "discussion of harassment and rape."[10] This is followed on the same network by *American Playhouse* (repeated later on another PBS channel). Its *Thousand Pieces of Gold* is about the trials of a Chinese woman on the western frontier. A special on 20/20 presents a special on "The New Rules of Love." The new rules are those demanded by women, not men.

Thursday, 30 April: The topic discussed on *Oprah* (repeated later that afternoon) is domestic violence. First Choice repeats its broadcast of *Switch*. On *Street Stories,* the cops fail to protect a woman from the man who threatens to kill her. On *The Human Factor,* "staffers take sides when a brilliant but cold-hearted oncologist files a sex-discrimination suit."[11]

Friday, 1 May: On *Oprah,* the topic is male stalkers. Later on, the episode in which Christine's law professor proves himself worthless is rerun on *Night Court.* One of the late movies is *Abducted,* in which "a young woman ... is held captive in the wilderness by a disturbed mountain man."[12]

The trend continued without a break through the mid-1990s. Consider the weeks of 29 January 1994 and 30 April 1994:
Saturday, 29 January: The misandric weekend begins this afternoon with an episode of *City Kids* in which "Nikki ... cries 'foul' when she's forced out of participating in an all-male basketball game."[13] The rest of the weekend is quiet.

Monday, 1 February: In the morning, *Sally Jessy Raphael* presents a show on the sexual abuse of children (repeated that afternoon). The Movie Network shows *Connections,* about "a reporter ... working in Europe [who] goes undercover to attract a killer whose victims were all registered with dating agencies."[14] That night, the ABC movie is *Lies of the Heart: The Story of Laurie Kellogg,* which "reconstructs a sensational Pennsylvania murder case in which a battered wife ... [is] accused of arranging her husband's murder.[15]

Tuesday, 2 February: The next instalment of *Sally Jessy Raphael* (repeated this afternoon) is on the obsession of some women with serial murderers. The CBS movie that night is *Cries Unheard: The Donna Yaklich Story,* about a "mother whose years of physical and emotional abuse by her husband ... a local cop and bodybuilder, compel her to plan his murder." Note the word "compel" in this case. An hour later, NYPD *Blue* presents a segment in which Kelly "moonlights as a security guard for a very wealthy woman who has a very bad marriage.[16]

Wednesday, 3 February: The morning begins with a talk show, *Bertice Berry,* about married men and exotic-dance clubs. At the same time, *Donahue* shows women how to get back at abusive husbands. In the evening *Unsolved Mysteries* presents a segment on the search for a New Mexico rapist. Tim buys an unsuitable present for Jill on *Home Improvement. E.N.G.* presents two stories. In one, "Mike's past failures as a father resurface with a visit from his daughter." In the other, "Copeland's romantic overtures toward a young researcher threaten to lead to a sexual harassment suit.[17]

Thursday, 4 February: The morning instalment of *Sally Jessy Raphael* (repeated in the afternoon) is about serial murders. The evening is more eventful. E.N.G. is repeated yet again. Connie Chung reports on what happens when teachers are accused of child molestation. And an episode of L.A. *Law* presents several stories. In one of them, "Mullaney's romantic involvement with Judge Walker (Joanna Cassidy) raises misconduct charges from a defense attorney." In another "a woman charges her boyfriend ... with sexual fraud."[18]

Friday, 5 February: The day includes an episode of *Step by Step* in which "Cody follows Dana to a college interview in Chicago to protect her from an attacker he saw in his dreams."[19] Later on that night, *Picket Fences* is about relationships: "Carter ... is smitten by a widow [who, after learning that he had concealed a walkie-talkie so that Stacey could tell him how to sound sophisticated on his first date, charges him with rape]," and young "Zack finds his first love [but touches her breast and is charged with sexual harassment by the school board]."[20] The week concludes with a special broadcast of *Nightline* called "Is Abuse an Excuse?" in which panelists discuss the trials of Lorena Bobbitt and the Menendez brothers.

Saturday, 30 April: The misandric week begins with an episode of *The Commish*: "Rachel ... supports a woman who says her ex-husband molested their daughter, but Tony has to arrest the woman for taking the child from her ex, who has legal custody."[21] A similar theme is explored back to back on *Street Justice*: "The biological mother of an adopted child fears that her son is being abused, so Beaudreaux ... steps in to investigate."[22] One of the late movies is *Cape Fear* (discussed in chapter 6).

Sunday, 1 May: CBS presents *The Oldest Living Confederate Widow Tells All*, in which an innocent young woman discovers the torments of marriage (albeit torments inflicted by a man who had been a victim himself). Meanwhile, on *Married with Children*, "a legendary guru of machismo [is] sought by Al and his men's club pals to teach them how to battle political correctness."[23] The main point of this episode is to mock machismo – that is, men.

Monday, 2 May: In the morning (and again in the afternoon), viewers can tune in to *Sally Jessy Raphael* for a discussion of children who accuse their parents, mainly fathers, of abuse. The NBC movie is *Moment of Truth: Cradle of*

Conspiracy: "A disturbing, fact-based drama about a couple's efforts to rescue their pregnant daughter from the cad who seduced her with the intention of selling their baby."[24]

Tuesday, 3 May: This is a red-letter day for misandry. It begins on *Good Morning America* with a discussion of Gloria Steinem's new book and its essay on Freud's sexism. Later on, *Geraldo* focuses attention on police officers and accusations of rape. Around the same time, the Movie Network presents *Careful*, an "avant-garde telling of incest among the inhabitants of a tiny 19th-century Alps village."[25] Meanwhile (and again several hours later), *Oprah* discusses date rape and the use of condoms. In the evening, *Home Improvement* entertains viewers with another of its routine satires on men. On CBS, *The Oldest Living Confederate Widow Tells All* concludes. At ten o'clock, on NYPD *Blue*, "the mistress of Kelly's wealthy, volatile pal ... is murdered."[26]

Wednesday, 4 May: The day begins on *Geraldo* with a discussion of infidelity, mainly that of husbands. In the evening, *Home Improvement* is repeated on no fewer than three other channels at various times. *Cutting Edge* presents "three dramas dealing with emotional and physical abuse [primarily of women] and the healing process."[27] Later, *Now* presents an "expanded report on stalking [that] focuses on the case of Susannah Manley, a California judge's daughter who went into hiding after the lawyer who was convicted of stalking her was set free. Also: security expert Gavin de Becker on how to recognize stalking."[28] Or, viewers can tune in to Vision TV for a discussion of sexual and physical abuse. On *Law and Order* they can see an episode about the physical abuse of a young girl by her foster-mother's boyfriend.

Thursday, 5 May: Shirley Solomon and her daytime guests discuss emotionally abused women. The afternoon concludes with an episode of *In the Heat of the Night*: "An unemployed man tries to disguise his wife's retaliation against her harassing boss."[29] At ten o'clock, Connie Chung presents a segment on "cyberstalkers, people who harass victims via computer."[30]

Friday, 6 May: The Movie Network shows *Raise the Red Lantern*, a Chinese movie about an innocent young woman who must adjust to life as the concubine of a wealthy man. The misandric week ends fittingly, at nine o'clock, with a showing of *Thelma and Louise* (discussed in chapter 4).

By the late 1990s, some feminists were beginning to discuss the problem of sexism in their own movement. But you would hardly know it from what was seen on television. That is partly because significant changes often require years or even decades to be felt at every level society or in every cultural venue.

Here, at any rate, is the tally of misandric shows for the week of 9 January
to 15 January 1999 (a week that featured, in addition, minute-by-minute
details of the Clinton scandal in Washington).

Saturday, 9 January: At 2:15 in the afternoon, misandric viewers can enjoy a
made-for-television movie, *Fatal Vision*, described as "the true story of Green
Beret Dr Jeffrey MacDonald, who was convicted of killing his wife and
children."[31] At 2:30 p.m., those who have already seen that rerun can tune in
to another movie called *Man Trouble*: "An opera singer in the midst of a
divorce hires a disreputable guard-dog trainer after she's stalked by a psycho."[32] But it is a quiet evening for misandric viewers.

Sunday, 10 January: The day begins slowly with another movie, *Guilty Conscience*, described as follows: "An egocentric lawyer ponders killing his
haughty wife."[33] By nightfall, things begin to heat up. At seven o'clock, viewers
can watch an episode of *Felicity* that focuses on Julie's rape. At eight, they can
watch yet another movie about women in jeopardy, *Murder in a Small Town*,
about "a famed Broadway director [who] tries to restart his life in a small
Connecticut town following the brutal murder of his wife."[34] (This movie is
repeated at ten o'clock and two o'clock the next morning.) Or they can watch
Thelma and Louise again. If they have seen that often enough, they can try
The Juror at 8:30 p.m. In this movie, a "single mother serving on the jury for
a mobster's trial is targeted by the crime lord's assistant in a bid to ensure a
not guilty verdict."[35] At midnight, *G.I. Jane* is shown: "A determined female
navy officer sets out to join the elite navy SEALs, and is faced with difficult
physical and emotional obstacles [courtesy of misogynistic men] en route to
her goal."[36]

Monday, 11 January: The misandric evening begins with no fewer than four
reruns of *Home Improvement* between five o'clock and seven. The rest of the
evening is light on misandry. But hardy viewers who stay up till dawn can
catch *Fire* on the Movie Network: "Two unhappily married Hindu women
find solace in each other as they cope with unloving husbands."[37]

Tuesday, 12 January: As usual, the schedule includes reruns of *Home Improvement* at five, six, and seven o'clock. An episode from the current season,
moreover, is shown at eight. On *Law and Order*, an "elevator repairman finds
the nude body of a young woman strangled to death."[38]

Wednesday, 13 January: After reruns of *Home Improvement* at the usual times,
misandric viewers can enjoy *Party of Five*. This episode is about the domestic
violence suffered by Julia at the hands of Ned. At ten o'clock, the Learning
Channel presents *The Human Sexes*, part of a series by Desmond Morris. *The*

Gender Wars "examines the historical power relationship between men and women, the societal obstacles which women have had to overcome in the struggle for equality, and the cost of such struggles."[39] *Law and Order*, at eleven o'clock, is about "the murder of a college coed that appears to be linked to a fellow classmate's fondness for online pornography."[40] Also at eleven is a presentation of the Arts and Entertainment network, *Agnes of God*, in which a "court-appointed psychiatrist tries to unravel the disturbing truth about a young nun who becomes pregnant and then kills her baby."[41]

Thursday, 13 January: Home Improvement reruns are broadcast, as usual, at five, six, and seven o'clock. Also at seven is Law *and Order*, this episode about "the death of a teenage [female] model ..."[42] At seven too is *Forever Knight*. In this episode, Nick investigates "the murder of a popular singer's mother. [He] suspects that the musician may have been programmed to be a killer while in therapy for drug addiction."[43] At eight, misandric viewers can enjoy an episode of *Due South* in which "Fraser and Ray bodyguard a Canadian country music star ... who is being stalked by an obsessed fan." At 2:15 a.m., those who missed *Fire* on Monday can try again.

Friday, 14 January: The week ends as usual with *Home Improvement* at five, six, and seven o'clock. At eleven *Law and Order* is about the "case of a murdered little girl [which] takes on a new twist when the child's mother kills the man suspected of the crime."[44] One of the late movies is *Rising Sun*: "Two detectives with opposing styles are assigned to the case of a young woman found murdered in the boardroom of a Japanese corporation."[45] The misandric week ends with a showing of *He Said, She Said* (discussed in chapter 3).

This is not a scientific study, of course.[46] Some weeks were probably less misandric than those mentioned here. Others were probably more so. Of interest here is the fact that *any* week could be so biased against an identifiable group and yet not provoke a public outcry.

Misandric Movie Genres

Throughout this book, we examine what could be called the "misandric genre." Movies in this proposed genre cut across all the conventional ones. And, if this book were addressed primarily to scholars in the field of film studies, we might have further subdivided by subgenres: misandric adventures; misandric comedies; misandric dramas; misandric melodramas; misandric historical dramas; misandric mysteries; misandric thrillers; misandric fantasies (animated features and science fiction); and misandric documentaries. For some purposes, this classification scheme might be very useful. But remember that movies can usually be classified in several ways, or in several genres, depending on which aspect you want to emphasize.

Think first about misandric *comedies*. According to the ancient Greeks, any play (funny or not) with a happy ending was a comedy. Any play with an unhappy ending – that is, with at least one major character who died – was a tragedy. In modern times, this distinction has evolved. Comedies are still supposed to have happy endings, but they are supposed to be funny as well, or at the very least, light rather than heavy in atmosphere. Viewers expect to smile or even laugh and cheer during the show. In this way, modern comedies are distinguished from genres that are serious, whether they end in death or not. In any case, misandry is now considered a standard source of cinematic comedy, just as misogyny once was. Examples discussed in this book would include *Switch* (chapter 2), for instance, and *He Said, She Said* (chapter 3).

The next subgenre, misandric *drama*, is very broad. In its most literal sense, "drama" refers simply to a play, any play. Here, however, the classification is reserved for what some people call "art films." These are intended to be provocative, inviting viewers to think about serious problems in the larger world of daily life. (Partly for convenience, similar movies set in the past are discussed elsewhere.) The "serious problem" is often identified explicitly, which is why movies of this type are sometimes called "message pictures." Often, other problems or related ones are introduced implicitly. Examples might include *I Shot Andy Warhol* (chapter 1), *Waiting to Exhale* (chapter 4), *Thelma and Louise* (chapter 4), *Polish Wedding* (chapter 4), *Kids* (chapter 6), and *Dolores Claiborne* (chapter 6).

Melodramas, whether misandric or not, have long been defined in connection with emotionalism. The experience is carried by feeling, whether crude or refined, not thinking. In this context, feeling usually means sentimentality. It should be noted that sentimental movies are not necessarily less misandric than more polemical ones. The difference is primarily one of strategy, or emphasis. Sentimental misandrics, for example, focus attention on the warm and cosy features of womanhood, contrasting them pointedly with the sinister and threatening features of manhood. Polemical misandrics focus attention on the sinister and threatening features of manhood, contrasting them pointedly with the warm and cosy features of womanhood. Examples of misandric melodramas might include *How to Make an American Quilt* (chapter 4) and *Little Women* (chapter 4).

Until recently, historical dramas were often classified simply as costume dramas. These were associated with frivolous romps in the boudoirs of Versailles or epic battles in the streets of ancient Rome. They were notable primarily for their lavish costumes and sets. Yet even in the early days of cinema, it would have been a mistake to dismiss them all as trite entertainment. Movies set in the past often were, and are, insightful or even provocative. Some stories are given historical settings, in fact, mainly as a safe way of commenting on social, cultural, or political conditions in the present.

A good example is an adaptation of Arthur Miller's *The Crucible* (Nicholas Hytner, 1996), ostensibly about the historical witch hunts held in colonial Salem. It is actually about the witch hunts intended by Senator Joseph McCarthy to round up communists and even, perhaps, the witch hunts intended to round up those suddenly "remembered" to have been involved in "satanic ritual abuse." Another example, with a much more obvious political subtext, is *Dangerous Beauty* (Marshal Herskovits, 1997). Its protagonist is low-born but ambitious. Her mother, a former courtesan, teaches her the one way in which women can become educated and independent. Eventually, the Inquisition throws her in jail as a witch – that is, the movie indicates, for disrupting the social norm of female domesticity. This movie is not discussed here, however, because it does not quite fit into the misandric genre. For one thing, the local matrons side with the Inquisition, not the victimized woman (whose freedom they envy). Then too, one her former clients has enough courage to rouse the population against clerical tyranny, which would end their enjoyment of extramarital liaisons. Even so, this movie makes its point. In case anyone did not get it, promos made it obvious, observing that the movie is set in the sixteenth century, "when women were the property of men."

It is with all that in mind – the attempt to ground contemporary feminism in history, especially recent history, and the attempt to use history for political purposes – that this subgenre should be understood. At issue here is not whether there are good reasons for the historical development of feminism (because there clearly are) or even the authenticity with which historical periods are recreated – the problems of inaccuracy and bias are found in all literary works set in the past, of course, as well as in all theatrical and cinematic productions – but the particular school of feminism being propagated. Other examples might include *The Color Purple* (chapter 1), *Little Women* (chapter 4), *Fried Green Tomatoes* (chapter 4), *Mr and Mrs Bridge* (chapter 5), and *The Long Walk Home* (chapter 5).

There is a fine line between *thrillers* and *mysteries*, whether misandric or not. Generally speaking, mysteries have had a slightly more cerebral tone. Viewers are asked, at least in theory, to figure out who did what to whom (as in the classic mysteries of Arthur Conan Doyle, for example, and Agatha Christie). By the 1990s, when cinematic misandry was becoming popular,[1] far more thrillers than mysteries were being made. In misandric thrillers, the narrative mystery is subservient to political theory. Thrillers also involve a mystery but depend more on suspense – that is, on scaring viewers. The story, for example, might include some shocking revelation. Both the visual imagery and the musical score contribute to the effect of dread or horror. In misandric productions, however, there is an additional element – the ideological one – that should inspire dread or horror among sociologists, philosophers, ethicists, and any anyone who cares about the future of our society. Examples would include *Deceived* (chapter 6), *Sleeping with the Enemy* (chapter 6), *A Kiss before Dying* (chapter 6), *The Silence of the Lambs* (chapter 6), and *Cape Fear* (chapter 6).

The protagonists of misandric *adventures* are usually male (even though one of the most famous movies that could be included in this genre, *The Wizard of Oz*, has a female protagonist). These movies often take the form of traditional folk tales, which in turn are often derived from mythic prototypes. A boy sets out to seek his fortune, right a wrong, or perform some other task. He either takes some friends with him on the quest or meets them along the way. Together, they undergo many ordeals. These are, in fact, tests. The story ends when the hero, having accomplished his goal and thus passed the test, is suitably rewarded. In movies heavily influenced by tradition, even if indirectly, one subtle or not-so-subtle implication is that the hero has done more than survive physically: he has grown both psychologically and spiritually. In fact he has come of age. He is ready to enter society and assume the responsibilities of an adult man. Not all adventure movies are so influenced by traditional lore. Many are just excuses to enthral viewers with technological gadgets or allow them the vicarious experience of physical sensations. But this genre is very ancient and probably universal as well. It should surprise no one that the protagonists of modern "road pictures" or "buddy movies," both traditional and non-traditional, are now sometimes women. The most famous recent example, which could be classified also as a road movie or coming-of-age movie, is *Thelma and Louise* (chapter 4). Other examples might include *Switch* (chapter 2), *Polish Wedding* (chapter 4), *How to Make an American Quilt* (chapter 4), *Little Women* (chapter 4), *The Long Walk Home* (chapter 5), and *Sleeping with the Enemy* (chapter 6).

One misandric subgenre might be considered the most innocuous of all: misandric *fantasies*. But it is sometimes considered the most sinister, because many examples of it are explicitly addressed to children. We are no longer surprised by Disney productions such as *Mulan* (Barry Clark and Tony Bancroft, 1998), which present girls with assertive, independent, even aggressive paradigms. Not all of these productions do only that. Some present in addition what we consider more disturbing messages. It is worth noting that some fantasies are addressed to adults, moreover, not only to children. An example discussed in this book is *Beauty and the Beast* (chapter 6).

Populist or Elitist?
Talk Shows in
the Context of Democracy

The problem of misandry on talk shows is related to a much deeper one, illustrated by the way talk-show hosts and other cultural observers defend these productions. The focus of debate is often on the relation between talk shows and participatory democracy. Defenders argue that talk shows are manifestations of democracy in action. When attacked by journalists for promoting sensationalism, for instance, hosts routinely argue that they are merely making the public aware of important problems that would otherwise be either ignored or presented in terms accessible only to the educated elite. In that sense, they are clearly furthering the project of democracy. But there is more to all this than meets the eye.

By watching these shows often enough, it becomes clear that some points of view are much more likely to be promoted than others. Partisanship per se is not undemocratic, but talk shows seldom acknowledge partisanship. Even though many of them overtly foster tolerance and compassion and other commonly accepted notions, they often covertly foster very controversial positions. In theory, they present a free market of ideas (or at least of opinions). In fact, they promote some but not others. It is this ambiguity, not partisanship, that undermines democracy.

In theory, nonetheless, hosts foster the idea that truth can be decided democratically and that they are the neutral "facilitators" or "enablers" required for the process. But they have opinions of their own. They have power, and they use it to promote their opinions. Phil Donahue never left his viewers in doubt about his support for some guests and his thinly concealed contempt or open hostility for others. And he expected members of the studio audience, along with viewers at home, to follow his lead. In a very literal sense, he used what Teddy Roosevelt had once called the "bully pulpit." Other hosts, including Oprah Winfrey, do the same thing in more subtle ways. They use passive aggression more often than not, instead of outright aggression. But here is our point: Western societies are representative democracies, not direct democracies. People are elected, presumably on the basis of some expertise, to represent their constituents. Talk show hosts are not elected. In other words, they are not responsible to anyone within the institutional framework of government.

(They are responsible to their networks or production companies for ratings, to be sure, but those bodies are not responsible to anyone at all.) Unlike citizens running for election, moreover, talk-show hosts have daily access to the airwaves. Oprah Winfrey has enormous power not only within the television industry but also within the film industry and the publishing industry. Her opinion matters far more to many people, it could be argued, than that of any elected official. The same thing could be said, though in a relatively minor way, of any talk-show host. To the extent that they influence voters, talk-show hosts can be said to participate fully in the democratic process without actually running for election or holding office. If that does not undermine representative democracy, what would?

The talk shows can undermine democracy in more subtle ways too. Viewers, whether in the studio or at home, are supposed to feel comfortable with the show's point of view. Otherwise, after all, they would not watch. Sometimes, that position is clear from the names of guests or the titles of specific shows. Just to be on the safe side, Donahue routinely asked members of his audience to indicate their response to statements made by guests. Popular ones were applauded and unpopular ones booed. Today's hosts seldom bother to ask; their studio audiences know the drill and respond accordingly. But the underlying assumption and inevitable implication, that popular ideas are correct and unpopular ones incorrect, indicates a serious misunderstanding of democracy. By definition, democracy is the rule of the majority. Unfortunately, the majority opinion is often assumed to be not only normal in the statistical sense but also normative in the moral sense. If most people believe that some position is wrong, then it must be so. Returning to our case study from chapter 3, most people in the audience believe that men have no legitimate reason for feeling threatened by feminism. Ergo, it must be so. But democracy has nothing whatever to do with truth, because truth cannot be established by counting heads. Sometimes popular ideas are false. Sometimes unpopular ones are true. Thus, even though talk shows support democracy in the limited sense of glorifying majority positions, they undermine democracy in a broader sense by preventing people from accepting its limits.

Democracy functions best when citizens can evaluate ideas and are thus able to make rational choices, which is why, until very recently, democracy was always limited to an educated elite (not that education per se always produces insightful or even rational citizens). Although talk-show hosts explicitly encourage the free exchange of ideas, they often do so in ways that implicitly or explicitly encourage the venting of emotion instead. On the *Donahue* show discussed in chapter 3, both the host and his audience take feelings far more seriously than ideas. Donahue's aims are dominated by the desire to make women feel good about themselves, not to explore the moral ambiguities and complexities of gender. Hosts function not as neutral (and thus responsible) "facilitators" or "enablers" but as pop psychologists or secular priests. The result could technically be called democracy in action, but a better analogy would be group therapy in action.

Underlying all of these arguments is the question of populism versus elitism. Talk shows, it is often said, take ordinary people seriously and thus foster populism. Populism is the grass-roots expression of democracy. Ergo, talk shows foster democracy. And there is some truth in that: talk shows do encourage ordinary people to discuss public controversies. But they do so, as we say, in highly manipulative ways. Ironically, moreover, they do so in ways that are better classified as elitist than populist.

As often as not, talk shows appeal to authority. It is not enough, obviously, to show ordinary people sounding off about this or that public controversy; experts are invited in as guests to "guide" discussions – but also, and not incidentally, to promote the opinions of hosts (and possibly those involved behind the scenes).[1] But experts are by definition members of an elite. Several ways of resolving that contradiction have been tried. Experts might be invited, for instance, because they have just written books that translate academic works or complex ideas into simplistic terms accessible to the masses. Somehow, they are thus both elite and popular.

The function of talk shows in a democracy is not quite as clear as their defenders imagine. In one sense, they really are thoroughly populist in that they allow public discussion of important problems. But they do so by relying more heavily on emotional catharsis than on intellectual rigour. When you consider the history of populist political movements often involving racism and anti-Semitism, this is hardly surprising. In other ways, however, the talk shows are populist only in a very ambiguous way. They certainly provide an outlet for the frustrations of many people, but they do so primarily for particular groups. These become, in effect, new elites. They allow even the most ignorant callers or members of the studio audience to speak, but they allow carefully selected "experts," in addition, to set the tone. At this point, the dividing line between populism and elitism virtually disappears.

The conflict between populism and elitism is hardly a recent development in the United States. The new nation rejected hereditary monarchy and aristocracy, but it was founded and led by members of a highly educated gentry. They did not assume that membership in the human race, or even in their own race, conferred whatever was necessary to form legitimate opinions about public affairs. On the contrary, they assumed that democracy could flourish only if citizens were both willing and able to make rational arguments about the way society should be organized or administered. The problem was, and is, that not everyone can be considered both willing and able to do so.

The distinction between populism and elitism is more complex than many people imagine. A parallel conflict is demonstrated every day on the talk shows. In the crudest terms, it could be described as the conflict between those who value feeling most and those who value thinking most.[2]

On the populist side are those who believe that legal, moral, and political problems – the problems that are discussed every day, no matter how superficially, on the talk shows – can be handled most effectively in *emotional* terms. If justice were discerned primarily through feeling, it could be defined in terms of collective hopes or fears. Decisions affecting public policy and private life would need not make sense intellectually if they provided satisfaction psychologically. Affirmative action makes no sense intellectually, for example, because it is based on a contradiction in logic: that inequality can be institutionalized in the name of equality. Nevertheless, affirmative action appeals strongly to many people, and not only to those who stand to benefit directly from the new inequality. They usually argue that the new inequality is just a practical way of eliminating the old, but this is based on the dubious assumption that ends can justify means. When pushed to the wall, they assert that the new inequality merely replaces an old one, but that is based on the equally dubious assumption that revenge is synonymous with justice. The problem of inequality has not been solved, merely placed in a highly emotional context of fear, resentment, and self-righteousness on both sides.

On the elitist side are those who still believe that legal, moral, and political problems are examined most appropriately in *intellectual* terms. Justice is discerned for them, therefore, primarily through thinking. Some are hostile to emotion, true, but others are not. Even if only because they are accustomed to rigorous thought, they realize that emotion must be accounted for as a fundamental feature of human existence. Obviously, they argue, we need both intellectual discipline and emotional sensitivity, not one or the other. Because the former requires a particular kind of training that most people now lack, however, a special effort must be made to maintain the integrity of human experience – that is, to integrate thinking and feeling. As intellectual heirs of the Judaeo-Christian tradition like most other people in our society, moreover, elitists acknowledge that justice must always be tempered by mercy, or, to put it another way, that law must always be balanced by love, or compassion. They do not deny that justice should be emotionally satisfying, but they do insist that it be founded on principles that are logically coherent and consistently applied. Tell that to the irate mothers and alienated daughters and abused wives who find their way to the talk-show studios every day. They are not interested in analysis, by and large. They want action.

In a world more concerned with feeling than thinking, more attentive to pollsters than philosophers, it is hardly surprising that those who engage in oxymoronic "advocacy journalism" are more influential than those who engage in critical analysis. Because legislation in democracies is based ultimately on popular opinion, not intellectual consistency or even moral integrity, the consequences can be grave. The two inherent dangers of democracy, as the founders of American democracy knew well, are demagoguery and, its likely result, mobocracy. Both are illustrated well on the talk shows. Today, demagogues need not run for election. They need only run talk shows. And mobs need not run screaming through the streets. They can cheer and boo on national television.

Anyone familiar with recent feminist theories will realize by now that yet another level of complexity has been added. The conflict between populism and elitism, feeling and thinking, has been reconceptualized as a conflict between femaleness and maleness. Followers of Carol Gilligan[3] and Marilyn French,[4] among others, routinely stereotype the sexes in connection with their different modes of perception. Men are supposedly those who prefer the abstract, logical, linear, impersonal, or instrumental. Women are supposedly those who prefer the concrete, emotional, intuitive, personal, or relational. (Whether implicitly suggested or explicitly stated, "female" qualities are considered superior to "male" ones.) The extent to which any of this is actually true or false can be ignored for the time being. The point for now is that an intense effort has been made to legitimate the "lateral thinking" or "alternative logic" of women.

In this atmosphere, it is no wonder that far more attention is paid on talk shows to the emotional implications of this or that topic than to the intellectual ones. This situation should not be blamed entirely on feminism, however, or on the fact that most viewers happen to be women. Many other factors are involved. Anti-intellectualism has a long history in the United States and Canada, for instance, and has proven very useful in political movements. Of importance here is that so many therapeutic movements, all emphasizing the priority of emotional support and personal self-esteem, have been de rigueur for over twenty years.

Most people, including those who defend the talk shows, admit that the focus on sensationalism and emotionalism is disturbing, which is why some hosts have agreed, at least in theory, to clean up their shows. But distaste for vulgarity and prurience is not the same as concern for democracy. As some critics have pointed out, there can be a direct cause-and-effect relation between the kind of pop psychology and anti-intellectualism promoted by talk shows and the decline of fundamental institutions. One special broadcast of *Nightline*[5] featured a panel discussion of the Menendez trials. At one extreme was Alan Dershowitz, who claimed that the jurors had been inadequately trained to evaluate complex moral, philosophical, and legal problems. In fact, he called them a bunch of ignorant fools. At the other extreme were those who claimed that the jurors had been adequately trained for a very limited task and, using common sense, had performed admirably under difficult circumstances. But here is our point: several panelists pointed out that responsibility for turning trials into circuses lay with journalists – primarily talk-show hosts – who, for twenty years, had used their enormous influence to foster a worldview that undermined the notion of individual responsibility, whether psychological, moral, or legal, and thus of democracy.

Sally Jessie Raphael and Montel Williams represented the talk-show hosts. Raphael scoffed at the attack, calling it "ludicrous." She argued in effect that her show supports democracy because it encourages citizens to talk about important social problems they would otherwise try to ignore. Unfortunately, that argument is deceptive. The topics she had in mind, both important and trivial, are no longer ignored. On the contrary, they are discussed relentlessly day after day, week after week, month after month, year after year. Whatever benefit the talk shows might have conferred in that respect has long since been dissipated. Moreover, talk is not enough to sustain a healthy democracy, unless the talk is based on sound *thinking.*

Consider that problem in connection with Lorena Bobbitt, who cut off her abusive husband's penis while he slept. The event and the trial were given extensive coverage on the talk shows. And hosts seldom felt any need to prompt callers or members of studio audiences. Whichever side they took, callers and members of the studio audience were motivated primarily by emotion rather than reason. (Sometimes, those two things complement each other, but not always.) Did Lorena deserve pity as someone who had suc-cumbed to "temporary insanity"? Or did she deserve praise as someone who rose up with perfect sanity to defend herself? Many of those who supported the verdict relied on not one but both justifications. They believed that the official verdict involving "temporary insanity" was right, because it got Lorena off the hook. But the unofficial and contradictory verdict involving self-defence was right, too, because it provided legitimation for other women to take the law into their own hands whenever "necessary." This second justification, of course, was what really counted most on the talk shows; after all, most of the viewers were women. Its popularity was not due to logic, which had to account for such complexities as the symbolism of castration and the possibility of vigilantism. It was due to emotion, which expressed the solidarity of all women with those who are abused.

No durable solution to these underlying conflicts in our society is likely to emerge, certainly not in the near future. Some are endemic and have been for centuries. In any case, it would be naive to imagine that the talk shows will produce any solution. On the contrary, they have already exacerbated the conflict by undermining the democratic institutions in which these conflicts might have been resolved.

Deconstructionists and Jacques Derrida, Founding Hero

Jacques Derrida might or might not disapprove of the way his theories have been used by ideological opportunists, but he has generally refrained from saying so. You might well ask how he presumes to do two things that are mutually contradictory: enjoy the sheer play of deconstructing any text and promote revolution. In *Against Deconstruction* John Ellis[1] curiously misses this fundamental conflict. Although he has carefully documented all the components of ideology in the strategies of deconstruction, he stops short of arguing the obvious: that deconstruction is the handmaid of ideology. Rather, he concludes that Derrida's real purpose is merely to demonstrate the "play" of meaning. This being the case, feminists and Marxists who appropriate deconstruction to make their marginal views privileged, whether they admit that or not, will be shocked some day to find critics deconstructing their points of view.

In 1981, interviewers tried to make Derrida admit his kinship with Marxism. They knew that he had acknowledged inspiration by the anti-institutional spirit of 1968 in France.[2] But Derrida replied that the works of Marx and Lenin have yet to be read "in a rigorous fashion which could draw out their modes of rhetorical and figurative working."[3] For Derrida, observes Christopher Norris, "the language of dialectical materialism is shot through with metaphors disguised as concepts and themes that carry along with them a whole unrecognized baggage of presuppositions."[4] In short, Marxism itself should be deconstructed. This has not stopped the Althusserian Marxists from appropriating deconstruction to attack their enemies. To avoid sliding into relativism, however, they "halt the process at a point where science can extract the hidden message of ideology."[5] But Norris points out that the idea of arresting the process of deconstruction has already been deconstructed by Derrida himself in "Force and Signification." He has asserted his moral righteousness by adopting "politically correct" causes but simultaneously asserted his intellectual freedom by suggesting that he is willing to challenge these same causes (at least in the case of Marxism).

On another occasion too, Derrida made it clear that he was politically oriented, not relativistic. Responding to Francis Fukuyama's *The End of History and the Last Man*,[6] in which the author claims that capitalism and liberal democracy have finally and permanently triumphed over all rival systems, Derrida noted that celebrations were premature. Never before in all of human history, he averred, has there been so much suffering.[7] It is ironic that after so many years of playing cat and mouse on the question of whether he is sympathetic to Marxism, ostensibly to protect his claim that deconstruction is a method that can be applied anywhere and anytime – that is, to "texts" of *any* persuasion – he feels obliged to defend Marxism against the triumphalism of its historic adversaries. Having failed to make his support for Marxism explicit in the past, he does so now that Marxism has been transmuted into feminism and other ideologies that depend on deconstruction. All of these are based on Marxist analysis but substitute gender, race, and other categories for class. Derrida is the bad conscience, as Richard Appignanesi and Chris Garratt put it, at Marx's funeral. By his deconstructing Fukuyama but never deconstructing Marx, despite the claim that it should be done, his own political ideology became evident.

Scrutiny of Derrida's writings shows that he himself is always against sexism, racism, Eurocentrism, and other politically correct causes. To expose these problems, he uses a technique called "intertextual freeplay." The idea is to assault normal expectations by creating incongruous juxtapositions and undermining one "text" by means of the other. This, he believes, equalizes the authors by preventing any "privileged voice" from dominating the "discourse." In theory, this allows for "freeplay." In practice, the "play" is anything but "free." Juxtapositions are cleverly chosen and visually arranged to reveal hidden assumptions or intentions in "texts" that he dislikes, usually on political or ideological grounds; in short, this technique of "freeplay" is more like free manipulation. With word plays, future plays, and intertextual freeplays, who could ever speak of striving for objectivity? In *Glas*, for instance, Derrida juxtaposes passages from Hegel and Genet, arranging them on the page in a peculiar manner so as to assault academic expectations. Is the juxtaposition between Hegel and Genet really "intertextual freeplay" or has this merely been staged by Derrida to expose Hegel's covert sexism? Observes Norris,

He incorporates passages on love, marriage and the family from Hegel's letters and other biographical material; examines the way that his reading of Sophocles' *Antigone* turns upon this same dialectical overcoming of woman's interests in the name of male reason and political order. He then goes on to show through a series of elaborately staged intertextual readings, how other philosophers (including Kant) have likewise managed to repress or to sublimate woman's voice while claiming to speak in the name of universal humanity and absolute reason. All this in counterpoint with the passages from Genet (chiefly *Our Lady of the Flowers* and *The Thief's Journal*) which supply not so much an ironic gloss as an adversary language which progressively invades and disfigures the discourse of Hegelian reason. Thus *Glas* opens up the domain of male dialectical thought to a series of

complicating detours and *aporias* that cannot be subsumed by any logic of speculative reason ... the effects of meaning come about through chance collocations,
unlooked-for homonyms and everything that holds out against reduction to a stable
economy of words and concepts.[8]

In short, Derrida has "destabilized" Hegel's "discourse." More importantly,
his so-called freeplay has been carefully contrived with a purpose: to subvert
Hegel's claim to speak for and to humanity by exposing his sexism.

But Derrida and deconstruction are not synonymous. What Derrida himself
says or does not say, in connection with feminism, is irrelevant except to
biographers. What his followers say or do not say, on the other hand, *is*
relevant. These deconstructionists understand fully the implications of a
method by which to deconstruct all "texts" *except* their own or those they
favour. It is as if the rhetoric of individualism, inclusion, and pluralism is
nothing but a front for the real business of revolution, a way to deconstruct
the exclusivity of privileged positions by insisting on inclusivity. In *The Last
Integrationist*, novelist Jake Lamar observes that there are "no people left in
the United States of America; only your own people. Only races, genders,
ethnicities, sexual orientations, cultures."[9]

We do acknowledge that this strategy – silencing all opposing voices as
politically incorrect – is extremely sophisticated, even brilliant. And it has been
extremely effective. It will remain so until people begin to challenge the
fundamental, but almost always *unacknowledged*, principles on which deconstruction rests.

If you think that all of this applies only to the humanities and other "soft"
disciplines, think again. Postmodernism in general and deconstruction in particular have been used to attack science too, allegedly the strategy par excellence of a patriarchal conspiracy. Science is guilty, claim postmodernists, of
refusing to acknowledge "women's ways of knowing." Belatedly, after ignoring
the problem for thirty years, scientists are fighting back.[10]

Film Theory and
Ideological Feminism

Nothing is self-evident when it comes to interpreting the artifacts of popular culture (or any other cultural artifacts, for that matter). As a result, academics have come to the rescue with theories purporting to explain what ordinary people see and hear at the movie house. These theories filter down, usually in primitive but potent forms, to journalists and reviewers.

By far the most influential theory of cinema at the moment, and the one most obviously relevant here, is common in ideological feminism. To explain our own approach to the study of movies (and television), therefore, we must present at least a brief account of this theory and raise at least a few questions about its adequacy. Our film analyses should be seen in the light of this debate over theory. At issue is not an arcane academic debate but a pervasive social and cultural conflict over sex and gender that consciously or unconsciously affects the daily lives of everyone in our society.

In *Male Subjectivity at the Margins*,[1] Kaja Silverman makes the following argument, which has dominated academic film studies since the 1980s: (1) Ideology is a way of thinking or perceiving that is manufactured by powerful and sinister "others"; (2) it promotes "misrecognition" (that is, distorted or fictional versions of reality that nevertheless give the impression of being very real); (3) several ideologies can operate at any one time and place; (4) each is propagated by groups seeking dominance; (5) to be successful, each must correspond in fundamental ways to the "dominant fiction" (master ideology) that underlies all the others (which could be called "spinoffs"); (6) the underlying "dominant fiction" is determined by sex, not social or economic class; (7) boys begin from birth to absorb the "dominant fiction" of their superiority over girls; and (8) it thus becomes a "constitutive" feature of their "subjectivity," or identity.

Much of this could be described as warmed-over Marxism. Silverman's theory is based directly on Louis Althusser and Antonio Gramsci. These Marxists took the primitive idea of "false consciousness" and turned it into the somewhat more sophisticated notion of "cultural hegemony." Silverman's main departure from Marxism is the replacement of class by sex (not gender) as the ultimate source of ideology. To do so, she draws on notions of subjectivity and identity in the work of Sigmund Freud, Jacques Foucault, and Jacques Lacan (the latter two having become virtual icons of the deconstructionists).

Of importance here are the implications of her theory. She does not actually say that men are evil. She says only that men produce the "dominant fiction" underlying all others and that is how men acquire dominance. Because "dominance" is merely a polite or academically respectable word for "sexism," however, and because sexism is generally considered evil, the implication is clearly that men are evil. She does not actually say, moreover, that men are inherently evil. She says only that men begin acquiring dominance at birth. But because many things that begin at birth are indeed innate, the obvious implication is that men might just as well be considered innately evil. She refrains from actually eliminating the distinction, because she does not want to let men off the moral hook. If their behaviour were determined by genes, after all, they would be incapable of making moral choices. Men are not evil because of social, political, and economic systems that encourage them to exploit or oppress others. On the contrary, she implies, these derivative or lesser "fictions" are evil as the creations of men. It could be argued that Silverman has merely replaced economic determinism with sexual determinism. Because it is not stated directly, readers are spared the necessity of confronting their own moralistic assumptions. In the academic world, the ideal of being "value free" still has a tenuous hold. Making overtly moralistic statements is considered gauche even among feminists who, when it serves their purposes, condemn this approach as "the male model."

What does any of that have to do with movies? Precisely this: it encourages the belief that men are incapable of producing movies that do anything other than propagate their own hatred of women and buttress their own power over women. What else could the purpose of film criticism be, then, but to expose movies as the nefarious productions of men, by men, and for men? What we have called the "conspiracy theory of history" is clearly paralleled by what could be called the "conspiracy theory of film." According to the former, as we have said so many times, men and women once lived together in peace, equality, and harmony – the idyll remembered as a lost golden age, or paradise – until men destroyed it. According to the latter theory, this "memory" of human history is expressed in the microcosmic terms of the individual. All people originate, after all, in what could be considered (and has been by both theologians and psychoanalysts) their very own lost golden age, or paradise: the womb. Even males, as individuals, are free of misogynistic conditioning during the nine months inside women.

Silverman's aim is to show that movies, being produced primarily by men,[2] add up to nothing more and nothing less than a convenient "discourse" designed to propagate the "ideology" of men and thus their "hegemony." Silverman is by no means unusual. This approach is de rigueur in academic circles. And the results can be seen every day in newspapers and on talk shows.

In this book, we show what happens when specific movies are understood as a collective "discourse" of ideological feminists.

Novelist Joyce Carol Oates says the same thing, from a non-academic point of view, in an op-ed piece for the *New York Times*. She discusses the relation between Hollywood's version of *The Scarlet Letter* (Rolande Joffe, 1995) and Nathaniel Hawthorne's book. Oates seems at first to agree with critics of the movie. It "represents American film making at its most spectacularly superficial. Or perhaps it's the medium of film, in contrast to prose, that is superficial." Oates is interested in neither the film nor the book, as such. What does interest her is the opportunity to score political points for women. The book has an unhappy ending. This, she observes, displeased Hawthorne's wife. The movie has a happy ending, on the other hand, which pleases women. "The new Disney version of 'The Scarlet Letter,' a lushly photographed and luridly orchestrated ode to the power of romantic love, might be described as Sophia Hawthorne's belated revenge. Indeed, it's a backlash against every great American prose classic in which happy endings are denied in the service of mythopoeticized "male" issues of courage, conscience, and destiny. Why not, for once, a romantic ending, the lovers united?"[3]

What does any of this have to do with men and women? According to Oates, the answer is simple: men like unhappy endings and women like happy ones. But this does not mean that men see reality more clearly than women do – on the contrary, she argues. Clearly influenced by the misandric wing of feminism, Oates explains herself in frankly polemical terms:

The trajectory of what we might call the female vision, as distinct from the male, is toward accommodation, not repudiation; life, not elevated death; the survival of the individual as a member of a species itself bent upon survival as the highest, perhaps the only, good. The female vision seeks compromise in order that the next generation and the next come into being. There is nothing diminished or contemptible in such a vision, our knowing that our mothers would have wished us life at any cost, including, most likely, their own suffering or humiliation. This is, after all, the life force. Who would wish to argue against it? Yet the wish-fulfillment happy endings of such films as "The Scarlet Letter" make us recoil in disbelief and disdain: what a cynical contrivance, to exploit female yearning in this way, mocking the genuine plight of many millions of women. The idea that male dominance melts before a woman's physical attractiveness and outspokenness is a melancholy fantasy in 1995 when, unlike the movie's Hester Prynne, so many woman [sic] are still stalked, beaten or killed by possessive lovers, or left to raise a child on their own. The collective hunger for happy endings is predominantly female, in our time as much as Sophia Hawthorne's, and there is no mystery why.[4]

To buy this argument, readers must first accept the notion that there is a single female vision and a single male vision. Do we know that men, not necessarily all men but men in general, are innately drawn to unhappy endings? If so, you could not look to the ancient Greeks for proof. Their great authors, most or all of them males, produced classic plays of *two* kinds: comedies (anything with a happy ending) and tragedies (anything with an unhappy ending). The same could be said of world mythology, and even of Christian lore. The story of every individual, including Jesus, involves suffering. The story of human existence, nevertheless, is what Dante called it: a divine comedy. But there is no need to look so far afield to challenge Oates.

It is not men who are notable for preferring happy endings. Nor is it the men who make movies and sitcoms as distinct from those who write novels. (At least half of all novels are now produced by women. And many of these, apart from romance novels, have distinctly unhappy endings.) It is modern Americans, both male and female, who have a taste for happy endings. This has been well known for a long time. In the early part of this century, observers noted a fundamental difference between American and European movies. The former invariably had happy endings, and the latter often had unhappy ones. Indeed, happy endings were routinely tacked onto the unhappy ones of European movies in order to attract American viewers. There have always been snobs who believed that gritty European reality was more "mature" than American fantasy. And there have always been others who believed that hopeful American idealism was more "healthy" than European cynicism. What those on both sides keep forgetting is the human need of both men and women for both.

And in the larger context of modern civilization as a whole, due to a curious division of labour, people have always been provided with both. From Europe come the "serious films" that academics and critics considered high art. In the avant-garde tradition, these focus attention on the chaos that lies just beneath conventional order. Protagonists suffer, of course, for daring to challenge the status quo. From America, on the other hand, come the popular "movies" that function as secular myths. These focus attention on the order that lies just beneath apparent chaos. Protagonists incarnate, as archetypal images, the ultimate triumph of truth and justice. This dichotomy between preferences in endings on the part of men and women, at any rate, is a false one. Even the dichotomy between European and American preferences is a facile one. In our time, for example, American directors usually see themselves as artists in the avant-garde European sense. Consequently, no one can assume any longer that their movies will end up with everyone healthy and happy.

There is always the possibility that Oates is being not merely superficial in her reasoning but opportunistic. What if the situation were reversed? What if someone were to take a popular romance novel and turned it into a tragedy? Chances are that Oates, or someone like her, would applaud this as an effort to show more realistically how women are treated by men. And she would probably go on to argue that "the female vision" involves unhappy endings, and "the male vision" happy ones, because only women are victims and only women know what it means to suffer.

Some feminists, however, go to the opposite extreme. Mary Gaitskill, for example, thinks the whole feminist debate over movies is a waste of time. Movies are not dangerous for women, according to her, even if they do represent the fantasies of men. Her point is worth examining here because our aim in this book is to show not that movies present no dangers to women but that they present dangers to both women *and* men.

In an otherwise brilliant essay for *Harper's Magazine*,[5] Gaitskill argues that too much is made of the symbolic messages conveyed by movies. If women want to stop thinking of themselves as victims, she argues, they will have to define themselves and not be defined by other people:

When I was in my late teens and early twenties, I could not bear to watch movies or read books that I considered demeaning to women in any way; I evaluated everything I saw or read in terms of whether it expressed a "positive image" of women. I was a very P.C. feminist before the term existed, and, by the measure of my current understanding, my critical rigidity followed from my inability to be responsible for my own feelings. In this context, being responsible would have meant that I let myself feel whatever discomfort, indignation, or disgust I experienced without allowing those feelings to determine my entire reaction to a given piece of work. In other words, it would have meant dealing with my feelings and what had caused them, rather than expecting the outside world to assuage them. I could have chosen not to see the world through the lens of my personal unhappiness and yet maintained a kind of respect for my unhappiness. For example, I could have decided to avoid certain films or books because of my feelings without blaming the film or book for making me feel the way I did.[6]

Gaitskill denies that she was motivated by some need to be a victim. She was merely doing what mainstream (and feminist) critics had long been doing: judging works of art on the basis of their moral or political messages. She was troubled, therefore, by a message that could be interpreted as attack on her and other women. She is now even more troubled, however, by those who claim the authority for telling her what to think or how to feel about either herself or her world. Who speaks for the entire community, or even for a particular community within the larger one, when it comes to establishing the moral or philosophical standards by which to evaluate literary or cinematic messages? "The lengthy and rather hysterical debate about the film *Thelma and Louise*, in which two ordinary women become outlaws after one of them shoots the other's potential rapist, was predicated on the idea that stories are supposed to function as instruction manuals, and that whether the film was good or bad depended on whether the instructions were correct. Such criticism assumes that viewers or readers need to see a certain type of moral universe reflected back at them or, empty vessels that they are, they might get confused or depressed or something."[7]

But Gaitskill's theory breaks down here. In this case, ironically, both the feminists and their opponents are probably standing on firmer ground than she is. It is true that the cinematic value of this or that movie has nothing to do with its message or "instructions." As long as people accept the avant-garde dictum of "art for art's sake," the only criterion that can be used is effectiveness. Does the work convey feelings or ideas effectively? If so, then it is good art. But art is understood differently in other societies and has been even in our own society until very recently. In virtually every other time and place, the function of art has been precisely to support communally shared worldviews. Sometimes the function has been understood broadly, so that art focuses attention on universally understood symbols. At other times, its function has been defined more narrowly. Works of art might be used to instruct the community (about its past, say, or which plants are edible), glorify the wealth and prestige of powerful clans, or whatever. But since the late nineteenth century, Western art has acknowledged only one function: subverting the traditional worldview (whether "bourgeois" or "patriarchal") by trying to shock people.

To argue, in any case, that art is somehow removed from the realm of values[8] is either to trivialize it beyond recognition or to deny the obvious. Nothing illustrates more dramatically the danger of Gaitskill's position than the case of Leni Riefenstahl. Half a century after falling into professional disfavour, she remains the most famous (or infamous) female film director of all time. As a member of Hitler's entourage, she was commissioned to produce films documenting the Nuremberg Party Rally of 1934 and Berlin's Olympic Games in 1936, *Triumph of the Will* and *Olympia*. No one has ever denied the greatness of these films in terms of cinematic art. They are brilliant in technical terms. They are brilliant in political terms, too. Riefenstahl herself, however, claims to have been apolitical and interested only in art. The fact that she provided the Nazi regime with its most effective advertising, she claims, was irrelevant.[9] According to Gaitskill, the debate over Riefenstahl's films is a tempest in a teapot.

To dismiss the effect of art on the way people think and feel is to ignore the obvious. Of course *Thelma and Louise* sends messages to viewers, albeit different ones to men and women. Of course it was shaped by powerful social and cultural forces. Of course it plays a role in shaping the evolution of those forces. This movie, like so many others, does indeed confirm the hopes or fears of viewers. Its popularity can be understood as a legitimation of its political message. It is foolish to argue, therefore, that it is anything other than a cultural artifact of profound importance, especially for anyone trying to understand our society.

There is a point to what Gaitskill writes about personal psychology: "As I've grown older, I've become more confident of myself and my ability to determine what happens to me, and, as a result, those images no longer have such a strong emotional charge. I don't believe they will affect my life in any practical sense unless I allow them to do so. I no longer feel that misogynistic stories are about me or even about women (whether they purport to be or not) but rather are about the kinds of experience the authors wish to render and therefore are not my problem."[10] But this is probably much easier for a woman to say than for a man. Even though misogyny is still a problem out there, it has been challenged very effectively by a *mass movement* of women. A whole cultural and social universe – books, movies, talk shows, law reformers, political groups and so forth – has been established to foster high self-esteem and self-confidence among women. The same is not yet true for men. The traditional universe on which men relied for self-esteem and self-confidence is crumbling. A suitable replacement has not yet emerged. And almost any attempt to create one is quickly denounced, whether correctly or incorrectly, as misogynistic. Gaitskill's own attitude is possible not only because she has grown up, please note, but also because she has grown up (no matter how recently) in a context that provides her with the emotional and intellectual resources necessary to support a healthy identity as a woman. That very context, unfortunately, is to a large extent precisely what denies men the resources they need to support healthy identities as men. Gaitskill's point of view will make sense only when this discrepancy has disappeared.

Besides, Gaitskill might have an ulterior motive of her own for dismissing the impact of a movie considered hostile to men: "A respected mainstream essayist writing for *Time* faulted my novel *Two Girls, Fat and Thin* for its nasty male characters," she writes, "which he took to be a moral statement about males generally. He ended his piece with the fervent wish that fiction not 'diminish' men or women but rather seek to 'raise our vision of' both, in other words, that it should present the 'right' way to the reader, who is apparently not responsible enough to figure it out alone."[11] The reviewer's point, in any case, was not that Gaitskill should be censored but that our society desperately needs artists and intellectuals who want to foster healing and reconciliation between the sexes.

It is not merely naive but irresponsible as well for Gaitskill to ignore the context – whether social or political, intellectual, or emotional – in which books and movies are experienced. Whatever the personal motivations of their creators, the impact on readers and viewers becomes a legitimate concern once books or movies enter the public realm. It is true that adults should be able to read books or see movies without feeling threatened enough to fall apart. It is true also, however, that adults should be able to acknowledge the link between their own feelings and the cultural forces that induce them. Women are not merely childish for doing so. And men are not merely childish, or (unduly) "threatened," for doing exactly the same thing. That is one point of this book.

Into the Twenty-First Century

When it comes to the portrayal of men in popular culture, nothing much has changed since the 1990s. In chapter 2, we discussed the movie *Switch* (referring also to *Some Like It Hot*, a classic that involved men disguised as women). The same motif has generated one episode of *Twice in a Lifetime*.[1] This show has an invariable premise. Flawed characters die and appear before a heavenly judge. He gives them three days to go back in disguise (helped by one Mr Smith, also in disguise) and convince their evil selves to change. Salvation is the reward for success; they get to continue their earthly lives, beginning at the moment of moral redemption.

Despite the episode's title, "Some Like It ... Not," its real prototype is *Switch*. Dr Greiner is a dentist who hires female assistants only to have brief affairs with them before moving on. Heavenly Judge Othniel orders him, therefore, to "walk a mile in a woman's shoes" – literally. He is sent back disguised as Mandy, Greiner's assistant (and the equally sexist Smith is sent back as "Lorraine," Greiner's bookkeeper). Greiner falls for Lorraine and learns, due to her prompting, that his refusal to love women is due to the early death of his mother. Watching himself in action through Mandy's eyes, meanwhile, he realizes what a jerk he was and convinces his former self to repent. Greiner is saved.

Like *Switch*'s disguised protagonist ("Amanda"), Greiner is saved by obligatory "sensitivity training." Like its undisguised protagonist (Steve), moreover, Greiner is hardly a mass murder. Even so, promiscuity apparently justifies what amounts to the death penalty. For a show that purports to focus on some cosmic moral law, albeit one that gives evildoers a chance to mend their ways, this should be a serious problem. No one noticed the problem in *Switch*, and, judging from the absence of any public controversy over "Some Like It ... Not," no one is noticing now.

Notes

1 Jules Isaac, *The Teaching of Contempt: Christian Roots of Anti-Semitism* (New York: Holt, Rinehart and Winston, 1964) 17–18.

2 William Shakespeare, *The Merchant of Venice,* 3.1.

3 David Thomas, *Not Guilty: The Case in Defense of Men* (New York: Morrow, 1993) 14–19.

4 For all intents and purposes, the Jews had long since ceased to exist as a community in England. Even after the expulsion, however, a few Jews could be found there. Like many other monarchs of the time, Queen Elizabeth relied on the services of a Jewish physician, one Roderigo Lopez. Shortly before the play was written, Lopez had been executed for his role in a plot to kill the queen and the Portuguese ambassador, Antonio Perez. Not coincidentally, perhaps, Antonio is also the name of Shylock's intended victim.

5 The word "anti-Semitic" is anachronistic here. Until the nineteenth century, hostility towards Jews was expressed primarily in theological terms. This was, to be precise, anti-Judaism. In the nineteenth century, however, traditional anti-Judaism was "translated" into the secular terms of racism. Technically speaking, therefore, anti-Semitism did not exist in earlier times.

6 Not everyone is willing to give Shakespeare the benefit of the doubt: see Montagu Frank Modder, *The Jew in the Literature of England: To the End of the 19th Century* (Philadelphia: Jewish Publication Society of America, 1939). For our purposes, however, the attitude of Shakespeare himself is irrelevant. Of great relevance, on the other hand, is Shylock's speech itself – whatever the original intention of its author in creating him.

7 We disagree with feminists who claim that all of history can be reduced to conflict over gender. Because human history is extremely complex, we disagree with other forms of historical reductionism as well (the most popular being theories of conflict over class, race, or religion). On the

other hand, we do recognize that that the lives of women in many societies have been focused heavily on their families – including or primarily their husbands.

8 The term "popular culture" is a problematic term among specialists. Usually, it is defined as the folk culture of early modern and modern societies. The distinction between folk culture and popular culture often includes a parallel distinction between oral (rural) and written (urban) culture, which can involve differing levels of technology. Popular culture, unlike folk culture, is mediated at first by the printed word and then by the broadcast word. It is now mediated also by the Internet. For our purposes in this book popular culture refers to mass-mediated artifacts (such as books, comic strips, or magazines) and productions (such as movies or television shows).

9 By definition, hatred is culturally propagated. We have added the qualifier to avoid confusion. The word "hatred" is often used in popular parlance as a synonym for "anger," which is an emotion and therefore spontaneous, personal, and ephemeral. Hatred is not an emotion. It is a way of thinking deliberately fostered by society and passed down from one generation to the next. We discuss this more fully chapter 7.

10 We discuss the misandry of elite culture in the next two volumes.

11 "Declaration on the Relationship of the Church to Non-Christian Religions (Nostra Aetate)," in *The Documents of Vaican II*, ed. Walter Abbot (New York: Herder and Herder, 1966): 660–8. Pope John Paul II has made important efforts to promote reconciliation between Christians and Jews. Early in his reign, he became the first pontiff to attend a synagogue liturgy. Later on, he recognized the State of Israel. During the Holy Year of 2000, he made a highly publicized statement of repentance for the centuries of hostility shown by Catholics towards Jews and others. This was followed up a few weeks later by a visit to Yad Vashem, Jerusalem's memorial museum dedicated to victims of the Nazis. His statement of repentance was directed more specifically towards Jews. Although he was criticized for not actually apologizing, most Jews acknowledged that he had gone far beyond any other pope – or any other Christian leader, for that matter – in trying to heal the ancient rift between Christians and Jews.

12 Analogies of this kind are extremely dangerous, so we make them with what we hope is due caution. Elie Wiesel and many other observers have noted that the Nazi Holocaust – what is more appropriately called the *shoah* (Hebrew for catastrophe) – is now routinely exploited for a variety of purposes. In the most egregious cases, people exploit it for personal gain. And we are not referring primarily to those who find ways of making money by marketing, in effect, the suffering of others, but primarily to people who do something more insidious. There are those

who find ways of earning prestige by building academic or political careers on the suffering of others. Although the proliferation of "Holocaust studies" in universities is a good thing in many ways, even necessary, it does support what is widely known as the "Holocaust industry." Not everything written about that event, by any means, is profound. Even more disturbing, from some points of view, is the extent to which the *shoah* (along with ethnicity and nationalism) has come to replace Judaism. Something like a cult of death, it has become a "secular religion" focused not so much on memory (which is highly desirable) but on the manipulation of emotions such as guilt and anger (which is not).

At issue here, however, are merely analogies to the *shoah*. Some people argue that it has no historical analogue and that any attempt to find one is tantamount to disrespect for the victims (or even to anti-Semitism). They claim that the *shoah* is not merely unique, as every event is, but *uniquely unique* – a metaphysical category indicating that the event happened outside of history. And if no analogy can be made between the *shoah* and other historical events, ironically, it would be *irrelevant*. Other people, including Wiesel, argue that some – not many, but some – analogies are legitimate. This is why he has loudly condemned atrocities committed in Bosnia and elsewhere. The problem is to distinguish between appropriate and inappropriate analogies. Any analogy that trivializes the *shoah* would clearly be highly inappropriate.

Our analogy is a very limited one. The analogy is not between the death camps and anything likely to be experienced by men (or women, for that matter). It is between two forms of hatred. The fact that Nazi hatred eventually *resulted* in death camps is not part of our analogy. To put it simply, we believe that hatred is *inherently* evil. It is evil, in other words, no matter what the results might be.

But why resort to such an extreme analogy? Precisely *because* it is extreme. Very few readers are likely to agree with the Nazis. Nazi beliefs are now virtually synonymous with evil and mistaken beliefs. Even neo-Nazis realize that much, and spare no efforts to convince people that the death camps never really existed. Therefore, anything resembling Nazi beliefs is, and should be, highly suspect.

13 Women are told that only they are portrayed in a negative way. Every year, the Lucy Awards are presented by Women in Film. According to its advertisement in *Entertainment Weekly* (Women in Film, advertisement for the 1995 Lucy Awards, presented on 9 September 1995 at the Beverly Hills Hotel, *Entertainment Weekly*, 8 September 1995: 17), this is "the foremost organization for women in the global communications industry. It offers members a wide range of educational services and networking programs designed to foster professional growth and greater public awareness of the positive strides being made by talented women

in film and television ..." Among other laudable aims (such as the pursuit of "equal opportunities for women, fair employment practices ... and increased recognition for the contributions women have made to the industry"), WIF aims to foster "a more positive depiction of women in film and television." The word "equality" is conspicuously absent here. WIF believes either that men are depicted in a positive way, which is hardly the case, or that the depiction of men is irrelevant.

14 Owen Gleiberman, "The Family Plot," *Entertainment Weekly*, 17 January 1992: 40.

15 Gloria Steinem, "Hollywood Cleans up *Hustler*," *New York Times*, 7 January 1997: A-17. On the same topic, Steinem was interviewed by Charlie Rose on *Charlie Rose*, PBS, WETK, 9 January 1997.

16 "He and She," *Today*, NBC, WPTZ, Plattsburgh, N.Y., 10 November 1994.

17 Popular music allows an obvious exception. Some genres, especially rap, are notorious for their verbal attacks on women (and gay people). Composers and performers such as Eminem often reply to criticism by arguing that their grotesque language should not be taken literally. Of interest here is the mere fact that they are forced to reply and at least try to legitimate what they are doing. But they would never get that far in movies or on television. Productions aimed specifically at adolescent boys often focus attention on machismo, but that does not necessarily involve misogyny. On the contrary, the same mentality is often attributed to women. More and more often in popular culture, macha women join macho men or even replace them. The most significant new genre to emerge in the late twentieth century, in fact, is one that glorified female fighters – which explains the current popularity of *Xena: Warrior Princess, The Bionic Woman, Wonder Woman, Buffy the Vampire Slayer, Charlie's Angels*, and so on.

18 The word "evil" is problematic. Although virtually everyone is familiar with it, few would use it in everyday life. Most people understand it as a synonym for the bland, vague, and overused word "bad" or the more interesting but somewhat archaic word "wicked." They might think of it also as a synonym for the legalistic word "immoral," although this often has specifically sexual connotations. The word "evil" is stronger than "bad" and more general than "immoral." That is because of its theological connotations. To say that people are immoral is to say only that they have chosen to do specific things considered immoral. With more loving parents or better teachers in the past, they might have made different choices. Under different circumstances in the future, they might yet make different choices. To say that people are evil, however, is to say that there is something *inherently* wrong with them. Even under the best of circumstances, they are predisposed to malice. Immorality, then, can

be explained in terms of the social sciences. Evil, on the other hand, is best explained in metaphysical terms. We have nevertheless decided to use the word "evil" here for two reasons. First, it is a way of provoking readers into carefully examining precisely what is being said about men in the movies under discussion. Second, it expresses our own conviction that what is being said about men goes beyond whatever is connoted by either "badness" or "immorality."

It is important to remember here that this distribution of good (virtue, or moral behaviour) and evil (vice, or immoral behaviour) is quite unlike that of earlier genres. There have always been sinister male villains and innocent female victims. Popular culture, however, included at least some good men and evil women. Feminists have pointed out that female villains were particularly common in the genre of film noir. They often forget that the *femme fatale* was almost always matched by a male counterpart. In *Double Indemnity* (Billy Wilder, 1944), the nefarious Phyllis Diedrichson is bent on murdering her husband for the insurance money. Nevertheless, Walter Neff is the equally nefarious character who actually plans and executes the murder. In *Mildred Pierce* (Michael Curtiz, 1945), the selfish Veda makes life miserable for her mother and murders Monty. Still, Monty himself is the equally selfish character who exploits Mildred rather than going to work, eventually stealing her business, and encourages the dissolute ways of Veda. In the new genre under discussion here, the *homme fatal* is not matched by a female counterpart.

19 The word "propaganda" usually refers to the propagation of evil ideas or points of view. Theoretically, however, it refers to the propagation of *any* idea or point of view. In some cases, moreover, it has been used for the promotion of ideas considered inherently worthy. It is still used that way by the Vatican. In this sense, the art of Giotto, Bernini, Michelangelo, and virtually all European artists until the eighteenth century could be called "propaganda." But because that word has been used most recently and most dramatically for the propagation of what we consider unpopular ideas – the Nazis had a Ministry of Popular Enlightenment and Propaganda – it has come to mean in popular usage the manipulative and sinister propagation of ideas people do not like for purposes they do not consider legitimate. Doing the same thing with ideas people do like for purposes they do consider legitimate is never called "propaganda." Instead, it is called "public relations," "education," "consciousness raising," "education," or, at worst, "indoctrination." What is truth to some is propaganda to others, and what is propaganda to some is truth to others. In short, this word has no objective definition. As a subjective slur on anything people do not like, it can hardly be used effectively in this book.

Most critics agree nevertheless that some books and movies are "better" than others. They disagree only over precisely what makes some better than others. Usually, the topic is discussed in terms of art, or aesthetics. Great fiction, for instance, is great art. Artistic greatness, according to current notions, is attributed to a novel or a play or a movie because it expands our sense of humanity, what we all share by virtue merely of being human. Through literary art, for example, we recognize in ourselves the flaws we normally attribute only to other people. Through literary art, we extend to other people, no matter how alien or unpleasant they might seem, the dignity we normally reserve for ourselves. For that sort of thing to happen, writers and directors must feel at least some compassion for the characters they create, especially for those whose narrative function is negative. Otherwise, what they produce is something other than great art, something other than art of any kind, something people tend to call "propaganda."

20 The dividing line between popular and elite, or "literary," fiction is not always easy to make. In this context, it is enough to say that we refer to neither romance novels nor to those addressed only to a literary intelligentsia.

21 Robert Plunket, "Switching Channels," review of *Welcome to the World, Baby Girl!* by Fannie Flagg, *New York Times Book Review,* 1 November 1998: 11.

22 Laura Zigman, *Animal Husbandry* (New York: Doubleday, 1998).

23 Laura Miller, "Barnyard Romance: A First Novel Suggests That the Mating Habits of Men Have Much in Common with Those of Cattle," review of *Animal Husbandry,* by Laura Zigman, *New York Times Book Review,* 25 January 1998: 23. Miller is not particularly impressed with this book. Worth noting, however, is the fact that this book was reviewed in such an august literary journal.

24 Suzanne Ruta, "The Luck of the Irish," *New York Times Book Review,* 21 December 1997: 19.

25 Benilde Little, *The Itch* (New York: Simon and Schuster, 1998).

26 Lori L. Tharps, "Books," review of *The Itch,* by Benilde Little, *Entertainment Weekly,* 26 June 1998: 121.

27 Valerie Frankel, "Love's Arrows," review of *Cupid and Diana,* by Christina Bartolomeo, *New York Times Book Review,* 12 July 1998: 19.

28 Frankel, 19.

29 Joanne Harris, *Chocolat* (New York: Viking Press, 1999).

30 Marilyn French, *Beyond Power: On Women, Men, and Morals* (New York: Ballantine, 1985).

31 Alice Walker; quoted by Francine Prose in her review of *By the Light of My Father's Smile, New York Times Book Review,* 4 October 1998: 18.

32 Tobin Harshaw, "My Heart Belongs to Da," review of *44: Dublin Made Me,* by Peter Sheridan, *New York Times Book Review,* 13 June 1999: 11.

33 Bruce Fretts, "TV Saves the World; While the Season's Movies Fall Flat, the Small Screen Flies High!" *Entertainment Weekly,* 20 October 1995: 24.

34 Elizabeth McGovern; quoted in Fretts.

35 Kristen Baldwin, "Jerry's Jubilee," *Entertainment Weekly,* 23 January 1998: 16.

36 Dick Kurlander; quoted in Baldwin.

37 Greg Dawson, "Men Drag Down TV," *Montreal Gazette* 11, January 1993: C-3 (reprinted from the *Orlando Sentinel*).

38 Ken Tucker, "Men Behaving Badly," *Entertainment Weekly,* 13 September 1996: 68.

39 "The Color Purple Controversy," *Donahue,* NBC, WPTZ, Plattsburgh, N.Y., 11 April 1986.

40 April Selley, "Close Encounters of the Purple Kind: Spielberg's Film and Walker's Novel," paper presented at the 17th Annual Popular Culture Association meeting held in conjunction with the 9th Annual American Culture Association meeting, Montreal, 28 March 1987.

41 To get some idea of what might have been had *Purple* truly been approached with art in mind, you have only to consider it in relation to another movie set in the rural South between the wars, *Sounder* (Martin Ritt, 1972). According to that movie, the ability to transcend poverty, degradation, brutality, and hopelessness is a distinctly human quality, not a uniquely female or even black one. All people – male and female, black and white – can see their own humanity reflected in the characters. It emphasizes the particular, to be sure, but not as an end in itself. Without trivializing or distorting the specific condition of black people, it illuminates the condition of all people. In doing so, of course, it unites people instead of polarizing them.

42 Sociologists sometimes make a distinction between "social" and "societal." The former is a more general category than the latter, which refers specifically to institutions and society as a whole. But that distinction is not particularly useful here, especially because of the overlap in many cases. Moreover, even sociologists are by no means consistent. To be consistent, many terms in common usage, certainly among non-sociologists, would have to be changed. The term "social anthropology," for instance, would have to be replaced by "societal anthropology." In this book, we use only the broad term "social."

43 This term is discussed at length by Paul Nathanson in *Over the Rainbow: The Wizard of Oz As a Secular Myth of America* (Albany: State University of New York Press, 1991).

44 Some people distinguish between the words "moral" and "ethical." Unfortunately, doing so is seldom helpful. The distinctions are either too subtle or fail to account for ambiguity and overlap. The latter is sometimes said to indicate careful "reflection" on problems (usually by

"experts"), for example, and the former either personal or communal standards that are seldom questioned. But that distinction is not always useful, let alone necessary. Even worse, those who make distinctions of this kind seldom agree among themselves on precisely which distinctions are to be made. For practical purposes, therefore, we use these words interchangeably. We prefer "moral," however, because it lacks the elitist connotation of "ethical."

CHAPTER TWO

1 Greg Howard and Craig MacIntosh, *Sally Forth*, *Montreal Gazette*, 10 November 1994: D-6.
2 Brett Butler; quoted in *Entertainment Weekly*, 29 December 1995: 125.
3 Whoopi Goldberg, *Sixty-Sixth Annual Academy Awards*, ABC, WVNY-TV, Burlington, Vt., 21 March 1994.
4 Whoopi Goldberg; quoted in "Oscar's List," *Entertainment Weekly*, 1 April 1994: 6–7.
5 Jay Leno, *Tonight*, NBC, WPTZ, Plattsburgh, N.Y., 8 February 1996.
6 Susan Schindehette and Craig Thomashoff, "The Color of Funny," *People*, 11 November 1991: 128.
7 Jim Carrey; quoted in Schindehette and Thomashoff, 127.
8 Charlie Gibson, *Good Morning America*, ABC, WVNY-TV, Burlington, Vt., 31 March 1994.
9 Commercial for Polaroid, Global, CKMI, Montreal, Que., 18 October 1999.
10 Commercial for Pontiac Sunfire, CTV, CFCF-TV, Montreal, Que., 1 April 2000.
11 Nancy Linn-Desmond, *Men Who Hate Women and the Women Who Hate Them: The Masochistic Art of Dating* (New York: Carol Publishing Group, 1992).
12 David A. Rudnitsky, *Men Who Hate Themselves: And the Women Who Agree with Them* (New York: Sure Sellers, 1994).
13 Susan Forward and Joan Torres, *Men Who Hate Women* (New York: Bantam, 1987).
14 Thomas Whiteman and Randy Petersen, *Men Who Love Too Little* (Nashville: Olver-Nelson, 1995). The title refers to another book, which was discussed on every talk show: Robin Norwood's *Women Who Love Too Much: When You Keep Wishing and Hoping He'll Change* (Los Angeles: Tarcher, 1985). Norwood says that women are too morally sensitive for their own good, even though the phenomenon she describes is neuroticism rather than love in any moral sense.
15 Jennifer Berman, *Why Dogs Are Better Than Men* (New York: Pocket Books, 1993).

16 John Gray, *Men Are from Mars, Women Are from Venus: A Practical Guide for Improving Communication and Getting What You Want in Your Relationship* (New York: HarperCollins, 1993). Gray became not only a bestselling author but a successful entrepreneur. His glorification of sexual differences, many of them stereotypical, has become an industry.

17 John Gray, *Mars and Venus in the Bedroom: A Guide to Lasting Romance and Passion* (New York: HarperCollins, 1995).

18 Greg Howard, *Sally Forth*, Montreal Gazette, 3 August 1992: E-8; 4 August 1992: F-7; 6 August 1992: D-6; 7 August 1992: A-11; 8 August 1992: L-5.

19 Greg Howard and Craig MacIntosh, *Sally Forth*, Montreal Gazette, 5 July 1995: B-6. See also 6 July 1995: E-8 and 9 July 1995: I-5.

20 Jim Unger, *Herman*, Montreal Gazette 6 November 1998: E-8.

21 Gary Wise and Lance Aldrich, *Real Life Adventures*, Montreal Gazette, 28 October 1998: G-8.

22 Ibid., 10 September 1994: J-7.

23 Ibid., October 1994: C-11.

24 Ibid., 26 April 1997: K-6.

25 Dick Browne, *Hagar the Horrible*, Montreal Gazette, 8 November 1996: F-8.

26 Jim Mullen, *Hotsheet*, Entertainment Weekly, 15 January 1999: 8.

27 Mort Walker, *Beetle Bailey*, Montreal Gazette, 8 January 1997: F-6.

28 Andrea Dworkin, *Intercourse* (New York: Free Press, 1987).

29 Belinda Luscombe, "People," *Time*, 7 July 1997: 50; Antonia Zerbisias, "Star Dismisses Beetle Bailey," *Montreal Gazette*, 12 July 1997: E-10.

30 This trend gained momentum in 1990 with the publication of *Twisted Sisters*, a collection edited by Aline Kominsky-Crumb and Diane Noomin. It sold well not only in comic-book stores but also in ordinary bookstores. The phenomenon is worth noting not merely because it shows that women are, once again, moving into a domain formerly run by men but because it shows that women, at last, can be just as honest about themselves as men. "Happily," writes Roberta Smith, "underground women cartoonists are not setting a good example; like their male counterparts in the underground, they are telling unvarnished truths. So doing, they offer evidence that women are subject to the same feelings, torments and desires, and capable of the same unspeakable acts and fantasies as men. Like the so-called sitcom 'Roseanne' and the ironically violent 1992 movie, 'My New Gun,' their work removes women from either doormat or and [sic] pedestal status and seeks to put them on an equal footing with men" (Roberta Smith, "A Parallel Art World, Vast and Unruly," *New York Times*, 20 November 1994: 2: 1; 42–3).

Even though few American women are willing to acknowledge their own darker fantasies, many Japanese women are. Whether they talk about it or not, they buy these fantasies in the form of comic books. The staple feature of these "ladies' comics" is violence, especially sexual violence. They revel in torture and pain. Even worse, they glorify rape. Almost a third of *Amour*'s issue for December 1995 issue was devoted to scenes of rape. Most disturbing to American women, however, is that the women depicted usually enjoy what begins as rape.

This phenomenon should not be dismissed as the exploitation of women by men. These comic books are by *female* artists and authors. The customers who buy them are women. "These magazines are not found in the average woman's shoulder bag," writes Nicholas Kristof ("In Japan, Brutal Comics for Women: Mass-Market Rape Fantasies," *New York Times*, 5 November 1995: 4: 1.), "but neither are they a tiny fringe of the market. *Amour*, which is six years old, claims a circulation of 400,000, and its readership may be several times that since copies are often passed around among friends ... Publishers say the buyers are overwhelmingly women, mostly in their 20's and 30's, and the ads are all for women's products."

Yayoi Watanabe is one of these artists. "Men read these kinds of comic books," she says, "so why shouldn't women as well? Women seem to be starting to say, 'Hey, we lust, too,' and 'We're also thinking of porn and promiscuity.'" Yes, but what about all the rape scenes? Obviously, women do not want to be raped. Rape is by definition an *un*wanted sexual encounter. Wanting to be raped, therefore, makes no sense in purely logical terms. "Women don't want to be raped," observes Watanabe, "but women can be aroused by imagining it. That's true of me, too" (Yayoi Watanabe; quoted in Kristof, 1). It is at least possible, moreover, that something similar might be true of both women and men. Not all men who are aroused by pornography, after all, actually want to attack the women they see or know in real life.

You need not be a psychoanalyst to realize that when it comes to the human imagination, fantasy, and its relation to reality, something much more complex than reason is involved. This makes no political sense. If women can enjoy fantasies of being raped, some Japanese feminists have begun to worry, maybe they really do not want to be liberated. Nevertheless, everyone in Japan was outraged by the notorious real-life rape, allegedly by three American soldiers, of a girl in Okinawa. Whether the rape fantasies of women make political sense or not, however, they do make psychological sense. They must. Otherwise, they would not exist. The possible explanations are many. In a general sense, the "ladies' comics" are just like any other form of entertainment. They allow people to deal with stress before returning to the workaday world. According to Chie Miya, another artist, the rapists depicted are always very handsome young men. "So readers don't really take it as a rape. They see it as an assault by a person whom they are attracted to but whom they could not have as a partner in real life" (Chie Miya; quoted in Kristof, 6).

31 Gerri Hirshey, "Happy? to You," *New York Times Magazine*, 2 July 1995: 27.

32 Ibid., 27.

33 Ibid., 43.

34 Kathy Jackson, "Man Jokes Make Bucks," *Montreal Gazette*, 30 March 1992: C-1.

35 Jackson, C-1.

36 Helen Reddy; quoted in "Overheard," *Entertainment Weekly*, 11 November 1991: 15.

37 Gene Shalit, "Critic's Corner," *Today*, NBC, WPTZ, Plattsburgh, N.Y., 16 May 1991; Gene Siskel, CBS *This Morning*, CBS, WCAX-TV, Burlington, Vt., 17 May 1991.

38 *Equal Justice*, CBC, CFCF-TV, Montreal, 22 May 1991. Even cases of "pre-emptive self-defence" are morally dubious, though, because they amount to vigilantism. Instead of encouraging people to take the law into their own hands, legal and other institutions should protect people in danger of assault.

39 In both Judaism and Christianity, two notions of the soul's origin and destiny coexist uneasily. According to one, the soul exists in eternity, is incarnated during the life cycle, and then returns to eternity. According to the other, the soul is incarnate from the beginning, separates from the body at death, and is then reunited with it on the day of resurrection.

40 Marilyn French, *Beyond Power: On Women, Men, and Morals* (New York: Ballantyne, 1985).

41 *Some Like It Hot*, however, is about men who dress in the clothing of women (a homosexual subtext) and *Switch* is about a man who inhabits the body of a woman (a transsexual subtext).

42 Rebecca Ascher-Walsh, "Lady and the Chump," *Entertainment Weekly*, 8 December 2000, 28.

43 Ibid.

44 Ibid., 33–4.

45 The term "cultural studies" is not a synonym for "cultural anthropology." A better name would "ideological studies," because it is a school of analysis that relies heavily on Marxist and Marxist-derived theories. (See chapter 7 for a detailed discussion of ideology.)

46 The same two approaches are characteristic of many other genres. Crime or legal shows – *Cagney and Lacey*, L.A. *Law*, *Miami Vice*, *Homicide: Life on the Street*, *The Practice*, NYPD *Blue*, *Brooklyn South*, *Law and Order*, *Law and Order: Special Victims Unit* – refer explicitly to sexual politics by presenting case studies of topical "issues." Viewers are not only entertained, presumably, but also informed by way of personal

testimonies at interrogations and expert witnesses at trials. Westerns – *Dr Quinn, Medicine Woman*, say, or *The Magnificent Seven* – refer implicitly to sexual politics by anachronistically ascribing the politically correct notions of our time to characters living in an earlier time and thus calling attention to these notions. For some reason, science-fiction shows – *Star Trek: Voyager, Star Trek: The Next Generation*, and *Star Trek: Deep Space Nine* – have been relatively free of sexual politics. The most likely reason is that women will have already achieved their goals in future worlds.

47 Ginia Bellafante, "Cool, Dude," *Time*, 27 January 1997, 48.

48 Ken Tucker, "Boos to 'Men,'" *Entertainment Weekly*, 27 September 1996: 62. Tucker observes that Sarah too acts badly from time to time. A nurse, she "says of her patients, 'Sometimes, I wish they'd all die so I could sleep in.'" But remarks of this kind from her occur so seldom that the humour derives as much from anomaly as anything else. She can say silly things occasionally without changing our perception of her, just as Kevin can say intelligent things occasionally without changing our perception of him.

49 Tom Werner; quoted in Barbara Righton, "Men Are Dogs," review of *Men Behaving Badly, Montreal Gazette, TV Times*, 21 September 1996: 6.

50 *Men Behaving Badly*, CTV, CFCF-TV, Montreal, Que., 27 November 1996.

51 Kathy Spear and Terry Grossman, "Blanche's Little Girl," *The Golden Girls*, CBS, WCAX, Burlington, Vt., 6 January 1988.

52 *Men*, ABC, WVNY-TV, Burlington, Vt., 25 March 1989–22 April 1989.

53 Christopher Loudon, "Power," *TV Guide*, 28 March 1998: 13.

54 Mike Boone, "Male Chauvinism in for a Jolt in Terrific New Sitcom, Home Improvement," *Montreal Gazette*, 18 February 1992: B-6.

55 Ibid.

56 Richard Zoglin, "Prime-Time Power Trip," *Time*, 31 May 1993: 60. Zoglin notes "that *Home Improvement*, for all its macho strutting is actually more popular among female viewers than men. (The show typically ranked higher than even *Roseanne* among women ages 18–49.)" On the same topic: "Allen, Tim," *Current Biography*, May 1995: 13.

57 Ken Tucker, "Comforts of 'Home,'" *Entertainment Weekly*, 21 May 1993: 36.

58 Ibid.

59 Mark Morrison, "Man of the House," *Us*, November 1991: 66.

60 Unlike misogyny, misandry was the height of fashion in the 1990s in stand-up comedy. Male comedians who would never dream of ridiculing women were quite willing to ridicule men. Jerry Seinfeld, for example, told the audience of *Tonight* (WPTZ, Plattsburgh, N.Y., 26 September 1991): "You know, men are not good at relationships. A lot of women

think: 'Not my guy. He's coming along. I'm working on him. He's improving, you know ... twenty years ... he's gonna commit, I know it. I feel it.' I think the only thing that enables a man to keep a woman attracted to him is flowers. We give them the flowers. That's why they keep us around. If there were no flowers on earth, there'd be men and lesbians."

61 Morrison, 66.
62 Tim Allen; quoted in ibid.
63 Morrison, 66.
64 Carmen Finestra, David McFadzean, and Matt Williams, [pilot episode], *Home Improvement*, ABC, WVNY-TV, Burlington, Vt., 24 September 1991.
65 Tim Allen; quoted in Morrison, 66.
66 John T.D. Keyes, "In Review," *TV Guide*, 28 September 1991: 32.
67 Leo Benvenuti, quoted in Tim Appelo, "Sleighing 'Em," *Entertainment Weekly*, 18 November 1994: 25.
68 Mark Harris, review of *Martin*, *Entertainment Weekly*, 28 August 1992: 54.
69 Brian Garden; quoted in Andrew Ryan, "Is This 'Studs' for You?" *TV Guide*, 28 September 1991: 30.
70 Ken Tucker, "His Show of Shows," *Entertainment Weekly*, 4 December 1992: 48.
71 Ibid.
72 Ibid., 49.
73 David M. Wolf, "The Little Women," *The Wonder Years*, ABC, WVNY-TV, Burlington, Vt., 31 March 1993.
74 Richard Helm, "Role Was Right up Her Ally," *Montreal Gazette*, 24 January 1998: D-9.
75 James Collins, "Woman of the Year," *Time*, 10 November 1997: 81.
76 Benjamin Svetkey, "Everything You Love or Hate about Ally McBeal," *Entertainment Weekly*, 30 January 1998: 22.
77 Joanne Watters; quoted in Svetkey, 23.
78 Susan Carroll; quoted in Svetkey, 33.
79 Svetkey, 24.
80 Kinney Littlefield, "New Sitcom Lets Women Win in Battle of the Sexes," *Montreal Gazette*, 6 April 1998: C-3.

CHAPTER THREE

1 Anna Quindlen, interviewed on *Live with Regis and Kathie Lee*, CBS, WCAX-TV, Burlington, Vt., 15 April 1993.
2 Shere Hite, *The Hite Report on Male Sexuality* (New York: Knopf, 1981).

3 There would be no point in maintaining their marriages at all, of course, if extramarital relations were more frequent.

4 Michael Segell, "Sexual Performance," *Esquire*, March 1994: 122.

5 In real life, many women are unlike Lorie in one important way. They want exciting careers, to be sure. But they want children too. In order to "have it all," they must make a sacrifice. Even under the best of circumstances – helpful husbands and enough money to hire servants – they must divide their time and energy between career and family. But the "debate" in *He Said, She Said* either ignores or avoids the more complex situation of ambivalent women.

6 Vanessa V. Friedman, review of *Divided Lives*, by Elsa Walsh, *Entertainment Weekly*, 4 August 1995: 52.

7 *Statistical Abstract of the United States: The National Data Book* (Washington, D.C.: U.S. Department of Commerce, Economics and Statistics Administration; Bureau of the Census, 1997). In 1970, 123.3 per thousand divorced women remarried; 204.5 per thousand divorced men did. In 1990, 76.2 per thousand divorced women remarried; 105.9 per thousand divorced men did. In 1970 10.2 per thousand widowed women remarried; 40.6 per thousand widowed men did. In 1990, 5.2 per thousand widowed women remarried; 20.8 widowed men did.

8 This explains why there is a difference between men and women in the rate of extramarital sex. Segell cites cross-cultural studies to argue that men want sexual variety very much, despite strong cultural sanctions, but also want marriage. This, he says, is the result of an evolutionary compromise: men want to spread their genes as widely as possible but agree to provide special support for the children of one woman.

9 Women want security and stability from men, resources and status, not variety.

10 In 1948, Alfred Kinsey reported that half of American men were having extramarital affairs. Kinsey has since come under attack for "cooking" the statistics, mainly by recruiting as informants friends known to prefer deviant sexual practices (Norman Doidge, "Human Nature," *Medical Post*, 9 June 1998: 17). In 1994, the first comprehensive survey of American sexual behaviour since Kinsey's reported that 75 per cent of married men and 85 per cent of married women say that they have been faithful to their spouses. Of both married and unmarried Americans, 83 per cent reported having had one or zero sexual partners during the preceding year. Over his entire lifetime, a typical man might have only six partners and a typical woman two. Nevertheless, 54 per cent of the men think about sex daily; only 19 per cent of the women do (Philip Elmer-Dewitt, "Now for the Truth about Americans and Sex," *Time*, 17 October 1994: 46–54). According to several other studies, moreover, almost all men have sexual fantasies, but only about half of all women do (Segell, 119–26).

11 Next to some movies, *He Said, She Said* seems mild. And we are not
   referring here to those that explore truly hideous forms of psychopathology. Consider *Arousal* (Sharon Hyman, 1998), an indie produced only a
   few years after *He Said, She Said* and exhibited at the Montreal World
   Film Festival. This movie should have been called simply *She Said*. It too
   is about the ways in which men and women "relate" to each other, but
   only as experienced by women – two women, in fact, who live next
   door to each other. One of them is surfacing after an emotionally
   destructive relationship, the victim of overt "abuse." The other woman
   is burdened by an equally but less obviously destructive relationship. Her
   mate is supposedly sensitive but in fact self-centred and thus indifferent
   to her. One man represents the old version of manhood, the other a new
   one. The implicit, possibly unwitting, message is that men, whichever
   stereotype they have assimilated, are no good for women. In her review,
   Heather Solomon notes that the reaction of men is anger. But Hyman,
   the director, responds as follows: "The angrier people get, the more I
   think I'm obviously showing them something that's hitting a nerve. Isn't
   that what art is supposed to do? I hold up a mirror to people so they're
   forced to look at, not just what they like, but at what scares them, what
   shocks them, what they wish weren't there" (Heather Solomon, "Film
   Examines How Men and Women Relate," *Canadian Jewish News*,
   17 September 1998: 60). Hymen's definition of art does fit that of Western societies since the late nineteenth century, a highly idiosyncratic definition. Even so, she construes her artistic duty very narrowly. As she sees
   it, her artistic duty is to "shock" only men. She feels free to tell women,
   on the other hand, what they want to hear.
12 Richard Threlkeld, *This Morning*, CBS, WCAX-TV, Burlington, Vt., 19
   April 1993.
13 Diane Slaine-Siegel, "Life in the 90s," *PrimeTime Live*, ABC, WVNY-TV,
   Burlington, Vt., 8 April 1993.
14 Anna Quindlen, *Thinking Out Loud: On the Personal, the Political, the
   Public, and the Private* (New York: Random House, 1993).
15 Quindlen, *Live with Regis and Kathie Lee*, CBS, WCAX-TV, Burlington,
   Vt., 15 April 1993.
16 Quindlen, *Black and Blue* (New York: Random House, 1998), 320.
17 Deborah Tannen, *You Just Don't Understand Me: Women and Men in
   Conversation* (New York: Ballantine, 1990).
18 Carol Gilligan, *In a Different Voice: Psychological Theory and Women's
   Development* (Cambridge: Harvard University Press, 1982).
19 We tried several times to contact *Today* and NBC *News* for an exact date
   but received no response. The interview took place within a few days,
   however, of the book's publication in 1990.
20 Marilyn French, *Beyond Power: On Women, Men and Morals* (New York:
   Ballantine, 1985).

21 For two excellent studies of the enthusiastic support women gave to Hitler, see Claudia Koonz, *Mothers in the Fatherland: Women, Family Life, and Nazi Ideology, 1919–1945* (New York: St Martin's Press, 1987); and Alison Owings, *Frauen: German Women Recall the Third Reich* (New Brunswick, N.J.: Rutgers University Press, 1995).

22 Grant Brown draws attention to the following case: "Throughout the supplement [produced by the Status of Women Committee for a bulletin of the Canadian Association of University Teachers] we are shown cartoons involving dinosaurs such as the 'Pteranodon,' about whom it is said: '... changes in the academic terrain which he observes beneath him leave him unaffected, other than cuts in the travel budget, which produce outraged screams and daring attacks on undefended secretarial staff.' The clear purpose of the cartoons is to suggest that whoever disagrees with the supplement is a 'dinosaur'" (*CAUT Bulletin* 9.14 [October 1992]: 18). What makes this inappropriately gender-specific language particularly ironic is that the cartoon is credited to a member of the 1990 Task Force on Bias-Free Communication!

23 Talk shows in two categories do not fit this pattern and are not discussed here. In the first category are those devoted to celebrity chitchat and popular culture. Examples include *Rosie O'Donnell* (although its host does occasionally treat her viewers to political harangues) and late-night counterparts such as Jay Leno's *Tonight* show and David Letterman's *Late Show*. In the second category are talk shows devoted to serious discussion. The most obvious examples, and possibly the best, are *Charlie Rose* and Ted Koppel's *Nightline*. Some of these shows are discussed elsewhere, as newsmagazine shows, but in connection with specific topics rather than the talk-show format.

24 For a discussion of what Nathanson has called the "secular religion" of emotionalism, see "I Feel, Therefore I Am: The Princess of Passion and the Implicit Religion of Our Time," *Implicit Religion*, 2.2 (1999): 59–87.

25 Charles Krauthammer, "Not Enough Conversation: On Matters of Race, We Need Civility, Not More Self-Expression," *Time*, 22 December 1997: 22.

26 Ibid.

27 Ibid.

28 Dialogue is not the same as debate. The latter, which is very useful in universities and courtrooms, relies on the expectation that one side will win and the other lose. The former, which has been tried with moderate success in churches, relies on two basic expectations: that both sides have valuable things to say and that neither side intends to defeat the other. Dialogue is much more difficult than debate, because it requires restraint and reaching beyond individual or collective self-interest. Our research has led us to conclude that the only hope for improving

relations between men and women and establishing the foundation for a new social contract lies in what we call "intersexual dialogue," although that must be defined much more carefully and practised much more rigorously than it usually is. We intend to discuss dialogue in the third volume of this trilogy.

29 *Donahue*, NBC, WPTZ, Plattsburgh, N.Y., 26 January 1990.

30 Throughout this trilogy, we discuss the double moral standard that makes misogyny intolerable but misandry tolerable. That double standard is expressed in countless double messages to both men and women about their own sex and the opposite sex. We cannot do that topic justice within the scope of this volume but will to do so in the next one.

31 Andrea Dworkin, *Intercourse* (New York: Free Press, 1987).

32 Laurel Holliday, *The Violent Sex: Male Psychobiology and the Evolution of Consciousness* (Guerneville, Calif.: Bluestocking Books, 1978).

33 Mary Daly, *Gyn/Ecology: The Metaethics of Radical Feminism* (Boston: Beacon Press, 1978).

34 Magazines, for example, emphasize the political problems immediately affecting the personal lives of readers. This is sometimes done by publishing excerpts from the works of feminist writers. At other times, it is done by focusing attention on practical advice. This means that the problems are considered in a somewhat "sanitized" atmosphere that nonetheless has been defined in polarized terms.

35 Consider the case of Shirley Solomon. Debating the merits of castrating child molesters, Solomon glibly asserts the following: "What really is so bad about the idea? We castrate women all the time, but we call it a hysterectomy. Let's face it – we live in a patriarchal society. Men make the rules" (quoted by Victor Dwyer in "Cross-Border Talking: Shirley's Relevance and Fun Win over ABC," *Maclean's*, 18 January 1993: 57).

That remark was made during an interview, not on her show. As much as anything that she actually said or implied on television every day, though, it revealed her underlying mentality, her way of thinking, her political perspective. The "moral" foundation of her remark – revenge – is primitive, to say the least. Besides, if it is wrong to "castrate" women, how could it be right to castrate men? And if it is wrong for men to "make the rules," how could it be right for women to do the same thing? The possibility that some courses of action are always wrong, no matter how emotionally gratifying they might seem to those who propose them, obviously never occurred to Solomon. Why was she, like Donahue and the others, considered a moral maven, someone whose opinions on moral problems are worth taking seriously? Certainly not because of any serious training or even a demonstrable interest in ethics.

36 French Stewart on *Politically Incorrect*, ABC, WVNY-TV, Burlington, Vt., 19 November 1998.

37 Link Byfield, "Censorship: Some Stories Are Just Too Hot to Handle," *Montreal Gazette*, 19 July 1997, D-3.

38 "The New Rules of Love," *20/20*, ABC, WVNY-TV, Burlington, Vt., 29 April 1992.

39 Maia Samuel and Marilyn Heck, associate producers; Diane Doherty, senior production associate, "Mothers with a Mission," *PrimeTime Live*, ABC, WVNY-TV, Burlington, Vt., 17 March 1994.

40 Elizabeth Herron and Aaron Kipnis, "He and She," *Today*, NBC, WPTZ, Plattsburgh, N.Y., 11 March 1994.

41 Marna LoCastro, "He and She," *Today*, NBC, WPTZ, Plattsburgh, N.Y., 9 March 1994.

42 Joe Ferules, dir., Ann Shannon, ed., "Hit or Miss?" *Dateline*, NBC, WPTZ, Plattsburgh, N.Y., 15 December 1997.

43 Mark Harmon, *Today*, NBC, WPTZ, Plattsburgh, N.Y., 24 September 1991.

CHAPTER FOUR

1 Gary Dontzig, Steven Peterman, and Korby Siamis, *Murphy Brown*, CBS, WCAX-TV, Burlington, Vt., 14 September 1992.

2 Andrea Dworkin, *Intercourse* (New York: Free Press, 1987).

3 In episode 6 ("Baby Love," CBS, WCAX, Burlington, Vt., 12 December 1988), Murphy decides to have a baby and considers artificial insemination. In a later episode ("You Say Potatoe, I Say Potato," 21 September 1992, she responds to Dan Quayle's comments about single motherhood.

4 Margaret Carlson, "Why Quayle Has Half a Point," *Time*, 1 June 1992: 46.

5 Dan Quayle; quoted by Lance Morrow, "But Seriously, Folks ...," *Time*, 1 June 1992: 46.

6 Barbara Dafoe Whitehead, "Dan Quayle Was Right," *Atlantic Monthly*, April 1993, 55.

7 In the film industry too, directors often deliberately insert covert political or ideological "messages" into their productions. Richard Donner, for example, included the following in *Lethal Weapon 3*: a T-shirt that says "Pro-choice"; a truck with the slogan "Only animals should wear fur"; a sign in the police station warning people to "Recycle"; and so forth (Susan Spillman, "Wielding a 'Weapon' for Causes," USA *Today*, 22 May 1992: D-2).

8 Ken Tucker, "Single Mother Theory," *Entertainment Weekly*, 5 June 1992: 20.

9 Meg Greenfield, "Quayle and 'Family Values,'" *Newsweek*, 22 June 1992: 76.

10 Gary Dontzig, Steven Peterman, and Korby Siamis, "You Say Potatoe, I Say Potato," *Murphy Brown*, CBS, WCAX-TV, Burlington, Vt., 21 September 1992.

11 Candice Bergen, *This Morning*, CBS, WCAX-TV, Burlington, Vt., 21 September 1992. This phrase is repeated in the episode itself. Recalling the broadcast (on single-parent families) that she had just given at the newsroom, Murphy tells her infant that "Mommy took the high road."

12 John Leo, "A Pox on Dan and Murphy," US *News and World Report*, 1 June 1992: 19.

13 Canadian statistics do not present quite such a dramatic picture, but the picture is startling enough all the same. Citing one study from 1971 (Census of Canada 1971, vol. 2, pt. 2) and another from 1996 (Families, Number, Type and Structure, Statistics Canada cat. no. 93–312), the Ottawa-based Vanier Institute for the Family notes that the number of single-parent families increased by 138 per cent during roughly the same period as that covered by the American figures. This rate of increase was much higher, moreover, than the rates of any other family type: two-parent families increased by 30 per cent, families with children by 45 per cent, and families of all types by 55 per cent.

14 Dee La Duke and Mark Alton Brown, "Picking a Winner," *Designing Women*, CBS, WCAX-TV, Burlington, Vt., 14 October 1992.

15 Gail Parent, "The Accurate Conception," *The Golden Girls*, NBC, WPTZ, Plattsburgh, N.Y., 14 October 1989.

16 Ken Tucker, "Lifetime Achievement," *Entertainment Weekly*, 4 September 1998: 62.

17 Barbara Dafoe, Whitehead, *The Divorce Culture* (New York: Knopf, Random House, 1997).

18 *Donahue*, NBC, WPTZ, Plattsburgh, N.Y., 26 January 1990.

19 This topic is extremely complex. It involves not only the gradual marginalization of the male body over a period of at least ten thousand years, after all, but also the implications of that process for masculine identity. It requires a much more thorough examination than any we could possibly provide within the narrow scope of this book.

20 This is not science fiction, according to Margaret Somerville, director of the McGill Centre for Medicine, Ethics and Law. In fact, the advent of an artificial womb is imminent. Cf. M.L. Lupton, "Artificial Reproduction and the Family of the Future," *Medical Law* 17.1 (1998): 93–111.

21 Among the most active of these organizations is the Feminist International Network of Resistance to Reproductive and Genetic Engineering. Members virulently oppose most forms of reproductive technology. It is true that they favour those technologies (such as artificial insemination and abortion) that have given women reproductive autonomy, but they oppose anything (such as artificial wombs and surrogate motherhood) that might give men the same kind of autonomy.

22 Karen De Witt, "For Black Women, a Movie Stirs Breathless Excitement," *New York Times*, 31 December 1995: 1: 1, 25.

23 Owen Gleiberman, "What's Love Got to Do with It?" *Entertainment Weekly*, 12 January 1996: 40.

24 Angela Bassett; quoted in Rebecca Asher-Walsh, "Back in the Groove," *Entertainment Weekly*, 14 April 1998: 41.

25 CBS *Evening News*, CBS, WCAX-TV, Burlington, Vt., 4 January 1995.

26 Anne Bancroft; quoted in Karen Karbo, "Just Sew Stories," *Entertainment Weekly*, 13 October 1995: 38.

27 Ibid., 36.

28 Ibid., 37.

29 Owen Gleiberman, "Ryder, Burstyn at the Seams," *Entertainment Weekly*, 13 October 1995: 56.

30 Caryn James, "Marriage, Betrayal and Turning Points," review of *How to Make an American Quilt*, New York Times, 6 October 1995: C-12; emphasis added.

31 Anne Hollander, "Portraying 'Little Women' through the Ages," *New York Times*, 15 January 1995: 2: 11.

32 Richard Schickel, "Transcendental Meditation," review of *Little Women*, Time, 9 December 1994: 74.

33 Forget about the story for a moment. This movie can be examined not only as a series of events but also as a collection of symbolic contrasts. A "paradigmatic" analysis of misandric productions would focus attention on: (1) male versus female; (2) culture versus nature; (3) city versus country; (4) evil, psychotic, or inadequate versus good or healthy. These contrasts do not emerge accidentally. They correspond to major themes in misandric forms of feminism, as we have noted, ones that were highly influential during the 1980s and 1990s. As we will see in the case of *Sleeping with the Enemy*, the primary contrast in *Thelma and Louise* and many other movies of this genre is ontological or even metaphysical: male versus female. This is mediated in terms of symbolic contrasts: culture (often technology in particular) versus nature; city (or suburb) versus country (whether farmland or wilderness). These are then evaluated in terms of a moral or psychological contrast: evil, psychotic, or inadequate versus good or healthy.

34 Alice Hoffman, "Ten Movies That Shaped Our Decade: *Thelma and Louise*," *Premiere*, October 1997: 69.

35 Callie Khourie, "Life after Oscar," *Us*, April 1994: 39.

36 In this respect, it is unusual but hardly unique. Several female protagonists went through the same kind of experience in Hollywood's "golden year" of 1939 alone: *Gone with the Wind* (Victor Fleming), *The Wizard of Oz* (Victor Fleming), and *Ninotchka* (Ernst Lubitsch), to name just a few. Still, these movies have been less common in the recent past.

37 Michelle Bowers, "*Thelma and Louise* Debuts," *Encore*, 23 May 1997: 74.

38 Hoffman, 69.

39 That topic too is so complex that we cannot do more than allude to it here. Our research indicates that the idea of a primaeval supreme goddess is based on severely flawed scholarship. See Katherine K. Young, "Goddesses, Feminists, and Scholars," in *Annual Review of Women in World Religions*, ed. Arvind Sharma and Katherine K. Young, (Albany: State University of New York Press, 1991): 105–79.

40 Owen Gleiberman called it a "feminist revenge tract." See "Dead Again, and Again: A Remake Takes Most of the Mystery out of *Diabolique, Entertainment Weekly*, 29 March, 1996: 44–5.

41 Sena Jeter Naslund, *Ahab's Wife, or, The Star-Gazer* (New York: William Morrow, 1999).

42 Stacey D'Erasom, "Call Me Una," review of *Ahab's Wife*, by Sena Jeter Naslund, *New York Times Book Review*, 3 October 1999: 12.

43 D'Erasmo, 12.

44 Not all groups see their identities in connection with contributions to the larger society and yet maintain what could be considered healthy identities. That would be true of the Amish, say, or the Hasidim. But these communities *withdraw* from the larger society. We are referring here to people who remain *within* the larger society and therefore identify themselves in some way with its destiny. Even though some isolationist communities do not see themselves in connection with the larger society, moreover, they do see themselves in a larger context. The Hasidim do not contribute much to the larger society (except by taking care of themselves and thus not becoming burdens on the economic system or the courts), but they do believe that they are contributing to the ultimate redemption of the entire cosmos. That belief lies at the core of their collective identity.

CHAPTER FIVE

1 Lynne Marie Lathan and Bernard Lechowick, "s.n.a.f.u.," *Homefront*, ABC, WVNY-TV, Burlington, Vt., 24 September 1991.

2 Sam Egan, "Lithia," dir. Helen Shaver, *Outer Limits*, Fox, WFFF, Burlington, Vt., 23 March 2000; originally broadcast in 1998.

3 Nothing, however, could be less characteristic of Christian fundamentalists than a preference for the Old Testament. Christian conservatives in general, and fundamentalists in particular, are profoundly Christocentric. Their entire worldview is preoccupied with salvation won by Christ as revealed in the New Testament. Indeed, the Old Testament is often seen as a mere precursor to the New. Characters in the Old Testament are merely prototypes of those in the New. Events in the Old Testament merely foreshadow those in the New. Christian liberals, on the other

hand, really are interested in the Old Testament. They like to emphasize their "Judaic roots," by which they refer mainly to the "prophetic tradition" and its focus on social justice. They often criticize conservatives or fundamentalists for perpetuating a dichotomy between the Old and New Testaments, one that dates back as far as the second century, when Marcion argued that the church should abandon the Old Testament altogether. The church preserved the Old Testament, as it happened, but mainly because it could be mined for proof texts and prophecies supporting claims in the New Testament.

Religious conservatives are not Christocentric only in the doctrinal or cognitive sense. They are Christocentric in the emotional sense as well. Evangelicals, in particular, are preoccupied with the experience of conversion. For them, religion is primarily about being personally saved by Jesus. Biblical inerrancy is important to them, in short, precisely because the text provides a dependable guide to salvation. (The same was true even of the Puritans, who really did take the Old Testament seriously.) In short, religious conservatives are probably the very last group of people who would be interested in promoting a revival of pre-Christian religion.

4 Ann Douglas, *Terrible Honesty: Mongrel Manhattan in the 1920s* (New York: Farrar, Straus and Giroux, 1995).

5 It includes daytime soap operas as well, of course, but these are best considered (for sociological reasons) a separate category.

6 Richard Zoglin, "The Way We (Maybe) Were," *Time*, 30 September 1991: 71.

7 Lathan and Lechowick.

8 Ken Tucker, "Next of Quinn," *Entertainment Weekly*, 1 April 1994: 41.

9 Rama Laurie Stagner, *A Passion for Justice: The Hazel Brannon Story*, ABC, WVNY-TV, Burlington, Vt., 17 April 1994.

CHAPTER SIX

1 Harry F. Waters, "Whip Me, Beat Me ... and Give Me Great Ratings: A Network Obsession with Women in Danger," *Newsweek*, 11 November 1991: 74.

2 This is not to say that mentally incompetent people are less than human or even less than fully human, because moral agency is not the *only* criterion by which humanity is defined. Besides, it is precisely on moral grounds that people without the particular capacity for making moral decisions must be included within the category of full humanity.

3 Allen Garr, "My Brother's Keeper," *Prime-Time News*, CBC, CBMT, Montreal, Que., 7 March 1995.

4 Ibid.

5 John Haslett Cuff, "Making a Strong Case for Capital Punishment," *Globe and Mail*, 7 March 1995: A-13.

6 John Miglis; directed by Robert Iscove, *Dying to Love*, CBS, WCAX-TV, Burlington, Vt., 16 March 1993.

7 Selma Thompson and Jeff Andrus; directed by Harry Winer, *Men Don't Tell*, CBS, WCAX-TV, Burlington, Vt., 14 March 1993.

8 Barbara Righton, "Maternity-Home Monster," *Montreal Gazette*: TV *Times*, 7 January 1995: 5.

9 Joe Cacaci; directed by Joyce Chopra, *Murder in New Hampshire: The Pamela Smart Story*, CBS, WCAX-TV, Burlington, Vt., 24 September 1991.

10 Dan Freudenberger; directed by Harry Winer, *Stay the Night*, ABC, WVNY-TV, Burlington, Vt., 26 and 27 April 1992.

11 Mimi Rothman Schapiro and Bill Wells (based on screenplay by Sharon Michaels); directed by Jud Taylor, *In My Daughter's Name*, CBS, WCAX-TV, Burlington, Vt., 10 May 1992.

12 Joe Cacaci; directed by Dick Lowry, *Her Final Fury: Betty Broderick, the Last Chapter*, CBS, WCAX-TV, Burlington, Vt., 1 November 1992.

13 Alan Carter, "Guilty, Guilty! Guilty!" *Entertainment Weekly*, 30 October 1992: 13–14.

14 Joe Cacaci; directed by Dick Lowry, *A Woman Scorned: The Betty Broderick Story*, CBS, WCAX-TV, Burlington, Vt., 1 March 1992.

15 Waters, 74–5.

16 Richard Zoglin, "Oh, the Agony! the Ratings! The U.S. Networks Court Women Viewers with a Parade of Heroines Who Are Betrayed, Battered and Bewildered," *Time*, 11 November 1991: 78–9.

17 Waters, 74.

18 Ibid.

19 Carole Lieberman; quoted in Waters, 75.

20 Mark Harris, "Dangerous Women," *Entertainment Weekly*, 24 April 1992: 38.

21 Zoglin, 78.

22 Waters, 74.

23 Zoglin, 79.

24 Waters, 75.

25 Harris, 38.

26 Waters, 75.

27 Ibid.

28 Richard Schickel, "Everybody's Good Girl," *Time*, 4 September 1995: 52.

29 Schickel, 52.

30 Caren Weiner, "Emboldened Girls," *Entertainment Weekly*, 21 March 1997: 81.

31 Tom Gliatto, review of *Kids*, *People*, 7 July 1995: 13.

32 Steve Kokker, "No Teen Flick," *Montreal Hour*, 3 August 1995: 13 (emphasis added).

33 Paul Delean, "Tough Children Make for Sharp Kids," *Montreal Gazette*, 28 July 1995: C-8.

34 The monarchs and the upper classes surely had the most elaborate funerary arrangements. And today their tombs are the ones that survive, or at least the ones that look most impressive. But Egyptians of other classes were by no means without hope for renewed life beyond the grave.

35 Marc Lépine murdered fourteen women at the University of Montreal in 1989, after which he shot himself. His stated reason was that women were ruining his life. But observers, including psychologists and psychiatrists, devoted a great deal of time and energy to possible underlying explanations. You do not have to be a Freudian to suggest that part of his rage originated in early childhood. His was an unhappy one. Apart from anything else, his father was violently abusive.

36 Elaine Showalter, "Ten Movies That Defined Our Decade: Beauty and the Beast," *Premiere*, October 1997: 66.

37 Ibid.

38 Beaumont's rendition was based directly on an earlier French one, *La jeune amériquaine, et les contes marins*, written by Gabrielle Susanne Barbot de Gallon de Villeneuve in 1740. This was written not for children but for the author's friends at court. The story had been written down even earlier, however, in other languages. The earliest might have been Giovanni Francesco Straparola's *Le Piacevoli Notti*, written in 1550. For a detailed account of versions in the English language, see Betsy Hearne's *Beauty and the Beast: Visions and Revisions of an Old Tale* (Chicago: University of Chicago Press, 1989).

39 In traditional versions, the sisters pretend to be happy with Beauty and thus prolong her stay at home beyond the week allotted to her by the Beast. Suddenly, looking into the magic mirror, she sees him weeping and decides to return at once. Because the evil sisters have been removed in the Disney version, another reason had to be found for Belle's sudden desire to see the Beast again; it is Gaston's horrid plot to place her father in an insane asylum that provides the motivation. Belle picks up the magic mirror to show him and the mob that the Beast really does exist and is not a figment of her father's imagination.

40 Hearn, 27.

41 Ty Burr, "The 'Beast' Goes On," review of *Beauty and the Beast*, *Entertainment Weekly*, 14 November 1997: 96.

42 These threats are well known but seldom acknowledged in current political debates over gender. The most important one involves identity. All children must assert their independence from Mother. Unlike girls, though, boys must also switch the focus of their identity from Mother to

Father. The transition, the assimilation of masculinity in one form or another, is extremely difficult. But it is of profound importance to both the boys themselves and to society as a whole. We will discuss the problem in another volume of this trilogy.

43 In traditional versions, he is successful as a merchant – less successful at maintaining family harmony, and extremely unsuccessful in raising all but one of his children.

44 Hearn, 132–3.

45 Hearn, 89.

46 Elaine Benken, "Mail," *Entertainment Weekly*, 29 July 1994: 6 (emphasis added).

CHAPTER SEVEN

1 Elizabeth G. Davis, *The First Sex* (New York: Dent, 1973): 351–2.

2 The Devil, or Satan, has always been considered male in Western folklore and theology. Consider a recent television commercial for Smart Ones (CBS, WCAX-TV, Burlington, Vt., 31 January 1998). A devil and an angel try to influence a shopper. The angel tells her to buy Brussels sprouts, carrots, rice cakes, seven-grain cereal, and everything wholesome or nourishing. The devil tells her to buy chocolate cake, cookie dough, pork rinds, and everything unhealthy or "sinful." The angel is female, of course, and the devil male.

There have been human representations of evil as well, among them, the witch. European witches were usually (though not always) female after the fifteenth century. They were said to be agents of Satan who were both metaphorically and literally seduced by him. But burning or hanging witches did not become an obsession until the sixteenth and seventeenth centuries. And witches were never considered the only human sources of evil.

There were at least two other major sources of evil in the Middle Ages: infidels (first Jews, then Muslims as well) and heretics (some of whom – the Albigensians, for instance – represented not the theological idiosyncrasies of individuals but the social and political goals of mass movements). And all were normally considered most threatening – most evil – in *male* form. This was partly because it was primarily men who expounded the doctrines and promoted the practices that competed directly with Christianity. In addition, it was because their threat, except in the case of Jews, was military as well as intellectual. As for the Jews, Montagu Frank Modder has written about their representation in English literature (*The Jew in the Literature of England to the End of the Nineteenth Century* [Philadelphia: Jewish Publication Society of America, 1939]). He points out that the evil Jew was usually represented by the father of an innocent and virtuous daughter who, after escaping his clutches through conversion, marries the Christian hero.

More recently, especially in American folklore, women have been associated with the opposite of evil. On the frontier and in small towns, women were involved in poetry readings, literary guilds, art societies, and whatever passed for "refinement." In addition, they were associated with piety and morality as missionaries, schoolmarms, and mothers. They were angels tending the domestic hearth. Men, on the other hand, were associated with evil. They were beasts that rode the range with their cattle or went off to work in the urban jungle. They had to be tamed or "civilized" by good women. In our own time, the demonization of men is so thorough and so pervasive that only those who never watch television, never see popular movies, and never read mass-market magazines can fail to be aware of it.

3 The classic pattern could change, now that God is sometimes shown as a woman. In *Dogma* (Kevin Smith, 1999), God is portrayed by Alanis Morissette. On one episode of *Popular*, God appears to Harrison as a woman ("Are You There, God? It's Me, Ann-Margaret," Fox, WFFF, Burlington, Vt., 8 December 2000). By 2000, not surprisingly, Jeniffer Love-Hewitt was preparing to play Satan in *The Devil and Daniel Webster*. Part of the appeal in all these cases, however, is precisely the shock value of overturned tradition.

4 Katherine K. Young, "Goddesses, Feminists, and Scholars," in *Annual Review of Women in World Religions*, ed. Arvind Sharma and Katherine K. Young (Albany: State University of New York Press, 1991): 105–79.

5 It ranked first in its first week. When *Silence of the Lambs* was released the next week, it moved to second place and remained in that position the following week ("Box Office," *Entertainment Weekly*, 21 February; 1 March; 8 March; 15 March; 22 March 1991).

6 Martin does not like Laura. He merely wants her to gratify his need for sexual release and, especially, his need for control and order. Although Ben too would like to control her, he can still like her as a person and enjoy being with her.

7 Marilyn French, *Beyond Power: On Women, Men and Morals* (New York: Ballantine, 1986).

8 Mary Daly has written several books about the transition from matriarchal to patriarchal religion, from Goddess to God. It has been a constant theme running throughout her work over several decades, although she is by no means the only feminist to have done so and argued for a return to the former. Cf. *Beyond God the Father: Toward a Philosophy of Women's Liberation* (Boston: Beacon Press, 1973); *Pure Lust: Elemental Feminist Philosophy* (Boston: Beacon Press, 1984); and *Quintessence – Realizing the Archaic Future: A Radical Elemental Feminist Manifesto*

(Boston: Beacon Press, 1998). We intend to discuss this goddess scenario in another volume.

9 Paul Nathanson, *Over the Rainbow: The Wizard of Oz as a Secular Myth of America* (Albany: State University of New York Press, 1992): 109–78.

10 Christians have usually assumed that the Torah is a burden from which Christ released them. Unlike Jews, they say, Christians do not have to prove themselves by obeying every commandment. They can be saved merely by faith in Christ (an event that, especially among Protestants, is a gift of divine grace rather than something achieved by sinners). For Jews, however, the Torah is anything but the burden imposed by a remote but strict God. It is the greatest and holiest gift of a compassionate God. It is the chief source of joy, moreover, not of anxiety. That is because the Jewish God is not a cosmic scorekeeper. Salvation is assumed, for all those who repent their inevitable failure to attain perfection, not earned (although Jews, unlike many Protestants, assume that people can at least cooperate with God in the creation of holiness.)

11 The same is true of Judaism. Every convert is immersed ceremonially in a *mikvah*. But Christian baptism is far better known both inside and outside the Christian community. Even many Jews are unaware of the same rite in their own tradition. That is partly because Jews have been reluctant to convert non-Jews (although a high rate of intermarriage is changing that) and partly because of the religious ignorance of many secular Jews.

12 John Dominic Crossan, *"The Dark Interval: Towards a Theology of Story* (Niles, Ill.: Argus communications, 1975). For Crossan, parables are stories that subvert or challenge a worldview. That is precisely what avant-garde art is supposed to do. The extent to which avant-garde art actually works that way is open to question. It could be argued that the avant-garde has by now become the mainstream, supported by conventional academic wisdom about the nature of art and often by government funding as well. Crossan says that myth, on the other hand, establishes, confirms, or sustains a worldview. That makes it a suitable analogy for popular art forms. But that too is open to question. Sometimes, popular art forms do subvert cultural norms. The most obvious examples would come from the contentious world of hip hop, heavy metal, and other forms of popular music that are associated with protest movements. But these analogies – parable and elite culture, myth and popular culture – refer to ideal types. They are useful in defining a continuum of possibilities.

13 As of 2001, we cannot say much more about the problem of "husband battering" than that it exists. In fact, there have "been almost no systematic studies of battered husbands since [Suzanne] Steinmetz created

the term" (Leslie Tutty, *Husband Abuse: An Overview of Research and Perspectives* [Ottawa: Health Canada, Family Violence Prevention Unit, 1999] 15) decades ago (Suzanne K. Steinmetz, "The Battered Husband Syndrome," *Victimology* 2 [1977–78]: 499). And the studies that have been done are methodologically flawed due to small samples of the population, ambiguous questions, cultural assumptions, and so on. In 1999, however, Health Canada produced a summary of the research. Leslie Tutty concluded that "more research on the experiences of abused men is essential to estimate the extent and severity of the problem. The little research conducted to date raises more questions than it answers" (Tutty 23). Elsewhere, she notes that the "existence of husband abuse is not an issue. Rather, the debate concerns how common it is and the degree of harm inflicted" (Tutty 4).

As for how common it is, preliminary evidence strongly suggests that the one-way-street theory of domestic violence – that only men are the perpetrators of domestic violence and that only women are the victims of it – is not tenable. Compare the evidence from two studies, one Canadian (Grandin and Lupri, 1986) and the other American (u.s. National Family Violence study, 1985). According to the American study, 1.2 per cent of the men – and 4.3 per cent of the women – admitted that they had committed "severe violence." According to the Canadian study, 9.9 per cent of the men – and 15.5 per cent of the women – admitted the same thing. Another Canadian study (Sommer 1994) found that "aggressive behaviour" was admitted by 17.3 per cent of the men – and 27.4 per cent of the women. It has been argued that fewer men than women are likely to admit their evil ways. But that is an argument from silence, or absence. We have no way of knowing, at least for the time being, how many men really are violent but either refuse to admit or fail to recognize it as a problem.

Maybe more men should be added to the statistics of perpetrators, but what are we to make of the women who admit to being perpetrators? It has been argued that women are more likely than men to acknowledge their own flaws. Once again, however, we do not know that. It has been argued, moreover, that much of what women admit to doing is of minor importance. That, of course, is a subjective position. Not so long ago, after all, many people believed that there was nothing so horrible about slapping or throwing things at a wife (or a child) now and then. Today, in a very different political atmosphere, that is a matter of considerable debate.

One major problem facing researchers is the fact that people interpret their own behaviour and that of their partners in a variety of ways. Some consider slapping and hitting part of normal life. Others consider these things abusive. Some consider them abusive when done by one sex but not when done by the other. Some interpretations are affected by the way behaviour is depicted in movies or on television. Others are affected by the way it is explained by ideological feminists or explained away by their opponents.

The discussion of husband abuse or battering often concludes with one obvious question: Where are the victims? We have already agreed that few men would want to admit their own violence, even if only to researchers. In all probability even fewer men would want to admit being the victims of violence – and still fewer would want to admit being the victims of violent women. As Tutty points out, the few male victims who do consult the police are often ridiculed. Until men have the incentive to admit vulnerability of any kind, let alone at the hands of women – something strictly forbidden by custom to men in our society – they are unlikely to show up looking for help. That would be the equivalent for men of the "fate worse than death" for women.

One common argument against government intervention on behalf of victimized men bypasses the one about prevalence. No matter how commonly men are victimized by their female partners, this argument goes, the harm inflicted is likely to be less severe than that inflicted by men. This is not necessarily an argument about men being more willing than women to injure their partners. It is based on the fact that men in general are bigger and stronger than women in general. When men resort to violence, they are likely to inflict more damage than women who do so.

Tutty says the same thing. She does "not deny that women use violent tactics, but suggest[s] that the results of at least some female violence need to be perceived differently and are less likely to have the same serious consequences as those used by men" (Tutty 11). For her, this argument is practical rather than moral. (Those who belong to the consequentialist school of ethics, believing that acts are good or evil depending on consequences rather than motivation, might disagree). Almost by definition, governments are less interested in the moral aspects of social problems than they are with practical measures – that is, with the allocation of tax dollars to shelters and other solutions to demonstrably widespread and urgent problems. It is assumed that victimized men have the financial resources to fend for themselves and need not rely on programs funded by the government (even though men might be reluctant to leave home for other reasons, including the welfare of their children, just as women are). In the absence of evidence one way or another, however, Tutty does acknowledge that further research might legitimate government intervention. Meanwhile, she notes, some victimized men are "helped" by being sent for group therapy intended for men who victimize their female partners!

Debate continues over the meaning, context, and perception not only of abuse and violence but even of murder (although the prevalence of murder, no matter what its meaning, context, or perception, is known). Consider murder rates in the United States and Canada. In the United

States, men and women kill each other in equal numbers. In Canada, there are roughly three times as many female victims as male ones. Is there something "innocent" about Canadian women and something "evil" about American women? That is unlikely, observes Tutty. She suggests that the "easy availability of handguns [in the United States] equalizes power so that both men and women are at about equal risk of being murdered by the other" (Tutty 13).

At the very least, we should try to separate what statistical evidence we have from moral or ideological claims. It is probably true, as Tutty observes, that "women differ from men in their perception of whether a situation might result in dangerous retaliation, such that women were less aggressive when they expected danger to be imminent." This claim is about the prudence of women in evaluating the likely behaviour of men, however, not about their moral superiority to men.

With all this in mind – lack of evidence for the prevalence of this problem and the likelihood that victimized women are in greater danger than victimized men – Tutty's report does not recommend immediate government intervention on behalf of victimized men.

14 Georges Dumézil, *Gods of the Ancient Northmen*, Publications for the UCLA Center for the Study of Comparative Folklore and Mythology, ed. Einar Haugen (Berkeley: University of California Press, 1973), 66–7. Because the tempests he brought provided rain for the crops, Thor was associated with fertility as well. Nevertheless, he was and is best known as the stormy and powerful god of thunder and lightning.

15 Ibid., 68.

16 Ibid., 19. Vulcan (in Greek mythology, Hephaestus) was a god of fire. Because fire was required for the working of metals, he became the divine blacksmith and patron of crafts and industries. Like Thor, the son of Odin, Vulcan was a son of Jupiter (Zeus).

17 Brian D. Johnson, "The Marrying Maniac: A Horrid Script Wrecks a Horrifying Story," *Maclean's*, 6 May 1991, 56.

18 They are rational, but only within an irrational context. Even though psychotics use sound logic to achieve their goals, for example, the goals themselves originate in irrational fears or delusions.

19 In ancient Rome, neither Vulcan nor the technology he represented was seen as malevolent.

20 Henry Miller, "Sexus," in *The Rosy Crucifixion* (New York: Grove Press, 1965).

21 Owen Gleiberman, "With a Vengeance," *Entertainment Weekly*, 22 November 1991: 56.

CHAPTER EIGHT

1 Jean Bethke Elshtain, *Women and War* (New York: Basic Books, 1987) 3.

2 Barbara Amiel, "Henpecked Men Carry Feminist Torch," *Montreal Gazette*, 23 November 1996: B-6.

3 E.O. Wilson, "Back from Chaos," *Atlantic Monthly* (March 1998): 58.

4 The origins of fascism are complex, dating back at least to the rise of Romanticism. In Germany, however, the Versailles Treaty was a major factor in the rise of National Socialism.

5 Nellie McClung is known in Canada as a pioneer feminist. Her book *In Times Like These* (1915; Toronto: University of Toronto Press, 1972) is concerned with World War I. It is a polemical statement of female superiority. Thinking about the war from her remote home on the prairies of western Canada, she blamed the war specifically on the kaiser but generally on men. Had they not restricted the vote to themselves, she argued, there would have been no war in the first place. "Although men like to fight, war is not inevitable. War is not of God's making. War is a crime committed by men, and, therefore, when enough people say it shall not be, it cannot be. This will not happen until women are allowed to say what they think of war. Up to the present time women have had nothing to say about war, except pay the price of war – this privilege has been theirs always" (page 15). Never mind that men too paid a price: being slaughtered en masse. Never mind that both women and men eventually opposed the war. In a comparative review of McClung's book and Charles Yale Harrison's *Generals Die in Bed* (1930; Hamilton, Ont.: Potlatch Publications, 1975), Allison Phillips notes a significant difference in perspective. "It might be possible to classify both of these authors as reformers in that neither wants the war to be repeated. It is difficult to make a comparison because the two authors are almost waging two completely different battles. Harrison is fighting for his mental and physical survival, while McClung's self-righteousness leads her to wage a war on society's immorality" ("A Comparative Review of *Generals Die in Bed* and *In Times Like These*," *Historical Discourses* 1 [April 1987]: 77) – that is, on *men's* immorality.

6 They based their claim on one or more of three major sources: the egalitarianism of the Enlightenment as filtered through the American and French Revolutions; the utilitarianism of John Stuart Mill; and the socialism of Karl Marx.

7 Ann Douglas, *Terrible Honesty: Mongrel Manhattan in the 1920s* (New York: Farrar, Straus and Giroux, 1995), 254.

8 Douglas, 255.

9 George Train; quoted in Douglas, 258.

10 Douglas, 254–7.

11 Meron Wondwosen; quoted in "Talk of the Streets," *Time*, 29 April 1996: 10.

12 Douglas, 258.

13 Ibid., 262.

14 Glen Jeansonne, *Women of the Far Right: The Mothers' Movement and World War II* (Chicago: University of Chicago Press, 1997). The author points out that even though these women were motivated partly by the desire to keep their own sons safe, they were motivated also by anti-Semitism. The war, as far as they were concerned, was the result of an anti-Christian conspiracy.

15 Elizabeth Kaye, "Ladies First: Power Isn't Always Pretty ..." *George*, September 1996: 143.

16 Some men argued the reverse. This was especially true of those who championed evolutionary theories. Charles Darwin himself was ambivalent on this matter. "It is generally admitted," he noted, "that with woman the powers of intuition, of rapid perception, and perhaps of imitation, are more strongly marked than in man; but some, at least, of these faculties are characteristic of the lower races, and therefore of a past and lower state of civilization" (Charles Darwin, *The Descent of Man and Selection in Relation to Sex* [New York: Appleton, 1871] 563).

17 Michael Bradley, *The Iceman Inheritance: Prehistoric Sources of Western Man's Racism, Sexism, and Aggression* (New York: Kayode, 1991). Christopher Lasch has noted parallels between the civil rights movement and the women's movement. Just as not all blacks adopt the ideology of black power, not all women adopt ideological forms of feminism. Those who do, however, make the same mistake as their black counterparts. Both claim "that a special history of victimization entitles them to reparations or justifies the very methods they condemn when their enemies use them. In the 1970s and 1980s, the art of political organization has more and more come to depend on the mobilization of resentment and the moral elevation of the victim" (page 19). Lasch points out that this sort of thing occurs on both the left and the right. For him, it is primarily the prevalence of this mentality that explains the steady deterioration of public life in a democratic society. But black leaders do not need white leaders to remind them of this.

18 Although ideology was a central concept for Marx, he did not define it. By piecing together his comments, John Torrance (*Karl Marx's Theory of Ideas* [Cambridge: Cambridge University Press, 1995] concludes that Marx understood ideology as a distortion of thought originating in and concealing social contradictions. More specifically, the material aspects of life, which should belong to everyone according to ability and need, are inverted by the bourgeois theoreticians into concepts of "ought" and "ought not." This cultural manipulation obscures the reality of the proletarian contribution to production. Also, it sublimates material culture and economics into prescriptive law. The latter becomes so embedded in culture – practical and theoretical views about living in society – that it seems to express what is natural or common sense. In other words, it seems to require neither explanation nor legitimation.

When prescriptive rules become even more deeply embedded in culture, they take the form of fetishism (power falsely ascribed to persons or objects), religious myth, doctrine, truth claims, and metaphysics. These explanatory theories are based on illusions, or "false consciousness," based in turn on social barriers to knowledge. To destroy "false consciousness," according to Marx, it is necessary to change the circumstances or practice of communal life, through revolution if necessary, to share material abundance and eliminate dependence. Marx assumed that reality could be defined solely in terms of material needs, emphasizing the "modes of production," and ignored any other possible human needs. Marx believed that his systematic examination of reality would make possible a rational and even scientific view of history. This would show how ideologies are formed and economic problems obscured. It would generate an ethic based on justice, moreover, and a historical goal (the full and free development of each person).

To Torrance's reconstruction of Marx's notion of ideology, the following should be added. Whereas Marx defined ideology as "false consciousness," the same thing could be said of his own view. This was certainly the case in communism, which reduced reality to the material realm of economics by ignoring the non-material needs addressed by religion. By obscuring important dimensions of reality to produce its own explanatory theory, which was based on a partial understanding of it, communism became embedded in ideology as Marx himself understood that word.

19 Yin is usually considered weaker than yang, but our point here is merely to note the possibility of two principles that complement rather than oppose each other.

20 In some cases, evil is said to be acquired but has nevertheless been so pervasive for so long that it might as well be considered ontological. Some feminists are unwilling to claim with their radical sisters that men are *innately* evil (by virtue of their biology), for example, but are willing to claim that men have been so contaminated by patriarchy that, for all intents and purposes, they can be considered *inherently* evil (by virtue of their history).

21 The transition from superiority to hatred is by no means inevitable. Parents can be considered superior to their children in many ways, after all, but most do not hate their children or hold them in contempt. On the contrary, they love their children and try to protect them. Men who feel superior to women do not necessarily end up hating them. And women who feel superior to men do not necessarily end up hating them. But hatred is an inherent danger associated with ideologies purporting to explain superiority and inferiority. It is not enough, therefore, to challenge those feminists who openly espouse female superiority, or sexism in

the form of misandry. It is necessary also to challenge those who directly or indirectly provide the intellectual foundation for it. Ideological feminism must not be conveniently swept under the carpet like a dirty secret. It must be examined as a logical development based on ideas inherent in other forms of feminism.

22 For a detailed study of paradise as understood in American popular culture and popular religion, see Paul Nathanson, *Over the Rainbow: The Wizard of Oz as a Secular Myth of America* (Albany: State University of New York Press, 1991).

23 Norman Rufus Cohn, *The Pursuit of the Millennium* (London: Secker and Warburg, 1957).

24 The extent of millenarianism within modern societies is startling. Cf. Daniel Wojcik, *The End of the World As We Know It: Faith, Fatalism, and Apocalypse in America* (New York: New York University Press, 1997). The author notes that modern versions of "otherworldly" salvation do not necessarily involve supernatural beings. Often, they involve superhuman but extraterrestrial beings.

25 Cynicism meant something very different to the ancient Greeks and Romans. Founded in the fifth century B.C., probably by Diogenes of Sinope, this school of philosophy taught that virtue depended on the cultivation of austere simplicity, self-control, asceticism, and a fiercely independent will. About all its adherents had in common with the cynics of today is contempt for the artificial conventions of society and those who live by them.

26 A few scholars have begun to challenge the prevailing atmosphere of cynicism. Marilynne Robinson has argued against the idea that disillusionment is a sign of wisdom. As she puts it, "when a good man or woman stumbles, we say, 'I knew it all along,' and when a bad one has a gracious moment, we sneer at the hypocrisy. It is as if there is nothing to mourn or admire, only a hidden narrative now and then apparent through the false surface narrative. And the hidden narrative, because it is ugly and sinister, is therefore true" (Marilynne Robinson; quoted in Roger Kimball, "John Calvin Got a Bad Rap," review of *The Death of Adam*, by Marilynne Robinson, *New York Times Book Review*, 7 February 1999: 14). Even Richard Rorty has advised academics on the left, for example, to abandon their characteristic cynicism (Richard Rorty, *Achieving Our Country: Leftist Thought in Twentieth-Century America* [Cambridge: Harvard University Press, 1998]).

27 Alan Ryan, "The New New Left," review of *Achieving Our Country* by Richard Rorty, *New York Times Book Review*, 17 May 1998: 13.

28 John Torrance, *Karl Marx's Theory of Ideas* (Cambridge: Cambridge University Press, 1995).

29 George L. Mosse, *Germans and Jews: The Right, the Left, and the Search for a "Third Force" in Pre-Nazi Germany* (New York: Grosset

and Dunlap, 1970): 116. Mosse refers to Arnim Mohler, *Die Konservative Revolution in Deutschland* (Stuttgart, 1950) and Klemens von Klemperer, *Germany's New Conservatism* (Princeton: Princeton University Press, 1957).

30 The Nazis were ambivalent about bourgeois society. On the one hand, they refrained from destroying it. On the other, they introduced policies that conflicted with the bourgeois mentality. Hitler believed that women should stay home and take care of their families, but he encouraged young people to put class interests aside in the interest of the New Order. The *Lebensborn* program, for example, created stud farms at which SS officers could mate with women of pure Aryan extraction and thus produce the master race.

31 There are those who would disagree. In *Hitler's Willing Executioners: Ordinary Germans and the Holocaust* (New York: Knopf, 1996), Daniel Goldhagen made his career by arguing that Nazi anti-Semitism was nothing more than traditional German anti-Semitism. On that basis, he argued that "ordinary Germans" welcomed the opportunity to murder Jews. There were precedents for the murder of Jews, to be sure, and not only in Germany. (Our word "pogrom" comes from the Russian.) Ergo, it would make no sense to speak of a Nazi revolution. But Goldhagen never provided an adequate definition of "ordinary," one that could account for variables such as class, education, region, travel, and so on. In *Nazi Terror: The Gestapo, Jews, and Ordinary Germans* (New York: Basic Books, 1999), Eric A. Johnson found that these people were anything but ordinary according to standard psychological and sociological indicators. Granted that "eliminationist" anti-Semitism had a long history in Germany (and elsewhere), but why had it not been released for centuries as mass murder? The answer is that the Nazi regime did what no other regime had done in modern times: it created a revolution strong enough to override centuries of inhibiting factors.

32 The term "secular religion" has been defined by Paul Nathanson as a worldview that functions in most, but not all, ways as a religion. It does not mediate the sacred, defined in connection with an experience that cannot be reduced adequately to an idea or a feeling or an "ultimate concern," but it is like religion in almost every other way. It generates myths and rituals, for instance, that provide people with a sense of origin, destiny, identity, meaning, and purpose. It is expressed in venerated books or essays. It organizes society according to a code of political or personal morality. It is experienced on special days and in special places. The list could go on. Examples of secular religion include not only the "civil religions" of many countries or communities but also political ideologies such as communism, nationalism, and at least some forms of feminism. Less obvious are the worldviews that underlie those ideologies. Among the most important of these would be neo-romanticism, a

worldview that glorifies feeling, whether emotion or sensation, as an end in itself and usually at the expense of reason. See Paul Nathanson, *Over the Rainbow: The Wizard of Oz As a Secular Myth of America* (Albany: State University of New York Press, 1991) and "I Feel, Therefore I Am: The Princess of Passion and the Implicit Religion of Our Time," *Implicit Religion*, 2.2 (1999): 59–87. The closely related term "implicit religion" is used by scholars in Britain. They do not, however, see any inherent distinction between religion and implicit religion. The latter corresponds more closely, therefore, to Paul Tillich's notion of religion as "ultimate concern."

33 Mircea Eliade, *Myths, Dreams and Mysteries: The Encounter between Contemporary Faiths and Archaic Realities* (New York: Harper, 1960).

34 Ibid., 25.

35 For Marxists, this means the functional annihilation of an evil class. It means in addition the physical annihilation, if necessary, of any people who have continued to oppose the supposedly inexorable flow of history. Other people might become reconciled to it, but only by obliterating their old identities (if that is possible) and taking on new ones. The culmination of history for ideological Christians would involve the abolition of Judaism and, possibly through conversion, the Jewish community that perpetuates it. Similarly, the culmination of history for Marxists would involve the abolition of capitalism and, through consciousness raising or revolution, the middle and upper classes that perpetuate it. There is no room in the Marxist utopia for both classes to coexist, let alone to cooperate in harmony. In fact, there is no room in any ideological utopia – religious or secular, traditional or modern, right wing or left wing – for groups of people who fail to conform, who swim against the tide.

It could be argued that Marxism is more like other secular ideologies than religious ones for another reason as well. Like secular ideologies, it is primarily about collectivities or classes, not individuals. But Western religions are about individuals (personal destiny in the hereafter) *and* collectivities (in connection with the conclusion of history), not one or the other. When these religions become ideological, therefore, the result is equally dualistic – in spite of the official belief that everyone can choose freely between truth and error.

To the extent that specific communities are believed to be influenced by supernaturally evil forces, and to the extent that this influence is institutionalized in the error of their beliefs and practices, they can be considered inherently or ontologically evil on a collective basis. Religious ideologies have thus identified whole groups of people as evil and targeted them for either conversion or persecution (the difference not always being obvious to those on the receiving end).

Likewise, many Marxists have identified specific *classes* of people (the workers and peasants) as inherently good and others (the bourgeois) as inherently evil, a few exceptional individuals on either side notwithstanding. In theory, it is true, members of the bourgeoisie can "convert" by mending their ways, joining the workers or peasants in their struggle, and becoming part of the new world order. In practice, however, this possibility is seldom taken seriously.

On the other hand, Marxism might seem more like secular ideologies than religious ones. Like the former, Marxist ideology defines the enemy class functionally, not ontologically or metaphysically. But when Christianity took on ideological form, as we have already noted, it made no significant distinction between the function of Jews in society or even history and the nature of their being. The obvious conclusion was drawn in late mediaeval Spain, when membership in the Christian community was defined not by baptism but by purity of blood (*limpieza di sangre*). There was something inherently sinister even about Jews who became Christians. From this, it is clear that anti-Judaism and anti-Semitism are just two different ways of talking about the same kind of hatred and thus two different labels for the same phenomenon.

36 Arthur Marwick; quoted in Ellen Willis, "On the Barricades," review of *The Sixties: Cultural Revolution in Britain, France, Italy, and the United States* by Arthur Marwick, *New York Times Book Review*, 8 November 1998: 16.

37 Consider the context in which early twentieth-century Canadian feminists debated the relative merits of men and women. Some feminists, including social-Darwinist Charlotte Perkins Gilman, believed that men were innately and irremediably warlike – that is, evil. Thus only woman suffrage could prevent war and maintain the race. Nellie McClung, a believing Christian, disagreed. Far from being God's intention, she argued, war was not merely a crime but also a sin of men. Because men had the ability to choose between good and evil, they could not be considered inherently inferior to women. But the distinction was fuzzy. For all intents and purposes, men had created a world in which their own inclinations, including war, were fostered and those of women were not. See Randi R. Warne, *Literature as Pulpit: The Christian Social Activism of Nellie L. McClung*, Dissertations SR, vol. 2 (Waterloo, Ont.: Wilfrid Laurier University Press, 1993) 137–83.

38 Mary Daly, *Pure Lust: Elemental Feminist Philosophy* (Boston: Beacon Press, 1984) ix–xii.

39 Naomi Goldenberg, *Returning Words to Flesh: Feminism, Psychoanalysis, and the Resurrection of the Body* (Boston: Beacon Press, 1990) 189.

40 David L. Kirp, Mark G. Yudof, and Marlene Strong-Franks, *Gender Justice* (Chicago: University of Chicago Press, 1986) 48.

41 How can we oppose ideologues for setting up dualistic dichotomies of this sort, readers might well ask, when we ourselves seem to be doing the very same thing? We will no doubt be accused of contradicting ourselves. For a rebuttal, see chapter 8.

42 No one should have been surprised, therefore, that some feminists have felt the need for a second cable network. Like Lifetime, Oxygen is devoted to productions made primarily by and for women. Co-founder Caryn Mandabach notes, for example, that business shows featuring numbers have no inherent appeal to women. "When a woman sees a car, she thinks about whether it will work for car pool or carrying groceries. Her concerns about others prompt her buying decisions" (Caryn Mandabach; quoted in James Poniewozik, "Will Women Take a Breath of Oxygen?" *Time*, 31 January 2000: 50.) Her "concerns" are not only different from those of men, in other words, but superior as well. That leads directly to the next feature of ideological feminism.

43 Anthropologists have recognized some small-scale societies as virtually egalitarian despite the fact that they emphasize the differences between men and women. Examples would include the Iroquois and the Central Eskimo in North America; the !Kung, the Mbuti, the Hudza, and the Gebusi in Africa; and the Semai in Asia. Theoretically, then, focus on difference need not result in hierarchy. In this case, however, ideological rhetoric was involved. Feminists began saying not that men and women were alike in spite of a few differences but that men and women were unlike in spite of a few similarities. The aim was frankly polemical. A move towards the rhetoric of superiority was inevitable.

44 Much has been written about this. Radical positions on motherhood and family life, for example, have alienated many women who do not believe that motherhood and family life are parts of a sinister plot to keep women from becoming autonomous. They want husbands and children. But many other examples come to mind. In response to the self-righteous and intimidating attitude of some feminists towards women who choose to have hysterectomies, thus unwittingly buying into what they consider the oppression of a male medical establishment, Jane Gross argues that hysterectomies sometimes serve the real needs of real women. She refers to one female physician who advised her to resist the guilt-inducing polemics of these feminists because their tactics had "the effect of silencing women who chose to have politically incorrect procedures and 'don't want to be pummeled by the ideologues.' Dr Greenwood also noted that the hectoring tone of this literature is 'part of the male model' and thus best avoided. 'To be so aggressive about your point of view and not concede anything to the other side,' she said, 'as women, we should not be adopting this tactic" (Sadja Greenwood; quoted in Jane Gross, "Our Bodies, but My Hysterectomy," *New York Times*, 16 June 1994, sec. 4: 1, 1.).

45 "Women's League Challenges Non-Sexist Ads for Players," *Montreal Gazette*, 12 May 1988: B-2; "A Few Girls Here, a Few Boys There," *Montreal Gazette*, 12 April 1988: B-2.

46 As a result, it is often assumed that the world and all of history revolve around women. At the height of conflict in Hebron, after a massacre of Palestinians at prayer, the *Montreal Gazette* (8 March 1994: A-1) decided that International Women's Day would be the leading story. At the top of page one, the headline read: "Feminism in the '90s: Movement Defies a Definition." Lower down, albeit in slightly bigger type, was "Arafat Meets with Israelis: First Parley since Hebron Aims to Revive Peace Talks."

47 Mary Daly; quoted in Virginia R. Mollenkott, "Against Patriarchy," review of *Gyn/Ecology*, by Mary Daly, *Christian Century*, 11 April 1979: 417.

48 The term "cultural revolution" requires an explanation. Maoist China went through a cultural revolution in a very general sense. Although radical cultural change was indeed a goal, it was attained by political means and in fact was organized and perpetrated directly by the state. We are talking about a cultural revolution in a much more specific sense: radical change in cultural perceptions but not accompanied by radical political change. Most feminists would be unwilling to subvert the state and topple its institutions. They want "merely" for citizens to see, or use, the state and its institutions in a new way.

49 Here is one example: "I maintain that upholding abortion on demand and without apology is profoundly moral," writes Mary Lou Greenberg, "because it puts women first" (Mary Lou Greenberg, "Letters," *New York Times*, 6 April 1997: 18). At issue here is not her point about abortion but her point about morality. The criterion is not whether something is right or wrong but whether it serves the interests of women. Abortion, whether right or wrong, is merely the means to an end.

50 Paul Nathanson, "I Feel, Therefore I Am: The Princess of Passion and the Implicit Religion of Our Time," 59–87.

51 David Sexton, "Nags, Shrews and Snools," *Spectator*, 23 February 1985: 23.

52 Wendy Kaminer, "Feminism's Identity Crisis," *Atlantic Monthly*, October 1993: 51–68.

53 Ibid., 67–8.

54 Ibid., 67.

55 By "deconstructing" deconstructive "texts," are we not doing the same thing ourselves? Not everything that looks like deconstruction, however, is deconstruction (just as not everything that looks like scholarship is scholarship). Those who advocate deconstruction for political purposes do so on an opportunistic basis. They deconstruct only in order to

replace an ideology they dislike with their own ideology. If we were deconstructionists, we would argue in this book that popular culture is saturated with misandry and use that as a pretext for reasserting misogyny or patriarchy, or male dominance, or whatever. But our aim is not to deconstruct misogyny as a way of promoting the interests of men exclusively. Our aim is not to replace feminism with masculinism. Our aim is to clear the air so that scholars can do their job properly by exploring truth wherever that quest might lead them. Merely by acknowledging ambiguity, we establish ourselves outside the boundaries of fashionable deconstruction with its intensely, though often covert, political "agenda." In theory, these deconstructionists could say the same thing about their own work. But in fact, as we have argued, their work and its heavy influence on political ideologies would not support that claim. Without adopting the theory of deconstruction, we have tried to show what would happen if the technique of deconstruction were used to examine cultural artifacts and productions normally considered exempt from it.

56 The label "deconstructionist" is seldom used by those who practise deconstruction. We use it here mainly in order to avoid the continual repetition of clumsy locutions such as "those who use deconstructive techniques" or "those who have adopted deconstruction as an analytical tool."

57 According to Derrida himself, "deconstruction, if there is such a thing, takes place as the experience of the impossible" (quoted in Mitchell Stephens, "Jacques Derrida," *New York Times Magazine*, 23 January 1994: 22.

58 John M. Ellis, *Against Deconstruction* (Princeton, N.J.: Princeton University Press, 1989).

59 These ideas are brought out by Derrida in his discussion of the French verb *différer*, which means both "to differ" and "to defer." Words and ideas differ in meaning from one context to another, say the Derrideans, which generates interactive meanings. Never knowing how one meaning might interact with another at any particular moment, we can never have a fixed or standard "reading." Any exhaustive interpretation must be deferred indefinitely, moreover, because new readers will always have new responses.

60 By way of illustration, consider an example from Derrida's own writings. In one essay, written for the catalogue of an art exhibition assembled by the Association of Artists of the World against Apartheid in cooperation with the United Nations, he focuses on the future. He notes that this collection of art would form the basis of a future museum that some day might be presented to the "first free and democratic government of South Africa." In the meantime, it would travel from country to

country. It "does not yet belong to any given time or space that might be measured today. Its flight rushes headlong, it commemorates in anticipation not its own event but the one that it calls forth. Its flight, in sum, is as much that of a planet as of a satellite. A planet, as the name indicates, is first of all a body sent wandering on a migration which, in this case, has no certain end ... And if it never reaches its destination, having been condemned to an endless flight or immobilized far from an unshakable South Africa, it will not only keep that archival record of a failure or a despair but continue to say something, something that can be heard today, in the present" ("Racism's Last Word," trans. Peggy Kamuf, *Critical Enquiry* 12 [1985]: 293). In other words, as this imaginary change of perspective makes clear, meaning cannot be exhausted in the present. The current meaning of this exhibition is only a "trace" of what it will come to mean in the future.

61 Ellis, 69.

62 Ibid., 71.

63 Johnson; quoted in ibid., 6.

64 Ellis, 109.

65 Ibid.

66 Ibid., 141.

67 Ibid., 139.

68 Ibid., 96.

69 Ibid., 91–2.

70 Deconstruction is based on an inherent contradiction. By virtue of saying "there is no way to communicate objective truth," an attempt has been made to do just that. We could argue, therefore, that those who say this *think* they are deconstructionists but *in fact* are not, because that would be impossible on purely logical grounds. We prefer not to use this argument, however, because it leaves us ambivalent. On the one hand, it is self-evidently true. Besides, it should be possible to say that people are mistaken in their beliefs. Consider those who reject scripture in every sense but that of a vague moral guide: we could say that these people are secular. Some of them might even agree but still want to call themselves Jews, say, or Christians. The word "Jew" or "Christian" would become almost meaningless at that point because it could be used to mean almost anything. On the other hand, that argument is arrogant. Who are we, after all, to tell others who they are and are not? If people sincerely believe they are Christians, then maybe they are Christians (even if we think their beliefs are false or out of line with our own definition of religion in general or Christianity in particular). That is the identity they have chosen. We can think they are deluded, that they do not know what religion is or even what Christianity is, but can we say that their identity is other than what they themselves believe it to be? If

so, then we would surely have to agree with Karl Rahner who once averred that "enlightened" Jews or Buddhists were not really Jews or Buddhists at all but "anonymous Christians," people who were too stupid (although Rahner never put it that way) to define their own identity correctly. As we say, this kind of argument leaves us ambivalent. Common sense tells us one thing. Common decency tells us something else.

71 Because many critics take deconstructive theory seriously, believing that those who espouse it do so themselves, their arguments against it some times seem naive. Ellis points out that deconstruction, by its own logic, would force feminists to accept "male chauvinist and fascist voices" as no less legitimate than their own. He fails to see that hardly anyone (if anyone at all) actually takes deconstruction to its logical conclusion. According to Ellis, however, feminism and deconstruction are incompatible. He writes that "the vitality of feminism lies not simply in the fact that it has been a neglected perspective ... but rather in the fact that it is a neglected perspective that is too inherently valuable to ignore. The centre that ignored a female perspective was a defective centre specifically to the extent that it ignored that perspective." He does not realize that many deconstructionists *are*, in fact, feminists – even ideologically oriented feminists. We, at any rate, are unaware of any deconstructionist who has tried to deconstruct a feminist "text" (let alone a deconstructive one). In theory, feminism is legitimated in terms of deconstruction by arguing that it is merely about *restoring* women to the "centre." In fact, those who argue in this way try to do so by *replacing men at the centre with women* and *replacing women at the margin with men.* Those who use this theoretical legitimation do not worry about its logical implication (that fascists or male chauvinists too could claim their place at the centre) because they have no intention of following through with the inherent "logic" of deconstruction. If so, then deconstruction is a convenient rhetorical tool and nothing more. It can be discarded conveniently, therefore, once the "texts" of their adversaries have been "problematized," or "demystified." Merely reversing the hierarchy obviously makes no sense from a strictly deconstructive point of view, but it makes a great deal of sense from an ideological point of view.

72 Nagarjuna, an early Buddhist philosopher from India, encouraged his followers to use a device called the *catuskoti*, which gives four alternative views on the true nature of things (affirmation, negation, both affirmation and negation, neither affirmation nor negation) to refute opponents by exposing contradictions, absurdity, or dogmatism through reductio ad absurdum and ad hominem arguments. The immediate goal is to transcend all perspectives and realize emptiness. The ultimate goal is to realize that everything is interrelated and interdependent. The

catuskoti is used only for philosophical debates, however, and spiritual quests. (See *The Dialectical Method of Nagarjuna (Vigrahavyavartani)*, trans. Kamaleswar Bhattacharya [Delhi: Motilal Banarsidass, 1978]: 5–8.) Unlike the deconstructive attack on social structure today, with its goal of ushering in a new world order, classic Buddhist texts conveniently make attacks of this kind off-limits. Because Buddhist texts rarely comment on social norms in any case, deconstructing the latter would have to be considered either irrelevant or dangerous. Accordingly, Buddhists have posited two levels of truth: lower and higher. The lower level is known in everyday life, be it religious or secular, of ordinary people living in the world. The higher level can be known only through monastic disciplines based on meditation leading to enlightenment. Hindus, with a great deal of their own to say about two levels of truth and reality, have found it convenient to avoid deconstructing the "lower level" of existence. The social structure is protected, therefore, by a tacit consensus of intellectuals, philosophers, and theologians.

73 Although we reject the idea that all of history can be reduced to a conspiracy of "them" against "us," we acknowledge that specific times and places do generate conspiracies. This was true, for example, of the English court during the sixteenth and seventeenth centuries when Protestants and Catholics manoeuvred furtively for control of the throne. It might be true today on university campuses, though in a much more diffuse way, when ideologues of one kind or another manoeuvre covertly for control of academic (and, ultimately, of political) debate.

74 It could be argued that the precedent for this in the West is found in the Gospel itself. To be sure, Jesus told his followers: "But many that are first will be last, and the last first" (Mark 10: 21). He referred to people, not theories. Those who adhered out of genuine conviction to a way of life universally acknowledged in that community as divine in origin, and thus eternal rather than ephemeral, would be given their rightful status in the Kingdom. Those who did so out of hypocrisy or opportunism, on the other hand, would lose theirs. It could be argued that Jesus tried to reverse the political hierarchy, in short, but not the moral hierarchy: "Think not that I come to abolish the law and the prophets. I have come not to abolish them but to fulfil them. For truly I say to you, till heaven and earth pass away, not an iota, not a dot, will pass from the law until all is accomplished" (Matthew 5: 17). Presenting deconstruction as a redemptive message, a secular *kerygma*, can be seen as an attempt to legitimate secular ideologies that promise salvation in this world to some at the expense of others. (It is worth noting here that Christians have sometimes failed to understand this very principle. When they see the church as a *replacement* for Israel, the result has always been the replacement of theology by anti-Jewish ideology.)

75 For a discussion of this problem, see Charles Taylor, *Multiculturalism and "the Politics of Recognition"* (Princeton: Princeton University Press, 1992): 39.

76 We do not assume that feminism is monolithic, that all feminists are alike, or even that all feminists are ideological. Those who do adopt an ideological worldview have often been compared in this book to the advocates of other ideologies.

77 According to feminists themselves, there are two major fault lines. One is based on ethnicity: white feminists versus African-American "womanists" and Hispanic "*mujeristas.*" The other is based on method: radical separatists (who want total revolution) versus more egalitarian reformers (who want a modified version of the current system).

78 Mort Walker and Dik Browne, *Hi and Lois, Montreal Gazette,* 7 April 1994: D-11.

79 Nevertheless, hatred is related to emotion. The emotion most closely related is fear, though, not anger. Racism has always been present in Canada, the United States, and every other heterogeneous society. But overt expressions of racism are more common or more extreme at some times than others. What accounts for the recent upsurge in overt racism – that of the Aryan Nation, say, or anti-Semitism in the Nation of Islam – at this time? Obviously, many factors are involved. One of them is surely fear: some people are afraid of losing their jobs, but others are afraid of losing their identity. This is obviously true in communities with a long history of persecution or marginalization. To this day, many black Americans struggle merely to feel good about being black. Precisely the same thing is true for many Jews, including those who are financially secure. The fact is that members of any group under attack or even the threat of attack will eventually feel the pressure and respond to it in one way or another.

For members of minority groups, it might seem hard to understand how the same problem can afflict members of majority communities or representatives of "the dominant culture." Nevertheless, it happens. Men have far more to fear from women than competition for jobs, although it would be a mistake to underestimate the importance of that fear. Their deepest fear, though seldom consciously acknowledged even now, is that they will be left either with a negative identity (as incarnations of evil) or with no identity at all (as second-rate women). Will there be room in the new society, they might well ask, for men *as such*? If women can do everything as well or better than men, what could it possibly mean to be a man? One way of responding to this, unfortunately, is to exaggerate the value of anything at all that can still be identified with maleness and diminish the value of anything associated with femaleness. That is misogyny. And misogyny, as one form of sexism, is a form of racism (hostility to a *biologically defined* group).

80 There are positive stereotypes, and women have used many of these to describe themselves, but they are not germane to the discussion of prejudice.

81 "Racist Women," *Sally Jessy Raphael*, NBC, WPTZ, Plattsburgh, N.Y., 9 January 1991.

82 *Donahue*, NBC, WPTZ, Plattsburgh, N.Y., 23 January 1993.

83 This was discussed following the 1995 assassination of Itzhak Rabin, the prime minister of Israel, by someone who had succumbed to the rhetoric of revenge. By trading land for peace, it was said by some Israelis, Rabin had been responsible for terrorist attacks that took the lives of settlers in the West Bank. With that in mind, they not only fostered the desire for revenge but openly advocated Rabin's murder. Barreca does not soil her hands with such hideous things. It would be easy for her to distinguish between murder and the simple pleasures of verbal put-downs. The joy some women take in watching men squirm, or vice versa, might be perfectly natural, but it is still inherently wrong from a moral point of view. People are cultural beings, after all, not purely natural beings. We can choose to *foster* some ways of feeling or thinking rather than others.

84 Annette Insdorf; quoted in Benjamin Svetkey, "Blood, Sweat, and Fears," *Entertainment Weekly*, 15 October 1999: 31.

85 Regina Barreca, *Sweet Revenge: The Wicked Delights of Getting Even* (New York: Harmony Books, 1995).

86 Ibid., 262.

87 Ibid.

88 Jeffrie G. Murphy, "Getting Even: The Role of the Victim," *Social Philosophy and Policy* 7, no. 2 (Spring 1990): 209–25.

CHAPTER NINE

1 Amy Pascal; quoted in Anne Thompson, "Opening Pandora's Box Office: Daring Movies, Record Grosses, and a Town in Transition – The Lessons of 1999," *Premiere*, January 2000: 47.

2 Jim Mullen, "Hot Sheet," *Entertainment Weekly*, 8 July 1994: 10.

3 Ken Tucker, "Potty Animals," *Entertainment Weekly*, 16 January 1998: 54.

4 Not everyone would agree that sexual polarization is a problem. Some women, for instance, believe that they have more to gain politically by sustaining or even increasing sexual polarization.

5 Howard Bloch and Frances Ferguson, eds., *Misogyny, Misandry, and Misanthropy* (Berkeley: University of California Press, 1989). It is worth noting that the Library of Congress lists only three books under the subject heading of "misandry." The other two are Judith Levine, *My Enemy, My Love: Man-Hating and Ambivalence in Women's Lives* (New York:

Doubleday, 1992) and Daphne Patai, *Heterophobia: Sexual Harassment and the Future of Feminism* (Lanham, Md.: Rowman and Littlefield, 1998). By contrast, seventy-five books are listed under "misogyny."

6 Richard Corliss, "Caution: Male Fraud," *Time*, 26 August 1997: 40.

7 Colin Brown, "Controversy Theory," *Screen International*, 15 August 1997: 13.

8 Tom Bernard; quoted in Corliss, 41.

9 Ibid., 42.

10 Ken Tucker, "Men Overboard!" *Entertainment Weekly*, 25 June 1999: 111.

11 John Gray, *Men Are from Mars, Women Are from Venus: A Practical Guide for Improving Communication and Getting What You Want in Your Relationships* (New York: HarperCollins, 1992).

12 Owen Gleiberman, "Cosmos Guy," *Entertainment Weekly*, 10 March 2000: 47.

13 Germaine Greer, *The Whole Woman* (New York: Knopf, 1999).

14 Katherine K. Young, "Goddesses, Feminists, and Scholars," in *Annual Review of Women in World Religions*, ed. Arvind Sharma and Katherine K. Young, (Albany: State University of New York Press, 1991): 105–79.

15 Many authors made this claim in the 1970s and 1980s (although less sophisticated versions had been proposed in the late nineteenth century and the early twentieth), but they were mainly ideologues. Among the better known was Marilyn French, whose massive compendium, *Beyond Power: On Women, Men and Morals*, has already been noted here on several occasions. Among the very few scientists who made the same claim was anthropologist Melvin Konner. In *The Tangled Wing: Biological Constraints on the Human Spirit* (New York: Holt, Rinehart and Winston, 1982), he argued that men were, in fact, responsible for just about everything bad in human existence and that women should rule the world. The popularity of this theory can be gauged by the fact that Konner's theory was published under the heading "The Aggressors" in the *New York Times Magazine*, 14 August 1988: 34. By the late 1980s, the argument was being taken seriously among scientists as one that had to be challenged. In *Social Structure and Testosterone: Explorations of the Socio-Bio-Social Chain* (New Brunswick, N.J.: Rutgers University Press, 1990), for example, Thomas Kemper focused on the properties of testosterone itself and concluded that "moral toxicity" is not one of them. In *Peacemaking among Primates* (Cambridge: Harvard University Press, 1989), Frans de Waal looked at genetics in a more general sense, that of the relation between men and other primate males (mainly bonobos) and concluded that the tendency to seek reconciliation, no less than aggression, is hard-wired into primate males. Male biology, in short, is not the cause of brutality (although, given cultural conditioning, it can be used effectively for that purpose).

16 See, for example, Camille Paglia, *Vamps and Tramps: New Essays* (New York: Random House, 1994); Donna Laframboise, *The Princess at the Window: A New Gender Morality* (Toronto: Penguin, 1996); Kate Fillion, *Lip Service: The Truth about Women's Darker Side in Love, Sex and Friendship* (Toronto: HarperCollins, 1996); Katie Roiphe, *The Morning After: Sex, Fear, and Feminism* (Boston: Little, Brown, 1994); Christina Hoff Sommers, *Who Stole Feminism?* (New York: Simon and Schuster, 1994); Rene Denfeld, *The New Victorians: A Young Woman's Challenge to the Old Feminist Order* (New York: Warner Books, 1995); Jean Bethke Elshtain, *Women and War* (New York: Basic Books, 1987), *Power Trips and Other Journeys: Essays in Feminism as Civic Discourse* (Madison: University of Wisconsin Press, 1990) and *Meditations on Modern Political Thought: Masculine/Feminine Themes from Luther to Arendt* (Univeristy Park: Pennsylvania State University Press, 1992); and Cathy Young, *Ceasefire! Why Men and Women Must Join Forces to Achieve True Equality* (New York: Free Press, 1999).

17 Susan Faludi, for instance, has clearly changed her mind since writing *Backlash! The Undeclared War against American Women* (New York: Crown, 1991). In *Stiffed: The Betrayal of the American Man* (New York: William Morrow, 1999), she takes the problems of men seriously – especially those with economic roots. Even she, however, has little to say about misandry.

18 Anne McIlroy, "Do Men Deserve to Be Studied?," *Montreal Gazette*, 8 June 1995: A-5. The implication is that not all people "deserve" to be studied and must therefore prove themselves worthy before scholars take them seriously.

19 Judith Schuldevitz, "Prematurely Correct," review of *Real Politics: At the Center of Everyday Life* by Jean Bethke Elshtain, *New York Times Book Review*, 14 December 1997: 18. "Large though they loom in her essays, radical feminists were a marginal bunch even within feminism itself. It is true that Shulamith Firestone, the author of 'The Dialectic of Sex,' railed against heterosexual love as an epiphenomenon of biological tyranny, and that the writer Ti-Grace Atkinson viewed men as the enemy. But these are straw women. One of Elshtain's main charges is that the revolutionary rhetoric of radical feminism ignores the realities of female life, but she herself, by shifting radical feminism from the fringes to the center, ignores the realities of American feminism."

20 This information was supplied in the confidential letter of someone working at that university.

21 Many women are hired at the junior level, which is where the new positions are. And, thanks to affirmative action programs, there are many of these. Statistical signs of change at the *senior* level, of course, will take a generation to show up. Nonetheless, real change has already occurred. Because there are still few senior women *available* at the top, the pool of

candidates is small but growing all the same. Also worth considering is the fact that some women do not choose prestigious jobs because of the mobility or pressure that goes along with them. Statistics show rapid improvement, at any rate. Between 1983 and 1993 in the United States, according to the cover story in a business journal, "the percentage of white, male professionals and managers ... dropped from 55% to 47%, while the same group of white women jumped from 37% to 42%" (Michele Galen and Ann Therese Palmer, "White, Male and Worried," *Business Week*, 31 January 1994: 51).

22 Although women do indeed continue to have serious problems, reality is much more complex than many feminists are willing to admit. To take only one example, researchers find it impossible to ignore a growing gender gap in confidence levels and aspirations. After admitting that schoolgirls do, in fact, have a great deal of self-confidence and are out-performing boys, for instance, Janet Bagnall cannot help noting rather sourly, "Instead of congratulating girls, Quebec, like every other West-ern society, is wringing its hands over what all this means for boys and whether the school system has somehow gone wrong" (Janet Bagnall, "Why Girls Get Ahead," *Montreal Gazette*, 23 October 1996: A-1).

23 The threat to identity is not necessarily due to misandry in particular. One threat is gynocentrism in general. For some men, especially those in the "mythopoetic" movement associated with Robert Bly, gynocentrism has highlighted qualities that could benefit men no less than women. They have tried to feminize themselves, to emphasize their "feminine side." Unlike male feminists, they reject (or do not see) the negativity of ideological feminism. One journalist put it this way: "What lies behind the Men's Movement is this: we have evolved into a status society where people get their place not from being individuals but from belonging to a group. We are so group conscious that if we wanted to practice a pri-vate vice we'd need a group to do it. We are women, blacks, native peo-ples, Muslims, visible minorities or defined by our sexual proclivities. It was inevitable that men would want to join the status society by estab-lishing men's studies and men's support groups. Why be left out? The trouble is that unlike feminism with its clear agenda to seize power and socially engineer society to suit its own purposes, the Men's Movement has no real agenda. They dance only to the tune of feminism, falling in with its line about the need of men to be more 'sensitive' and to 'bond' ... Now we are attempting to make female instincts, reactions and behaviour normative for all members of society. Unsurprisingly, it is our feeble-minded, trendy, henpecked males who are leading this movement. It won't work, it can't work, but meanwhile, groups of men will steal into the forest to be sensitive, caring, bonding and drink beer, swap girlie mags, tales of ludicrous sexual-harassment charges and play at

being Tarzan. Our only hope is that just as women still like being Cleopatra or Audrey Hepburn, men will turn their backs on the nice nerd such as Hugh Grant or the steroid exaggeration of an Arnold Swchwarzenegger and once again rediscover the sophisticated take-charge masculinity of a David Niven or Cary Grant (Barbara Amiel, "Henpecked Men Carry Feminist Torch: Feminized Society Deprives Women of Take-Charge Men," *Montreal Gazette*, 23 November 1996: B-6).

24 "Kill Wife Beaters Who Go Free, Feminist-Rights Activist Urges," *Montreal Gazette*, 13 May 1991: A-7.

25 Donna Laframboise, "It's V-Day Today, But Not in the Way You Thought," *National Post*, 14 February 2000: A-1.

26 Hoff-Sommers, A-2; quoted by Laframboise.

27 According to the author of *Vagina*, Eve Ensler, "Most of the women in the world spend their lives either defending against violence or anticipating violence or recovering from it" (Eve Ensler; quoted by Laframboise, A-2). The V-Day website, moreover, used the American statistic that "22% to 35% of women who visit emergency rooms are there for injuries related to on-going abuse" (Laframboise, A-2; citing V-Day website). The Canadian pamphlet points out that 51 per cent of women in Canada have experienced violence.

28 Laframboise, A-2.

29 Camille Paglia; quoted in ibid.

30 Taryn McCormick; quoted in ibid.

31 Ibid.

32 Arvind Sharma, "On Tolerating the Intolerant: Hindu Perspectives," *Vidyajyoti*, 51 (1987): 29–32.

33 Even though we see convincing evidence that these artifacts and productions have harmful effects on society, we see no reason to advocate censorship. Banning misandric movies, for instance, would do nothing but prevent people from seeing and challenging political presuppositions that are now pervasive. The solution would be to help people do those things just as they now do in connection with misogyny.

APPENDIX ONE

1 Given the academic war going on over the Western "canon," we use that word with due caution.

2 John Griffin, "Piano Is Best Film in a Long, Long Time," *Montreal Gazette*, 20 November: D-1.

3 Jane Campion, interviewed on CBS *This Morning*, WCAX-TV, Burlington, Vt., 24 November 1993.

4 Owen Gleiberman, "Tone Poem," *Entertainment Weekly*, 19 November 1993: 68.

5 Ibid.
6 Ibid., 69.
7 Griffin, D-1.
8 Ibid., D-2.
9 Owen Gleiberman, "Family Plot," *Entertainment Weekly*, 17 January 1992: 40.
10 This observation was made by Maureen Garvie, our editor.
11 Richard Schickel, "The Ultimate Other Woman," *Time*, 20 January 1992: 50.

APPENDIX TWO

1 On *Days of Our Lives* in May 1994, several misandric story lines could be followed (which does not mean that the series as a whole must be considered misandric). Jamie is sexually molested by her father. A porn star now on heroin reveals that she had been raped by her father. Her husband's affair unhinges Laura. And, just in case anyone misses the message, every woman in town is threatened by a serial rapist.
2 We have deliberately avoided weeks during which news events dictated particularly heavy emphasis on themes such as rape or domestic violence. A case in point was the week of 18–24 June, with the arrest of O.J. Simpson for the murder of his wife and another man. Day after day, coverage of domestic violence on the talk shows, morning shows, and news specials was extensive. That was not, therefore, a typical week.
3 These two words, "typical" and "characteristic," do not mean quite the same thing. The study of Torah is characteristic of Jewish life, for example, but by no means typical of it in many modern Jewish communities.
4 *TV Guide*, 25 April 1992: P-18.
5 Ibid.
6 Ibid., P-46.
7 Ibid., P-58.
8 Ibid., P-60.
9 Ibid., P-68.
10 Ibid., P-72.
11 Ibid., P-88.
12 Ibid., P-102.
13 Ibid., 29 January 1994: P-12.
14 Ibid., 1 February 1994: P-38.
15 Ibid., P-45.
16 Ibid., P-56.
17 Ibid., P-67.
18 Ibid., P-79.
19 Ibid., P-91.

20 Ibid., P-92.
21 Ibid., P-24.
22 Ibid.
23 Ibid., P-38.
24 Ibid., P-50.
25 Ibid., P-55.
26 Ibid., P-63.
27 Ibid., P-73.
28 Ibid.
29 Ibid., P-82.
30 Ibid., P-90.
31 Ibid., 9 January 1999: P-16.
32 Ibid.
33 Ibid., 9 January 1999: P-32.
34 Ibid., P-39.
35 Ibid., P-40.
36 Ibid., P-42.
37 Ibid., P-64.
38 Ibid., P-78.
39 Ibid., P-96.
40 Ibid.
41 Ibid., P-99.
42 Ibid., P-109.
43 Ibid., P-110.
44 Ibid., P-132.
45 Ibid., P-133.
46 To establish that on a scientific basis would mean actually watching (as distinct from relying merely on occasional program notes) every show on every channel in order to catch every possible reference.

APPENDIX THREE

1 By the 1990s, feminism had become mainstream (even if the label itself had not), the result was a direct or indirect glorification of emotion (supposedly representing some female essence) at the expense of reason (representing some male essence), even though that undermined academic and professional women who claimed that they were just as rational as men. (For a discussion of emotionalism in its larger historical and sociological context, see Paul Nathanson, "I Feel, Therefore I Am: The Princess of Passion and the Implicit Religion of Our Time, *Implicit Religion*, 2, no. 2 [1999]: 59–87). Executives in the entertainment industry have always understood the power of stereotypes, but the old stereotype of *men* has been replaced by a new one. The equivalent of sentimentality, for men, is

no longer intellect but raw sensation (which explains the current prevalence of car chases and explosions).

1 The talk shows are seldom impartial in any democratic sense when it comes to the selection of experts. These are chosen for their probable appeal to specific groups of viewers, not the population at large. That could mean appealing to groups ranging from religious fundamentalists – not all talk shows are aimed at secular liberals – to radical feminists. To avoid the charge of manipulating opinion, two experts might be chosen. The impact of unpopular ones can always be "balanced," therefore, by popular ones. The burden of convincing viewers usually falls on the former, not the latter. And if all else fails, hosts themselves can always provide the necessary "balance" as mediators. Donahue liked to play devil's advocate occasionally but was careful to do so in ways that seldom hid his own position, seldom took the "devil's" position seriously, and thus seldom altered the balance of power.

2 Although the word "populist" is adequate here, because everyone can experience powerful feelings, the same cannot be said for "elitist." Virtually everyone can think, it is true, but not everyone has been trained or even encouraged to think in a disciplined way. Because this latter is precisely what many elitists want, they too are "populists." (In this, they resemble another group sometimes accused of elitism: the early rabbis were neither aristocrats nor peasants but members of the middle class. When their movement began, the rabbis were a highly educated elite. But their goal was not to remain an elite. On the contrary, they wanted *all* Jews to become rabbis and study Torah for themselves. They never fully achieved this goal, but they did succeed to a remarkable extent over the course of two thousand years. Even relatively uneducated Jews eventually came to place a high value on the study of Torah, and even secular Jews to place a high value on learning.) Their motivation is not necessarily noble. They realize that their own future in a democracy depends on the ability of *most* citizens to think clearly. Whatever their motivation, the fact remains that harmony in a democracy cannot be sustained unless the majority of citizens or voters are able to make intelligent choices. And intelligent choices cannot be made without intellectual effort.

3 Carol Gilligan, *In a Different Voice: Psychological Theory and Women's Development* (Cambridge: Harvard University Press, 1982).

4 Marilyn French, *Beyond Power: On Women, Men, and Morals* (New York: Ballantine, 1985).

5 *Nightline*, ABC, WVNY-TV, Burlington, Vt., 4 February 1994.

APPENDIX FIVE

1 John M. Ellis, *Against Deconstruction* (Princeton: Princeton University Press, 1989).
2 Mitchell Stephens, "Jacques Derrida," *New York Times Magazine*, 23 January 1994): 24.
3 Christopher Norris, *Deconstruction: Theory and Practice* (London: Methuen, 1982) 74.
4 Ibid., 75.
5 Ibid., 84.
6 Francis Fukuyama, *The End of History and the Last Man* (New York: Free Press, 1992).
7 Jacques Derrida, *Spectres de Marx: L'État de la dette, le travail du deuil et la nouvelle Internationale* (Paris: Galilée, 1993).
8 Christopher Norris, "Deconstruction, Post-modernism and the Visual Arts," in *What is Deconstruction?*, ed. Christopher Norris and Andrew Benjamin (London: Academy Editions, 1988), 15.
9 Jake Lamar, *The Last Integrationist* (New York: Crown, 1996), 317.
10 See Paul R. Gross and Norman Levitt, *Higher Superstition: The Academic Left and Its Quarrels with Science* (Baltimore: Johns Hopkins University Press, 1998); John Gilliott and Manjit Kumar, *Science and the Retreat from Reason* (New York: Monthly Review Press, 1997); and Paul R. Gross, Norman Levitt, and Martin W. Lewis, eds., *The Flight from Science and Reason* (New York: New York Academy of Sciences, 1996). E.O. Wilson made this very clear in "Back from Chaos," *Atlantic Monthly* (March 1998): 41–62.

APPENDIX SIX

1 Kaja Silverman, *Male Subjectivity at the Margins* (New York: Routledge, 1992).
2 According to Richard Corliss of *Time*, movies made by and for women "are about hugging, not punching; continuity, not apocalypses. Life's rough accommodations make survival, with wits intact, a kind of triumph. 'Women tend to honor and validate daily life and human transaction,' says Sarah Pillsbury, 'and recognize that within the mundane the miraculous often exists'" ("Women of the Year," *Time*, 13 November 1995: 63). Two things must be said about these statements. First, the end result is often a combination of saccharine sentimentality and sanctimonious self-righteousness (not to mention polemic). Second, these qualities (aside, perhaps, from the hugging and kissing) correspond to virtues promoted by traditional religions such as Judaism and Christianity – that is, *patriarchal* ones.

3 Joyce Carol Oates, "Rewriting 'The Scarlet Letter': Hawthorne's Heroine Goes Hollywood," *New York Times*, 15 October 1995: 15.

4 Ibid., 15.

5 Mary Gaitskill, "On Not Being a Victim: Sex, Rape, and the Trouble with Following Rules," *Harper's Magazine*, March 1994: 35–44.

6 Ibid., 42.

7 Ibid., 43.

8 Even scientists no longer, if they ever did, claim complete freedom from the realm of values. Many are prepared to make only the more modest claim of trying to transcend bias.

9 Janet Maslin, "Just What Did Leni Riefenstahl's Lens See?" *New York Times*, 13 March 1994: H-15, H-23.

10 Gaitskill, 43.

11 Ibid.

APPENDIX SEVEN

1 Lance Kinsey, "Some Like It ... Not" (episode 231), *Twice in a Lifetime*, CFCF-TV, Montreal, Que., 9 June 2001.

Index

Because every page of this book is about "men" (as represented in popular culture), "masculinity," and "misandry," the list of entries under these headings would have been extremely long. We have replaced these headings (except for a definition of misandry), therefore, with what would have been subheadings. Although "popular culture," "gyno-centrism," and "feminism" (referring specifically to misandric, or ideological, forms of feminism) are mentioned nearly as often, we have used these headings. But most other headings refer to these too, in one way or another.

To help readers navigate the virtually uncharted waters of a new approach to the study of men – to help them link apparently disparate topics or use terms in unfamiliar ways – we have supplied many "see also" references.

This book is about commonly held *perceptions* about men and the resulting *symbolic representations* of them, not about the social sciences. Words are thus often used evocatively rather than with technical precision (although we have either maintained or introduced some forms of precision, such as using "sex" in connection with the biology of maleness or femaleness and "gender" in connection with cultural systems of masculinity or femininity). To put it another way, many selected keywords are heavily laden with connotations. Some represent one phenomenon but allude to several closely related ones (such as "dualism," "essentialism," and "hierarchy," each of which implies the others and cannot be understood properly in isolation). Other keywords represent one phenomenon but at more than one level (such as "women," which refers to both cultural and biological phenomena). We could not always refer directly, in short, from the specific keywords used as headings to passages in the text; even when keywords do appear there, they do not necessarily refer to the concept being indexed (and have therefore been omitted in those cases). Still, the basic concepts should match.

To the extent that an index can "say something," make its own contribution to the learning process by encouraging readers to make new connections, this one probably does.